Interdimensional Theology

The Law and Fulfillment of the Sabbath

Written by
James Albert Richardson

Edited by
Isaiah James Richardson

Copyright © 2020 James Richardson.

All rights reserved. This book or parts thereof may not be reproduced in any form, stored in any retrieval system, or transmitted in any form by any means—electronic, mechanical, photocopy, recording, or otherwise—without prior written permission of the publisher, except as provided by United States of America copyright law. For permission requests, write to the publisher, at "Attention: Permissions Coordinator," at the address below.

Bowker an affiliated business of ProQuest:
630 Central Ave., New Providence, NJ 07974

ISBN: 978-1-7360320-0-8 (PDF)
ISBN: 978-1-7360320-1-5 (Paperback)
ISBN: 978-1-7360320-2-2 (EPUB)

Front and back cover graphic generated from the lunar-calendar Python utility created by codebox Rob Dawson at the below URL.

https://github.com/codebox/lunar-calendar

Paperback printed by Kindle Direct Publishing in the USA.

Frist printing edition 2020.

Contact Auther/Publisher at:
Apostles-Creed.Org

Table of Contents

Preface i
Introduction 1

Chapter 1 - First Day Sabbatarian 9
   1. The Westminster Confession of Faith 9
      a. The Puritans 9
   2. The Church Fathers 11
      a. Augustine 11
      b. Athanasius 11
      c. Thomas Aquinas 12
   3. Christ is the Lord of the Sabbath 12

Chapter 2 - Seventh Day Sabbatarian 15
   1. The Seventh Day Adventist or SDA 15
      a. Ellen White 16
      b. The Modern SDA 17
   2. The Beast of Revelation 18
   3. The Sabbath and the Lord's Day 21
      a. The Sabbath is for man 22
      b. Worship and the Sabbath 23
      c. Working in the Church 23

Chapter 3 - Antinomian Non-Sabbatarian 25
   1. Dispensationalism 25
      a. Classic Dispensationalism 26
      b. Progressive Dispensationalism 28
      c. Dallas Theological Seminary 30
   2. There is no distinction between Jew and Greek 32
   3. Law and Grace 33

Chapter 4 - The Law 35
   1. The three-part structure of the Law 35
      a. Dispute or Controversy 35
      b. Judge 36
      c. Ordinances or Judgments 36
      d. Laws 37
      e. Statutes 37
      f. Appointed feasts or assemblies 38
      g. Sabbaths 39
   2. Identifying the Law 39
      a. God established the Government 41
      b. The Westminster Confession of Faith .. 43
      c. Objections to the three-part structure of the Law 44
   3. The Moral Law 47
      a. The Moral Law in Genesis 48
      b. The Sabbath is our duty to our neighbor 49
   4. The Judicial Law 50
      a. Civil Tort law 51
      b. The malleability of the Law 52
   5. The Ceremonial law 54
      a. Sacrifices and the Law 55
      b. Christ fulfilled the Ceremonial Law 56
      c. The Law changes with the change of the priesthood 56

Chapter 5 - The Calendar 59
   1. The different calendars 59
      a. Solar Calendar 59
      b. Lunar Calendar 61
      c. Lunisolar calendar 63
   2. The Jewish Calendar 64
      a. The Days 64
      b. The Months 64

  c. The Years 65
 3. The choice of the solar calendar 66
 4. Sabbaths or sevenths as calendar markers 69
 5. The inaccuracy of calendars 70
  a. Calculating Dates 70
  b. Missing years of the Jewish chronology 71

Chapter 6 - The Sabbath 77
 1. Definition of the Sabbath 78
 2. The Sabbath and three-part structure of the Law 80
  a. Statutes and Judgments 80
  b. Ceremonial Laws conflict with the Fourth Commandment 81
 3. The Moral Law and the Sabbath 82
  a. Breaking the Sabbath and Israel 83
 4. Judicial Law and the Sabbath 84
 5. The Ceremonial Law and the Sabbath 85
  a. The Sabbath and healthcare 87
  b. Doing good on the Sabbath 89

Chapter 7 - Modern Day Consequences 93
 1. Workaholism 93
 2. Servants and Animals 94
  a. Livestock and pollution 95
 3. Cultivating Land 96
  a. Deforestation 97
  b. Enslavement of farmers 98
 4. Immigrant exploitation 99
 5. Wasting food, water, and energy 101
 6. Effects of bad debt 103

Chapter 8 - The Ceremonial Law fulfilled in Christ 105
 1. The Sabbath 106
 2. The Passover 110
  a. Christ's blood of the covenant 111
 3. The Feast of Unleavened Bread 112
 4. The Feast of First Fruits 114
 5. The Feast of Weeks 116
 6. The Feast of Trumpets 119
  a. The resurrection of the dead 120
  b. The Sadducees denied the afterlife ... 121
 7. The Day of Atonement 123
  a. The day of Judgment 124
 8. The Feast of Booths 126
  a. Mount Sinai and Mount Zion 127
  b. The City of God 127

Chapter 9 - The Feasts and the end times ... 130
 1. The fulfillment of the Law for all time ... 132
  a. Christ was "slain from the foundation of the world" 133
  b. Old Testament Saints were saved by faith in Christ 134
 2. Differing views on the fulfillment of the feasts 135
  a. The Futurist 135
  b. The Historicist 136
  c. The Preterist 137
  d. The Interdimensional 138
 3. The Intermediate State 139
 4. The Seventy Weeks of Daniel 141
  a. This generation will not pass till all is fulfilled 143
  b. The daily sacrifices were prophesied to cease 146
 5. Heaven and Earth 148
  a. Heavenly dimension 149
  b. Children of God 151

    c. Children of wrath 153
    d. Traversing heaven and earth 154
    e. The heavens open up 155
  6. The coming of Christ 156
    a. Coming in the clouds 158
    b. The resurrection at death 159
    c. Coming quickly 160
  7. The New Jerusalem, the City of God 164
    a. The throne of God 164
    b. The Fathers house 166
    c. The bride 168
    d. Descending from heaven 170

Chapter 10 - The Christian Day of Worship . 175
  1. The designated day for worship in the Old Testament 175
    a. The assembly and the first day 175
    b. Daily offerings in the Old Testament . 177
  2. The designated day for worship in the New Testament 178
    a. Christ and the Apostles worshiped daily 180
  3. Communion breaks the Sabbath 182
    a. Socialism or Communism 183

    b. Helping the needy 185

Chapter 11 - Conclusion 189

Appendix I 197
  The Didache 198
  The Letter of Barnabas 198
  Ignatius of Antioch 198
  Justin Martyr 198
  Tertullian 200
  Constitutions of the holy apostles 202
  Origen 202
  Peter, Archbishop of Alexandria 202
  Cyprian 203
  Victorinus 203
  Eusebius of Caesarea 203
  Council of Laodicea 204
  John Chrysostom 204
  Augustine of Hippo 205

Appendix II 207
Appendix III 211
Appendix IV 214
Index 216
Works Cited 228

Preface

The perspective of the author is what is known as "confessionalism." *The Collins English Dictionary* defines "confessionalism" as,

> *The belief that a religion, esp Christianity, should have a set of essential doctrines to which members of that religion must adhere.* [1]

The creeds and confessions throughout the Christian church are a paper trail of what the church has taught from the beginning. *The Apostles Creed, Nicene Creed*, confessions, catechisms, and the writings of the early Church Fathers are indispensable to the Christian faith. This book adheres to "The Westminster Standard." The Westminster Standard is the doctrinal standard found in *the Westminster Confession of Faith, the Westminster Shorter Catechism*, and *the Westminster Larger Catechism. The Westminster Confession of Faith* is the primary confession referenced in this book. Even though this book teaches a form of confessionalism, this does not mean the confessions and writings of the Church Fathers are equal to the Bible itself. Even though *the Westminster Confession of Faith* is used as a primary source, there are some doctrines in the confession that are shown to be false. The confessions and the writings of the Church Fathers are how we know what Christians taught throughout history. When it comes to deciding what is absolutely true about God, the Bible is the final authority. The Bible is the only way anyone can discern what is good or evil. The Apostle Paul wrote,

> *But evil men and impostors will proceed from bad to worse, deceiving and being deceived. You, however, continue in the things you have learned and become convinced of, knowing from whom you have learned them; and that from childhood you have known* **the sacred writings which are able to give you the wisdom** *that leads to salvation through faith which is in Christ Jesus.* ***All Scripture is inspired by God and profitable for teaching, for reproof, for correction, for training in righteousness; that the man of God may be adequate, equipped for every good work****. (2Ti 3:13-17 NAS)*

The Bible alone is the sole arbiter of truth when it comes to anything pertaining to life and godliness. The Bible is the written Word of God. In Deuteronomy, God said that the commandments given to the Israelites while they wandered in the wilderness were to show them that man does not live by bread alone, but by the Word of God.

> ***All the commandments that I am commanding you today you shall be careful to do, that you may live and multiply,*** *and go in and possess the land which the LORD swore to give to your forefathers. "And you shall remember all the way which the LORD your God has led you in the wilderness these forty years, that He might humble you, testing you, to know what was in your heart, whether you would keep His commandments or not. "And He humbled you and let you be hungry, and fed you with manna which you did not know, nor did your fathers know,* ***that He might make***

> *you understand that man does not live by bread alone, but man lives by everything that proceeds out of the mouth of the LORD. (Deu 8:1-3 NAS)*

Keeping His commandments is so that "you may live." The Bible, both the Old and New Testaments, are the Word of God. Every book in the Bible applies to the Christian. The entirety of the Old and New Testaments are centered on Jesus Christ.

> *And **beginning with Moses and with all the prophets, He explained to them the things concerning Himself in all the Scriptures**.... Now He said to them, "These are My words which I spoke to you while I was still with you, that all **things which are written about Me in the Law of Moses and the Prophets and the Psalms must be fulfilled**. (Luk 24:27,44 NAS)*

The view that the entire Old and New Testament is centered on Jesus Christ is called "Christocentric" theology. "Christocentric" is defined as,

> *Of systems of theology which maintain that God has never revealed Himself to humanity except in the Incarnate Christ.* [2]

The entire theological view of this book is centered on Jesus Christ and the salvation we have in Him. Jesus Christ is the truth that comes from the Father.

> *Jesus said to him, "I am the way, and the truth, and the life; no one comes to the Father, but through Me." (Joh 14:6 NAS)*

> *I came forth from the Father, and have come into the world; I am leaving the world again, and going to the Father. (Joh 16:28 NAS)*

The reason why the Old and New Testaments of the Bible are centered on Jesus Christ is because Jesus Christ is the Word of God (John 1:1; Rev 19:13). The Bible is the written Word of God and Jesus is the Word of God. The Word of God and Jesus Christ are one person and not two different entities. You will find no scripture making the distinction between the Word of God and the Son of God. The Word of God created all things.

> *By faith we understand that the worlds were prepared by the word of God, so that what is seen was not made out of things which are visible. (Heb 11:3 NAS)*

Jesus Christ, the Word of God, created all things from eternity. He was born of the virgin Mary and became man.

> *In the beginning was the Word, and the Word was with God, and the Word was God. He was in the beginning with God. All things came into being by Him, and apart from Him nothing came into being that has come into being...And the Word became flesh, and dwelt among us, and we beheld His glory, glory as of the only begotten from the Father, full of grace and truth. (Joh 1: 1-3,14 NAS)*

Jesus Christ proceeded from or is begotten from God.

Preface

> *Jesus said to them, "If God were your Father, you would love Me; for I proceeded forth and have come from God, for I have not even come on My own initiative, but He sent Me." (Joh 8:42 NAS)*

While Christ was born of the virgin Mary at a specific time in earth's history, Christ is also begotten from eternity before creation. Paul taught the Son was begotten from eternity when he wrote,

> *For He delivered us from the domain of darkness, and transferred us to the kingdom of His beloved Son, in whom we have redemption, the forgiveness of sins. And **He is the image of the invisible God, the first-born of all creation. For by Him all things were created, both in the heavens and on earth**, visible and invisible, whether thrones or dominions or rulers or authorities-- **all things have been created by Him and for Him**. (Col 1:13-16 NAS)*

Paul said *"His beloved Son"* is the "first-born of all creation" and "by Him all things were created." Paul did not make the distinction between the Word and the Son as existing at different times. Nowhere does the Bible teach the Word of God is a different person than the Son of God. Nor does it teach the Word of God is a person and Christ the man is a separate person. Christ, the Son of God, is "the beginning and the end."

> *I am the Alpha and the Omega, the first and the last, the beginning and the end. (Rev 22:13 NAS)*

To teach the Old Testament and the New Testament is to teach Jesus Christ. The Christocentric application of the Old Testament and New Testament is critical for interpreting any of the Bible's meaning. What is true of Christ is true of God.

> *And we know that the Son of God has come, and has given us understanding, in order that we might know Him who is true, and we are in Him who is true, in His Son Jesus Christ. This is the true God and eternal life. (1Jo 5:20 NAS)*

Understanding Christ as the Eternal Word of God necessitates the teaching of an eternal kingdom. There must be a distinction between the eternity and the historical timeline of earth. This concept must be kept in mind when reading this book. The eternal realm and the earthly realm are separate dimensions of reality. So, while it is true, Jesus Christ was born of the virgin in the earthly realm, Jesus Christ is also from eternity. There are two realities, the earthly world and eternal world. This is clearly seen in both the Old and New Testaments of the Bible.

> *But as for you, Bethlehem Ephrathah, Too little to be among the clans of Judah, From you One will go forth for Me to be ruler in Israel. His goings forth are from long ago, **From the days of eternity**. (Mic 5:2 NAS)*

> ***Even from eternity I am He**; And there is none who can deliver out of My hand; I act and who can reverse it? (Isa 43:13 NAS)*

Preface

> *And He was saying to them, "You are from below, I am from above; **you are of this world, I am not of this world.**" (Joh 8:23 NAS)*
>
> *Jesus answered, "**My kingdom is not of this world**. If My kingdom were of this world, then My servants would be fighting, that I might not be delivered up to the Jews; but as it is, My kingdom is **not of this realm**." (Joh 18:36 NAS)*
>
> *Now to the **King eternal**, immortal, invisible, the only God, be honor and glory forever and ever. Amen. (1Ti 1:17 NAS)*
>
> *Therefore, brethren, be all the more diligent to make certain about His calling and choosing you; for as long as you practice these things, you will never stumble; for in this way the entrance into **the eternal kingdom of our Lord and Savior Jesus Christ** will be abundantly supplied to you. (2Pe 1:10-11 NAS)*

The eternal realm is also called heaven. It is important to keep the earthly and heavenly realms in mind when reading this book.

Another important concept to understand in this book is that God ordained and created everything from all eternity. This is a "supernaturalist" viewpoint. Supernaturalism is not referring to non-substantial or invisible beings like angels, spirits, or a devil. Supernaturalism is the belief that all things are created and maintained by God. The opposite view is naturalism where the universe maintains itself by its own laws and random course. The view in this book is that God created everything past, present, and future, across all time and space, in six days. This means all things are done and finished from God's perspective; but from our perspective, it is a linear timeline. He predestined everything, controls everything, and set all things in place so that nothing is random; yet, creation simultaneously works according to its free agency. This book is coming from a "Supralapsarian Calvinist" view. Supralapsarian Calvinism is strictly supernaturalist theology. The *Merriam-Webster dictionary* defines "super-naturalism" as,

> *Belief in a supernatural power and order of existence.* [3]

"Naturalism" is the opposite view. The *Merriam-Webster Dictionary* defines "naturalism" as,

> *A theory denying that an event or object has a supernatural significance specifically: the doctrine that scientific laws are adequate to account for all phenomena.* [4]

Pure naturalism teaches that the universe runs on its own random course. Most Christian theology is a mixture of supernaturalism and naturalism. This is the teaching that God created everything to sustain itself while God interferes with creation. "Infralapsarian Calvinism," also known as T.U.L.I.P., is also a mixture of naturalism and supernaturalism. The view of this book rejects the T.U.L.I.P. form of Calvinism. Supralapsarian Calvinism is different than the T.U.L.I.P. teaching held by most Calvinists. The Infralapsarian view teaches that God predestined some people after Adam sinned. The T in T.U.L.I.P. stands for "Total Depravity." The U in T.U.L.I.P. stands for "Unconditional Election." The reason the T comes before the U is because Infralapsarians teach that Adam became a totally depraved sinner

Preface

before God chose certain people throughout history to be His elect. This doctrine follows the standard of *the Belgic Confession of Faith*. *The Belgic confession* teaches that after Adam sinned and then God predestined some to heaven and left the rest behind to perish in hell. *The Belgic Confession* states,

> *We believe that God, after all the offspring of Adam thus fell head over heels into perdition and destruction by the guilt of the first man, demonstrated and put forth His very self as such a kind as He is: both merciful and also just. Indeed, merciful in freeing and saving from damnation and ruin those whom in His eternal council He elected, out of gratuity apart from any work, according to His goodness through our Lord Jesus Christ. Truly just, in leaving behind others in their fall and ruin into which they threw their very selves head over heels.* [5]

This form of predestination teaches that God only intervenes in the life of certain people for salvation while leaving everyone else to their own demise. The Supralapsarian view teaches that God predestined everything because He created it and governs it through His providence. Predestination is not contingent on the actions or events of creation. Predestination refers to God ordaining everything in creation supernaturally from eternity. Predestination is not referring to God ordaining some people to heaven. *The Westminster Confession of Faith* states,

> **God, from all eternity**, did, by the most wise and holy counsel of his own will, freely, and **unchangeably ordain whatsoever comes to pass**: yet so, as thereby neither is God the author of sin, nor is violence offered to the will of the creatures. [6]

The Westminster Standard is that all creatures are predestined and all creatures freely choose according to their own will simultaneously. This supernaturalist concept is explained further in *the Westminster Larger Catechism*.

> Q. 14. How doth God execute his decrees?
> A. God **executeth his decrees in the works of creation and providence**, according to his infallible foreknowledge, and the free and immutable counsel of his own will. [7]

This means that God predestined everything by creating all things: past, present, and future. They are predestined because He created them. This view is vastly different than the T.U.L.I.P. Calvinist view. The supernaturalist view teaches that the Law of God is fixed in God's creation and not just a set of rules available for people to willingly keep or not keep. God's Law is just like the Law of Gravity, an integral part of the cosmos. With these concepts in mind, the reader should be able to understand the perspective of the book going forward.

Preface

Introduction

It is not breaking news to point out that the Christian Church has divided over theological doctrines throughout its existence. There are so many instances of Christians debating, dividing, and breaking fellowship with one another over doctrines that, in some instances, are completely trivial. Throughout the history of the Christian Church, the Fourth Commandment "to keep the Sabbath holy" is one of the most neglected and confused laws in the entire Old Testament. The Christian Church has discussed, fought, divided, and ripped itself apart over this commandment time and time again. Whole denominations were created over the doctrine of the Sabbath. The Reformed, Seventh Day Adventists, Evangelical, and Roman Catholic churches all teach different views on the Sabbath. The division on the Fourth Commandment has always boggled my mind as a Christian. There are many times in my Christian experience where Church pastors, elders, and other church leaders, push Christians out of "their" church over unbiblical doctrines. The divisions in the Church largely overlook the main purpose of the Christian message. The purpose of the Church is to preach salvation in Jesus Christ. Paul wrote,

> *And when I came to you, brethren, I did not come with superiority of speech or of wisdom, proclaiming to you the testimony of God. For I determined to know nothing among you except Jesus Christ, and Him crucified. (1Co 2:1-2 NAS)*

The Church is not to divide and start a new Church every time someone disagrees with a doctrine taught by a Church leader and their followers. Paul pointed this out to the Corinthian church. Paul wrote,

> *For you are still fleshly. For since there is jealousy and strife among you, are you not fleshly, and are you not walking like mere men? For when one says, "I am of Paul," and another, "I am of Apollos," are you not mere men? What then is Apollos? And what is Paul? Servants through whom you believed, even as the Lord gave opportunity to each one. (1Co 3:3-5 NAS)*

Divisions in the Church are as old as the Church itself. The Corinthians caused strife between each other about whether to follow Paul, Apollos, or Cephas. It seems to be a sad inevitability for Christians to follow Church leaders instead of Christ. Christ gave one simple command,

> *This I command you, that you love one another. (Joh 15:17 NAS)*

Yet, specific teachers have used the Fourth Commandment "to keep the Sabbath holy" as fuel to divide the Christian church. These divisions have wrought devastating results in the unity of the Christian church. The Apostle Paul specifically said not to divide the Church over disputes about the Law. Paul wrote,

> *But shun foolish controversies and genealogies and strife and disputes about the Law; for they are unprofitable and worthless. Reject a factious man after a first and second warning, knowing that such a man is perverted and is sinning, being self-condemned. (Tit 3:9-11 NAS)*

Paul points out the fact that some men want to teach strange doctrines and myths that lead to pure speculation. Paul wrote,

> *As I urged you upon my departure for Macedonia, remain on at Ephesus, in order that you may instruct certain men not to teach strange doctrines, nor to pay attention to myths and endless genealogies, which give rise to mere speculation rather than furthering the administration of God which is by faith. (1Ti 1:3-4 NAS)*

Those who teach myths and speculations about the Law while not knowing anything about the Law are to be rejected. The object of preaching the gospel of Christ is from love and sincerity. Paul further states,

> *But the goal of our instruction is love from a pure heart and a good conscience and a sincere faith. (1Ti 1:5 NAS)*

Faith in Christ is the object of instruction and not strange prophetic predictions or leading people astray with twisted interpretations of the Law. Paul wrote,

> *For some men, straying from these things, have turned aside to fruitless discussion, wanting to be teachers of the Law, even though they do not understand either what they are saying or the matters about which they make confident assertions. (1Ti 1:6-7 NAS)*

The doctrine of the Sabbath must be derived from the Bible alone and not from the point of view of a theologian. The word "sabbath" has several meanings when studying the Bible. Sometimes it is referring to the Fourth Commandment, sometimes the weekly ceremonial sacrifice, and sometimes a calendar day. One anomaly is how the word "sabbath" is inconsistently capitalized in the Bible and in people's writings. In regards to capitalizing the word "sabbath," *the Religion Stylebook* says,

> *The day of the week observed for rest and worship. Most Christian traditions observe the Sabbath on Sunday. Judaism — along with some Christian traditions such as Seventh-day Adventists — observes the Sabbath on Saturday. (Jews' observance of the Sabbath begins at sundown Friday [and is often referred to by the Hebrew word Shabbat].)* **Capitalize in religious references but lowercase when talking about periods of rest.** *[8]*

An example of the inconsistency found in the capitalization of the word "sabbath" is seen in *the New American Standard* (NASB) and *the King James* (KJV) Bibles. In *the New American Standard* and *the King James* Bibles, the word "sabbath" is lower case through all of the Old Testament, while it is capitalized through all of the New Testament. Both Hebrew and ancient Greek characters in the Bible are caseless, so it is a choice done by the translators. The inconsistency in capitalizing the word "sabbath" does impact the English rendering. Throughout this book, the word "sabbath" is capitalized only when it is a proper noun. When the word "sabbath" is used as a common noun it is not capitalized. The different authors quoted in this book use inconsistent capitalization. The capitalization within quotes used in this book were not changed from the original authors usage.

Introduction

Only a Bible that uses a translation of the original Greek and Hebrew should be used. Using a literal translation of the Bible is imperative. This is so the original Greek or Hebrew word can be looked up, defined, and verified. An example of a translation that is not literal is *the Living Torah* translated by Rabbi Aryeh Kaplan. An example of a word not in the original text in *the Living Torah* is found in Leviticus 23:3.

> *You may do work during the six weekdays,* **but Saturday** *is a Sabbath of Sabbaths. It is a sacred holiday to God, when you shall do no work. Wherever you may live, it is God's Sabbath.* [9]

Rabbi Aryeh Kaplan inserted the word "Saturday" into the text. The ancient Israelites did not use the word Saturday in the original text. Nowhere is the word "Saturday" found in the Bible. "Saturday" is a modern word that comes from the modern calendar. Rabbi Aryeh Kaplan inserted this word into the text himself. According to Rabbi Aryeh Kaplan, the literal translations, like *the King James Version* are scholarly; however, they do not agree with the Jewish traditions.

> *Most previous translations of the Torah can be divided into categories. The "traditional" ones are, for the most part, based on the King James translation.* ***Although a superb scholarly work, this translation is not rooted in Jewish sources, and often goes against traditional Jewish teachings.*** *Furthermore, the language is archaic and difficult for the modern reader. Both of these shortcomings remain in most "traditional" translation.* [10]

The reason the Jewish tradition conflicts with the Bible is because the Jewish tradition does not come from the Bible. Bible translators who insert their words into the text in order to fit their theology must be rejected. God condemns those who use their own words in place of God's Word.

> *But the prophet who shall speak a word presumptuously in My name which I have not commanded him to speak, or which he shall speak in the name of other gods, that prophet shall die. (Deu 18:20 NAS)*

The Bible is not a matter of a person's personal religious tradition or their own theological interpretation. The Apostle Peter explains this clearly.

> *But know this first of all, that no prophecy of Scripture is a matter of one's own interpretation, for no prophecy was ever made by an act of human will, but men moved by the Holy Spirit spoke from God. (2Pe 1:20-21 NAS)*

To add or remove words from Scripture is condemned by the Apostles and the Prophets. The book of Revelation says,

> *I testify to everyone who hears the words of the prophecy of this book: if anyone adds to them, God shall add to him the plagues which are written in this book; and if anyone takes away from the words of the book of this prophecy, God shall take away his part from the tree of life and from the holy city, which are written in this book. (Rev 22:18-19 NAS)*

Introduction

Therefore, the only translations used in this book are literal translations that have a Bible concordance where the Greek and Hebrew word can be looked up. The literal translations used in this book are *the New American Standard* and *the King James Version* Bibles.

The intent of this book is to dispel all myths and speculations that theologians produce with their false interpretations of the Law, especially in relation to the Fourth Commandment "to keep the Sabbath holy." This is for the purpose of bringing back unity and faith in the gospel of Jesus Christ. The following seven points will prepare you for what will be discussed going forward.

1. In order to pin point the exact error in most Church doctrines of the Sabbath, we must briefly cover three prevalent views in the Church. Many Christian Churches hold "Sabbatarian" theology. A "Sabbatarian" is someone who holds the theological position that the Sabbath is the specific designated day for worship. There are typically two types of Sabbatarians; the "First Day Sabbatarian" and the "Seventh Day Sabbatarian." Those who hold that the Law is abolished are called "antinomian." Antinomians believe the Fourth Commandment "to keep the Sabbath holy" and all of the Law in the Old Testament is no longer applicable to the Church. Most Christians in general will fall into one of these three theological positions. Each of these views will be scrutinized and refuted.

2. The Law of God, God's Law, and the Law of Moses are all referring to the same Law found in the Old and New Testaments of the Bible. The Law of God is understood in three separate parts. Some call this the "tripartite" structure of God's Law. The three-part structure of God's Law is the Moral Law, the Ceremonial Law, and the Judicial Law. The Law of God contains either statutes or judgments. The Moral Law is summed up in the Ten Commandments. The Ceremonial Laws are the duties of the priests regarding sacrifices, feasts, new moons, and sabbaths. The Judicial Laws are civil and criminal laws. The three-part structure of the Law must be applied to the doctrine of the Sabbath. Jesus fulfilled all of what was spoken of Him in the Law of Moses and the Prophets in His messianic work.

> *He said to them, "These are my words that I spoke to you while I was still with you, that everything written about me in the law of Moses and in the prophets and psalms must be fulfilled." (Luk 24:44 NAB)*

Christ did not just fulfill one part of the Law. He fulfilled ALL of the Law. How Christ fulfilled the Law is thoroughly explained. The messianic work of Christ and how He fulfilled the Law is outlined in *the Apostles Creed*.

3. In order to understand the Ceremonial Laws, it is necessary to study how the calendar works in general. The Bible does not have enough information to establish a specific calendar. The phases of the moon were used to determine the months in the Bible. Sabbaths, new moons, feasts, festivals, and sacrifices are calendar events that established the seasonal cycles required for agriculture. The events that establish the Jewish holidays are delineated in the book of Leviticus chapter 23. These events were primarily memorials of events that happened when the Israelites left captivity in Egypt. The Ceremonial Laws foreshadow the promises of God fulfilled in the messianic work of Jesus Christ. The events on the Jewish calendar are a timeline of what Christ did for us in His messianic work. How the ancient Israelites kept track of their calendar significantly differs from the Gregorian calendar we use today.

Introduction

Understanding the workings of these calendars is necessary for coming to the correct understanding of the Ceremonial Law. It is impossible to set accurate dates when calculating prophecy and historical events because the ancient Jewish and Gregorian calendars differ significantly. All dates derived in this book are only for approximations of historical events. It is impossible to accurately determine the dates of Biblical prophecies. This is largely due to the fact that each society had conflicting calendar systems and that there are no documents establishing the chronological events in certain parts of history. Attempting to predict future prophetic events is contrary to the gospel and must be rejected.

4. From an appropriate study of the Law and the Jewish festivals, we can ascertain the facts about the Sabbath. The core concept of the Fourth Commandment is to rest from labor and to rest the land. The command mentions nothing about religious worship services. The command is specific to labor, land, and commerce. Not just an individual's labor, but all people in society as well. The priests, sacrifices, or any worship activities are not mentioned in the commandment at all. The fact that religious worship is not mentioned in the commandment is key to understand what God intended in the Fourth Commandment.

5. The Fourth Commandment "to keep the Sabbath holy" is extremely important and relevant to any society of any generation. Many actual detrimental issues we face in society today are caused by breaking the Fourth Commandment. Climate change is one problem caused by breaking the Fourth Commandment. By climate change, I am referring to the change in environmental weather patterns and the sustainability of the earth's ecosystem. In this book, climate change has nothing to do with the "Greenhouse Gas Effect." Attending a church service on Saturday or Sunday is irrelevant to labor, land, and commerce. Worshiping God on a specific day has nothing to do with breaking the Fourth Commandment. Nowhere in the Bible does God reprimand His people for failing to worship Him on the Sabbath. Every instance where Israel breaks the Fourth Commandment "to keep the Sabbath holy" is in reference to working labor, land, and commerce. The fact is, observing the Fourth Commandment is just as critical for our modern world as it was for ancient Israel.

6. The purpose of God's Law is to lead His people into the glorious salvation we have in Jesus Christ. Without the Law of God, there is no salvation.

> *For it is not those who hear the law who are just in the sight of God; rather, those who observe the law will be justified. (Rom 2:13 NAB)*

The ancient Israelites observed the Ceremonial Law as a memorial of the salvation of God's people from slavery in Egypt and to keep the promise of the future Messiah. The observances of the feasts, new moons, and sabbaths in the Old Testament foreshadowed what Jesus Christ did for His people as the promised Messiah. The salvation of God's people is clearly seen in the fulfillment of the Law in Christ. The timeline of the feasts, new moons, and sabbaths corresponds to the Christian gospel. Jesus Christ fulfilled the promises in His being born of the virgin, crucifixion, resurrection from the dead, ascending to heaven, and His judging the living and the dead. The fulfillment of Christ as the promised Messiah is articulated in *the Apostles Creed*. The prophecies of the Old Testament are completely fulfilled in the messianic work of Jesus Christ.

Introduction

7. Studying the Fourth Commandment "to keep the Sabbath holy" undeniably leads to the conclusion that the commandment has nothing to do with a worship service. Nor does the Fourth Commandment establish a specific day for worship. The Fourth Commandment was never intended to establish a worship day. Likewise, the observance of holidays like Easter and the Passover are completely subjective and not worthy of Church divisions. Accurately teaching the Law of God and the fulfillment of the Law is essential to appropriately loving God and our neighbor. Theological doctrines that neglect an adequate study of God's Law must be rejected. Those who neglect the Law of God in their life are deluding themselves.

> *Be doers of the word and not hearers only, deluding yourselves. For if anyone is a hearer of the word and not a doer, he is like a man who looks at his own face in a mirror. He sees himself, then goes off and promptly forgets what he looked like. But the one who peers into the perfect law of freedom and perseveres, and is not a hearer who forgets but a doer who acts, such a one shall be blessed in what he does. (Jam 1:22-25 NAB)*

In addition to the seven points just explained, it is important to address any preconceived notions. The theological position proposed in this book is a unique doctrine called "Interdimensional theology" and is not a regurgitation of another systematic doctrine. Interdimensional theology does not contain "futurist" or "historicist" predictions of Bible prophecy. Date setting and "end times" predictions are the antithesis to Interdimensional theology. Interdimensional theology does not teach any position against the ethnicity of Jews or for any ideas that may be construed as "Anti-Semitic." Interdimensional theology does not establish any position on the restoration of the Nation of Israel in 1948. Zionism is not taught in Interdimensional theology. In other words, God can establish the Nation of Israel at any time in history He so chooses, past, present, or future according to His sovereign choice determined solely by His Will alone. The restoration of the Nation of Israel in 1948 or Zionism has nothing to do with the teachings in this book. Only ancient Israel found in the Old Testament is discussed. The theology propounded in this book teaches that the Law of God found in the Old Testament is for Jews and Gentiles alike.

> *For I am not ashamed of the gospel, for it is the power of God for salvation **to everyone who believes, to the Jew first and also to the Greek**. (Rom 1:16 NAS)*

> *Or is God the God of Jews only? Is He not the God of Gentiles also? **Yes, of Gentiles also.** (Rom 3:29 NAS)*

> *And He did so in order that He might make known the riches of His glory upon vessels of mercy, which He prepared beforehand for glory, even us, whom He also called, **not from among Jews only, but also from among Gentiles**. (Rom 9:23-24 NAS)*

This book does not teach any "futurist" predictions or fulfilments of prophecy or date setting for the "second coming of Christ." Date setting, prophetic predictions, or any matching up of Bible prophecy to future events is contrary to the teachings of Interdimensional theology. The doctrine called "the second coming of Christ," as taught by Futurists, Historicists and Preterists, is rejected as false.

Introduction

Interdimensional theology does not teach that the coming of Christ happened at AD 70 as some Preterists teach. This does not mean Interdimensional theology denies the coming of Christ. The teaching of the coming of Christ in this book appears to be paradoxical. Interdimensional theology holds paradoxes as true in reasoning. *The Merriam-Websters Dictionary* defines the word "paradox" as,

> *a statement that is seemingly contradictory or opposed to common sense and yet is perhaps true. [11]*

An example of a paradox in Christian theology is the nature of Christ. Christ is fully God and fully man at the same time.

The teaching to follow God's Law in this book does not mean to mindlessly follow all government laws. The government laws must match the Law of God. If the government creates statutes legalizing murder, such as abortion, Christians are obligated to speak against and disobey these laws. Also, the theology in this book is strictly for the purpose of teaching the gospel and breaking down the divisions in the church. Hating other Christians for their theological position is contrary to the teachings found in this book. Reformed, Seventh Day Adventist, Evangelical, Roman Catholic, and ALL Christians are to be respected and loved equally as brothers in Christ. Pointing out the differences between Christian theological groups does not necessitate breaking fellowship with those groups. Whether one group wants Saturday or Sunday worship should not be a point of division in the Church.

Finally, the view provided in this book does not exhaustively cover every single view in Christianity. The Reformed, Seventh Day Adventist, and Dispensationalist views are addressed because they are the most common views that are encountered. The purpose of this book is not to represent every known doctrinal view on the Sabbath known to man. Different theological positions are included generically for the purpose of understanding Interdimensional theology. The views of non-Christian cult groups such as the Church of Jesus Christ Latter Day Saints, Jehovah Witnesses, and so forth will not be discussed in this book. When the word "Church" is used, it is referring to all Christian denominations as a whole. The Church as a whole is the "ecumenical" or "Catholic" church. The word "Church" or "Catholic" does not mean "Roman Catholic." Lastly, all bolded text in quotes throughout this book are done by the writer and not the original author of the quote.

> *Grace and peace be multiplied to you in the knowledge of God and of Jesus our Lord; seeing that His divine power has granted to us everything pertaining to life and godliness, through the true knowledge of Him who called us by His own glory and excellence. For by these He has granted to us His precious and magnificent promises, in order that by them you might become partakers of the divine nature, having escaped the corruption that is in the world by lust. Now for this very reason also, applying all diligence, in your faith supply moral excellence, and in your moral excellence, knowledge; and in your knowledge, self-control, and in your self-control, perseverance, and in your perseverance, godliness; and in your godliness, brotherly kindness, and in your brotherly kindness, love. For if these qualities are yours and are increasing, they render you neither useless nor unfruitful in the true knowledge of our Lord Jesus Christ. (2Pe 1:2-8 NAS)*

Introduction

Chapter 1 - First Day Sabbatarian

A predominant Sabbath doctrine in Christianity is First Day Sabbatarian theology. First Day Sabbatarian's teach that the Fourth Commandment "to keep the Sabbath holy" was changed from the seventh day to the first day of the week. The Presbyterian, Reformed Baptist, Dutch Reformed, and other "Reformed" churches have First Day Sabbatarian creeds. *The Westminster Confession of Faith of 1647* clearly teaches the Sabbath was changed to the first day of the week. *The Westminster Confession of Faith* expressly teaches that the Sabbath is the designated day for worship called the "Lord's Day."

1. *The Westminster Confession of Faith*

The Westminster Confession of Faith calls the Sabbath the Lord's Day teaching that the Sabbath changed to the first day of the week as the day of worship.

> *As it is the law of nature, that, in general, **a due proportion of time be set apart for the worship of God**; so, in his Word, by a positive, moral, and perpetual commandment binding all men in all ages, he hath particularly appointed one day in seven, **for a Sabbath**, to be kept holy unto him: which, from the beginning of the world to the resurrection of Christ, was the last day of the week; and, from the resurrection of Christ, **was changed into the first day of the week, which, in Scripture, is called the Lord's day**, and is to be continued to the end of the world, as the **Christian Sabbath**. [12]*

The Westminster Confession of Faith teaches that the Sabbath requirement to do no work is applied to the first day, not the seventh day. It establishes the "Christian Sabbath" as THE day for worship.

> *This Sabbath is then kept holy unto the Lord, when men, after a due preparing of their hearts, and ordering of their common affairs beforehand, do not only **observe an holy rest, all the day, from their own works, words, and thoughts about their worldly employments and recreations**, but also are taken up, the whole time, in the public and private **exercises of his worship**, and in the duties of necessity and mercy. [13]*

This view was widely taught by the Puritan theologians.

a. The Puritans

Thomas Watson, along with the other Puritans of his time, propounded this view heavily. Thomas Watson wrote,

> ***The old seventh-day Sabbath, which was the Jewish Sabbath, is abrogated, and in the room of it the first day of the week, which is the Christian Sabbath**, succeeds. The morality or substance of the fourth commandment does not lie in keeping the seventh day precisely, but keeping one day in seven is what God has appointed. [14]*

Chapter 1 - First Day Sabbatarian

The Puritan "Christian Sabbath" doctrine is founded upon a conclusion drawn from tradition. In an attempt to prove the necessity of observing the Fourth Commandment, the Puritans came to the conclusion that the Sabbath changed from the seventh day to the first day. They introduced the name "Christian Sabbath." Thomas Watson draws the conclusion from tradition in his following explanation.

> *The change of the Sabbath from the last day of the week to the first was by Christ's own appointment. He is 'Lord of the Sabbath.' Mark 2: 28. And who shall appoint a day but he who is Lord of it? He made this day. 'This is the day which the Lord has made.' Psa 118: 24.* **Arnobius and most expositors understand it of the Christian Sabbath,** *which is called the 'Lord's-day.' Rev 1: 10. As it is called the 'Lord's Supper,' because of the Lord's instituting the bread and wine and setting it apart from a common to a special and sacred use; so it is called the Lord's-day, because of the Lord's instituting it, and setting it apart from common days, to his special worship and service. Christ rose on the first day of the week, out of the grave, and appeared twice on that day to his disciples, John 20: 19, 26, which was to intimate to them,* **as Augustine and Athanasius say, that he transferred the Jewish Sabbath to the Lord's day.** *[15]*

Relying on authorities like Arnobius, Augustine, or Athanasius as sufficient evidence is the fallacy of "appealing to an authority." The authorities themselves must be proven correct first. Even though Thomas Watson wrote, "Augustine and Athanasius say, that he transferred the Jewish Sabbath to the Lord's day," neither Church Father is quoted. Even if the Church Fathers did say the Jewish Sabbath was transferred to the Lord's Day, this is the fallacy of appealing to an authority. The "appeal to authority" fallacy is defined as,

> *Insisting that a claim is true simply because a valid authority or expert on the issue said it was true, without any other supporting evidence offered. [16]*

Being great in the church does not necessitate they are correct in their theology. The Scriptures quoted by Thomas Watson do not support the argument that the Sabbath changed to the first day. The verse "Lord of the Sabbath" (Mar 2: 28) simply means Christ is God and the supreme authority of the Sabbath. "This is the day which the Lord has made" (Psa 118: 24) clearly is referring to every day of the week. The quote "the Lord's Day" (Rev 1: 10) in Revelation is too vague and does not state which specific day John was referring to. The context of the verse that Jesus "appeared twice on that day to his disciples" (Joh 20: 19, 26) does not mention or reference the Sabbath at all. Christ raising from the dead on the first day and the institution of the Lord's Supper does not support the claim that the Sabbath changed from the seventh to the first day.

The reasons given by Thomas Watson do not logically lead to the conclusion that there is a Christian Sabbath or that the Sabbath changed from seventh day to the first day. Thomas Watson clearly rationalized the conclusion. When someone offers a false explanation that does not support the conclusion, they are rationalizing. Rationalizing is defined as,

> *Offering false or inauthentic excuses for our claim because we know the real reasons are much less persuasive or more embarrassing to share, or harsher than the manufactured ones given.* [17]

When approaching Scripture, it is important to use deductive reasoning when coming to the knowledge of truth. The evidence presented in an argument must logically follow to the conclusion. Studying the writings of Augustine and Athanasius leads to a different conclusion than what was given by Thomas Watson.

2. The Church Fathers

Saints are often quoted to support First Day Sabbatarian theology. Thomas Watson maintains Augustine and Athanasius taught the Christian Sabbath. Neither Augustine nor Athanasius taught the Sabbath was changed from the seventh day to the first day.

a. Augustine

According to Augustine, the eighth day is the Lord's Day after the Sabbath. Christ was in the tomb on the Sabbath and rose from the dead on the eighth day. Augustine taught the Lord's Day was when Christ rose from the dead after the Sabbath. Augustine did not teach the Lord's Day became the new Sabbath day. Augustine wrote,

> *He brought it about that **His body rested from all its works on Sabbath in the tomb**, and that His resurrection on the third day, which **we call the Lord's day, the day after the Sabbath**, and therefore the eighth, proved the circumcision of the eighth day to be also prophetical of Him.* [18]

Augustine clearly taught the Sabbath and the Lord's Day were separate distinct days.

b. Athanasius

There is a specific quote allegedly from Athanasius *On Sabbath and Circumcision*. The source text attributed to Athanasius *On Sabbath and Circumcision* appears to not be available to date. At least, I have not been able to find it. In fact, it is disputed that Athanasius even wrote this quote.

> *AD 345. Athanasius: "**The Sabbath was the end of the first creation, the Lord's day was the beginning of the second**, in which he renewed and restored the old in the same way as he prescribed that they should formerly observe the Sabbath as a memorial of the end of the first things, so we honor the Lord's day as being the memorial of the new creation."* [19]

Athanasius' writing *On Sabbath and Circumcision* is an unknown document that does not appear to exist. Regardless, even if the quote is genuine, Athanasius still does not teach the Sabbath is the Lord's Day. The quote says the Sabbath is the "end of the first creation" and the Lord's day is "the beginning of the second." Clearly the author of this quote understood the Sabbath and the Lord's Day as two different events. This is similar to what Augustine taught. There are no other quotes in any of the works of Athanasius that states anything substantial about the Sabbath. Evidence shows neither Augustine nor Athanasius taught the Sabbath changed from the seventh day to the first day of the week.

c. Thomas Aquinas

The Puritans studied Saint Thomas Aquinas heavily. The confusion of the Sabbath and the Lord's Day can be construed from the Catechism of Saint Thomas Aquinas.

> *The Jews kept holy the Sabbath in memory of the first creation; but Christ at His coming brought about a new creation. For by the first creation an earthly man was created, and by the second a heavenly man was formed: "For in Christ Jesus neither circumcision availeth anything, nor uncircumcision, but a new creature." This new creation is through grace, which came by the Resurrection: "That as Christ is risen from the dead by the glory of the Father, so we also may walk in newness of life. For if we have been planted together in the likeness of His death, so shall we also be in the likeness of His resurrection."* **And thus, because the Resurrection took place on Sunday, we celebrate that day, even as the Jews observed the Sabbath on account of the first creation.** [20]

The teaching of Saint Thomas does not teach the first day or the Lord's Day is the Christian Sabbath either. Saint Thomas clearly taught that as the Jews worshipped God in relationship to the first creation, the Sabbath, and Christians worship God in relation to the new creation, the resurrection day. Any way you look at the doctrine of the Christian Sabbath, it cannot be found in the Church Fathers teaching. The Sabbath and the Lord's Day are always separated as different days with different purposes. For more on what the Early Church Fathers taught see Appendix I on the "Early Church Fathers on the Sabbath and Lord's Day." The first day was made a national day for Christians to go to Church by Emperor Constantine throughout the Roman Empire in the Edict of Milan AD 313. This was to remove Jewish influence from Christianity. It was not a change of the Sabbath from the seventh day to the first day. This is discussed further in the chapter on "the Calendar."

3. Christ is the Lord of the Sabbath

There is confusion on the expression "the Lord of the Sabbath." Somehow, the Puritans used the following verses to establish the doctrine of the Christian Sabbath.

> *For the Son of Man is Lord of the Sabbath. (Mat 12:8 NAS)*
> *Consequently, the Son of Man is Lord even of the Sabbath. (Mar 2:28 NAS)*
> *And He was saying to them, "The Son of Man is Lord of the Sabbath." (Luk 6:5 NAS)*

There is no logical way to interpret the phrase "the Lord of the Sabbath" as referring to attending church on Sunday. There are no references to attending worship services in Matthew 12, Mark 2 or Luke 6 at all. The phrase that Christ is "the Lord of the Sabbath" clearly shows Christ equated Himself to God. Only God can rightly be called "the Lord of the Sabbath." Christ, the Eternal Word, created all things and rested on the seventh day. Paul wrote in Colossians.

For He delivered us from the domain of darkness, and transferred us to the kingdom of His beloved Son, in whom we have redemption, the forgiveness of sins. And He is the image of the invisible God, the first-born of all creation. **For by Him all things were created, both in the heavens and on earth, visible and invisible, whether thrones or dominions or rulers or authorities all things have been created by Him and for Him.** *And He is before all things, and in Him all things hold together. (Col 1:13-17 NAS)*

Christ is "the Lord of the Sabbath;" therefore, Christ Himself has the right, the knowledge, and everything in His power to judge how the Sabbath is to be observed. Inserting Sunday worship into the phrase "the Lord of the Sabbath" is completely contrary to the context of the gospels. The conclusion is that First Day Sabbatarian theology is only built upon tradition. The Fourth Commandment "to keep the Sabbath holy" is only referring to labor, land, and commerce, not a day of worship. This is discussed in detail later in the chapter on "the Sabbath."

It is impossible to find any teaching in the Bible or the Church Fathers that the Fourth Commandment "to keep the Sabbath holy" was changed from the seventh day to the first day. The Sabbath on the seventh day is always differentiated from the Lord's Day. When the council of Nicaea met in AD 325, they discussed which day to celebrate Easter. At the time, Christians celebrated Easter on two different days of the year. Christians celebrated Easter according to the Jewish calendar and the other on the Julian calendar. Eusebius wrote,

> *And first of all, it appeared an unworthy thing that in the celebration of this most holy feast we should follow the practice of the Jews, who have impiously defiled their hands with enormous sin, and are, therefore, deservedly afflicted with blindness of soul.* **For we have it in our power, if we abandon their custom, to prolong the due observance of this ordinance to future ages, by a truer order, which we have preserved from the very day of the passion until the present time.** *Let us then have nothing in common with the detestable Jewish crowd; for we have received from our Saviour a different way. A course at once legitimate and honorable lies open to our most holy religion.* [21]

The establishment of Sunday as the day of worship was partly to remove the Jewish Sabbath and festivals from Christianity entirely. There was no change. The dates to celebrate Easter, Christmas, the Lord's Day, and all Christian festivals were established on dates that have nothing to do with the Jewish calendar. How the Jewish calendar works is discussed further in the chapter on "the Calendar."

The "Christian Sabbath" doctrine and the alleged switch of the Sabbath from the seventh day to the first day completely lacks evidence. The Sabbath on the seventh day was always distinguished from the Lord's Day on the first day. The doctrine of the "Christian Sabbath" is an "Ad Hoc Rescue" fallacy. The definition of the Ad Hoc Rescue fallacy is,

> *Very often we desperately want to be right and hold on to certain beliefs, despite any evidence presented to the contrary. As a result, we begin to make up excuses as to*

why our belief could still be true, and is still true, despite the fact that we have no real evidence for what we are making up. [22]

The only conclusion is that the Christian Sabbath doctrine is not supported by the Bible or the Early Church Fathers.

Chapter 2 - Seventh Day Sabbatarian

Seventh Day Sabbatarian theology is another prevalent Sabbath doctrine in Christianity. Seventh Day Sabbatarians teach that worship services should be performed on the seventh day or Saturday. They teach that the Fourth Commandment is referring to worship services and resting from labor. Seventh Day Sabbatarians emphasize Christian worship on Saturday and not Sunday. The Seventh Day Adventist church is the biggest proponent of Seventh Day Sabbatarian theology. Seventh Day Adventists teach the Lord's Day is the same day as the Sabbath on the seventh day. Because Seventh Day Adventists are the biggest proponent of the Seventh Day Sabbatarian's, the Seventh Day Adventist view is represented here.

1. The Seventh Day Adventist or SDA

The SDA church adheres strictly to Seventh Day Sabbatarian doctrine. The SDA church teaches true Christian worship is to be held on the seventh day (Saturday specifically). *The 28 Fundamental Beliefs* of the Seventh Day Adventist Church states the Fourth Commandment is for rest, worship, and ministry.

> *The gracious Creator, after the six days of Creation, rested on the seventh day and instituted the Sabbath for all people as a memorial of Creation. The fourth commandment of God's unchangeable law requires* **the observance of this seventh-day Sabbath as the day of rest, worship, and ministry in harmony** *with the teaching and practice of Jesus, the Lord of the Sabbath. The Sabbath is a day of delightful communion with God and one another. It is a symbol of our redemption in Christ, a sign of our sanctification, a token of our allegiance, and a foretaste of our eternal future in God's kingdom. The Sabbath is God's perpetual sign of His eternal covenant between Him and His people. Joyful observance of this holy time from evening to evening, sunset to sunset, is a celebration of God's creative and redemptive acts.* [23]

The Sabbath is key to all SDA worship activities. *The 28 Fundamental Beliefs* of the Seventh Day Adventist Church magnifies worship as the most important duty on the Sabbath.

> *The Sabbath is central to our worship of God. The memorial of Creation, it reveals the reason why God is to be worshiped: He is the Creator, and we are His creatures.* **"The Sabbath, therefore, lies at the very foundation of divine worship, for it teaches this great truth in the most impressive manner, and no other institution does this.** *The true ground of divine worship, not of that on the seventh day merely, but of all worship, is found in the distinction between the Creator and His creatures. This great fact can never become obsolete, and must never be forgotten." It was to keep this truth forever before the human race that God instituted the Sabbath.* [24]

The fact is the Fourth Commandment to "keep the Sabbath holy" has nothing to do with Christian worship. Similar to the First Day Sabbatarian, the SDA church rationalizes the Fourth Commandment as the foundation of Christian worship. Actually, the SDA church goes far beyond teaching the Sabbath as a day for worship. They delve deep into hysterical interpretations. The radical interpretation of the Sabbath originates in the teachings of Ellen White.

a. Ellen White

Seventh Day Adventism was founded by Ellen White in 1863. The SDA church considers her a prophetess. The core theological teaching of the SDA church on the Sabbath involves their "end times" theology. For example, Ellen White taught that the United States is the fulfillment of the "Image of the beast" found in the book of Revelation. She wrote,

> "Saying to them that dwell on the earth, that **they should make an image to the beast**." Here is clearly presented a form of government in which the legislative power rests with the people, a most striking evidence that **the United States is the nation denoted in the prophecy**. [25]

Ellen White draws the conclusion that the United States "blue laws" (laws prohibiting certain activities, such as shopping and working, on Sunday) fulfill the prophecy of the beast in the book of Revelation. According to Ellen White, changing worship from Saturday to Sunday is a sign of the "mark of the beast."

> As the sign of the authority of the Catholic Church, papist writers cite "the very act of changing the Sabbath into Sunday, which Protestants allow of;... because by keeping Sunday, they acknowledge the church's power to ordain feasts, and to command them under sin."--Henry Tuberville, An Abridgment of the Christian Doctrine, page 58. **What then is the change of the Sabbath, but the sign, or mark, of the authority of the Roman Church--"the mark of the beast"**? [26]

It is an egregious abuse of scripture to apply the prophecies of "the beast" and "the mark" to the United States "blue laws." Ellen White taught that keeping the Sabbath is the true test of loyalty to God in the end times. According to Ellen White, those who attend Church on Sunday will receive the "mark of the beast."

> **The Sabbath will be the great test of loyalty,** for it is the point of truth especially controverted. When the final test shall be brought to bear upon men, then the line of distinction will be drawn between those who serve God and those who serve Him not. **While the observance of the false sabbath in compliance with the law of the state, contrary to the fourth commandment, will be an avowal of allegiance to a power that is in opposition to God,** the keeping of the true Sabbath, in obedience to God's law, is an evidence of loyalty to the Creator. While one class, by accepting the sign of submission to earthly powers, **receive the mark of the beast,** the other choosing the token of allegiance to divine authority, receive the seal of God." [27]

Ellen White draws a divide between Christians. She literally taught those who worship on Saturday are "loyal to the creator" while those who worship on the "false sabbath" or Sunday "receive the mark of the beast." This is why SDA members are so adamant about Saturday worship. They literally believe worshiping on Sunday is following Satan. Faith, repentance, and good works are secondary factors for who is loyal to God in the SDA church. Worshiping on Saturday is the measure of the true follower of God according to Ellen White. This doctrine is designed to scare members from leaving the SDA church for other denominations that worship on Sunday. The United States of America fulfilling the prophecy of the beast is an irreparable heresy that causes division between believers in Christ. It is irreparable because it cannot be fixed only abandoned.

b. The Modern SDA

The SDA church continues to affirm the teachings of Ellen White on Saturday worship. *The Adventist Review* in 2015 talks about "end times scenarios" of Satan changing the Sabbath to Sunday.

> ***Satan's ability to replace Sabbath with Sunday culminates in Revelation's end-time scenario,*** *which centers on the true day of worship (Rev. 13:11-17; 14:9; cf. the ability of the little-horn power of Daniel 7:25 to "change times and law" [NKJV]). [28]*

The SDA church focuses solely on the "true day of worship." The connection between Saturday worship and end times prophecy is the central theme in SDA doctrine. Ted C. Nelson in *the Adventist Review* affirms Ellen Whites teaching. *The Adventist Review* quotes Ellen Whites "The Great Controversy" as authoritative regarding Sunday worship and receiving the "mark of the beast."

> *The second animal in this chapter, which represents the United States, creates the image of this beast. A definition of the image is given on page 443 of The Great Controversy......**The mark of the beast—observance of a day other than the seventh-day Sabbath**—is an institution that clearly sets forth the authority of the beast. One world church boldly boasts that it has changed the seventh-day Sabbath instituted at Creation from Saturday to Sunday. Other churches indicate that they worship on Sunday as a memorial of Christ's resurrection. Neither assertion is found in Scripture. As a result, the recognition due the Creator is removed. [29]*

Ellen White is considered to be a prophetess in the SDA church to this day. The SDA church indoctrinates their church members to believe they will be persecuted for attending church worship on Sunday. Ted C. Nelson, in *the Adventist Review*, continues to teach their members that the world will hate and persecute them for worshiping God on Saturday.

> *Apostate religious leaders will not be able to refute scriptural evidence for the sacredness of Saturday as the Sabbath, and this fills them with anger. As a result,* ***Sabbath keepers will be persecuted and imprisoned.*** *Amid all these events, the proclamation of the third message will have an effect that has not been seen before. People will see that prophecies in Daniel, Matthew, Mark, Luke, Revelation, and elsewhere in Scripture are being fulfilled exactly as commandment keepers said they would.* ***The formation of the image of the beast and the enactment of the Sunday law will lead to national and international ruin.*** *[30]*

The Sabbath teaching of the SDA church is a scare tactic and not a Biblical fact. Scare tactics are used to retain church membership. The SDA church teaches their members to not associate with Christians who attend church on Sunday. Likewise, SDA church members are prohibited to attend a Christian church on Sunday. The logical conclusion to SDA church doctrines is that associating with Sunday Christians is equal to associating with the followers of Satan.

2. The Beast of Revelation

Because the beast of Revelation is central to the SDA doctrine of the Sabbath, it is important to explain the beast of Revelation. Teaching that the United States of America is the beast is false prophecy. The interpretation that the Beast of Revelation is the United States of America is completely absurd. Ellen White's interpretation of the beast is completely false when analyzing the Bible and historical facts. There is no reason for anyone to be confused on the beast. The angel explained who the Beast is.

> *And the angel said to me, "Why do you wonder?* ***I shall tell you the mystery of the woman and of the beast*** *that carries her, which has the seven heads and the ten horns." (Rev 17:7 NAS)*

According to the angel, the Beast was and is not, and is about to come. The angel explained,

> ***The beast that you saw was and is not, and is about to come up out of the abyss and to go to destruction.*** *And those who dwell on the earth will wonder, whose name has not been written in the book of life from the foundation of the world, when they see the beast,* ***that he was and is not and will come.*** *(Rev 17:8 NAS)*

The angel specifically said the beast is "about to come up out." Clearly the coming of the beast is an imminent event at the time the book of Revelation was written and not an event 2000 years into the future. The angel explains what this means.

> *Here is the mind which has wisdom. The* ***seven heads are seven mountains*** *on which the woman sits, and* ***they are seven kings; five have fallen, one is, the other has not yet come****; and when he comes, he must remain a little while. (Rev 17:9-10 NAS)*

Clearly, the beast comprises seven kings, five of the kings had already passed away. One of the kings was reigning during the time the book of Revelation was written. The final king was to come after the king who was reigning at that time. This placed the beast and all his attributes during the time of the Apostle John and not far into the future. Therefore, the United States cannot possibly be the beast of Revelation. Historicists attempt to change the word "kings" into "kingdoms" in order to fit the beast of Revelation into future historic events. The kings spoken of by the angel are NOT kingdoms. They are specific individuals who reign over the Roman Empire. The attempt to change the word "kings" into "kingdoms" not only twists the words of the text, but also is easily refuted by researching the seven mountains. The seven mountains are clearly in reference to the seven hills of Rome. Rome is known as the city founded upon seven hills. Researching seven "mountains" or "hills" will immediate result in the reference to the city of Rome. Anyone reading the book of Revelation at the time the book was written would clearly understand this. From the *Encyclopedia Britannica, Seven Hills of Rome [31]*, the seven hills are: Palatine, Capitoline, Quirinal, Viminal, Esquiline, Caelian, and Aventine.

It is not possible for people during the time of the Apostle John to apply the seven hills to the United States of America. The United States of America did not exist yet. There are approximately 73,301 mountains in the United States of America which is not even close to seven. The people of the Apostle John's time would automatically know that seven mountains or hills was referring specifically to Rome. This fact clearly identifies Rome and the Roman Caesars as the beast of Revelation. It makes interpreting the beast of Revelation that much easier knowing that the kings are the Roman Caesar's. Looking at the history of the Roman Caesars from the *Encyclopedia Britannica, List of Roman emperors [32]*, it is evident that the Roman Empire is the beast of Revelation. Just reviewing the history of the Roman Caesars, it becomes obvious that the book of Revelation was written during or around the reign of Vespasian. The five fallen kings in Revelation 17:10 were,

1. Augustus (31 BCE–AD 14)
2. Tiberius (AD 14–37)
3. Caligula (AD 37–41)
4. Claudius (AD 41–54)
5. Nero (AD 54–68)

While Vespasian was away from Rome in battle, there was a power struggle to take the throne in Rome. Within a year, three Roman generals tried to seize the throne while Rome was in a civil war. These generals were, Galba (AD 68–69), Otho (January–April AD 69), and Aulus Vitellius (July–December AD 69). Josephus writes about the civil war.

> *Now as Vespasian was returned to Cesarea, and was getting ready with all his army to march directly to Jerusalem, he was informed that Nero was dead, after he had reigned thirteen years and eight days.... how also the war in Gall ended; and **how Galba was made emperor** and returned out of Spain to Rome; and how he was accused by the soldiers as a pusillanimous person, **and slain by treachery in the middle of the market-place at Rome**, and **Otho was made emperor**; with his expedition against the commanders of Vitellius, and **his destruction thereupon**; and besides what troubles there were under Vitellius, and the fight that was about the capitol; as also **how Antonius Primus and Mucianus slew Vitellius**, and his German legions, and **thereby put an end to that civil war**;... So Agrippa resolved to go on to Rome without any terror; on account of the change in the government; but Titus, by a Divine impulse, sailed back from Greece to Syria, and came in great haste to Caesarea, to his father. And now they were both in suspense about the public affairs, **the Roman empire being then in a fluctuating condition**, and did not go on with their expedition against the Jews, but thought that to make any attack upon foreigners was now unseasonable, on account of the solicitude they were in for their own country. [33]*

These three "Caesars" are not included in the list of Caesars because Rome was in a civil war during this time. This is for the same reason the Confederate president Jefferson Davis during the American Civil War is not considered a president of the United States. The three Roman generals who tried to seize power only reigned for months before they were removed. These three "Caesars" are not included in the lineage of the kings of Rome in the book of Revelation. When Vespasian came back from war, he became Caesar. The king who was reigning around the time the book of Revelation was written would be,

6. Vespasian (AD 69–79)

The final king who was to shortly to come after Vespasian was,

7. Titus (AD 79–81)

Titus reigned "a little while," approximately 2 to 4 years. According to Bible prophecy, the sacrifices were to end and the abomination of desolation was to make the temple desolate (Dan 11:31). Jesus said,

> *Therefore, **when you see the abomination of desolation** which was spoken of through Daniel the prophet, **standing in the holy place** (let the reader understand), then let those who are in Judea flee to the mountains. (Mat 24:15-16 NAS; Mar 13:30; Luk 21:32)*

The abomination of desolation, according to Jesus was to occur during the generation of those to whom Christ was speaking. Jesus said,

> *Even so you too, when you see all these things, recognize that He is near, right at the door. "Truly I say to you, **this generation will not pass away until all these things take place**. Heaven and earth will pass away, but My words shall not pass away." (Mat 24:33-35 NAS)*

The city of Jerusalem was completely destroyed by Titus around AD 70 while serving as general under his father Vespasian. Titus became the seventh Caesar of Rome after Vespasian's reign ended. Titus was one of the generals under Caesar, "the eighth" and later became the seventh Caesar. Titus is the one who went to destroy Jerusalem thus "he goes to destruction."

> *And the beast which was and is not, is himself also an eighth, and is one of the seven, and he goes to destruction. (Rev 17:11 NAS)*

Many futurist and historicist theologians disagree with this interpretation. They insist the beast of Revelation is a far-off prophecy referring to an event thousands of years into the future. The beast of Revelation can only be interpreted as occurring during the time the book of Revelation was written. The very first verse of the book of Revelation states "the things which must shortly take place."

> *The Revelation of Jesus Christ, which God gave Him to show to His bond-servants, **the things which must shortly take place**; and He sent and communicated it by His angel to His bond-servant John. (Rev 1:1 NAS)*

The word "shortly" cannot be interpreted far into the future. *The NASB Concordance* defines "shortly" as,

<5034> τάχος (tachos)
Meaning: *speed*
Origin: *from 5036*
Usage: *quickly(2), shortly(3), soon(1), speedily(1).*
Notes: *Or, signified Joh 17:8; Rev 5:7 Rev 22:6 Dan 2:28f.; Rev 1:19 Rev 17:1; Rev 19:9f.; Rev 21:9; Rev 22:16 Rev 1:4, Rev 1:9; Rev 22:8. [34]*

The explanation of the beast of Revelation given by the angel cannot possibly be applied to the United States of America 2000 years after the time the book of Revelation was written. Lastly, the Seventh Day Adventist Church are by no means persecuted for attending church in the United States of America. Nobody in the United States of America prevents or even cares that Seventh Day Adventists attend church on Saturday.

3. The Sabbath and the Lord's Day

In SDA theology, the Lord's Day is the same day as the Sabbath. The only verse in the entire Old and New Testament that says the phrase "the Lord's Day" is in the book of Revelation.

> *I was in the Spirit on the Lord's day, and I heard behind me a loud voice like the sound of a trumpet. (Rev 1:10 NAS)*

Besides the fact that the book of Revelation never mentions the Sabbath, the phrase "the Lord's Day" in Revelation 1:10 is too ambiguous to support any view on the Sabbath. John could be referring to the "Day of the Lord" referred to in Acts 2:20 or Matthew 24:42 or any day of the week as in Psalms 118:24. There is no logical reason to conclude that Revelation 1:10 is referring to the Sabbath. The Early Church Fathers made a clear distinction between the Lord's Day and the Sabbath. The Church Fathers always taught the Lord's Day is the day Christ rose from the dead. The closest possible Old Testament reference is in Isaiah. God says "My holy day" and "holy day of the Lord."

> *If because of the sabbath, you turn your foot from doing your own pleasure on **My holy day**, and call the sabbath a delight, **the holy day of the LORD honorable**, and shall honor it, desisting from your own ways, from seeking your own pleasure, and speaking your own word. (Isa 58:13 NAS)*

Isaiah calls the day "the Sabbath" and not the Lord's Day. The expressions "My holy day" and "holy day of the Lord" are descriptors of the Sabbath and not the titles of the Sabbath. Nobody in the Old or New Testament called the Sabbath the "Lord's Day." The Bible does not support the conclusion that the Lord's Day is the same day as the Sabbath. If John was referring to the Sabbath in Revelation 1:10, he would have said "the Sabbath" and not the "Lord's Day." This line of reasoning is a fallacy called arguing from a "semantic ambiguity." If a word or phrase contains more than one meaning, the word or phrase can lead to multiple conclusions. All the Apostles specifically designated the Sabbath day with the name "Sabbath" and not "Lord's Day." The only reasonable conclusion is that the "Lord's Day" mentioned in Revelation 1:10 is too ambiguous to build an entire doctrine from it.

a. The Sabbath is for man

In Luke 6:5, the Pharisees complained that the disciples were harvesting food to eat on the Sabbath. They believed it was a violation of the Law found in Exodus 16:5, 16:21-28, 31:14 and Numbers 15:32-36. Christ perfectly gave the purpose of the Sabbath in one sentence. Jesus said,

> *The Sabbath was made for man, and not man for the Sabbath. (Mar 2:27 NAS)*

Jesus Christ, being the architect of the Law and the creator of all things from the beginning, knows the minutia of the Law. The verse, "the Sabbath was made for man, and not man for the Sabbath" unlocks the entire meaning of the Sabbath. Exodus plainly says "**you** shall have a holy day."

> *For six days work may be done, but on the seventh day **you shall have a holy day**, a sabbath of complete rest to the LORD; whoever does any work on it shall be put to death. (Exo 35:2 NAS)*

The Sabbath is not the Lord's Day at all. The Fourth Commandment "to keep the Sabbath holy" is specifically for the people, land, and commerce. The Sabbath is man's day. The Sabbath is specifically commanded for everybodys benefit. Breaking the Sabbath is sin committed towards our neighbor and not a failure to worship God. It is our duty to our neighbor. The SDA view that worship is the central purpose of the Fourth Commandment and that Sunday worship is receiving the "mark of the beast" is false and extremely divisive. All creation, whether in heaven or on earth, is to worship God every day forever.

> *So I will sing praise to Thy name **forever**, That I may pay my vows **day by day**. (Psa 61:8 NAS)*

> *Every day I will bless Thee, And I will praise Thy name **forever and ever**. (Psa 145:2 NAS)*

> *And **every day, in the temple** and from house to house, they kept right on teaching and preaching Jesus as the Christ. (Act 5:42 NAS)*

> *And the four living creatures, each one of them having six wings, are full of eyes around and within; **and day and night they do not cease** to say, "Holy, holy, holy, is the LORD God, the Almighty, who was and who is and who is to come." (Rev 4:8 NAS)*

God has no restrictions set on what day we can attend a Church service or worship Him. This is not to say the Sabbath should not be observed. Society itself needs to enforce the Fourth Commandment "to keep the Sabbath holy" for the good of the land, workers, families, and the whole world. In the United States, there are labor laws restricting employers from working their employees for too many consecutive days. The five-day work week is an example of how workers are rested in the United States. How the Fourth Commandment applies to our situation today is discussed in the chapter on "Modern day consequences."

b. Worship and the Sabbath

The Fourth Commandment should not be confused with the Christian worship service. This is the largest problem with the SDA view on Saturday worship. The Sabbath was not instituted to mandate a worship service. The ancient Israelites did not assemble for a worship service. The convocations or assemblies on the Sabbath were specifically for the purpose of performing sacrifices and offerings on behalf of the people. Leviticus states this plainly.

> *These are the appointed times of the LORD which you shall proclaim as holy convocations,* ***to present offerings by fire to the LORD-- burnt offerings and grain offerings, sacrifices and libations****, each day's matter on its own day. (Lev 23:37 NAS)*

The duties of the priests conflicted with the Fourth Commandment to "keep the Sabbath holy." The ceremonial duties performed by the priests broke the Sabbath. The Christian worship service, if work is done on the Sabbath, also breaks the Sabbath. This is because Christian worship service includes paid musicians and pastors, cooking food, collecting money, travel, and a host of other activities. All these activities are work. Christian worship services are not central to the Sabbath. Jesus said, the priests in the temple broke the Sabbath.

> *Or have you not read in the Law,* ***that on the Sabbath the priests in the temple break the Sabbath****, and are innocent? (Mat 12:5 NAS)*

God never intended the Sabbath to be a ceremony or Christian Church service. The duties of the priest on the Sabbath is discussed further in the chapter on "the Sabbath." The obvious message that dominates the Fourth Commandment "to keep the Sabbath holy" is regulating labor, land, and commerce in an occupation. The institution of the Sabbath in the Law of Moses is in Exodus 16. There are no references to a day of worship or ceremonies in the establishment of the Fourth Commandment. Worship is nowhere mentioned. The SDA doctrine that worship is central to "keeping the Sabbath holy" is false.

c. Working in the Church

Clearly the Church service should be minimal on the Sabbath because Christian activities are work. For this reason, the first day of the week is an appropriate day to commence Christian Church activities. There should be no occupational work in the Church on the Sabbath, especially when Church volunteers work in an occupation all week. For example, when parents work all week and then volunteer their time on the Sabbath for Church activities, it can interfere with their responsibility as a parent towards their family. This does not mean the Church should be completely closed to the public on the Sabbath. This simply means the major activities that are done in the church such as selling property and possessions should be done on a different day. Jesus and the Apostles were in the temple teaching and preaching the gospel every day. The early Christians would sell their possessions and property and distribute them to those in need. Luke wrote in Acts,

> *And all those who had believed were together, and had all things in common; and* ***they began selling their property and possessions****, and were sharing them with all, as anyone might have need. And day by day continuing with one mind in the temple,*

and breaking bread from house to house, they were taking their meals together with gladness and sincerity of heart, praising God, and having favor with all the people. And the Lord was adding to their number day by day those who were being saved. (Act 2:44-47 NAS)

Many Christian Church services include collecting food for food banks, distributing food to the needy, cooking meals for the community, distributing clothing, selling goods to obtain funding, giving money to support the Church mission, and much more. These activities were never a part of the Sabbath. If someone is seen starving or in need of medical attention on the Sabbath, it does not break the Sabbath to help them. Collecting money, buying and selling, distributing food and clothing, and other activities do break the Sabbath. There are plenty of reasons why Christian Church service and the Sabbath are not the same institution. This is discussed in detail in the chapter on "the Sabbath" and in the chapter on "the Christian day of Worship."

Chapter 3 - Antinomian Non-Sabbatarian

The Non-Sabbatarian or "antinomian" view teaches the Law of God is no longer to be observed. The antinomian view has a wide grasp on Christianity. The Dispensationalist view is the most prevalent proponent of antinomian theology. A large number of Evangelical and non-denominational churches teach this view. *The American Heritage dictionary* defines the word "Dispensationalism" as,

> *A doctrine prevalent in some forms of Protestant Christianity that divides history into distinct periods, each marked by a different dispensation or relationship between God and humanity. Dispensationalism further holds that Christian believers will be transported to heaven without warning and that soon thereafter there will be a period of tribulation, followed by the Second Coming. [35]*

Because Dispensationalists divide the Scriptures into "periods" or "dispensations," they relegate the Law of God to some era of human history other than the Church. In doing this, Dispensationalists nullify or abolish ALL of God's Law for the Christian. The Dispensationalist view is inescapably antinomian. *The Merriam-Websters dictionary* defines the word "antinomian" as,

> *One who holds that under the gospel dispensation of grace (see GRACE entry 1 sense 1a) the moral law is of no use or obligation because faith alone is necessary to salvation. [36]*

Dividing Scriptures into dispensations where God changes His relationship with people is contrary to Scripture. Dispensationalists teach "the Law" is the "dispensation" of the Nation of Israel and "Grace" is the "dispensation" of the Church. Dispensationalism is antinomian by definition. The Apostle Paul expressly wrote not to associate with those who have no regard for God's Laws.

> *But actually, I wrote to you not to associate with any so-called brother if he should be an immoral person, or covetous, or an idolater, or a reviler, or a drunkard, or a swindler-- not even to eat with such a one. For what have I to do with judging outsiders? Do you not judge those who are within the church? But those who are outside, God judges. Remove the wicked man from among yourselves. (1 Co 5:11-1 NAS)*

1. Dispensationalism

The Dispensationalist theological viewpoint separates God's Law from God's Grace in a linear framework. According to Dispensationalists, the Law is part of a previous administration (the Nation of Israel) that was postponed by the new administration of Grace (the Church). According to Dispensationalism, the messianic work of Christ started the Church era called "the Administration of Grace." As a result of this separation between the Law and Grace, they separate the identity of the Nation of Israel and the Church. According to Dispensationalist theology, the Old Testament Law is nullified and abolished for the Christian. This means the Law does not apply to the Christian believer today. This not only abolishes the Fourth Commandment; it abolishes the requirement for Christians to observe any of God's Law. To describe dispensationalism in my own words, it's a cookie cut theological framework that is used to mindlessly generate doctrines based on that framework and not on sound Biblical Hermeneutics.

a. Classic Dispensationalism

Clarence Larkin is a prevalent theologian who taught "classic Dispensationalism." Because of the inherent unscriptural teachings in Dispensationalism, Dispensationalist theology has gone through revisions. Classic Dispensationalism is what the original Dispensationalists taught. According to classic Dispensationalism, the "Jewish Sabbath" was not changed to the "Christian Sabbath." The Sabbath is not abolished with this view either. Clarence Larkin taught God's Law does not apply to Christians or the Church. Clarence Larkin wrote,

> *As an institution of Judaism, the Sabbath, with all the "Feast Days" and other ritualistic ceremonies and offerings of Judaism, ceased to function with the close of the Jewish Dispensation.* **The JEWISH Sabbath was not changed to the CHRISTIAN Sabbath,** *any more than "Circumcision" was changed to "Baptism." There is no such thing as the "CHRISTIAN Sabbath."* **"Sabbath" has to do with LAW, and "Christian" with GRACE, and to join "LAW" and "GRACE" is to unite what God has forever separated.** *[37]*

According to Clarence Larkin, "God has forever separated" the Law of God and the Grace of God. This antinomian view makes God's Law null and void for the Christian. Clarence Larkin argues that the Sabbath day belongs to the Nation of Israel alone. According to Clarence Larkin, the Sabbath will be observed again when Nation of Israel is restored in the end times.

> **The command to observe the Sabbath was given to Israel EXCLUSIVELY.** *It was not given to the Gentiles. It was given to Israel as the "SIGN" of the "Mosaic Covenant." "Verily my Sabbaths ye shall keep: for it is a 'SIGN' between me and you* **throughout your generations."** *Ex. 31:13; Eze. 20:12, Eze. 20:19-21. The Sabbath Day then belongs to the Jews alone and is not binding on the Gentiles (the world), or on the Church (Christians). Nowhere in the Bible do you find God finding fault with any nation or people, except the Jewish nation, for not observing the Sabbath. As a Jewish ordinance it has never been abrogated, changed, or transferred to any other day of the week, or to any other people. It is now in abeyance as foretold in Hosea 2:11 it would be.* **It is to be resumed when the Jews are nationally restored to their own land.** *Isa. 66:23. Eze. 44:24; Eze 44:46; 1-3 [38]*

According to classic Dispensationalism, the Law of God is ONLY for the Nation of Israel ON THE LAND. The absurdity of this claim is manifest in the fact that the verse Larkin uses as proof is from Exodus, before the Jews received or occupied the land. The verse Larkin quotes says "throughout your generations." The verse does not say while you are on the land Nationally. Moreover, the Bible verse Larkin provides also says that the Law is never abolished, but "ye shall keep... throughout your generations" making the commandment a constant requirement forever. There is no possible way to deduce that the requirement to keep the commandment is abolished or postponed. Furthermore, the command is not solely for those who are genetically Jewish. The command is for native born and immigrant people as well.

> *But as for you, you are to keep My statutes and My judgments, and shall not do any of these abominations, **neither the native, nor the alien who sojourns among you.** (Lev 18:26 NAS)*

> *As for the assembly, there shall be one statute for you and for the alien who sojourns with you, **a perpetual statute throughout your generations; as you are, so shall the alien be before the LORD**. (Num 15:15 NAS)*

If the Law of God is abolished for the church, sin becomes a complete mystery for the Christian. If the Law is not the measurement of our sinfulness, how are we supposed to repent? The Apostles main message was repentance from sinning against the Law of God. Paul speaking to King Agrippa said,

> *Consequently, King Agrippa, I did not prove disobedient to the heavenly vision, but kept declaring both to those of Damascus first, and also at Jerusalem and then throughout all the region of Judea, and even to the Gentiles, that **they should repent and turn to God, performing deeds appropriate to repentance**. (Act 26:19-20 NAS)*

There are no distinctions between the Nation of Israel and Gentiles in keeping the Law of God. Repentance and turning to God is required by all people. Sin can only exist when there is law. If there is no law, there can be no sin. Paul said,

> *Therefore, just as through one man sin entered into the world, and death through sin, and so death spread to all men, because all sinned-- for until the Law sin was in the world; but **sin is not imputed when there is no law.** (Rom 5:12-13 NAS)*

The idea that all people have sinned and broke God's Law is critical to the gospel of Christ. The Law holds all people accountable. There is no distinction. All people will be judged by the measure of the Law. By God's Law, the whole world is held accountable. Paul wrote,

> *Now we know that whatever the Law says, it speaks to those who are under the Law, that every mouth may be closed, and **all the world may become accountable to God**; because by the works of the Law no flesh will be justified in His sight; for **through the Law comes the knowledge of sin**. But now apart from the Law the righteousness of God has been manifested, being witnessed by the Law and the Prophets, even the righteousness of God through faith in Jesus Christ for all those who believe; **for there is no distinction; for all have sinned and fall short of the glory of God**. (Rom 3:19-23 NAS)*

Because we all sinned, Jesus Christ died for our sins as a substitute. This is to satisfy God's requirement of absolute obedience to the Law of God. God did this as a gift to us. Not because we can keep the Law perfect, but because He is merciful.

> *Being justified as a gift by His grace through the redemption which is in Christ Jesus; whom God displayed publicly as a propitiation in His blood through faith. This was to demonstrate His righteousness, because in the forbearance of God He passed over the sins previously committed. (Rom 3:24-25 NAS)*

The Classic Dispensationalist theology destroys the central purpose of the gospel. The Law in the Old Testament is inseparable from God's grace in Christ dying for our sins.

b. Progressive Dispensationalism

Craig A. Blaising and Darrell L. Bock are prevalent proponents of "Progressive Dispensationalism." They also taught the "Nation of Israel" is a separate entity from the "Christian Church." Progressive Dispensationalists explain the "Law" as two covenants: the "Mosaic Covenant" or "Old Covenant" and the "New Covenant." They taught the Mosaic Covenant was replaced by the New Covenant in Christ.

> *The promises of the New Covenant, however, looked to a time when the Mosaic Covenant would be replaced. It would come to an end and be replaced by the New Covenant. [39]*

The Progressive Dispensationalists taught a reconstructed version of Classic Dispensationalism. According to Progressive Dispensationalism, the New Covenant Law is a different Law than the Old Covenant Law. In the same fashion as the Classic Dispensationalist, the New Covenant Law is a complete enigma. It begs the question. How do Dispensationalists extract any meaningful Law for Christians without referencing the Old Testament Laws? The Apostles did not make this distinction in the Law. The distinction between the New Covenant and Old Covenant is contrived to escape the antinomian label. Dispensationalists attempt to fix the inherent antinomianism in their own theology.

> ***The progressive dispensationalism of the New Testament theology is not antinomianism.*** *For while it teaches that the Mosaic Covenant law has ended dispensationally, it also teaches that it has been replaced by the new covenant law, and it presents this dispensational change as an integral to God's plan of redemption which affirms and fulfills the divine demand for righteousness and holiness even as it saves and eternally blesses the redeemed. [40]*

The Bible makes no distinction between a New Covenant Law and Old Covenant Law. Making this distinction goes against the nature of God. God is not fickle nor does He change his mind.

> *God is not a man, that He should lie, Nor a son of man, that He should repent; Has He said, and will He not do it? Or has He spoken, and will He not make it good? (Num 23:19 NAS)*

> *And also the Glory of Israel will not lie or change His mind; for He is not a man that He should change His mind. (1Sa 15:29 NAS)*

> *Every good thing bestowed and every perfect gift is from above, coming down from the Father of lights, with whom there is no variation, or shifting shadow. (Jam 1:17 NAS)*

Chapter 3 - Antinomian Non-Sabbatarian

God does not say something is sinful at one point of human existence, then change the rules for a different set of people. What was sinful then, still continues to be sinful now. What is sinful for a Jew is equally sinful for a non-Jew. Sin is sin regardless of your ethnicity. How else can we be considered sinners unless we have the requirement of God's Law? God's Law is our standard. Christ died for our sin against God's Law. Christ dying for our transgressions against God's Law is the most basic teaching in Christianity. If there was no necessity to keep God's commandments, which were set from the beginning and written in stone by God Himself, there would be no need for Christ to die for our sins.

The distinction between New Covenant law and Old Covenant law does not exist in the Bible. It is an impossible task to even know what the difference would be. The New Testament writers only referred to the one Law given in the Old Testament. Distinguishing between the New and Old Covenant Law was created to salvage Dispensationalist theology. It's a dizzying endeavor to figure out what portion of the Bible applies to the Christian Church and what part applies to the Nation of Israel. The most obvious Bible verses devastate this view. In Romans, Paul said only the doers of the law will be justified.

> *For all who have sinned without the Law will also perish without the Law; and all who have sinned under the Law will be judged by the Law; for not the hearers of the Law are just before God,* ***but the doers of the Law will be justified.*** *(Rom 2:12-13 NAS)*

Paul is talking about the Old Testament Law. The Apostle Paul continues saying the Gentiles have the Law written in their hearts and their conscience bears witness to the truth of the Law.

> *For when Gentiles who* ***do not have the Law do instinctively the things of the Law****, these, not having the Law, are a law to themselves, in that they show the work of the Law written in their hearts, their conscience bearing witness, and their thoughts alternately accusing or else defending them. (Rom 2:14-15 NAS)*

Clearly the Apostle is connecting the keeping of the Law with the justification for our salvation. Jesus said we are to show our good works which comes from keeping the Law and the Prophets.

> *Let your light shine before men in such a way that they may see your good works, and glorify your Father who is in heaven.* ***Do not think that I came to abolish the Law or the Prophets; I did not come to abolish, but to fulfill.*** *(Mat 5:16-17 NAS)*

Good works are the evidence of repentance that comes from keeping God's commandments. Jesus said,

> *If you love Me, you will keep My commandments. (Joh 14:15 NAS)*

We are to shine the light of the Law of God before men by keeping His commandments. Paul expressly taught good works.

> *Instruct them to do good, to be rich in good works, to be generous and ready to share. (1Ti 6:18 NAS)*

The Christian Church is required to do good works in keeping with God's Law. The Progressive Dispensationalist New Covenant Law doctrine is useless. Nobody knows where this New Covenant Law can be found or what it even is. Learning the Law accurately and performing good works is absolutely necessary to the Christian faith. The Law of God is the foundation of the gospel message.

c. Dallas Theological Seminary

Theologian Joel T. Williamson Jr. continues the Dispensationalist tradition that the Law or the Sabbath does not apply to the Christian Church. He says "at face value" the Sabbath does not apply to the Church.

> *One simply interprets Scripture as any other written text, taking it at face value within its context. Approached this way, Sabbath passages lead inevitably to the conclusion that the Old Testament command to keep the Sabbath does not apply to the New Testament church.* [41]

What does "taking it at face value" even mean? It appears a deep study of the subject is discouraged. The Scripture either says something in the text or it doesn't. Williamson Jr. continues to argue that the Sabbath is abolished. He uses Galatians to prove this.

> *In the New Testament, the legal requirement to keep Sabbath is abolished. While individual Christians are allowed to keep Sabbath, the practice is never imposed on the church. Two major Pauline passages prove this. The first is Galatians 4:10–11: "You observe days and months and seasons and years. I am afraid for you, lest I have labored for you in vain."* [42]

Williamson Jr. conflates the Ceremonial Laws in Galatians 4:10–11 with the Fourth Commandment "to keep the Sabbath holy." Dispensationalists do not make a distinction between Moral, Judicial, and Ceremonial Laws in the Bible. Paul's point is that Christians should not hold people accountable for Ceremonial Laws that are foreshadowing the work of Christ. There is a difference between the Fourth Commandment to "keep the Sabbath holy" and the ceremonies scheduled around the Sabbath called the "sabbaths, new moons, and feasts." The Moral Law (Ten Commandments), Ceremonial Law (sacrifices, sabbaths, new moons, and feasts), and the Judicial Law (Criminal and Civil Laws) are discussed in detail in the Chapter on "the Law." Williamson Jr. switches from the Classic Dispensational view that the Sabbath is abolished to "keeping Sabbath is optional."

> *Law is mandatory, not optional. In the Old Testament, the Sabbath is a matter of law. Failure to keep it brings capital punishment (Exod 31:14-15; 35:2).11 In the New Testament, however, keeping Sabbath is optional; breaking it brings no negative consequences. If the Sabbath is no longer mandatory, the Sabbath is no longer law. The conclusion is inescapable.* [43]

Williamson Jr. argues that because "breaking it brings no negative consequences," therefore "the Sabbath is no longer law." It is important to point out that the Bible never teaches the Sabbath is optional. With that said, having no consequences for breaking the Law does not make the law no longer mandatory. The Israelites did not enforce the Sabbath in the Nation of Israel; yet, God did not destroy them because of His mercy.

> *Because they rejected My ordinances, and as for My statutes, they did not walk in them; they even profaned My sabbaths, for their heart continually went after their idols.* **Yet My eye spared them rather than destroying them, and I did not cause their annihilation in the wilderness.** *And I said to their children in the wilderness, "Do not walk in the statutes of your fathers, or keep their ordinances, or defile yourselves with their idols." (Eze 20:16-18 NAS)*

The enforcement of the Sabbath is not the criteria for its moral legal status. If a Nation makes murder legal, like abortion, this does not make murder abolished in God's eyes. As for God, God is Love. Our Lord does not impose "negative consequences" because He is merciful. The Psalmist wrote,

> *The LORD is gracious and merciful; Slow to anger and great in lovingkindness. (Psa 145:8 NAS)*

Dispensationalists directly conclude that all of God's Law is abolished for the Christian. Williamson Jr. uses "logic" and concludes all of the Law of God is nullified.

> *The abolition of the Sabbath implies a second thing: that all of the commandments of the Mosaic code are now nullified. Here again, the logic is easy to follow, and the Scriptural support is overwhelming. [44]*

Williamson Jr. is creating a "false dichotomy." This logical fallacy limits the choices available on an argument. A false dichotomy or false dilemma is,

> When only two choices are presented yet more exist, or a spectrum of possible choices exists between two extremes. [45]

In this case, Williamson Jr. makes the argument that the Law is either mandatory or it's not mandatory, removing any other possibilities. Williamson Jr. concludes that the "the Sabbath is no longer mandatory" therefore "all of the commandments of the Mosaic code are now nullified." The fact is there are many variations that can be logically deduced from his argument. The black and white extreme Joel T. Williamson Jr. presents in his reasoning is unacceptable in logic. The Dispensationalist view is grossly in error. It is missing the most important part of the gospel. The fact is we are sinners and in need of a Savior. Because ALL transgressed the Law, we need a savior. This is the gospel. Christ clearly taught that those who annul any commandment in the Law are least in the kingdom of Heaven. Jesus said,

> *Do not think that I came to abolish the Law or the Prophets; I did not come to abolish, but to fulfill. For truly I say to you, until heaven and earth pass away, not the smallest letter or stroke shall pass away from the Law, until all is accomplished. Whoever then annuls one of the least of these commandments, and so teaches others, shall be called least in the kingdom of heaven; but whoever keeps and teaches them, he shall be called great in the kingdom of heaven. (Mat 5:17-19 NAS)*

God is not an evil angry unjust god who destroys His people in retribution for breaking his law.

2. There is no distinction between Jew and Greek

Before Israel existed, the Law of God was in effect. God's Moral Law can be seen throughout the book of Genesis. The Laws applied to both native born Israelites and the foreigner. The Law clearly states,

> *There is to be one law and one ordinance for you and for the alien who sojourns with you. (Num 15:16 NAS)*

God does not divide His people between Jews who are required to keep the Law and Gentiles who are not required to keep the Law. Gentiles were allowed to be a part of ancient Israel. Gentiles were not removed from the Nation based on ethnicity. All the people, including foreigners and those who were not native, were required to keep the Law of God. The notion that God's Law does not apply to Gentiles is grossly in error. Paul clearly taught we are all heirs of the promise, not just "Jews." All of Christ's people are the children of Abraham.

> *There is neither Jew nor Greek, there is neither slave nor free man, there is neither male nor female; for you are all one in Christ Jesus. And **if you belong to Christ, then you are Abraham's offspring**, heirs according to promise. (Gal 3:28-29 NAS)*

Paul clearly taught salvation is for ANYONE who calls upon the name of the Lord.

> *For there is no distinction between Jew and Greek; for the same Lord is Lord of all, abounding in riches for all who call upon Him; for "**Whoever will call upon the name of the LORD will be saved**." (Rom 10:12-13 NAS)*

The apostle James said to make no distinctions between people or show favoritism in regards to class. James wrote,

> *My brethren, do not hold your faith in our glorious Lord Jesus Christ with an attitude of personal favoritism. For if a man comes into your assembly with a gold ring and dressed in fine clothes, and there also comes in a poor man in dirty clothes, and you pay special attention to the one who is wearing the fine clothes, and say, "You sit here in a good place," and you say to the poor man, "You stand over there, or sit down by my footstool," **have you not made distinctions among yourselves, and become judges with evil motives?** (Jam 2:1-4 NAS)*

The apostle James demonstrates that making distinctions between each other is contrary to God's Law. James references the Ten Commandments as the criteria for evaluating sin. James continues,

> *If, however, you are fulfilling the royal law, according to the Scripture, "You shall love your neighbor as yourself," you are doing well. But if you show partiality, **you are committing sin and are convicted by the law as transgressors. For whoever keeps the whole law and yet stumbles in one point, he has become guilty of all.** For He who said, "Do not commit adultery," also said, "Do not commit murder." Now if you do not commit adultery, but do commit murder, you have become a transgressor of the law. So speak and so act, as those who are to be judged by the law of liberty. For judgment will be merciless to one who has shown no mercy; mercy triumphs over*

judgment. What use is it, my brethren, if a man says he has faith, but he has no works? Can that faith save him? If a brother or sister is without clothing and in need of daily food, and one of you says to them, "Go in peace, be warmed and be filled," and yet you do not give them what is necessary for their body, what use is that? ***Even so faith, if it has no works, is dead, being by itself.*** *(Jam 2:8-17 NAS)*

Faith in Christ and the works of the Law are inseparably tied together. The Apostles did not teach to distinguish the requirement to keep God's Law between the "Jews and Gentiles." The Sabbath Law included the sojourner, foreigners, and those who are not Israelites.

But the seventh day is a sabbath of the LORD your God; in it you shall not do any work, you or your son or your daughter or your male servant or your female servant ***or your ox or your donkey or any of your cattle or your sojourner who stays with you****, so that your male servant and your female servant may rest as well as you. (Deu 5:14 NAS)*

Even animals and the land are to keep the Sabbath. Nowhere does the Bible teach that Gentiles and Jews have different Laws. The Fourth Commandment to "keep the Sabbath holy" is ingrained into the fabric of the cosmos like thou shalt not kill or any other commandment. I will add that the One who said "Do not commit murder" also said to "keep the Sabbath holy."

3. Law and Grace

The Apostle Paul explained clearly how the Law works with the grace of God. All the world is accountable to God through His Law. Through His Law comes the knowledge of sin.

*Now we know that whatever the Law says, it speaks to those who are under the Law****, that every mouth may be closed, and all the world may become accountable to God****; because by the works of the Law no flesh will be justified in His sight;* ***for through the Law comes the knowledge of sin****. (Rom 3:19-20 NAS)*

It is our sinfulness in transgressing God's Law that brings us to faith in Christ. Faith in Christ does not nullify or abolish God's Law.

Do we then nullify the Law through faith? May it never be! On the contrary, we establish the Law. (Rom 3:31 NAS)

It is the Law that establishes our faith in Christ. Likewise, God's Grace does not nullify or abolish His Law.

What shall we say then? Are we to continue in sin that grace might increase? May it never be! How shall we who died to sin still live in it?... What then? ***Shall we sin because we are not under law but under grace? May it never be!*** *(Rom 6:1-2,15 NAS)*

The notion that there are two separate administrations of law and grace is completely foreign to Scripture. The Law is inseparable from God's grace. All the world is bound and subject to the Law of God until death.

Or do you not know, brethren (for I am speaking to those who know the law), that **the law has jurisdiction over a person as long as he lives**? *(Rom 7:1 NAS)*

The Apostle Paul clearly taught that all the world is bound to the Law of God as long as we live. The Law of God is central to the gospel of Christ. It is how we measure our behavior in society. To love your neighbor as yourself is integral in keeping God's Law. Jesus was asked which is the greatest commandment in the Law.

*"Teacher, which is the great commandment in the Law?" And He said to him, "'***You shall love the LORD your God with all your heart, and with all your soul, and with all your mind.***' "This is the great and foremost commandment. "The second is like it,* **'You shall love your neighbor as yourself.'** *On these two commandments depend the whole Law and the Prophets." (Mat 22:36-40 NAS)*

This is why the Ten Commandments is divided into two sections. It is our duty to God and our duty to our neighbor. We will be judged by ALL of God's Law found in the Ten Commandments, the Law, and the Prophets. The antinomian Dispensationalist teaching that the Law is abolished, nullified, unenforced, or superseded is contrary to the gospel of Christ in Scripture.

Chapter 4 - The Law

It is impossible to talk about the Fourth Commandment to "keep the Sabbath holy" without talking about the Law. In order to understand God's Law, we must learn how the law functions in society in general. For example, the legal system in the United States consists of criminal law, civil or tort law, punitive damages, remedies, statutes, and punishments. The purpose for the legal system is to dispense justice. If someone is killed, there must be a determination of how the person was killed. There are different types of killing: first degree murder, second degree murder, manslaughter, or wrongful death. In the case where someone is killed in a car accident, the charge could be vehicular manslaughter and not murder.

1. The three-part structure of the Law

The Ten Commandments are statutes called the "Moral Law." Breaking the Moral Law is a criminal offense. The laws determining judgments for breaking the Moral Law are called "Judicial Laws." Laws concerning sacrifices and festivals are called "Ceremonial Laws." These three classifications of the Law of Moses are called the "tripartite" or "three-part structure" of the Law. The three-part structure of the Law is clearly seen in Ezekiel 44. Both *the King James* and *the New American Standard version* Bibles are represented here.

> *And in a **dispute** they shall take their stand to **judge**; they shall judge it according to My **ordinances**. They shall also keep My **laws** and My **statutes** in all My appointed **feasts**, and sanctify My **sabbaths**. (Eze 44:24 NAS)*

> *And in **controversy** they shall stand in **judgment**; and they shall judge it according to my **judgments**: and they shall keep my **laws** and my **statutes** in all mine **assemblies**; and they shall hallow my **sabbaths**. (Eze 44:24 KJV)*

To apply God's Law correctly, it is critical to define the legal terms.

a. Dispute or Controversy

The Law is designed to resolve disputes and controversies. According to *the NASB concordance*, the Hebrew word "dispute" or "controversy" is,

> *<07379> רִיב or רִב (rib or rib) (936d)*
> **Meaning:** *strife, dispute*
> **Origin:** *from 7378*
> **Usage:** *adversary(1), case(11), cause(9), complaint(2), contend(1), contention(2), contentions(3), controversy(1), dispute(10), disputes(1), indictment(1), lawsuit(1), plea(1), plead a case(1), quarrel(2), strife(13), suit(2).*
> **Notes:** *[a] Deu 17:8, Deu 17:9; Deu 19:17; Deu 21:5; 1Ch 23:4; 2Ch 19:8-10 [b] Lev 23:2, Lev 23:4, 44 [c] Eze 20:12, Eze 20:20 [46]*

When disputes or controversies occur, the Law of God is needed in order to resolve the dispute. This requires an unbiased mediator to interpret the law in order to resolve the dispute. The unbiased mediator in a dispute is the judge.

b. Judge

Judges are required to interpret specific cases in order to come to an appropriate legal remedy between disputing parties. According to *the NASB concordance*, the Hebrew word for "judge" is,

> **<08199>** שָׁפַט *(shaphat) (1047a)*
>
> **Meaning:** *to judge, govern*
> **Origin:** *a prim. Root*
> **Usage:** *already acting a judge(1), argue a case(1), decide(2), defend(3), deliver(m)(1), dispense(1), enter into judgment(6), entered into judgment(1), entering into judgment(1), execute judgment(1), executing judgment(1), freed(2), governed(1), handed down(1), has a controversy(1), judge(96), Judge(5), judged(23), judges(39), judging(5), plead(1), pleads(1), pronounce judgment(1), rule(2), ruled(1), rulers(2), vindicate(6).*
> **Notes:** [a] *Deu 17:8, Deu 17:9; Deu 19:17; Deu 21:5; 1Ch 23:4; 2Ch 19:8-10* [b] *Lev 23:2, Lev 23:4, 44* [c] *Eze 20:12, Eze 20:20* [47]

Judges are necessary to apply the law in real case scenarios. If there are no judges, the law will be unfairly administered due to bias against one party. This is why it is important to have unbiased judges who show no partiality in judgment.

c. Ordinances or Judgments

Judgments are decisions made from specific cases that involve breaking statutes and previous court decisions. Judges make decisions in the judicial system. *The Oxford Advanced Learner's Dictionary* defines "judicial" as,

> *Connected with a court, a judge or legal judgement.* [48]

The newer Bible translations, like the NASB, use the word "ordinances" instead of the word "judgment." "Ordinance" is an incorrect word. The definition of "ordinance" differs significantly from the word "judgment." *The Oxford Advanced Learner's Dictionary* defines the word "ordinance" as,

> *a piece of legislation enacted by a municipal authority.* [49]

An ordinance is not a judgment. The Old Testament word is "judgment" not "ordinance." According to *the NASB concordance*, the Hebrew word is,

> **<04941>** מִשְׁפָּט *(mishpat) (1048b)*
>
> **Meaning:** *judgment*
> **Origin:** *from 8199*
> **Usage:** *arrangements(1), case(5), case*(1), cause(m)(7), charge(1), claim(1),*

court(m)(2), crimes(m)(1), custom(11), customs(2), decide(1), decision(2), decisions(1), deserving(1), destruction(1), due(1), injustice*(2), judge(1), judged(1), judgment(62), judgments(40), just(m)(4), justice(118), justly(m)(3), kind(1), manner(3), matters of justice(1), mode of life(1), order(1), ordinance(29), ordinances(79), plan(1), plans(1), practice(1), procedure(m)(4), properly(2), regulation(1), right(8), rightful place(1), rights(2), rule(m)(1), sentence(2), sentenced(m)(1), standard(m)(1), trial(m)(1), unjustly*(1), verdict(1), way prescribed(2), what is right(2), worthy(1).
Notes[a] *Exo 23:3, Exo 23:6; Deu 1:17; Deu 10:17; Deu 16:19 [50]*

Even though the Hebrew word is defined as "judgment," the NASB translators interpret the word מִשְׁפָּט (mishpat) as "ordinances" 108 times. This is completely unacceptable for the obvious reason that a judgment (civil law) is not an ordinance (statutory law). They have two totally different definitions. In Leviticus 19:5, the NASB interpreters use the correct word for מִשְׁפָּט (mishpat).

> *You shall do no injustice in **judgment**; you shall not be partial to the poor nor defer to the great, but you are to judge your neighbor fairly. (Lev 19:15 NAS)*

The King James version Bible correctly defines מִשְׁפָּט (mishpat) as judgment. Judgments based on the statutory laws are called the "Judicial Law."

d. Laws

The word "laws" in the Bible is the word "Torah." All the Laws of Moses in general are called "Torah." According to *the NASB concordance*, the Hebrew word is,

> **<08451>** תּוֹרָה *(torah) (435d)*
> **Meaning:** *direction, instruction, law*
> **Origin:** *from 3384*
> **Usage:** *custom(1), instruction(10), instructions(1), law(188), Law(1), laws(10), ruling(1), teaching(7), teachings(1).*
> **Notes:** [a] *Deu 17:8, Deu 17:9; Deu 19:17; Deu 21:5; 1Ch 23:4; 2Ch 19:8-10* [b] *Lev 23:2, Lev 23:4, 44* [c] *Eze 20:12, Eze 20:20 [51]*

When the word "law" is used, it is typically referring to all the Moral, Judicial, and Ceremonial laws together.

e. Statutes

Statutes are the codified laws made by law makers or a legislature. Statutes are not referring to judgments made by judges. The Moral and Ceremonial laws are statutes. According to *the NASB concordance*, the Hebrew word is,

> **<02708>** חֻקָּה *(chuqqah) (349d)*
> **Meaning:** *something prescribed, an enactment, statute*
> **Origin:** *fem. of 2706*

Usage: *appointed(1), customs(5), due(1), fixed order(m)(1), fixed patterns(m)(1), ordinance(5), ordinances(1), statute(25), statutes(62), statutory(2).*
Notes: *[a] Deu 17:8, Deu 17:9; Deu 19:17; Deu 21:5; 1Ch 23:4; 2Ch 19:8-10 [b] Lev 23:2, Lev 23:4, 44 [c] Eze 20:12, Eze 20:20 [52]*

Rules set by a law maker or legislature are called "statutes." This is no different than the laws in the United States today. *The Oxford Advanced Learner's Dictionary* defines "statute" as;

a law that is passed by a parliament, council, etc. and formally written down. [53]

The Moral Law specifically is statutory law.

f. Appointed feasts or assemblies

In Ezekiel 44:24, the New American Standard Bible uses the word "feasts" where the King James Bible uses the word "assemblies." Sometimes the word "convocation" is used. Sometimes the word "assembly" is used. There are a few Hebrew words used for the word "assembly." According to *the NASB concordance*, one Hebrew word means "appointed time."

<04150> מוֹעֵד *or* מֹעֵד *or* מוֹעָדָה *(moed or moed or moadah) (417b)*
Meaning: *appointed time, place, or meeting*
Origin: *from 3259*
Usage: *appointed(3), appointed feast(3), appointed feasts(11), appointed festival(2), appointed meeting place(1), appointed place(1), appointed sign(1), appointed time(21), appointed times(8), appointment(1), assemblies(1), assembly(2), definite time(1), feasts(2), festal(1), fixed festivals(3), meeting(147), meeting place(1), meeting places(1), season(4), seasons(3), set time(1), time(3), times(1), times appointed(1).*
Notes: *[a] Deu 17:8, Deu 17:9; Deu 19:17; Deu 21:5; 1Ch 23:4; 2Ch 19:8-10 [b] Lev 23:2, Lev 23:4, 44 [c] Eze 20:12, Eze 20:20 [54]*

The other Hebrew word "convocation" means,

<04744> מִקְרָא *(miqra) (896d)*
Meaning: *a convocation, convoking, reading*
Origin: *from 7121*
Usage: *assemblies(2), assembly(2), convocation(14), convocations(3), reading(1), summoning(1).*
Notes: *[a] Exo 20:9, Exo 20:10; Exo 23:12; Exo 31:13-17; Exo 35:2, Exo 35:3; Lev 19:3; Deu 5:13, Deu 5:14 [55]*

Another Hebrew word is "assembly."

<06951> קָהָל *(qahal) (874c)*
Meaning: *assembly, convocation, congregation*
Origin: *from an unused word*

> ***Usage:*** *army*(1), assembly(95), companies(1), company(15), congregation(8), crowd(1), horde(2) [56]*

These words all hold the idea of coming together as a group. The Law required the people to assemble on different days of the week. The feasts and assemblies were not required solely on the sabbath. This is why in Ezekiel 44:24 the "assembly" is separated from the "sabbath."

The Ceremonial law contains statutes and judgments as well. The judgments made by priests in the Ceremonial law are not case laws. The difference between the Judicial Law and the Ceremonial Law is that the judgment made in the Ceremonial Law is not a civil or criminal case. The Ceremonial Law is primarily for the priests to administer sacrifices for the sin of the people, to perform healthcare for the people, and to observe the seasons. This was to keep the memorials of the Israelites being freed from slavery in Egypt and to keep the promises of the coming of the Messiah.

g. Sabbaths

The word "sabbaths" has multiple meanings. According to *the NASB concordance*, the Hebrew word is,

> ***<07676>*** שַׁבָּת *(shabbath) (992a)*
>
> ***Meaning:*** *sabbath*
> ***Origin:*** *from 7673a*
> ***Usage:*** *every sabbath(2), sabbath(73), sabbaths(32).*
> ***Notes:*** *[a] Deu 17:8, Deu 17:9; Deu 19:17; Deu 21:5; 1Ch 23:4; 2Ch 19:8-10 [b] Lev 23:2, Lev 23:4, 44 [c] Eze 20:12, Eze 20:20 [57]*

The word "sabbath" can refer to the Fourth Commandment "to keep the Sabbath holy," a day on the Jewish calendar, or the Ceremonial Law. The definition of the word "sabbath" is discussed in detail in the chapter on "the Sabbath."

2. Identifying the Law

The biggest challenge most have with the law is identifying the parts of the law. God's **judgments** are laws based on specific **decisions of a judge**. God's **statutes** are decrees written by a **law maker** and not based on judicial cases. The **feasts, new moons, and sabbaths** are also statutes and judgments which are performed by **priests**. If the priest is required to keep the statute or make a judgment then the statute or judgment is a Ceremonial Law. Law makers write statutes; therefore, statutes are the Moral Law. If the judge makes a judgment in the law then it is a Judicial Law. The laws are distinguished from each other in regards to the statutes and judgments based on who is writing or judging the law. Throughout the Pentateuch, statutes and judgments are differentiated.

> *Therefore shall ye observe all my **statutes**, and all my **judgments**, and do them: I am the LORD. (Lev 19:37 KJV see also Exo 20:22, Num 9:3, Deu 4)*

Judicial Laws are administered by judges based on the statutes made by God. Judges interpret and apply the statutes. In the Bible, God wrote the statutes called the Moral Law. Judges enforce the statutes by ruling over a situation where a statute was broken called a "case." Judges use cases as precedence for future decisions. Both the statutes and the judgments are from God. God works through the "means" of judges. *The Oxford Advanced Learner's Dictionary* defines the word "means" as,

> *An action, an object or a system by which a result is achieved; a way of achieving or doing something. [58]*

They are His judgments even though they are made through a judge. This does not mean every judgment made by a judge is from God. Only rulings that reflect the justice found in the Law of God are His judgments. Specifically, only the Laws found in Scripture. The wicked statutes of lawmakers and wicked rulings of judges are not God's Law. Isaiah wrote,

> *Woe to those who enact evil statutes, And to those who constantly record unjust decisions, So as to deprive the needy of justice, And rob the poor of My people of their rights, In order that widows may be their spoil, And that they may plunder the orphans. (Isa 10:1-2 NAS)*

A modern example of a statute that steals from people is the "Death Tax." The Death Tax is a tax imposed on those who inherit property from a relative who died. For example, if a farmer's son inherits their parents farm, the government can take 40% of their farm. This causes farmers to lose their land, effectively destroying family businesses who farmed throughout their generations. This is a form of "legal theft." God commands His people to not pervert the law.

> *You shall not follow a multitude in doing evil, nor shall you testify in a dispute so as to turn aside after a multitude in order to pervert justice.... You shall not pervert the justice due to your needy brother in his dispute. "Keep far from a false charge, and do not kill the innocent or the righteous, for I will not acquit the guilty. (Exo 23:2,6-7 NAS)*

Judges who pervert justice are not acting on God's behalf. God does not pervert justice or act wickedly.

> *Surely, God will not act wickedly, And the Almighty will not pervert justice. (Job 34:12 NAS)*

The basic "rule of thumb" in determining the parts of the law in the Bible is by who is involved in the law; whether it is Moses or God (Moral and Ceremonial statutes), a judge (Judicial judgments), or a priest (Ceremonial judgments). All governments are required to administer justice for the Nation in a similar way as the Law of God. The Law of God was used in ancient Israel as their national legal system. The Law of God is just as applicable today. An example of a modern application of the Judicial Law from ancient Israel is when an ox kills someone. If an ox gored someone to death, the ox was to be put to death. If the owner knew and neglected to confine the ox, the owner was also to be put to death. The book of Exodus states,

> *And if an ox gores a man or a woman to death, the ox shall surely be stoned and its flesh shall not be eaten; but the owner of the ox shall go unpunished. If, however, an ox was previously in the habit of goring, and its owner has been warned, yet he does*

not confine it, and it kills a man or a woman, the ox shall be stoned and its owner also shall be put to death. (Exo 21:28-29 NAS)

In the United States, if an owner's dog attacks and kills someone, the dog is put to death. If the owner trained the dog and sent the dog to attack the person, the owner can be prosecuted as well. In the code of the State of Virginia in the United States,

Whenever an owner or custodian of an animal found to be a dangerous dog is charged with a violation of this section, the animal control officer shall confine the dangerous dog until such time as evidence shall be heard and a verdict rendered...Upon conviction, the court may (i) order the dangerous dog to be disposed of by a local governing body pursuant to § 3.2-6562 or (ii) grant the owner up to 30 days to comply with the requirements of this section, during which time the dangerous dog shall remain in the custody of the animal control officer until compliance has been verified. If the owner fails to achieve compliance within the time specified by the court, the court shall order the dangerous dog to be disposed of by a local governing body pursuant to § 3.2-6562. The court, in its discretion, may order the owner to pay all reasonable expenses incurred in caring and providing for such dangerous dog from the time the animal is taken into custody until such time that the animal is disposed of or returned to the owner. [59]

The difference between the enforcement of the Law of God in ancient Israel and the modern world is situational. Punishment for breaking God's Law manifests itself in every legal system that dispenses true justice. If a Nation dispenses justice appropriately then they are keeping God's Law.

a. God established the Government

Because the Moral Law is ingrained into the fabric of society, all governments have no choice but to make statutory laws similar to those in the Law of Moses. In Romans 13, Paul connects the laws of all rulers and authorities with the Moral and Judicial Laws of Moses. Paul says,

Let every person be in subjection to the governing authorities. For there is no authority except from God, and those which exist are established by God. Therefore he who resists authority has opposed the ordinance of God; and they who have opposed will receive condemnation upon themselves. (Rom 13:1-2 NAS)

God established all the governing authorities, not only the Nation of Israel. Governing authorities are God's avengers against those who practice evil. Paul continues,

For rulers are not a cause of fear for good behavior, but for evil. Do you want to have no fear of authority? Do what is good, and you will have praise from the same; for it is a minister of God to you for good. But if you do what is evil, be afraid; for it does not bear the sword for nothing; for it is a minister of God, an avenger who brings wrath upon the one who practices evil. Wherefore it is necessary to be in subjection, not only because of wrath, but also for conscience' sake. (Rom 13:3-5 NAS)

Chapter 4 - The Law

The governing authorities bear the sword against evil. Taxes are payed to rulers for the purpose of dispensing justice for the good of the people. The governing authorities are servants of God to do His will. Paul says,

> *For because of this you also pay taxes, for rulers are servants of God, devoting themselves to this very thing. Render to all what is due them: tax to whom tax is due; custom to whom custom; fear to whom fear; honor to whom honor. (Rom 13:6-7 NAS)*

We are to pay taxes for the purpose of administering justice. Loving your neighbor is fulfilling the law of the land. A nation that administers justice will not arrest someone for keeping God's commandments. The purpose of the Ten Commandments is to teach love. Love does no wrong. Paul says,

> *Owe nothing to anyone except to love one another; for he who loves his neighbor has fulfilled the law. For this, "You shall not commit adultery, You shall not murder, You shall not steal, You shall not covet," and if there is any other commandment, it is summed up in this saying, "You shall love your neighbor as yourself." Love does no wrong to a neighbor; love therefore is the fulfillment of the law. (Rom 13:8-10 NAS)*

Loving your neighbor cannot break the laws established by governing authorities. This of course depends on the degree the governing authority keeps the Law of God. An example is Daniel and the lion's den. Because Daniel distinguished himself from everyone else by his faithfulness to God's Law, the governors could not accuse Daniel of any wrong doing.

> *Then the commissioners and satraps began trying to find a ground of accusation against Daniel in regard to government affairs; but they could find no ground of accusation or evidence of corruption, inasmuch as he was faithful, and no negligence or corruption was to be found in him. (Dan 6:4 NAS)*

The only way they could accuse Daniel of any wrong doing was to make a law that went against God's Law.

> *Then these men said, "We shall not find any ground of accusation against this Daniel unless we find it against him with regard to the law of his God." (Dan 6:5 NAS)*

In an attempt to remove Daniel from office, the governors of the kingdom of the Medes made a law to force all in the kingdom to worship a statue of king Darius only.

> *The governors have consulted together that the king should establish a statute and enforce an injunction that anyone who makes a petition to any god or man besides you, O king, for thirty days, shall be cast into the lions' den. (Dan 6:7 NAS)*

Daniel did not obey the law to worship the statue of the king. When the governors trapped Daniel, they accused Daniel before the king.

> *Daniel, who is one of the exiles from Judah, pays no attention to you, O king, or to the injunction which you signed, but keeps making his petition three times a day. (Dan 6:13 NAS)*

The king himself was upset about the intent of governors trapping Daniel with the law.

> *Then, as soon as the king heard this statement, he was deeply distressed and set his mind on delivering Daniel; and even until sunset he kept exerting himself to rescue him. (Dan 6:14 NAS)*

The next day, after Daniel was put in the lion's den, the king opened the den and spoke to Daniel.

> *The king spoke and said to Daniel, "Daniel, servant of the living God, has your God, whom you constantly serve, been able to deliver you from the lions?" (Dan 6:20 NAS)*

Daniel answered back to the king.

> *Then Daniel spoke to the king, "O king, live forever! My God sent His angel and shut the lions' mouths, and they have not harmed me, inasmuch as I was found innocent before Him; and also toward you, O king, I have committed no crime." (Dan 6:21-22 NAS)*

The king, in response, had all the governors who trapped Daniel along with the governor's family executed.

> *The king then gave orders, and they brought those men who had maliciously accused Daniel, and they cast them, their children, and their wives into the lions' den; and they had not reached the bottom of the den before the lions overpowered them and crushed all their bones. (Dan 6:24 NAS)*

A just nation will have laws that honor God's Law. The government has no right to make laws that cause people to disobey God's Law. God's Law always take precedence. For this reason, it is important to know how the Law of God is to be applied to society. The three-part structure of the Law correctly applies God's Law to a nation. The Moral Law, the Judicial Law, and the Ceremonial Law must be applied to the Law of Moses in order for it to make sense. The three-part structure of the Law is the most Biblical and relevant view. It is nonsense to teach that God's Law does not apply to the Christian Church. I cannot stress enough how unbiblical and dangerous the antinomian view truly is. The precedence for creating a legal system based on criminal and civil law originates with God's Law.

b. The Westminster Confession of Faith

The three-part structure of the Law is taught in *the Westminster Confession of Faith*. Failing to apply the three-part structure of the Law debilitates a Christians understanding of the gospel. *The Westminster Confession of Faith* states,

> *2. **This law**, after his fall, continued to be a perfect rule of righteousness; and, as such, was delivered by God upon Mount Sinai, in **ten commandments**, and written in two tables: **the first four commandments containing our duty towards God; and the***

> *other six, our duty to man.*
>
> *3. Beside this law, commonly **called moral**, God was pleased to give to the people of Israel, as a church under age, **ceremonial laws**, containing several typical ordinances, partly of worship, prefiguring Christ, his graces, actions, sufferings, and benefits; and partly, holding forth divers instructions of moral duties. All which ceremonial laws are now abrogated, under the new testament.*
>
> *4. To them also, as a body politic, he gave sundry **judicial laws**, which expired together with the State of that people; not obliging any other now, further than the general equity thereof may require. [60]*

In section four, the statement "further than the general equity thereof may require" refers to the court of equity. *Merriam-Websters Dictionary* defines "equity" as,

> *Trial or remedial justice under or by the rules and doctrines of equity. [61]*

General equity is the law created by judicial precedence. It is the difference between a civil and criminal case. *The Westminster Confession of Faith* teaches that the first four commands are our duties to God and the last six commands are our duties to man [62]. The view proposed in this book is that the first three are duties to God and the last seven are out duty to our neighbor. This makes the Fourth Commandment "to keep the Sabbath holy" as our duty to our neighbor. Knowing our duty to God and our neighbor pinpoints exactly how we sin against God's commandments. The sum of the Ten Commandments shows our duty to God and our neighbor. Jesus said,

> **You shall love the Lord** *your God with all your heart, and with all your soul, and with all your strength, and with all your mind;* **and your neighbor** *as yourself.* (Luk 10:27 NAS)

Making classifications in the Law is NOT to figure out which laws are to be ignored or abolished. Understanding statutes and judgments in the Law makes the Law relevant to your life. The three-part structure of the Law in regards to the Sabbath will be discussed in the chapter on "the Sabbath."

c. Objections to the three-part structure of the Law

Dispensationalists attack this teaching in order to support their antinomian theology. Dallas Theological Seminary theologian, Joel T. Williamson Jr. argues that the three-part structure is useful to prove the Law as binding and abrogated at the same time. Differentiating between the Moral, Judicial, and Ceremonial Law is not for the purpose of picking and choosing which laws to obey and which to not. Williamson Jr. also demonstrates the lack of understanding between the difference of a statutory, judicial, and ceremonial law. Williamson Jr. writes,

> *The tripartite division proves theologically useful to some since it suggests how the law can be both abrogated and binding at the same time. The problem is that the Old Testament itself suggests no such classification. The law makes no such distinction when arranging its commands. Everyone agrees that **Leviticus 19:18** **states a universally applicable moral principle**: "You shall not take vengeance, nor*

> *bear any grudge against the children of your people, but you shall love your neighbor as yourself: I am the LORD."* **The very next verse, however, is ceremonial** *and would thus be limited to Old Testament Israel: "You shall keep My statutes. You shall not let your livestock breed with another kind. You shall not sow your seed with mixed seed. Nor shall a garment of mixed linen and wool come upon you."* **Nothing in these verses or the surrounding context suggests that Israel saw them as qualitatively different. Indeed, why should the first be binding on the church but not the second.**
> [63]

Williamson Jr. is demonstrating a severe lack of understanding in what Leviticus is teaching. He confuses the breeding of livestock and the sowing of seeds with the Ceremonial Law. Breeding livestock, sowing seeds, and materials in a garment are all related to bearing false witness in the Moral Law. The Ceremonial Law is about the priests observing the feasts, festivals, new moons, and sabbaths and the priests performing an offering or sacrifice for those who broke law or became sick. All of Leviticus is a mixture of Moral, Judicial, and Ceremonial laws. The reason Leviticus mixes the Laws together as one Law or Torah is because when the Law is broken, a judgment must be made on the remedy and a sacrifice or offering must be made for the one who broke the Law. Because of sacrificial requirement, the priestly ceremony usually comes after whatever Law was broken. An example of this is in Leviticus 19:20-22.

> ***Moral Law: Thou shalt not commit adultery***
> *20 'Now if a man lies carnally with a woman who is a slave acquired for another man, but who has in no way been redeemed, nor given her freedom, there shall be punishment; (Lev 19:20 NAS)*
> ***Judicial Law: No death penalty. Public Humiliation and provide a ram***
> *they shall not, however, be put to death, because she was not free.*
> *21 'And he shall bring his guilt offering to the LORD to the doorway of the tent of meeting, a ram for a guilt offering. (Lev 19:20-21 NAS)*
> ***Ceremonial Law: Priest sacrifices the ram for the persons sin***
> *22 'The priest shall also make atonement for him with the ram of the guilt offering before the LORD for his sin which he has committed, and the sin which he has committed shall be forgiven him. (Lev 19:22 NAS)*

The judicial penalty is public humiliation because the offending party had to publicly appear in front of the community, acknowledge their sin, and provide a guilt offering. The ancient Israel community would look upon someone who broke God's Law with disdain. Public guilt was a serious punishment in ancient Israel that would affect the person's status. When reading Leviticus 19, it becomes obvious what is being taught. Leviticus 19 is a list of Moral Law infractions, their Judicial punishment, and the Ceremonial offering required for the forgiveness of the sin. In Leviticus 19, verse 3 talks about honoring your father and mother, verse 4 idolatry, verses 9 and 10 the Sabbath, verse 11 stealing, verse 12 taking the Lord's name in vain, 13 to 19 bearing false witness, verse 20 adultery, and so forth. Looking at verse 19, the verse Williamson Jr. claims is ceremonial, it is clear interbreeding, mixing seed, and mixing materials in a garment has to do with cheating or lying about the quality of a product. That's why God says,

> Therefore shall ye observe all **my statutes**, and all **my judgments**, and do them: I am the LORD. (Lev 19:37 KJV)

Not only are the Moral Laws to be kept, the judgements for breaking those laws are to be kept and the offering or sacrifice for the sin is to be kept. Offerings or sacrifices were not solely provided for breaking the Moral or Judicial Law. Offerings or sacrifices were made by the priests for those who recovered from an illness as well. An example of this is when a leper became well. Leviticus states,

> This shall be the law of the leper in the day of his cleansing. Now he shall be brought to the priest…Then the priest shall take the one male lamb and bring it for a guilt offering, with the log of oil, and present them as a wave offering before the LORD. (Lev 14:2,12 NAS)

The distinction between the Moral, Judicial, and Ceremonial law can be deduced from the Bible. The Bible makes no distinction between the "Old Covenant Law" and the "New Covenant Law" that Dispensationalists assert. The purpose for making classifications in the Law is for explaining how the Law functions in general. The three-part structure of the Law has nothing to do with abrogating laws. Nobody has the right to pick and choose which Laws are to be kept or not kept. We are to observe ALL of God's Law. To answer the question "why should the first be binding on the church but not the second?" The answer is ALL of Leviticus 19 is binding.

Jesus Christ as our high priest fulfilled the requirement of the Ceremonial Law by offering Himself for our sins. Ancient Israel was a theocratic kingdom. The United States is a Republic. The church is not to be a theocratic "religion" on earth because Christ's kingdom is in heaven. Jesus Christ is our Prophet, Priest, and King, then, now, and forever more. His government has no end. The Ceremonial Laws are fulfilled in Him, our Savior, Jesus Christ.

> Now He said to them, "These are My words which I spoke to you while I was still with you, that **all things which are written about Me in the Law of Moses and the Prophets and the Psalms must be fulfilled."** (Luk 24:44 NAS see also Mat 5:17-18)

He has fulfilled these laws in His dying, (John 19:18) raising from the dead, (Act 2:24) and sitting at the right hand of God (Act 2:32-33) from where He judges the living and the dead (1 Pet 4:5). Jesus Christ intercedes for us as our high priest in heaven on our behalf. (Rom 8:24; Heb 6:20) He purchased us with His blood (Act 20:28). We are partakers of His kingdom which has no end.

> He has made us to be a kingdom, priests to His God and Father; to Him be the glory and the dominion forever and ever. Amen. (Rev 1:6 NAS)

Keeping God's commandments is loving Christ. Jesus said,

> If you love Me, you will keep My commandments. (Joh 14:15 NAS)

God's Law is the standard for ALL law in society. The Moral Law is unchangeable and set in stone. The Judicial Laws are judgments rendered in criminal and civil offenses. Criminal laws are serious like murder and stealing. Civil laws are for damages caused by another person due to negligence. Judgments are also made by priests in determining the feasts, festivals, new moons, sabbaths, and sacrifices. Not every law in God's Law necessarily applies to modern times. For example, the mode of transportation in ancient Israel is not the same as today. Today, automobiles are the mode of transportation and not donkeys. An example of damages caused by neglect is an automobile accident. The negligent party can be sued for restitution. You must understand God's Law as a legal document in order to comprehend it.

3. The Moral Law

God's Moral Law has been in effect from the beginning of creation. The Ten Commandments are set by God in the very fabric of creation. The Moral Law is statutory law established by the Master Lawmaker God Himself. These are laws that are not based on decisions from a judge. *The Westminster Confession of Faith* specifically defines the Moral Law as summarily found in the Ten Commandments.

> ***This law***, *after his fall, continued to be a perfect rule of righteousness; and, as such, was delivered by God upon Mount Sinai,* ***in ten commandments***, *and written in two tables: the first four commandments containing our duty towards God; and the other six, our duty to man. Beside this law,* ***commonly called moral****.... [64]*

Transgressing any of the Ten Commandments is ALWAYS called sin and abhorrent to God. There is no time in human history where God allowed idolatry or murder. The Ten Commandments contain the criteria for what we call good or evil. The Ten Commandments are ingrained in nature from the beginning. Jesus stated,

> *He said to them, "Because of your hardness of heart, Moses permitted you to divorce your wives;* ***but from the beginning it has not been this way****. And I say to you, whoever divorces his wife, except for immorality, and marries another woman commits adultery." (Mat 19:8-9 NAS)*

Jesus expressly taught that adultery was sinful from the beginning of creation. God's Law was set in stone even before the tablets of stone were given to Moses on the mountain. Moses made judgments in the law that allowed divorce to keep the peace. This is no different than the United States today. There are plenty of examples of breaking the Law prior to the stone tablets. (Exo 20:3-17 NAS). Abraham kept God's commandments and God blessed him. In Genesis, God said,

> *Because Abraham obeyed Me and kept My charge,* ***My commandments, My statutes and My laws****. (Gen 26:5 NAS)*

The commandments Abraham obeyed are the Ten Commandments and the Laws are His Torah. The same language "My commandments, My statutes and My laws" is used by God in Deuteronomy.

Chapter 4 - The Law

> *If you obey the LORD your God to keep **His commandments and His statutes which are written in this book of the law**, if you turn to the LORD your God with all your heart and soul. (Deu 30:10 NAS)*

The phrase "turning your heart and soul to God" means the same thing as "to keep His commandments." This is the same as the gospel message. The main theme of the entire Bible is turning from your own way to keep God's commandments. Sin came into the world because Adam transgressed the Law of God. Paul explained this clearly.

> *Therefore, just as through one man sin entered into the world, and death through sin, and so death spread to all men, because all sinned-- for until the Law sin was in the world; but **sin is not imputed when there is no law**. Nevertheless death reigned from Adam until Moses, even over those who had not sinned in the likeness of the offense of Adam, who is a type of Him who was to come. (Rom 5:12-14 NAS)*

There can be no sin with no Law. It is irrefutable that the Moral Law has always existed.

a. The Moral Law in Genesis

The Law of God was in effect before the Law of Moses was written. The basic principles of the Ten Commandments are found in the book of Genesis. The Moral Law is expressed by God, when He said,

> *Abraham obeyed Me and kept My charge, My **commandments**, My **statutes** and My **laws**. (Gen 26:5 NAS)*

God put Abraham in charge of His commandments. The Hebrew word for "charge" in *the NASB concordance* is,

> *<04931> מִשְׁמֶרֶת (mishmereth) (1038b)*
> **Meaning:** *a guard, watch, charge, function*
> **Origin:** *fem. of 4929*
> **Usage:** *allegiance(1), charge(27), duties(15), duty(2), guard*(1), guard(2), guards(2), keep*(m)(1), keep(m)(1), kept(m)(5), obligation(4), obligations(4), offices(1), post(2), posts(1), safe(m)(1), service(2), service divisions(1), watch(4), worship(m)(1).*
> **Notes:** *¹ Lit., hearkened to My voice ᵃ Gen 22:16 [65]*

We are responsible and obligated to obey His commandments. The commandments, statutes, and laws are distinguished from each other and at the same time are one system of Law. The Nation of Israel did not come into being until after the ancient Israelites left the Egyptian captivity. This proves that God's Law is for all people, Jews and Gentiles alike, not only the Nation of Israel. The Law of God is the central theme of the entire Bible. To negate any part of the Law would destroy the meaning and purpose of the Bible. Table 4.1 on "the Ten Commandments in Genesis" shows how God's Law was in effect prior to the Ten Commandments given on Mount Sinai.

Table 4.1 - The Ten Commandments in Genesis		
Command	Explanation	Verse
First	Jacob is telling them to put their gods away and build an altar for God.	Put away your god's and make an altar for God (Gen 35:2-3 NAS)
Second	Jacob melted the idols.	They gave Jacob their gods and the silver rings (Gen 35:4 NAS)
Third	Cain was disingenuous about his relationship with God.	But for Cain and for his offering He had no regard. Cain became very angry and his countenance fell. (Gen 4:5 NAS)
Fourth	God rested on the seventh day and blessed it.	Then God blessed the seventh day and sanctified it, because in it He rested from all His work which God had created and made. (Gen 2:3 NAS)
Fifth	Cain dishonored His parents by murdering their son, his brother.	God has appointed me another offspring in place of Abel; for Cain killed him. (Gen 4:25 NAS)
Sixth	Cain murdered Abel.	Cain rose up against Abel his brother and killed him. (Gen 4:8 NAS)
Seventh	Abimelech was warned to not take a married woman as his own.	But God came to Abimelech in a dream of the night, and said to him, "Behold, you are a dead man because of the woman whom you have taken, for she is married." (Gen 20:3 NAS)
Eighth	Adam and Eve stole fruit which did not belong to them.	When the woman saw that the tree was good for food...she took from its fruit and ate; and she gave also to her husband with her, and he ate. (Gen 3:6 NAS)
Ninth	Cain lied to God about Abel.	Then the LORD said to Cain, "Where is Abel your brother?" And he said, "I do not know. Am I my brother's keeper?" (Gen 4:9 NAS)
Tenth	Cain coveted his brothers sacrifice.	But for Cain and for his offering He had no regard. So Cain became very angry and his countenance fell. (Gen 4:5 NAS)

b. The Sabbath is our duty to our neighbor

Traditionally, the Ten Commandments are classified into two parts: Our duty owed to God and our duty owed to man. The first four commandments traditionally are the duties man owes to God and the last six are duties man owes to his neighbor. *The Westminster Larger Catechism* states the Moral Law is summed in the Ten Commandments.

> Q. 98. Where is **the moral law** summarily comprehended?
> A. The moral law is summarily comprehended in the Ten Commandments, which were delivered by the voice of God upon mount Sinai, and written by him in two tables of stone; and are recorded in the twentieth chapter of Exodus; the **four first commandments containing our duty to God, and the other six our duty to man.**[66]

Chapter 4 - The Law

The distinctions between laws we owe to God and laws we owe to our neighbor are critical in understanding the Ten Commandments. One purpose of this book is to argue that the first three commands are duties to God. The last seven are duties towards our neighbor. It is appropriate to place the Fourth Commandment "to keep the Sabbath holy" under the classification of our duty towards our neighbor. Exodus states that the Sabbath is holy to YOU.

> *Therefore, you are to observe the Sabbath, **for it is holy to you**. (Exo 31:14 NAS)*

Traditionally, the Sabbath is a holy day to worship God. The Sabbath is not a day for worship. In actuality, the Sabbath is a day reserved holy for man. Jesus stated,

> *The **Sabbath was made for man**, and not man for the Sabbath. (Mar 2:27 NAS)*

It is necessary to classify the Ten Commandments into our duty to God and our duty to man. The Fourth Commandment "to keep the Sabbath holy" is our duty to man. God is requiring all people to give their employees, family, animals, land, and everything a day of rest from their labor. The Sabbath has nothing to do with worship. It is a statutory law enforced through judicial cases regulating labor, land, and commerce.

4. The Judicial Law

The Judicial Law contains the criminal and civil justice system of ancient Israel. Statutory Laws are enforced by judges making decisions on real life cases. The judgements written in the Bible are the Judicial Law. Many of the laws written in the Bible only show the judgments based on previous cases. The case itself is not always discussed. Many times, the written law is the decision only. An example of this is the dietary laws of Leviticus 11. The Law of God only lists what to and not to eat. It does not give the reasons why. At the time the Israelites were in the wilderness, there was a logical, scientific reason for the dietary laws.

The Judicial Law in the Bible is similar to the modern legal system in the United States. A common misinterpretation of the Law of God is in regards to the dietary Laws. A typical complaint is that "God says if you eat a pig you are sinning." They quote verses like Leviticus 11:6-8.

> *The rabbit also, for though it chews cud, it does not divide the hoof, it is unclean to you; and the pig, for though it divides the hoof, thus making a split hoof, it does not chew cud, it is unclean to you. You shall not eat of their flesh nor touch their carcasses; they are unclean to you. (Lev 11:6-8 NAS)*

Those who use this argument draw the conclusion that the Bible is in error because they believe there is nothing wrong with eating pigs. This logic is grossly in error. Pigs have parasitic infections that harm the wellbeing of a human being. It is not very smart to ignore intelligent scientifically based instructions on poor hygiene and parasitic infections such as tapeworms, nematodes, and flukes. Parasitic infections cause debilitating disease and poor quality of life. The passage in Leviticus 11:6-8 is similar to the modern-day Food and Drug Administration (FDA) regulations in the United States that govern food safety. For example, Coca-Cola soft drinks removed cocaine from their product because the drug is addictive and unhealthy to use. Cocaine was later added to the Dangerous Drug Act of 1920. The dietary laws in the Law of Moses are the precedence for governing food and drugs in a Nation. Criticizing the Law of God when the United States legislates similar laws today is ridiculous. The Kosher laws in the Law of Moses are a great dietary plan. Besides the precedence for the modern FDA regulations, the Law of Moses contains the precedence for modern civil and criminal law.

a. Civil Tort law

The Law of Moses contains a foundation for civil tort law. Tort occurs when someone causes damages to a person or property due to negligence. Torts are civil cases and not criminal. "Tort" is defined as,

> *An action that is wrong but can be dealt with in a civil court rather than a criminal court. [67]*

It is a fact that the modern American civil court system, also called "tort law," is taught in the Law of God. Louis W. Hensler from Regent Law writes,

> *So far as we know, there is no word in the Bible for 'torts.' Yet the 'norms' which the Creator told Moses to set before the Israelites, in the chapter of Exodus following the Ten Commandments, are filled with what we think of as 'tort' rules. [68]*

For example, modern personal injury is found in the book of Exodus. Louis W. Hensler points out that the Law of God has distinctions between personal injury and property damage. Hensler uses chapters 21 to 24 of the Law in the Book of Exodus or the "mishpatim." These are מִשְׁפָּט (mishpat) or judgments. Hensler writes,

> *The first organizational principle apparent within the tort law of the mishpatim is the distinction between personal injury and property damage: "The laws set out in Exodus 21:12–21:32 relate to acts adversely affecting persons, while those found in Exodus 21:33–22:15 concern injuries or damages to property." [69]*

The purpose of the legal system is for civil and criminal justice. The difference between the Judicial Law and the Moral Law is that the Judicial Law is based on cases and the Moral Law is based on statutes. There are no situations when murdering someone is not a sin. The punishment for killing varies based on the situation found in the Judicial Law. An example is when a thief was killed while breaking into someone's property. If a thief is killed breaking into somebody's home in ancient Israel, they did not have to be punished for the thief's death.

> *If the thief is caught while breaking in, and is struck so that he dies, there will be no bloodguiltiness on his account. (Exo 22:2 NAS)*

This situation is addressed in the laws of the United States today. Understanding the Law of God in this way makes far more sense than the antinomian Dispensationalist teaching. Teaching all of God's Law is abolished because we are under grace is ignorant and lazy minded. An excellent example of how tort law works in the Law of Moses is Exodus 21:33–34. Hensler explains an example of property damage in the Law of Moses.

> B. Property Damage in the Mishpatim (Exodus 21:33–22:6)
> 1. Property v. Property (Exodus 21:33–36)
> Paradigm #11: The Open Pit (21:33–34)

> **Protasis:** "When a man opens a pit, or digs a pit and does not cover it, and an ox or an ass falls into it . . . ."268
> **Apodosis:** "[T]he one responsible for the pit must make restitution; he shall pay the price to the owner, but shall keep the dead animal."269
> **Principle:** Strict liability extends to one who creates non-invasive risk. [70]

The basics of civil liability is established in God's Law.

b. The malleability of the Law

The Law of God changes in its application; but, not its purpose. The Law applies differently depending on the situation, society, geographical location, and other factors. There are laws that, over time become obsolete. An example of laws that become obsolete is the desuetude (des-wi-tood) of the Law. Desuetude of the law is when a law ceases to be used. Some laws become obsolete or unenforceable. The definition of "Desuetude" is,

> *The state of being unused; legally, the doctrine by which a law or treaty is rendered obsolete because of disuse. The concept encompasses situations in which a court refuses to enforce an unused law even if the law has not been repealed. [71]*

An example of the desuetude of law is the punishment of "ducking" or dunking a person into cold water. John F. Stinneford wrote,

> *Cruel and Unusual Punishments Clause makes statutes authorizing punishment for crime analogous to statutes that are declaratory of the common law. Although punishment statutes do not purport to "declare" custom, they are explicitly bound to custom by the Cruel and Unusual Punishments Clause. If they are harsher than custom (positive or negative) will permit, they are cruel and unusual. Thus, for example, the Pennsylvania Supreme Court declared in 1825 that the once traditional practice of subjecting a woman convicted of being a "common scold" to ducking in cold water had become unusual, and therefore illegal, because it had fallen out of usage at around the same time the practice of burning witches at the stake had fallen into disrepute a century before. Prior to 1958, the United States Supreme Court's decisions concerning the scope of the Cruel and Unusual Punishments Clause also relied on desuetude to determine which punishments were actually cruel and unusual. [72]*

The Eighth Amendment of the Constitution of the United States prohibits cruel and unusual punishments making the old ducking laws obsolete. This does not mean the Sabbath is abolished because of lack of use as Dispensationalist Joel T. Williamson Jr. argues. There is no time when God's

Law ceases to be law. Desuetude also refers to laws that are unenforceable. An example of a law that is unenforceable is a law in Rockville Maryland that states,

> *Sec. 13-53. Profanity; violation of section declared misdemeanor.*
> *(a) A person may not profanely curse and swear or use obscene language upon or near any street, sidewalk or highway within the hearing of persons passing by, upon or along such street, sidewalk or highway.*
> *(b) A person may not act in a disorderly manner by profanely cursing, swearing or using obscene language.*
> *(c) Any person who violates this section is guilty of a misdemeanor. [73]*

I guarantee Section 13-53 is broken constantly in Maryland with zero arrests. In *the Westminster Confession of Faith* Chapter 19 section 4, the statement "the general equity thereof may require" includes the desuetude of the law. The Judicial Law applies where it is required. The Judicial laws in general expired with the Nation of Israel because those laws are specific to the situation in ancient Israel. The desuetude of the law is expressed in the epistle to the Hebrews. The writer of Hebrews wrote,

> *When He said, "A new covenant," He has made the first obsolete.* **But whatever is becoming obsolete and growing old is ready to disappear**. *(Heb 8:13 NAS)*

There are many laws and punishments in God's Law that continue to be observed in God honoring governments. An example is capital punishment.

> *He who strikes a man so that he dies shall surely be put to death. (Exo 21:12 NAS)*

Some laws are not codified, but expected in a civil society. An example is if someone's animal is lost or in harm's way.

> *You shall not see your countryman's donkey or his ox fallen down on the way, and pay no attention to them; you shall certainly help him to raise them up. (Deu 22:4 NAS)*

If a neighbor's dog is stuck in a fence and could die, the dog should be helped out of the situation. There is no modern law requiring this. For example, if someone is in an automobile accident and has no aid, you should pull over to offer them aid. This is called the "duty to rescue."

> *Duty to rescue is a concept of tort law and refers to the duty of a person to rescue another who is in a dangerous situation. [74]*

This leads to the understanding that the Law is ordained by God to suit societal needs. This concept can be seen in Matthew. Jesus said Moses allowed a certificate of divorce. God did not ordain divorce law from the beginning.

> *And some Pharisees came to Him, testing Him, and saying, "Is it lawful for a man to divorce his wife for any cause at all?" And He answered and said, "Have you not read, that He who created them from the beginning made them male and female, and*

> *said, 'For this cause a man shall leave his father and mother, and shall cleave to his wife; and the two shall become one flesh'? "Consequently, they are no longer two, but one flesh. What therefore God has joined together, let no man separate." They said to Him, "Why then did Moses command to give her a certificate of divorce and send her away?" He said to them,* **"Because of your hardness of heart, Moses permitted you to divorce your wives; but from the beginning it has not been this way.** *"And I say to you, whoever divorces his wife, except for immorality, and marries another woman commits adultery." (Mat 19:3-9 NAS)*

Jesus said Moses permitted divorce because of the hardness of the people's heart. Moses had to make a decision on which sin is worse for society. Is allowing an evil person to divorce their wife worse than forcing them to remain married causing the woman be abused or murdered? Clearly, the Judicial Law, not the Moral Law found in the Ten Commandments, is malleable to address specific abuses in order to keep the peace. All government authorities are established by God to enforce God's Law (Rom 13:6). The Law of Moses is legal precedence from antiquity for the establishment of criminal and civil law. It is sheer ignorance to dismiss the entire Law of Moses and label the Law as "not applicable" to the Christian Church.

5. The Ceremonial law

Laws that establish the feasts, festivals, new moons, sacrifices, and all the priestly temple practices are Ceremonial Laws. Ceremonial Laws contain statutes and judgments. *The Westminster Confession of Faith* teaches that the Ceremonial Law is abrogated.

> *3. Beside this law, commonly called moral, God was pleased to give to the people of Israel, as a church under age, ceremonial laws, containing several typical ordinances, partly of worship, prefiguring Christ, his graces, actions, sufferings, and benefits; and partly, holding forth divers instructions of moral duties.* **All which ceremonial laws are now abrogated, under the new testament**. [75]

"Fulfilled" is a more accurate word than the word "abrogated." The Ceremonial Law is fulfilled by the messianic work of Christ and NOT abrogated or abolished. Besides that, the Confession distinguishes the Ceremonial Law well. We are not to hold each other accountable to observe the feasts, festivals, new moons and sacrifices because Christ fulfilled them. The festivals, new moons, and sabbaths are shadows of what is to come. In Colossians Paul wrote,

> *Therefore let no one act as your judge in regard to food or drink or in respect to a festival or a new moon or a Sabbath day--things which are a mere shadow of what is to come; but the substance belongs to Christ. (Col 2:16-17 NAS)*

Paul says, they are the "shadow of what is to come." Paul did not say the legal requirement to keep the Sabbath is abolished. It is important to understand that the word "sabbath" has different meanings throughout the Bible (Mat 12, Mar 2, Luk 6). The word "sabbath" is found in the Moral statutory Law (Exo 20:8), Ceremonial statutory Law (Num 28:10) and Judicial case Law (Num 15:32). In the Bible, there are disputes about how to observe the Sabbath; however, there are no questions of whether it should be observed. The purpose of the festivals, new moons, and sabbath days are for keeping the promises of the coming of the Messiah (Rom 9:4). More specifically, Christ fulfilled the requirement of the judgments and statutes in His messianic work as Prophet, Priest, and King. The Ceremonial Law in Leviticus 23 is a perfect timeline of what Christ did for us and our salvation. This is discussed in detail later in the chapter on "the Ceremonial Law fulfilled in Christ."

a. Sacrifices and the Law

Some of the sacrificial ceremonies were scheduled on the Sabbath, but not all of them. Just because the Jewish religion practices their worship service on the Sabbath does not mean the Bible teaches the Fourth Commandment "to keep the Sabbath holy" is for worship. The modern Jewish religion has no ability to keep the Law of Moses because the temple and the priests no longer exist. The sacrifices and ceremonies that were required on the Jewish calendar are fulfilled in the messianic work of Christ. The Fourth Commandment "to keep the Sabbath holy" is not a part of those ceremonies. The ceremonies in the Law of Moses were prophetic promises of the coming of the Messiah Jesus Christ (Rom 9:3,4). God clearly shows in Scripture that the sacrifices of bulls and goats never were appealing to Him. The writer of Hebrews wrote,

> *Therefore, when He comes into the world, He says, "Sacrifice and offering **Thou hast not desired**, But a body Thou hast prepared for Me; In whole burnt offerings and sacrifices for sin **Thou hast taken no pleasure** "Then I said, 'Behold, I have come (In the roll of the book it is written of Me) To do Thy will, O God.'" After saying above, "Sacrifices and offerings and whole burnt offerings and sacrifices for sin **Thou hast not desired, nor hast Thou taken pleasure in them.**" (which are offered according to the Law) (Heb 10:5-8 NAS)*

Also, the Bible does not teach that the sacrifices themselves forgave sins. The writer of Hebrews states,

> *For it is impossible for the blood of bulls and goats to take away sins. (Heb 10:4 NAS)*

Scripture is clear that the sacrifices were only foreshadowing or pointing to the true Sacrifice that was to come in ancient Israel. That sacrifice was Jesus Christ in His crucifixion on the cross. Hebrews says,

> *Then He said, "Behold, I have come to do Thy will." He takes away the first in order to establish the second. By this will we have been sanctified through the offering of the body of Jesus Christ once for all. And every priest stands daily ministering and offering time after time the same sacrifices, which can never take away sins; **but He, having offered one sacrifice for sins for all time, sat down at the right hand of God,** waiting from that time onward until His enemies be made a footstool for His feet. **For by one offering He has perfected for all time those who are sanctified.** (Heb 10:9-14 NAS)*

Therefore, God never intended for sacrificial offerings to be a part of the Sabbath. The Fourth Commandment to "keep the Sabbath holy" was never intended to be a day of worship. God wants us to worship Him every day. The day for worship is explained further in the chapter on "the Christian Day of Worship."

b. Christ fulfilled the Ceremonial Law

The purpose of the earthly ministry of Christ was to fulfill the prophecies found in the Old Testament. Jesus plainly said that "all things" spoken of Him in the Law of Moses were to be fulfilled. Luke wrote,

> Now He said to them, "These are My words which I spoke to you while I was still with you, that all things which are written about Me in the Law of Moses and the Prophets and the Psalms must be fulfilled. (Luk 24:44 NAS)

Jesus expressly stated He did not come to abolish the Law or the Prophets but to fulfill them.

> Do not think that I came to abolish the Law or the Prophets; I did not come to abolish, but to fulfill. (Mat 5:17 NAS)

The fulfillment of Old Testament prophecies about the coming of the Messiah is central to the Christian faith. The fact that Christ said He fulfilled all prophecies about Him is irrefutable evidence that the Ceremonial Laws were fulfilled in His earthly ministry. Jesus Christ is the Messiah promised in the Law and the Prophets of the Old Testament.

c. The Law changes with the change of the priesthood

Every time a new priest took over for the previous priest, the Law changed. It was necessary for the Law to change when Christ became our high priest. The writer of Hebrews wrote,

> For when the priesthood is changed, of necessity there takes place a change of law also. (Heb 7:12 NAS)

The change in the law can be seen in the work of Christ. The priest was required to provide a sacrifice for their own sins. Christ, our high priest, is sinless and needs no sacrifice for himself. For He Himself is the Sacrifice. The writer of Hebrews explains,

> For it was fitting that we should have such a high priest, holy, innocent, undefiled, separated from sinners and exalted above the heavens; who does not need daily, like those high priests, to offer up sacrifices, first for His own sins, and then for the sins of the people, because this He did once for all when He offered up Himself For the Law appoints men as high priests who are weak, but the word of the oath, which came after the Law, appoints a Son, made perfect forever. (Heb 7:26-28 NAS)

Christ also perfected the Law forever by offering Himself as the sacrifice for the sin of the people. The priests had to minister and offer sacrifices daily. Christ offered Himself for the sins of the people once and for all. His onetime offering of Himself satisfied the requirement for all people of all time.

> And every priest stands daily ministering and offering time after time the same sacrifices, which can never take away sins; but He, having offered one sacrifice for sins for all time, sat down at the right hand of God, waiting from that time onward

until His enemies be made a footstool for His feet. For by one offering He has perfected for all time those who are sanctified. (Heb 10:11-14 NAS)

The sacrifices were a memorial of the promises of God that required a substitutionary sacrifice for the sins of the people. This is clearly seen in the memorial of Passover where God passed over the Jewish people when God struck the first born in Egypt. The true sacrifice for their sins was performed by Jesus Christ on the cross. The Law of God was not abolished, it was fulfilled. Jesus Christ obeyed ALL the Law of God perfectly as our substitute. Because He is without sin, He fulfilled the requirement of the Law for His people. Christ satisfied the requirements of the law to observe the sabbaths, moons, festivals, and sacrifices in His messianic work. Christ, as our high priest has authority over His Own Law. His one act fulfilled ALL the Law of God for His people forever. This means when we sin, Christ's sacrifice for our sin grants us forgiveness. We are required to repent from our sin and confess our sin before the world. Christians are required to obey the truth of God's Law.

Therefore also God highly exalted Him, and bestowed on Him the name which is above every name, that at the name of Jesus every knee should bow, of those who are in heaven, and on earth, and under the earth, and that every tongue should confess that Jesus Christ is Lord, to the glory of God the Father. So then, my beloved, just as you have always obeyed, not as in my presence only, but now much more in my absence, work out your salvation with fear and trembling; for it is God who is at work in you, both to will and to work for His good pleasure. (Phi 2:9-13 NAS)

Chapter 4 - The Law

Chapter 5 - The Calendar

Christ's messianic work is foreshadowed in the Ceremonial Law. The Old Testament feasts, festivals, new moons, sabbaths, and sacrifices are all Ceremonial Laws. These Ceremonial Laws are taught in Leviticus 23, Numbers 28–29, and Deuteronomy 16. Jesus Christ fulfilled all of the requirements of the Ceremonial Law in His messianic work. The Jewish calendar is a picture of that very fulfillment. The Ceremonial Laws were scheduled on many different calendar days other than the seventh day.

Ancient Israel used a lunar calendar that follows the celestial behavior of the moon. The Gregorian calendar is a solar calendar that follows the celestial behavior of the sun. It is very common for Christians to teach Bible prophecies in reference to the solar calendar rather than the Jewish lunar calendar. In order for the Ceremonial Law to make sense, the functionality of the calendar must be studied. It is crucial to understand that, if the Ceremonial Laws are not fulfilled in Christ, then we are still obligated to perform them. We must believe Jesus Christ is the messiah that was promised in the Law and the Prophets. Jesus said Moses wrote about His work. John wrote,

> *For if you believed Moses, you would believe Me; for he wrote of Me. But if you do not believe his writings, how will you believe My words? (Joh 5:46-47 NAS)*

Moses and all the prophets spoke about the messianic work of Christ. Jesus explained to the Apostles what the Scriptures taught about Him. Luke wrote,

> *And He said to them, "O foolish men and slow of heart to believe in all that the prophets have spoken!" Was it not necessary for the Christ to suffer these things and to enter into His glory?" And beginning with Moses and with all the prophets, He explained to them the things concerning Himself in all the Scriptures. (Luk 24:25-27 NAS)*

Knowing the workings of the calendar helps understand how the scriptures are fulfilled in Christ.

1. The different calendars

There are three main calendar systems used throughout history: the solar, lunar, and lunisolar calendar systems.

a. Solar Calendar

The solar calendar uses the sun and the seasons as the metric for calculating the dates of the year. The solar calendar uses the position of the sun when it crosses the equinoxes to synchronize the seasons throughout each year. Calendars that do not synchronize the sun with the equinox can cause spring to start at the wrong time of the year. For example, it becomes difficult for farmers to predict the proper time to start agriculture when Spring is out of sync. The seven-day week on the solar calendar causes the Sabbath to always fall on Saturday. The Greeks and Romans used a solar calendar. Solar calendars have changed over time. There are two types of solar calendars, the "Sidereal" and the "Tropical." The Sidereal solar calendar bases the calculations of the time the Earth to complete an orbit around the sun

Chapter 5 - The Calendar

in relation to the fixed position of the stars. The Tropical calendar bases the calculations on the interval between equinoxes and solstices when the sun crosses the celestial equator. The Gregorian calendar is based on the tropical year. Figure 5.1 shows how the solar tropical year works.

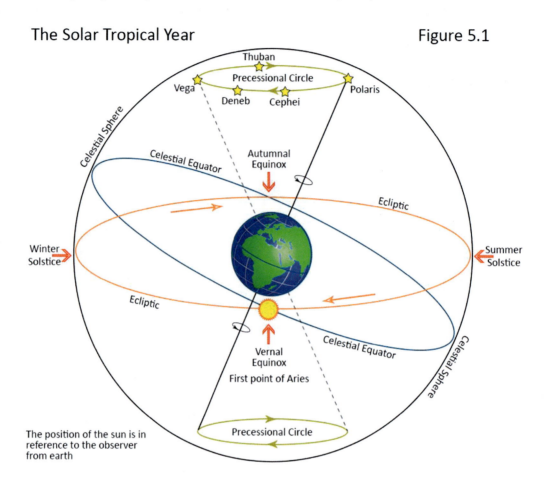

Solar calendars have approximately 365.25 years. Our modern Gregorian calendar comes from the Julian calendar based on the Tropical year. The precession of the Earth affects the calculation of the seasons. *The Dictionary of Geophysics, Astrophysics, and Astronomy* defines "precession" as,

> *The slow, conical movement of the rotation axis of a rotating body. [76]*

The axial precession of the Earth is approximately 1 degree every 72 years. We can find how long the Earth completes the precessional circle by multiplying the axial precession by 360 degrees which comes out to approximately 25,920 years. This calculation is based on current and previous mathematical data and most likely will change over future observations. It is possible the precession of the Earth could be gradually speeding up or slowing down. The precession of the Earth is why the North Star is not always the same star over time. The *Dictionary of Geophysics, Astrophysics, and Astronomy* in the definition of "precession" says,

> *A notable effect of precession is the changing of the North Star (today the north celestial pole is near the star Polaris, but around 2000 BC it was near the star Thuban) as the Earth's rotation axis points toward different locations in space. [77]*

Chapter 5 - The Calendar

The precession and tilt of the Earth causes the seasons to gradually change over time affecting the climate. The change in the Earth's orbit around the Sun (eccentricity), tilt (obliquity), and rotation (precession) all cause the solar calendar to be inconsistent requiring frequent adjustments. The change in the Earth's orbit that affects climate is called the "Milankovitch Cycle." The *Dictionary of Geophysics, Astrophysics, and Astronomy* defines the Milankovitch Cycle as,

> *Cyclic variations in climate driven by periodic changes in orbital and Earth orientation parameters. Climate in a particular area depends on the solar flux, and therefore on both the distance from the Earth to the sun and the angle between the surface of the area in question and the sun's rays over the course of a day (overhead sunlight leading to a greater flux than tangential sunlight). These both cause the seasonal variations in weather. [78]*

The Milankovitch Cycle is a form of climate change that causes the seasons to constantly shift. The variations of the Earth's orbit, tilt, and rotation will never be perfectly calculated since they are never constant and always changing. The variations of the Earth also cause different calendar systems to celebrate holidays on different days of the year. This constant change is also why astrological readings will never be reliable. When analyzing astrological readings, it becomes obvious that the sidereal calculations of the stars are completely different than the tropical calculation.

> *Not very many people are aware, but the most commonly used astrology in the western world (tropical astrology) sets the constellations to the seasons of the Earth, not the visible sky. This creates a growing variation of roughly one degree every 72 years from the true location of the constellations. At the moment the two systems are around 24 degrees apart, depending on which system is used. This translates to a difference of up to two zodiac signs away from the actual placements. [79]*

An example of this is a birth chart of someone born in 1973 with a tropical Capricorn zodiac sign could actually be a sidereal Sagittarius. For this reason, only the Bible should be trusted for truth and godliness and not astrological interpretations.

b. Lunar Calendar

The lunar calendar uses the phases of the moon for each month. There are approximately 354 days in a lunar calendar year. Each lunar cycle varies between 29 and 30 days a month. Lunar calendars synchronize the seasons with a leap year every two or three years by adding a 13th month. The insertion of an additional month to fix the calendar is called "intercalation" or "intercalary" day or month. The month starts over when the New Moon occurs. One popular lunar calendar used by some is called the "Creator's calendar" or the "Lunar Sabbath" calendar. The Creator's calendar uses the phases of the moon and starts each month with the new moon. The Creator's calendar is wholly independent of the solar calendar and is not synchronized to the Gregorian or the Jewish calendars.

Figure 5.2 shows the eight phases of the moon in relation to the position of the sun.

Chapter 5 - The Calendar

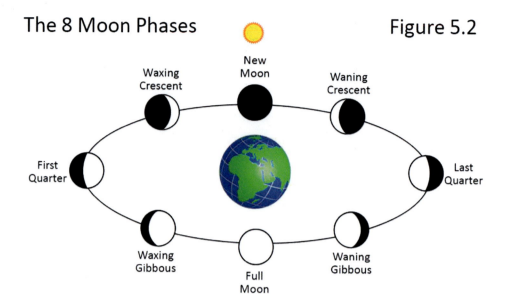

The Creator's calendar makes the Sabbath day consistently on the 8th, 15th, 22nd, and 29th day of each month. The first day of the month is always the new moon day. The 2nd day starts the work week making the 8th day the first Sabbath day of the week. Figure 5.3 shows how the days of the month are calculated in the Creator's calendar. [80]

Creator's Calendar — Figure 5.3

Lunar Sabbath						New Moon Day 1
Day 1	Day 2	Day 3	Day 4	Day 5	Day 6	Sabbath
2	3	4	5	6	7	8
9	10	11	12	13	14	15
16	17	18	19	20	21	22
23	24	25	26	27	28	29

Source: http://www.sabbathherald.com/biblical-calendar-for-this-month/

The problem many people have with the Creator's calendar is that the Sabbath day is not consistently on the seventh day and it does not synchronize to the seasons. The seasons gradually shift over time with lunar calendars due to the year being 354 days. The first day is the new moon and is a rest day. The first day of the work week starts on the 2nd day of the week making the Sabbath start on the eighth day and not the seventh day. The proponents of the Creator's calendar make the first day and thirtieth day a rest day. Each month has one or two days where the work week is not counted, breaking the seven-day week cycle. For example, in Appendix II, in the "Lunar Sabbath & Gregorian Calendar

Compared AD 2020-2021" chart, the month of Ziv has a transitional New Moon day at the end of the month on 30 Ziv and then a New Moon day on 1 Sivan. This creates a nine-day transition between the last Sabbath on 29 Ziv and the first Sabbath on 8 Sivan. When calculating the dates between the Creator's calendar and any solar calendar, the Sabbath days are rarely on Saturday. Also, when the Creator's calendar is compared to any solar calendar, the days of the week shift over time causing the feasts in Leviticus 23 to shift dates during the year. For more information on the comparison between the Creator's calendar and the Gregorian calendar, see Appendix II "Lunar Sabbath & Gregorian Calendar Compared AD 2020-2020." The shift in days during the month can be seen in the chart in Appendix II, the "Lunar Sabbath & Gregorian Calendar Compared AD 31."

c. Lunisolar calendar

Lunisolar calendars use the phases of the moon and the sun to calculate the year. The lunisolar calendar uses the phases of the moon to keep track of the months while using the sun to keep track of the week. This means the days of the month and the New Year will start on a different day than the solar calendar while the day of the week will continue to synchronize. Figure 5.4 shows how the lunar and solar calendars are combined.

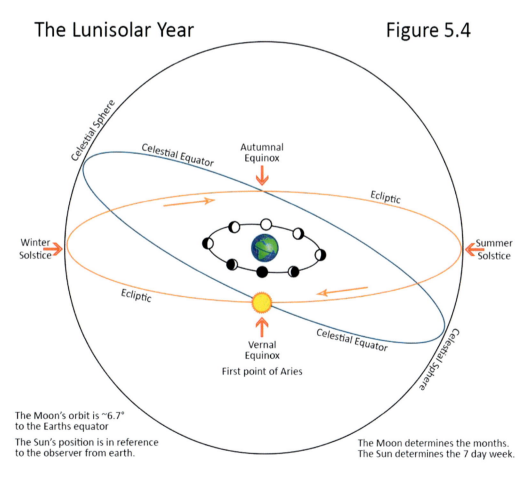

The lunisolar calendar synchronizes the lunar and solar calendar together to keep the seasons more accurate each year. Unlike the Creator's Calendar, the Sabbath is measured by the solar seven-day

Chapter 5 - The Calendar

cycle. The lunisolar calendar matches the days of the week to the solar calendar making Saturday the Sabbath day every week. The modern-day Jewish calendar is a lunisolar calendar.

2. The Jewish Calendar

The ancient Israelites did not use the same calendar the modern Jewish people use today. Prior to the destruction of the first temple, there are no remains left to determine what the ancient Israelites used for a calendar. If there is a copy of it, it is unavailable. The Bible does not teach any leap year, nor is there an established monthly cycle in the text. After the Jews were released from the Babylonian captivity, the Jews most likely used the lunisolar Babylonian calendar. The modern Jewish Talmudic Calendar is attributed to a Rabbi of the Sanhedrin named Hillel circa AD 358. The years gained or lost from the calendar system changes are unknown. This makes setting accurate dates impossible.

a. The Days

The Jewish calendar does not have formal names for the days of the week. Each day on the Jewish calendar is designated with a numeric value. On the Jewish calendar, the seventh day is the only day with a name, the "Sabbath." The Julian and Gregorian calendar inherited the names of each day from pagan gods. The Bible starts a day in the evening.

And there was evening and there was morning, one day. (Gen 1:5 NAS)

The solar days starts in the morning and ends in the evening. Table 5.1 compares both the Jewish and Gregorian calendar days of the week.

Table 5.1 - Comparison of the days in the Jewish and Gregorian calendars			
Hebrew	**Transliteration**	**English**	**Gregorian Calendar**
יום ראשון	Yom Rishon	First Day	Sunday
יום שני	Yom Sheini	Second Day	Monday
יום שלישי	Yom Shlishi	Third Day	Tuesday
יום רביעי	Yom R'vi'i	Fourth Day	Wednesday
יום חמישי	Yom Chamishi	Fifth Day	Thursday
יום שישי	Yom Shishi	Sixth Day	Friday
יום שבת	Yom Shabbat	Sabbath Day	Saturday
Source: [81]			

b. The Months

The Jewish month is based on the time it takes for the moon to go through the lunar cycle. This cycle is approximately 29.5 days. The start of the lunar cycle is called the "new moon" or "Rosh Chodesh." The Jewish calendar has twelve months and sometimes thirteen months depending on a leap year. The leap year synchronizes the lunar calendar with the seasons. Table 5.2 compares the months between the Jewish and Gregorian Calendars. For more information on how the Jewish calendar works in relationship to the Gregorian calendar, see Appendix II on the "Jewish & Gregorian Calendar Compared AD 2020-2021."

c. The Years

The New Year on the Jewish calendar starts on a different month than the solar calendar. For example, the Jewish New Year is 1 Tishrei year 5781 and begins on September 18th year AD 2020. The Jewish New Year begins in the month of Tishrei and not Nissan, even though the first month is Nissan. The Jewish calendar does not perfectly synchronize with the Gregorian calendar. The months are approximately 29.5 days long. There are approximately 29.5 times 12 equaling 354 days in a year. The addition of an intercalary month is called the Jewish leap year. The intercalation of the Jewish calendar is necessary to synchronize the calendar with the seasons.

> *The problem with strictly lunar calendars is that there are approximately 12.4 lunar months in every solar year, so a 12-month lunar calendar is about 11 days shorter than a solar year and a 13-month lunar is about 19 longer than a solar year. The months drift around the seasons on such a calendar: on a 12-month lunar calendar, the month of Nissan, which is supposed to occur in the Spring, would occur 11 days earlier in the season each year, eventually occurring in the Winter, the Fall, the Summer, and then the Spring again. On a 13-month lunar calendar, the same thing would happen in the other direction, and faster. [82]*

Table 5.2 – Comparison of months in the Jewish and Gregorian Calendars				
Hebrew	**English**	**Number**	**Length**	**Gregorian**
ניסן	Nissan	1	30 days	Mar-Apr
אייר	Iyar	2	29 days	Apr-May
סיון	Sivan	3	30 days	May-Jun
תמוז	Tammuz	4	29 days	Jun-Jul
אב	Av	5	30 days	Jul-Aug
אלול	Elul	6	29 days	Aug-Sep
תשרי	Tishrei	7	30 days	Sep-Oct
חשוון	Cheshvan	8	29 or 30 days	Oct-Nov
כסלו	Kislev	9	30 or 29 days	Nov-Dec
טבת	Tevet	10	29 days	Dec-Jan
שבט	Shevat	11	30 days	Jan-Feb
אדר א	Adar A	12	30 days	Feb-Mar
אדר ב	Adar II (Leap)	13	29 days	Feb-Mar
The Months of the Gregorian calendar can change in respect to the Jewish calendar over time. Source: [83]				

Chapter 5 - The Calendar

3. The choice of the solar calendar

After the early Church went through many years of Roman persecution, Emperor Constantine decriminalized Christianity with the Edict of Milan in AD 313. The ancient Nation of Israel was long gone by AD 313. A minority of Christians kept the festivals according to the lunar calendar. Most Christians at that time were using the Julian calendar to keep track of the Christian festivals. The early Church disagreed on the date to celebrate Easter from the time of the Apostles. This was not a sudden disagreement that arose because of Emperor Constantine. Some of the early Church followed the Jewish calendar and others the Julian calendar. Eusebius wrote,

> But **before this time another most virulent disorder had existed, and long afflicted the Church**; I mean the difference respecting the salutary feast of Easter. For while one party asserted that the Jewish custom should be adhered to, the other affirmed that the exact recurrence of the period should be observed, without following the authority of those who were in error, and strangers to gospel grace. [84]

To end the dispute, the First Council of Nicaea in AD 325 decided which day to celebrate Easter. At that time, the early Church would celebrate Easter twice in a year. Eusebius wrote,

> Hence it is that on this point as well as others they have no perception of the truth, so that, being altogether ignorant of the true adjustment of this question, **they sometimes celebrate Easter twice in the same year.** [85]

One group of Christians followed the lunar calendar and the other used the solar calendar. This clearly shows that the lunar and solar calendars never synchronized. The Council of Nicaea did not change the day for Easter to "Christianize" a pagan holiday. They chose the solar calendar over the lunar calendar, which was disputed since the early times of the Church. The early Church, during the time of the Roman Empire, celebrated Easter according to both the solar and lunar calendar from the beginning. The Roman Empire encompassed many different countries and lands during that time. The Julian calendar was used throughout the Roman Empire. The ecumenical church throughout the Roman Empire celebrated Easter according to the Julian calendar and not the Jewish calendar. Eusebius wrote,

> Since, therefore, it was needful that this matter should be rectified, so that we might have nothing in common with that nation of parricides who slew their Lord: and since that arrangement is consistent with propriety **which is observed by all the churches of the western, southern, and northern parts of the world, and by some of the eastern also**: for these reasons all are unanimous on this present occasion in thinking it worthy of adoption. And I myself have undertaken that this decision should meet with the approval of your Sagacities, in the hope that your Wisdoms will gladly admit that practice which is observed at once in the city of Rome, and in Africa; throughout Italy, and in Egypt, in Spain, the Gauls, Britain, Libya, and the whole of Greece; in the dioceses of Asia and Pontus, and in Cilicia, with entire unity of judgment. And you will consider not only that the number of churches is far greater in the regions I have enumerated than in any other, but also that it is most fitting that all should unite in

*desiring that which sound reason appears to demand, and **in avoiding all participation in the perjured conduct of the Jews**. [86]*

The Eastern Church primarily observed Easter according to the Jewish calendar. The Western Church and other churches throughout the Roman Empire primarily observed Easter according to the Julian calendar. Constantine and the early Church established the Julian calendar as the only calendar for the purpose of removing the Jewish festivals entirely. They wanted to establish only Christian festivals entirely separate from Jewish tradition. It would make no sense to force the whole world to change their calendar to a Jewish festival calendar since the feasts, festivals, new moons, and sacrifices were fulfilled in the messianic work of Christ. The early ecumenical Church, who resided across the world, chose the Julian calendar over the Jewish calendar for the purpose of ending an age-old dispute. Eusebius wrote,

> *In fine, that I may express my meaning in as few words as possible, it has been determined by the common judgment of all, that the most holy feast of **Easter should be kept on one and the same day**. [87]*

It was not Emperor Constantine acting as a tyrant imposing a calendar upon Christians against their will. This change made it possible to synchronize the Christian festivals with the world calendar, bringing the world in line with the Christian festivals. Establishing the Julian calendar fixed the festivals on a consistent date every year instead of the date changing every year like the dates on the Jewish calendar. Likewise, Emperor Constantine officially adopted the Lord's Day as the day of rest, prayer, and devotion to allow the Church to dedicate their time to religious worship unimpeded. Prior to the Edict of Milan in AD 313, the Christian Church was harassed, their property confiscated, they were murdered, and despicably treated. This was NOT a change of the Sabbath to the first day at all. The Sabbath and the Lord's Day were never confused as the same day. Constantine made it a crime to persecute Christians and take their property. Constantine established religious freedom. Eusebius wrote,

> **He ordained, too, that one day should be regarded as a special occasion for prayer: I mean that which is truly the first and chief of all, the day of our Lord and Saviour.** *The entire care of his household was entrusted to deacons and other ministers consecrated to the service of God, and distinguished by gravity of life and every other virtue: while his trusty body guard, strong in affection and fidelity to his person, found in their emperor an instructor in the practice of piety, and like him held the Lord's salutary day in honor and performed on that day the devotions which he loved. The same observance was recommended by this blessed prince to all classes of his subjects: his earnest desire being gradually to lead all mankind to the worship of God.* **Accordingly he enjoined on all the subjects of the Roman empire to observe the Lord's day, as a day of rest, and also to honor the day which precedes the Sabbath; in memory, I suppose, of what the Saviour of mankind is recorded to have achieved on that day.** *And since his desire was to teach his whole army zealously to honor the Saviour's day (which derives its name from light, and from the sun), he freely granted to those among them who were partakers of the divine faith, leisure for attendance on the services of*

Chapter 5 - The Calendar

> *the Church of God,* ***in order that they might be able, without impediment, to perform their religious worship****. [88]*

Yet, people like Ellen White want to insist that the Roman Catholic church changed the Sabbath to Sunday. Ellen White argued that the Pope and the Catholic church changed the Sabbath from Saturday to Sunday as a sign of the mark of the Beast.

> *Roman Catholics acknowledge that* **the change of the Sabbath was** *made by their church, and declare that Protestants* **by observing the Sunday** *are recognizing her power. In the Catholic Catechism of Christian Religion, in answer to a question as to the day to be observed in obedience to the fourth commandment, this statement is made: "During the old law,* **Saturday was the day sanctified***; but the church, instructed by Jesus Christ, and directed by the Spirit of God,* **has substituted Sunday for Saturday; so now we sanctify the first, not the seventh day***. Sunday means, and now is, the day of the Lord."*

> *As the sign of the authority of the Catholic Church, papist writers cite* **"the very act of changing the Sabbath into Sunday***, which Protestants allow of; . . . because by keeping Sunday, they acknowledge the church's power to ordain feasts, and to command them under sin."—Henry Tuberville, An Abridgment of the Christian Doctrine, page 58.* **What then is the change of the Sabbath***, but the sign, or mark, of the authority of the Roman Church--"the mark of the beast"?* [89]

The choice to use the Julian calendar festival dates was not for the purpose of converting people to Satan to make them receive the mark of the beast. The Bible has no Saturday, Sunday, and so forth; therefore, Saturday is a pagan day and not from the Bible. Ellen White clearly taught that the Sabbath is Saturday. It begs the question, if the Roman calendar is pagan, why would Seventh Day Adventist's observe Saturday as the Sabbath? The Sabbath was never a part of the Roman calendar in the first place. If the Sabbath is to be observed according to the Bible, wouldn't it make sense to follow the Creator's calendar or the Jewish calendar and not the Roman calendar? While the Seventh Day Adventists complain Sunday is a pagan day, they accept Saturday which is equally a pagan day. The differences between the solar, lunar, and lunisolar calendars make the exact Sabbath day observance completely subjective. *The Oxford Advanced Learner's Dictionary* defines "subjective" as,

> *Based on your own ideas or opinions rather than facts and therefore sometimes unfair.* [90]

Those upholding the Creator's calendar argue that the Sabbath is on a different day than Saturday. Those upholding the Jewish calendar argue the Sabbath is Saturday, but the festivals are not on the Gregorian calendar. Those upholding the Gregorian calendar argue the Jewish calendar should not be followed because Christianity does not follow the feasts, festivals, and new moons any more. Whether someone believes that Wednesday, Saturday, or Sunday is the Sabbath becomes a trivial argument. The more Christians argue about dates the more trivial they become. Those who uphold the Creator's calendar say Easter is pagan and we should celebrate Passover which is on April 21st AD 2020 placing the Sabbath on Wednesday April 22nd. The Western Church says not to celebrate the Passover at all, but Easter which is on April 12th AD 2020 placing the Sabbath on Saturday the 18th. The Eastern Church says that Easter is on April 19th AD 2020 placing the Sabbath on the 25th. Those who follow the Jewish calendar celebrate Passover and not Easter which is April 9th or 15 Nissan making the Sabbath on April 11th or 17 Nissan. This is only in reference to four different groups who follow different calendars. Imagine including other groups who also date festivals on different calendars like the Islamic, Ethiopian, Chinese, Coptic, Armenian, and so forth. This is why the Apostle Paul said,

> Therefore **let no one act as your judge in regard** to food or drink or in respect **to a festival or a new moon or a Sabbath day**-- things which are a mere shadow of what is to come; but the substance belongs to Christ. (Col 2:16-17 NAS)

The absurdity in arguing about dates, holidays, festivals, and so forth becomes clearer. The feasts, festivals, new moons, and sacrifices on the Jewish calendar foreshadowed the messianic work of Christ. The purpose of any festival is to glorify Christ. Causing divisions over trivial dates for sabbaths and festivals is contrary to the gospel. The feasts, festivals, new moons, and sacrifices correspond to the events that Jesus Christ fulfilled in His ministry. These depict the salvation we receive in Christ as our Prophet, Priest, and King. This basic understanding of the fulfillment of the feasts means that we are not to judge each other in regards to a festival, new moon, or a sabbath day. This is explained further in the chapter on "The Ceremonial Law fulfilled in Christ."

4. Sabbaths or sevenths as calendar markers

There are many passages that show the Ceremonial Laws are scheduled around the seventh or sabbath calendar day. The words "sabbath" and "seventh" are calendar days in which some of the sacrifices, feasts, and assemblies were scheduled. In the Bible, the word "sabbath" is not always referring to the Fourth Commandment, the Ceremonial Law, or the seventh day of the week. The word "sabbaths" is similar to saying the word "sevens." The book of Leviticus states,

> There shall be seven complete sabbaths. 'You shall count fifty days to the day after the seventh sabbath; (Lev 23:15-16 NAS)

Sometimes sabbaths are referring to years. The book of Leviticus states,

> You are also to count off seven sabbaths of years for yourself, seven times seven years, so that you have the time of the seven sabbaths of years, namely, forty-nine years. (Lev 25:8 NAS)

The sabbaths and new moons are used as markers of what day it was in the year. Second Kings says,

> And he said, "Why will you go to him today? It is neither new moon nor sabbath."
> And she said, "It will be well." (2Ki 4:23 NAS)

In 2 Kings 4:23, the new moon is once a month and the Sabbath once a week. It is imperative to understand the difference between the seventh or sabbath day of the week and the Fourth Commandment "to keep the Sabbath holy." The word "sabbath" and "seventh" are often simply referencing the day of the week. Second Kings says,

> *One third of you, who come in on the sabbath and keep watch over the king's house. (2Ki 11:5 NAS)*
>
> *One third of you, of the priests and Levites who come in on the sabbath, shall be gatekeepers. (2Ch 23:4 NAS)*

The 2 Kings 11:5 verse is similar to saying, "the police guarded the White House on Saturday." It would be absurd to interpret 2 Kings 11:5 and 2 Chronicles 23:4 as a command to post guards at the King's house in order to observe the Fourth Commandment. Isaiah used the expressions "new moon to new moon" and "sabbath to sabbath" to express a length of time.

> *And it shall be from new moon to new moon and from sabbath to sabbath, All mankind will come to bow down before Me, (Isa 66:23 NAS)*

In Isaiah 66:23, the expressions "sabbath to sabbath" and "new moon to new moon" are similar to saying "week to week," "month to month," or "year-round." The words "sabbath" and "seventh" are used in conjunction with the Ceremonial Laws because the ceremonies are scheduled on those days. The fact is the Sabbath day was not the only day ceremonies were performed.

5. The inaccuracy of calendars

Those who like to impose specific dates and make futuristic prophecies entirely overlook the imperfection of the calendar. The pagan calendars in antiquity changed frequently. It is impossible to know exactly how many days, months, or years were lost when governments imposed their calendars upon society. An example of this is when the Roman Catholic church changed from the Julian calendar to the Gregorian calendar. In February AD 1582, Pope Gregory XIII reformed the Julian calendar establishing the Gregorian calendar. The calendar needed to be reformed because the seasons were becoming out of sync with the months. With the Julian calendar, spring was beginning 10 days later than March 20th when the spring equinox was supposed to occur. The removal of the 10 days caused the date to go from Thursday October 4th to Friday October 15th in AD 1582. France, Italy, Poland, Portugal, and Spain removed 10 days from their calendar to fix the error. England lost 12 days when they changed their calendar from the Julian to the Gregorian calendar on September 2nd AD 1752. The next day was Thursday the 14th.

a. Calculating Dates

Problems arise when people try to calculate the dates in the Bible. It is impossible to calculate any accurate date due to the fact that the calendars used by pagan societies did not match the Jewish calendar. The calendars used by pagan societies frequently changed and did not consistently synchronize to the earth's seasons. There is no evidence that ancient Israel synchronized their calendar to pagan calendars. The accuracy of the seasons on the Jewish calendar relies on accurately observing the sabbaths, feasts, festivals, and new moons. The Jewish calendar contains spontaneous changes based on seasonal and lunar behaviors. The fact is that any measurement taken has a degree of error that must be considered. It is impossible to create a calendar or establish dates that are perfectly accurate. This is true when measuring anything. In regards to the error of measurement, physicist John R. Taylor wrote,

> Although many experiments call for measurement of a quantity whose accepted value is known, few require measurement of a quantity whose true value is known. **In fact, the true value of a measured quantity can almost never be known exactly and is, in fact, hard to define.** Nevertheless, the difference between a measured value and the corresponding true value is theoretically a very useful concept. As I have already mentioned, this difference if often called the error in the measurement, although some authors call it the true error to emphasize its relation to the true value. [91]

When looking at calendar data from the Bible, nowhere is there any mention of an intercalary day, month, or year. It is quite possible that the ancient Jewish calendar only went by the 12-month lunar cycle which would be approximately 354 days in a year. This means that after 500 years, there could be a loss of approximately 15 years in comparison to a solar calendar with 365 days in a year. The fact is that all calendar systems in the ancient world and in our current world are inaccurate and will continue to be inaccurate. Calendars used in ancient civilizations can only be used as rough estimates because of the frequent calendar failures and replacements.

b. Missing years of the Jewish chronology

Another extremely important problem of dating events is the "missing years" in the Bible chronology from the destruction of the First Temple to the construction of the Second Temple. These missing years are key to understanding the interpretation of the "Seventy Weeks" prophecy of Daniel 9:24. The discrepancy happens when Academic and Rabbinic scholars construct the timeline. Academic Bible Chronologists use the canon of Ptolemy to fill in the Persian Empire time period. Rev. Martin Anstey wrote,

> The Chronology of this period has never yet been accurately determined. **The received Chronology, though universally accepted, is dependent on the list of the Kings, and the number of years assigned to them in Ptolemy's Canon.** Ptolemy (AD 70–161) was a great constructive genius. He was the author of the Ptolemaic System of Astronomy. He was one of the founders of the Science of Geography. But in Chronology he was only a late compiler and contriver, not an original witness, and not a contemporary historian, for he lived in the 2nd Century after Christ. He is the only authority for the Chronology of this period. He is not corroborated. **He is contradicted, both by the Persian National Traditions preserved in Firdusi, by the Jewish National Traditions preserved in the Sedar Olam, and by the writings of Josephus.** [92]

The Canon of Ptolemy lists ten kings in the Persian Empire. The total length of time for the Persian Empire according to the Canon of Ptolemy is approximately 207 years. The method Ptolemy used to determine the length of the Persian Empire is dubious to say the least. Rev. Martin Anstey wrote,

> Ptolemy had no means of accurately determining the Chronology of this period, so he made the best use of the materials he had, and contrived to make a Chronology.

Chapter 5 - The Calendar

He was a great astronomer, a great astrologer, a great geographer, and a great constructor of synthetic systems. But he did not possess sufficient data to enable him to fill the gaps, or to fix the dates of the Chronology of this period, so he had to resort to the calculation of eclipses. **In this way then, not by historical evidence or testimony, but by the method of astronomical calculation, and the conjectural identification of recorded with calculated eclipses, the Chronology of this period of the world's history has been fixed by Ptolemy,** *since when, through Eusebius and Jerome, it has won its way to universal acceptance. It is contradicted by the national traditions of Persia, by the national traditions of the Jews, by the testimony of Josephus, and by the conflicting evidence of such well-authenticated events as the Conference of Solon with Croesus, and the flight of Themistocles to the court of Artaxerxes Longimanus, which make the accepted Chronology impossible. But the human mind cannot rest in a state of perpetual doubt.* [93]

Constructing history without using historical evidence is unreliable. Table 5.3 shows Ptolemy's list of Persian kings.

Table 5.3 - Persian Kings as Given in Ptolemy's Canon			
Persian Kings	**Reigns Nabonnassarian Era**	**BC Connumerary**	**BC Julian**
Cyrus	Reigned 9 years from 210	538	538
Cambyses	Reigned 8 years from 219	529	529
Darius I Hystaspes	Reigned 36 years from 227	521	521
Xerxes	Reigned 21 years from 263	485	486
Artaxerxes I Longimanus	Reigned 41 years from 284	464	465
Darius II Nothus	Reigned 19 years from 325	423	424
Artaxerxes II Mnemon	Reigned 46 years from 344	404	405
Artaxerxes III Ochus	Reigned 21 years from 390	358	359
Arogus or Arses	Reigned 2 years from 411	377	338
Darius III Codomannus	Reigned 4 years from 413	335	336
Alexander the Great	Reigned — years from 417	331	332
[TOTAL] ~207 years Source [94]			

Table 5.4 shows the Persian kings according to Josephus. He lists only six Persian and Median Kings. Using the same lengths of the reign of each Persian and Median king as Ptolemy used, the time frame would be approximately 117 years. In the Rabbinic tradition, the *Seder Olam Rabbah* teaches that the Persian and Median kings reigned only 52 years. The *Seder Olam Rabbah* states,

Chapter 5 - The Calendar

(Neh. 1:1) "The words of Nehemiah ben Hakhaliah . . ." Twelve years he was in the land of Israel, repairing the wall and returning every man to his town and his inherited land. And so it says (Neh. 13:6): "When all this happened, I was not in Jerusalem because in the year 32 of Artaxerxes I came to the king and after one year I took leave from the king." From year 20 to year 32 are 12 years. Behold, it says (Ezra 6:14): "The elders of the Jews did build and were successful, following the prophecy of the prophet Haggai, and Zachariah ben Iddo; **they built and perfected by the order of the God of Israel and by the order of Cyrus, and Darius, and Artaxerxes, the king of Persia.** *You find only two Persian kings, Cyrus and Darius, and for Media Darius and Ahasuerus.* **But Cyrus is Darius is Artaxerxes,** *since the kingdom was called Artaxerxes.* **The kings of Media and Persia ruled for a total of 52 years.** [95]

Table 5.4 - Persian Kings as Given in Josephus	
Persian Kings	**Reigns**
Cyrus	Book 11 Ch 1
Cambyses	Book 11 Ch 2
Darius I Hystaspes	Book 11 Ch 3
Xerxes	Book 11 Ch 5
Cyrus (son of Xerxes)	Book 11 Ch 6
Darius the last King	Book 11 Ch 7 Sec 2
[TOTAL] ~117 years	Source: [96] [97]

According to the *Seder Olam Rabbah*, the Kings of Persia had multiple names. Cyrus was called Darius and also called Artaxerxes. Table 5.5 shows the *Seder Olam Rabbah listing* only 4 Persian kings.

Table 5.5 - Persian Kings as Given in Seder Olam Rabbah	
Persian Kings	**Reigns**
Darius the Median	1 year
Cyrus	3 years
Cambyses (whom they identify with the Ahasuerus who married Esther)	16 years
Darius (whom they will have to be the son of Esther)	32 years
[TOTAL] ~52 years Source: [98]	

Chapter 5 - The Calendar

When calculating the length of the Persian and Median Empire, the Bible Chronology becomes overwhelmingly disputed. When matching dates to Greek history, the timeline becomes more disputed. Martin Anstey wrote,

> *It may be objected that in the Battle of Marathon, which was fought B.C. 490, Darius Hystaspes was defeated by the Greeks, and that the Greek Chronology, which was reckoned by Olympiads from B.C. 776 onward, cannot be at fault to the extent of 82 years. But that is just the very point in dispute. The Greeks did not make a single calculation in Olympiads, nor had they any accurate chronological records till sixty years after the death of Alexander the Great. All that goes before that is guess work, and computation by generations, and other contrivances, not the testimony of contemporary records. [99]*

Table 5.6, "Comparison of Bible Timelines," roughly shows how three different timelines will lead Bible expositors to make false prophecies. The only conclusion when studying the dates of any calendar or chronology of the Bible is that it is impossible to set any date and keep anyone accountable to feasts, festivals, sabbaths, or holidays. This is why the Apostle Paul said,

> *Therefore let no one act as your judge in regard to food or drink or in respect to a festival or a new moon or a Sabbath day-- things which are a mere shadow of what is to come; but the substance belongs to Christ. Let no one keep defrauding you of your prize by delighting in self-abasement and the worship of the angels, taking his stand on visions he has seen, inflated without cause by his fleshly mind, and not holding fast to the head, from whom the entire body, being supplied and held together by the joints and ligaments, grows with a growth which is from God. (Col 2:16-19 NAS)*

Because the discrepancies between the calendars and the incorrect timelines, it is inappropriate to divide over what day to worship God. Causing divisions over celebrating holidays, feasts, and prophecy is contrary to the gospel of Christ. Worshiping on a specific day, following a specific calendar, or setting mandatory dates is not the purpose for the Sabbath, nor is it the mission of the Church.

Table 5.6 - Comparison of Bible Timelines

*Ptolemy	**Josephus	***Seder Olam Rabbah
Destruction of 1st Temple 586		
Cyrus 538 BC		
Decree of Cyrus 537 BC		
Cambyses 529 BC	Hezekiah King of Judah 642 BC	
Darius I 521 BC	Renovation of the Temple 542 BC	First Ten Tribes exiled 574 BC
Temple Completion 515 BC	Babylonian Captivity 526 BC	Hezekiah King of Judah 562 BC
Xerxes 486 BC	Destruction of 1st Temple 507 BC	Tribes of Samaria exiled 556 BC
Artaxerxes I 465 BC	**Darius and Cyrus 460 BC**	Renovation of the Temple 458 BC
Ezra 458 BC	Decree of Cyrus 457	Babylonian Captivity 439 BC
Darius II 424 BC	**Cambyses 442 BC**	Destruction of 1st Temple 421 BC
Artaxerxes II 405 BC	**Darius I 434 BC**	**Darius and Cyrus 370 BC**
Artaxerxes III 359 BC	**Xerxes 398 BC**	**Cambyses 366 BC**
Arses 338 BC	**Cyrus 377 BC**	**Darius 350 BC**
Darius III 336 BC	**Darius 336 BC**	Second Temple Built 349 BC
Alexander the Great 332	Alexander the Great 332	Alexander the Great 332
†Jesus 5 BC	†Jesus 5 BC	†Jesus 5 BC
†Jesus Baptism AD 26	†Jesus Baptism AD 26	†Jesus Baptism AD 26
†Jesus Crucifixion AD 30	†Jesus Crucifixion AD 30	†Jesus Crucifixion AD 30
†Destruction of 2nd Temple AD 70	†Destruction of 2nd Temple AD 70	†Destruction of 2nd Temple AD 70

* Dates from [100]; Persian Kings from [101].
** Dates from [102]; Persian Kings from [103].
*** Dates from [104] [105]; Persian Kings from [106].

All dates are approximations
† The dates of the birth, baptism, crucifixion and destruction of Jerusalem are disputed

Chapter 5 - The Calendar

Chapter 6 - The Sabbath

The Sabbath is the only commandment in the Ten Commandments that specifically addresses working in an occupation and the use of land. Working in an occupation has many facets to it. The individual, family, servants, immigrant laborers, animals, land management, debt forgiveness, and many other laws are derived from the Fourth Commandment to "keep the Sabbath holy." The Fourth Commandment also addresses the conservation of resources. When resources are consumed incorrectly, the land becomes exhausted. This causes drought and negative climate phenomenon. In Genesis 2:2, God rested on the seventh day. God instituted the Sabbath as a law that is indelibly dyed into the fabric of creation. The Fourth Commandment to "keep the Sabbath holy" became codified in ancient Israel law after they left the captivity in Egypt. The essence of the Sabbath Law is found in Exodus 16. After Israel left Egypt, they wandered in the wilderness of Sin.

> Then they set out from Elim, and all the congregation of the sons of Israel came to the wilderness of Sin, which is between Elim and Sinai, on the fifteenth day of the second month after their departure from the land of Egypt. (Exo 16:1 NAS)

Because the wilderness of Sin is a desolate place, the Israelites complained that they were going to die of starvation. Exodus says,

> *Would that we had died by the LORD's hand in the land of Egypt, when we sat by the pots of meat, when we ate bread to the full; for you have brought us out into this wilderness to kill this whole assembly with hunger. (Exo 16:3 NAS)*

God provided bread from heaven for the Israelites called "manna." Verse four says,

> *Then the LORD said to Moses, "Behold, I will rain bread from heaven for you." (Exo 16:4 NAS)*

Moses directed the Israelites to gather manna enough to feed everyone.

> *Gather of it every man as much as he should eat; you shall take an omer apiece according to the number of persons each of you has in his tent. (Exo 16:16 NAS)*

The Israelites disobeyed Moses' command to gather all of the manna. As a result, the food spoiled.

> *And Moses said to them, "Let no man leave any of it until morning." But they did not listen to Moses, and some left part of it until morning, and it bred worms and became foul; and Moses was angry with them (Exo 16:19-20 NAS)*

The manna could not be gathered on the seventh day because it became inedible. Moses interpreted what the Lord meant from what had happened. Moses explains what the Lord meant.

> *This is what the LORD meant: "Tomorrow is a sabbath observance, a holy sabbath to the LORD. Bake what you will bake and boil what you will boil, and all that is left over put aside to be kept until morning. So they put it aside until morning, as Moses*

> *had ordered, and it did not become foul, nor was there any worm in it." And Moses said, "Eat it today, for today is a sabbath to the LORD; today you will not find it in the field. Six days you shall gather it, but on the seventh day, the sabbath, there will be none." (Exo 16:23-26 NAS)*

The Israelites tried ignoring the Lord by gathering food on the seventh day; but there was no food to gather. Moses explained further.

> *See, the LORD has given you the sabbath; therefore He gives you bread for two days on the sixth day.* **Remain every man in his place; let no man go out of his place on the seventh day**. *(Exo 16:29 NAS)*

As a result, the ancient Israelites were forced to stay home. Exodus 16 specifically says NOT to leave your house on the Sabbath. The Sabbath command is clearly talking about resting from gathering food and staying home on the seventh day. The final result of the Sabbath command is in the statement,

> *So the people rested on the seventh day. (Exo 16:30 NAS)*

There are no references to any ceremonial institutions or worship services on the Sabbath in Exodus 16. It is important to point out that references to sacrifices in the Law of Moses did NOT all occur on the seventh day. The Sabbath law as stated in the Fourth Commandment is NOT referring to sacrifices, offerings, or assembling the people. The Sabbath equally has nothing to do with a Christian day of worship. Christian worship is discussed further in the chapter on "the Christian Day of Worship." The fact that Moses scheduled the sacrifices around the Sabbath proves that "sabbaths" are the counting of days, weeks, months, and years in the increments of seven. The Fourth Commandment was not made for sacrifices, worship, or any ceremonies. The sacrifices, feasts, and new moons were scheduled in reference to "sabbaths" on a specific calendar day. They are not specifically referring to the Fourth Commandment.

1. Definition of the Sabbath

The difference between stating "seventh" and "sabbath" depends on the usage of the word. Sometimes it's a calendar day, one of the ten commandments, or a scheduled ceremonial day. The Strong's Concordance definition of "sabbath" in Hebrew is,

> **<07676>** שַׁבָּת *(shabbath) (992a)*
> **Meaning**: *sabbath*
> **Origin**: *from 7673a*
> **Usage**: *every sabbath(2), sabbath(73), sabbaths(32).*
> **Notes**: *[a] Exo 20:8 [b] Exo 31:17; Eze 20:12, Eze 20:20 [107]*

The Hebrew word for "seventh" is,

> **<07637>** שְׁבִיעִית **or** שְׁבִיעִי *(shebii or shebiith) (988c)*
> **Meaning**: *seventh (an ord. number)*
> **Origin**: *from 7651*

Usage: fourth(m)(1), seventh(96), seventh year(1).
Notes: [a] *Exo 20:8-11; Exo 31:17* [b] *Heb 4:4, Heb 4:10 [108]*

The New Testament Greek, word for "sabbath" is,

<4521> σάββατον (sabbaton)
Meaning: the Sabbath, i.e. the seventh day (of the week)
Origin: of Heb. or. 7676
Usage: Sabbath(58), Sabbaths(1), week(9) [109]

The Greek word for "seventh" is,

<1442> ἕβδομος (hebdomos)
Meaning: seventh
Origin: ord. from 2033
Usage: seventh(9).
Notes: [a] *Rev 4:3 [110]*

In both the Old and New Testaments, the word "seventh" is supplemented for the word "sabbath." The Old Testament frequently uses the word "seventh" day instead of the word "sabbath" day.

*And by the seventh day God completed His work which He had done; and **He rested on the seventh day** from all His work which He had done. Then God blessed **the seventh day and sanctified it**, because in it He rested from all His work which God had created and made. (Gen 2:2-3 NAS)*

*On **the seventh day is a holy convocation**; you shall not do any laborious work.'" (Lev 23:8 NAS)*

The interchanging of the word "seventh" and "sabbath" can be seen in Exodus.

*See, **the LORD has given you the sabbath**; therefore He gives you bread for two days on the sixth day. Remain every man in his place; let no man go out of his place **on the seventh day**. (Exo 16:29 NAS)*

God is establishing the seventh day as the last day of the week on the calendar. Because the words "seventh" and "sabbath" are interchanged in quite a few instances, it is important to define the words according to their context. When the day starts is different between the solar and lunar calendars. The solar calendars start the day on sunrise and the lunar calendar starts on sun down. The Jewish calendar starts the Sabbath on sun down (Friday evening) and ends on the next sundown (Saturday evening). Genesis shows that each day starts at night.

And there was evening and there was morning, one day. (Gen 1:5 NAS)

The Sabbath day is not Saturday morning to Saturday night as the Gregorian calendar has it. This establishes the seventh day as the last day of the work week. It also creates a seven-day week on the calendar.

2. The Sabbath and three-part structure of the Law

When approaching the subject of the Sabbath and the Fourth Commandment, the three-part structure of the Law must be applied. The words "sabbath" and "seventh day" have different meanings in reference to the Moral, Judicial, and Ceremonial Law. The Sabbath can refer to the Fourth Commandment to rest, a calendar day, timeframe for healing, debt forgiveness, and a host of social issues. "Sabbaths," in the plural form, typically refers to the sacrifices, new moons, and festivals and other Ceremonial Laws on the Jewish calendar. God did not ordain the Ceremonial Laws because He needed animal sacrifice to "appease" Him. The sacrifices were observed to keep the promises of the coming of the Messiah, Jesus Christ and as a memorial of the Exodus from Egypt. Ancient Israel was unfaithful in the keeping the Law. Therefore, God hated the new moons, sabbaths, and the calling of assemblies. Isaiah wrote,

> **Bring your worthless offerings no longer,** *Incense is an abomination to Me. New moon and sabbath, the calling of assemblies-- I cannot endure iniquity and the solemn assembly.* **I hate your new moon festivals and your appointed feasts,** *They have become a burden to Me. I am weary of bearing them. (Isa 1:13-14 NAS)*

God sent Babylon to destroy Israel for their unfaithfulness. Jeremiah said the Lord became like an enemy to Israel. The LORD in His indignation destroyed the appointed feast and sabbath in Zion. Lamentations states,

> *The Lord has become like an enemy. He has swallowed up Israel; He has swallowed up all its palaces; He has destroyed its strongholds And multiplied in the daughter of Judah Mourning and moaning. And He has violently treated His tabernacle like a garden booth; He has destroyed His appointed meeting place;* **The LORD has caused to be forgotten The appointed feast and sabbath in Zion,** *And He has despised king and priest In the indignation of His anger. (Lam 2:5-6 NAS)*

God hated the sacrifices and feasts performed by the Israelites. He never said He hated the observance of the Fourth Commandment "to keep the Sabbath holy." God is not referring to the Fourth Commandment. The Lord blessed the Sabbath as a forever statute.

> *The LORD blessed the sabbath day and made it holy. (Exo 20:11 NAS)*

> *It is to be a sabbath of solemn rest for you, that you may humble your souls; it is a permanent statute (Lev 16:31 NAS)*

a. Statutes and Judgments

Even though this is explained fully in the chapter on "the Law," I mention it again to show specifically how the three-part structure pertains to the Sabbath. As was discussed previously in the chapter on "the Law," the Law is comprised of statutes and judgments (incorrectly translated as ordinances). The Sabbath is a statute specifically to regulate working on the seventh day. Judgments are made based on the statutes. The Ceremonial Law consists of statutes and judgments. The judgments in the Ceremonial

Law are not civil or criminal laws. The distinctions between the different types of the Law can be seen in Nehemiah. Nehemiah wrote,

> Thou camest down also upon mount Sinai, and spakest with them from heaven, and gavest them right **judgments**, and true **laws**, good **statutes** and **commandments**: And madest known unto them thy holy sabbath, and commandedst them **precepts**, **statutes**, and **laws**, by the hand of Moses thy servant. (Neh 9:13-14 KJV)

God's commandments are organized into parts. God's law comprises of commandments, statutes, and judgments which we describe as Moral, Ceremonial, and Judicial Laws. In Numbers, they are called rites (KJV) or statutes (NASB) and ordinances (NASB, correctly translated as judgments) or ceremonies (KJV).

> *Now, let the sons of Israel observe the Passover at its **appointed time**. On the fourteenth day of this month, at twilight, you shall observe it at its **appointed time**; you shall observe it according to all its **statutes** and according to all its **ordinances**. (Num 9:2-3 NAS)*

> *Let the children of Israel also keep the passover at his **appointed season**. In the fourteenth day of this month, at even, ye shall keep it in his **appointed season**: according to all the **rites** of it, and according to all the **ceremonies** thereof, shall ye keep it. (Num 9:2-3 KJV)*

When looking at the difference between *the King James* and *the New American Standard* translations, the differentiation between the Moral, Judicial, and Ceremonial Law becomes more apparent. The Ceremonial Law specifically involves priests performing sacrificial offerings and observing the appointed seasons. The Moral Laws are criminal statutes and the Judicial Laws are judgments made when a Moral Law is broken.

b. Ceremonial Laws conflict with the Fourth Commandment

Scheduling the sacrificial laws, assemblies, and festivals on the weekly Sabbath breaks the Sabbath. The Fourth Commandment "to keep the Sabbath holy" is specific to rest from work only. The priests were required to perform much work on the Sabbath. Leviticus shows the convocations were specifically for presenting offerings.

> *These are **the appointed times of the LORD which you shall proclaim as holy convocations, to present offerings** by fire to the LORD-- burnt offerings and grain offerings, **sacrifices** and **libations**, each day's matter on its own day. (Lev 23:37 NAS)*

The sacrifices and assembly collide in contradiction to the Fourth Commandment to "keep the Sabbath holy." Jesus said in Matthew,

> *Or have you not read in the Law, that on the Sabbath the priests in the temple break the Sabbath, and are innocent? ... For the Son of Man is Lord of the Sabbath. (Mat 12: 5,8 NAS see Mar 2:28; Luk 6:5)*

For this reason, it is important to NOT perform worship services on the Sabbath that require work. The priests were required to perform circumcision and other medical practices on the Sabbath. That is why the priest were innocent in doing so. The sacrifices performed by the priests in Israel were on the Sabbath calendar day for the purpose of foreshadowing the messianic work of Christ. The Feasts in Leviticus 23 are a timeline of the events of Christ's crucifixion, resurrection, and sitting at the right hand of God. This is explained further in the chapter on "Ceremonial Law fulfilled in Christ."

3. The Moral Law and the Sabbath

The Fourth Commandment to "keep the Sabbath holy" is specific to work. The Sabbath is the resting of the people, land, workers, aliens, animals, and everything from doing labor. The Law of Moses clearly displays the Sabbath as a day of rest.

> But **the seventh day is a sabbath** of the LORD your God; in it **you shall not do any work.** *(Exo 20:10 NAS see Num 28:25, Deu 5:14, Deu 16:8)*

The Sabbath is a sign between God and the sons of Israel to cease from labor and to refresh themselves. Exodus 31 says,

> *It is a sign between Me and the sons of Israel forever; for in six days the LORD made heaven and earth, but on the* **seventh day He ceased** *from labor, and was refreshed. (Exo 31:14-17 NAS)*

There is nothing refreshing or restful about getting up early, getting your children dressed, cooking breakfast, and rushing to Church on time. The obvious intent of the Sabbath is for the people to rest. The land is also specifically included in the command "to keep the Sabbath holy."

> *You shall work six days, but* **on the seventh day you shall rest;** *even* **during plowing time and harvest** *you shall rest. (Exo 34:21 NAS)*

All the products of the land and all the workers domestic and foreign were to cease production. Leviticus 25 says,

> *And all of you shall have the sabbath products of the land for food; yourself, and your male and female slaves, and your hired man and your foreign resident, those who live as aliens with you. (Lev 25:6 NAS)*

In Second Chronicles, the desolation of the land of Israel was said to have enjoyed its sabbath rest.

> *To fulfill the word of the LORD by the mouth of Jeremiah, until the land had enjoyed its sabbaths. All the days of its desolation it kept sabbath until seventy years were complete. (2Ch 36:21 NAS)*

Second Chronicles correlates resting the land to the Sabbath which means the land was not worked agriculturally. The land was fallow.

Chapter 6 - The Sabbath

a. Breaking the Sabbath and Israel

The Bible never says failing to worship God breaks the Sabbath. Nehemiah talked about Israel continuing commerce on the seventh day, broke the Sabbath. Nehemiah pointed out that bringing grain or wares into the city to sell, broke the Sabbath.

> *As for the peoples of the land who bring wares or any grain on the sabbath day to sell, we will not buy from them on the sabbath or a holy day. (Neh 10:31 NAS)*

Bringing wine, sacks of grain, and all kinds of loads on a donkey was normal commerce in ancient Israel. This profaned the Sabbath day.

> *I saw in Judah some who were **treading wine presses** on the sabbath, and **bringing in sacks of grain and loading them on donkeys**, as well as wine, grapes, figs, and all kinds of loads, and they brought them into Jerusalem on the sabbath day... What is this evil thing you are doing, by **profaning the sabbath day**? (Neh 13:15,17 NAS)*

Making new products and importing new products into the land profaned the Sabbath. Doing evil or turning to your own way to obtain unjust gain profanes the Sabbath.

> *How blessed is the man who does this, And the son of man who takes hold of it; **Who keeps from profaning the sabbath**, And keeps his hand from doing any evil... And **the dogs are greedy**, they are not satisfied. And they are shepherds who have no understanding; They have all turned to their own way, Each one **to his unjust gain**, to the last one. (Isa 56:2,11 NAS)*

The evils that profaned the Sabbath were greed and unjust gain. Jeremiah also shows that bringing anything through the gates of Jerusalem breaks the Sabbath.

> *Take heed for yourselves, and do not carry any load on the sabbath day or bring anything in through the gates of Jerusalem (Jer 17:21 NAS)*

Amos specifically condemns open and dishonest markets on the Sabbath. The selling of grain in the wheat market and the cheating at the scales specifically broke the Sabbath.

> *Hear this, you who trample the needy, to do away with the humble of the land, saying, "When will the new moon be over, So that we may sell grain, And the sabbath, that we may **open the wheat market, To make the bushel smaller and the shekel bigger, And to cheat with dishonest scales**, So as to buy the helpless for money And the needy for a pair of sandals, And **that we may sell the refuse of the wheat**?" (Amo 8:4-6 NAS)*

Ancient Israel frequently fell into the trap of making money and opening markets on the Sabbath. All of these verses show that the commandment to keep the Sabbath is specific to commerce and unjust gain in the entire community. Sabbath breaking is in reference to the constant buying and selling in the market with no stop. This includes monopolistic business practices. This is particularly important in regards to the conservation of resources and helping the needy. The Bible never teaches failing to worship God on Saturday breaks the Sabbath.

4. Judicial Law and the Sabbath

The Law of Moses contains Judicial Laws for enforcing the Sabbath. As discussed in the chapter on "the Law," these laws are judgments based on specific cases. A judgment was required when someone broke or abused a commandment in one way or another. An example is when a thief is caught stealing. The general remedy to the victim in the Judicial Law is double.

> *For every breach of trust, whether it is for ox, for donkey, for sheep, for clothing, or for any lost thing about which one says, 'This is it,'* **the case of both parties shall come before the judges; he whom the judges condemn shall pay double to his neighbor.** *(Exo 22:9 NAS)*

The ancient Israelites while in the wilderness did not have a jail system. A thief who could not make restitution for their crime was sold as a slave.

> *If a man steals an ox or a sheep, and slaughters it or sells it, he shall pay five oxen for the ox and four sheep for the sheep. If the thief is caught while breaking in, and is struck so that he dies, there will be no bloodguiltiness on his account. But if the sun has risen on him, there will be bloodguiltiness on his account.* **He shall surely make restitution; if he owns nothing, then he shall be sold for his theft**. *(Exo 22:1-3 NAS)*

A Hebrew thief sold into slavery for not being able to pay restitution could not be held indefinitely. After six years the Hebrew slave was set free by law.

> *If you buy a Hebrew slave, he shall serve for six years; but* **on the seventh he shall go out as a free man without payment**. *(Exo 21:2 NAS)*

Setting the slave free after six years is a Judicial Law enforcing the Sabbath. The Judicial Law also contained judgments punishing those who worked on the Sabbath in their occupation. In Exodus, while the Israelites were wandering in the wilderness, those who broke the Sabbath were put to death. Exodus 35 says,

> For six days work may be done, but on the seventh day you shall have a holy day, a sabbath of complete rest to the LORD; **whoever does any work on it shall be put to death.** (Exo 35:2 NAS)

Continuing constant business activities on the Sabbath creates monopolistic and price gouging behaviors. In dire situations, like the ancient Israelites wandering in the wilderness, this behavior can be severely detrimental to society as a whole. This is because, while the whole of society is keeping the law, the few who exploit the law become wealthy by gathering all the resources for themselves and then selling them to others at high costs. This type of monopolistic behavior breaks the Sabbath. While the Israelites were in the wilderness, a person who repeatedly gathered wood on the Sabbath was given the death penalty. The book of Numbers says,

> *Now while the sons of Israel were in the wilderness, they found a man gathering wood on the sabbath day. And those who found him gathering wood brought him to Moses and Aaron, and to all the congregation; and* **they put him in custody**

because it had not been declared what should be done to him. Then the LORD said to Moses, "The man shall surely be put to death; all the congregation shall stone him with stones outside the camp." (Num 15:32-35 NAS)

The death penalty was given because the person horded the limited resources for the purpose of making dishonest gain. The Judicial Law can be understood in the statement, "it had not been declared what should be done." In the case of Numbers 15:32, there were no judgments yet made on the severity of the transgression. The Judicial Law sets the precedence for the penalty of those who break the Law in the future. Another example of the Judicial Law in the Fourth Commandment to "keep the Sabbath holy" is debt forgiveness. The Law of Moses provided judgments for debt forgiveness. The book of Deuteronomy says,

> At the end of every seven years you shall grant a remission of debts. And this is the manner of remission: every creditor shall release what he has loaned to his neighbor; he shall not exact it of his neighbor and his brother, because the LORD's remission has been proclaimed. (Deu 15:1-2 NAS)

The remission of debts is a Judicial Law enforcing the Sabbath. The judgments based on specific cases are classified as Judicial Laws by definition. Every instance where a person breaks the Sabbath Law always references labor and resources. This begs the question, should these Laws be in effect today? This is discussed in the chapter "Modern Day Consequences."

5. The Ceremonial Law and the Sabbath

The Ceremonial Law in regards to sacrifices, feasts, new moons, and sabbaths were never a part of the Sabbath Law from the beginning. The enforcement of the Sabbath Law degenerated in ancient Israel. The leaders of Israel during Christ's time did not properly enforce the Sabbath at all. An example of this is in the gospel of Mark. The Pharisees accused Jesus and the disciples of breaking the Sabbath. Mark wrote,

> *And it came about that He was passing through the grainfields on the Sabbath, and **His disciples began to make their way along while picking the heads of grain**. And the Pharisees were saying to Him, "See here, why are they doing what is not lawful on the Sabbath?" (Mar 2:23-24 NAS)*

Once Israel was able to plant crops, it was lawful for the homeless and needy to pick a single meal from the field on the Sabbath. The Sabbath is about labor and land in regards to commerce and not a homeless person eating a single meal. God commanded Israel to help the needy and poor in the land. Deuteronomy states,

> *For the poor will never cease to be in the land; therefore I command you, saying, 'You shall freely open your hand to your brother, to your needy and poor in your land.' (Deu 15:11 NAS)*

As a matter of fact, the farmers were required to leave the corners of the land for the poor people and the beasts to pick from. Exodus says,

Chapter 6 - The Sabbath

> *But on the seventh year you shall let it rest and lie fallow, so that the needy of your people may eat; and whatever they leave the beast of the field may eat. You are to do the same with your vineyard and your olive grove. (Exo 23:11 NAS see Lev 19:10, Lev 23:22)*

It is lawful for the needy or homeless to grab a single meal on the Sabbath from a farmer's land. Homeless people cannot store food in their homes. The homeless can only receive food as they need it. The Israelites during the time of Christ treated the poor and homeless people worse than beasts. The Fourth Commandment is about the land and the labor in regards to producing a profit and resources. It is not about a starving person grabbing a single meal. Jesus refuted the false teaching on the Sabbath with one sentence. Jesus said,

> *And He was saying to them, "The Sabbath was made for man, and not man for the Sabbath." (Mar 2:27 NAS)*

It is an irrefutable fact that the Sabbath is about labor and land in commerce and not the Ceremonial Law. The Sabbath clearly has NOTHING to do with Jewish or Christian worship ceremonies. The priests ceremonial duties actually conflicted with the Fourth Commandment to "keep the Sabbath holy." The Priest worked on the Sabbath (Mat 12:5). Being a priest was a lot of work. The priests had to mix oil with flour and offer two male lambs on every sabbath on behalf of the people. Numbers says,

> *Then on the sabbath day two male lambs one year old without defect, and two-tenths of an ephah of fine flour mixed with oil as a grain offering, and its libation: This is the burnt offering of every sabbath in addition to the continual burnt offering and its libation. (Num 28:9-10 NAS)*

It is crystal clear the Sabbath day and the Ceremonial Law are two separate conflicting laws. This does NOT mean the Bible is in error or that the God made a mistake. Nor does this mean God commands people to break His Law. This was for the purpose of keeping the promise that God was going to send the Messiah, His only begotten Son Jesus Christ, as the propitiation for the sins of the world (Rom 3:23; Heb 2:17; 1Jo 2:2; 4:10). The ceremonies coincided on the Sabbath calendar day in order to display the messianic work of Christ. Only faith in Christ's death, resurrection, ascension, and sitting at the right hand of God can we be forgiven for breaking God's Law (Rom 3:27-31; 4:13-16; Gal 2:16; 3:12-14; Phi 3:9-12).

> *Because by the works of the Law no flesh will be justified in His sight; **for through the Law comes the knowledge of sin**. (Rom 3:20 NAS)*

> *And according to the Law, one may almost say, all things are cleansed with blood, and **without shedding of blood there is no forgiveness**. (Heb 9:22 NAS)*

> *Who is the one who condemns? **Christ Jesus is He who died, yes, rather who was raised, who is at the right hand of God, who also intercedes for us**. (Rom 8:34 NAS)*

The Fourth Commandment to "keep the Sabbath holy" is not a Ceremonial Law. The Sabbath is not "the Christian Sabbath" on Sunday, worship on Saturday, nor was the Sabbath "abolished." The Sabbath is for resting laborers and the land.

a. The Sabbath and healthcare

The connection between the Sabbath and the healthcare responsibilities of the priest are for the most part ignored in Christian theology. The Law of Moses mandates healthcare provisions for the people. In the Bible, healthcare provisions are Ceremonial Laws. The Ceremonial Law contains both statutes and judgments. The judgments in the Ceremonial Law are NOT Judicial Laws. Judicial Laws are for criminal and civil cases. The Ceremonial Law required priests to make judgments in regards to the health of the people. One important duty the priest had was to make judgments for those who are sick. For example, the Law of Moses established quarantine procedures. Leviticus says,

> *As for the leper who has the infection, his clothes shall be torn, and the hair of his head shall be uncovered, and he shall cover his mustache and cry, 'Unclean! Unclean!' "He shall remain unclean all the days during which he has the infection; he is unclean. He shall live alone; his dwelling shall be outside the camp. (Lev 13:45-46 NAS)*

The judgments the priests had to make were extensive. They had to monitor childbirth, menstruation, circumcision, leprosy, and many other health issues of that time. The priests were the healthcare practitioners in ancient Israel. Notice that "sevenths" or "sabbaths" are the increments used to measure the duration of the healing process. For example, in the book of Leviticus, women were to rest seven days after child birth.

> *Speak to the sons of Israel, saying, 'When a woman gives birth and bears a male child, then **she shall be unclean for seven days**, as in the days of her menstruation she shall be unclean. 'And on the eighth day the flesh of his foreskin shall be circumcised. (Lev 12:2-3 NAS)*

God's Law contained provisions for treating those who had communicable diseases. The book of Leviticus states,

> *Then the LORD spoke to Moses and to Aaron, saying, "When a **man has on the skin of his body** a swelling or a scab or a bright spot, and it becomes an **infection** of leprosy on the skin of his body, then **he shall be brought to Aaron the priest, or to one of his sons the priest**. (Lev 13:1-2 NAS)*

These Laws are for the overall health of the population of the people. There are many healthcare provisions in the Law of Moses. An example is shaving and bathing a patient.

> *And it will be **on the seventh day that he shall shave off all his hair**: he shall shave his head and his beard and his eyebrows, even all his hair. He shall then wash his clothes and bathe his body in water and be clean. (Lev 14:9 NAS see Num 6:9)*

After someone is healed from the disease, on the seventh day, they are allowed back into the camp.

> *And you shall **wash your clothes on the seventh day and be clean**, and afterward you may enter the camp. (Num 31:24 NAS)*

It is an undeniable fact that the priests were required to perform the duties of a physician in the Law of Moses. Sacrifices, according to the Ceremonial Law, were also required by those who recovered from their health issue. The book of Leviticus says,

> *And when the days of her purification are completed, for a son or for a daughter, she shall bring to the priest at the doorway of the tent of meeting, a one year old lamb for a burnt offering, and a young pigeon or a turtledove for a sin offering. (Lev 12:6 NAS)*

Sevens or sabbaths were used in the healing cycle. The priests had to use their own judgment whether a person was healed based on the Ceremonial statutes. The healthcare duties performed by the priests were required on every day including the Sabbath. The priests performed the healthcare practice of circumcision on the Sabbath. In the gospel of John, Jesus said,

> *On this account Moses has given you circumcision (not because it is from Moses, but from the fathers), and **on the Sabbath you circumcise a man**. If a man receives circumcision on the Sabbath that the Law of Moses may not be broken, **are you angry with Me because I made an entire man well on the Sabbath**? (Joh 7:22-23 NAS)*

Healing people on the Sabbath was not contrary to the Law of Moses. In fact, the priests were required to heal people on the Sabbath. The healthcare requirement of the Law of Moses is not a popular topic, especially with the first century Pharisees. Jesus clashed with the leaders of Israel during His ministry on this topic many times. Jesus was actually performing proper priestly duties on the Sabbath. The leaders of ancient Israel did not keep the Law of Moses. They were only following their traditions. Jesus said,

> *And He answered and said to them, "And **why do you yourselves transgress the commandment of God for the sake of your tradition**?... And thus you invalidated the word of God for the sake of your tradition." (Mat 15: 3,6 NAS)*

During Christ's time, the leaders of Israel exalted their tradition over God's Law. It is sad the Pharisees refused their obligations to God's Law. The Pharisees constantly accused Christ of breaking the Sabbath, especially for healing. In fact, Jesus scolded the synagogue officials and the teachers in Israel for not carrying out the Law. John wrote,

> *Did not Moses give you the Law, and yet **none of you carries out the Law**? Why do you seek to kill Me? (Joh 7:19 NAS)*

Nobody, except Christ, kept the Law of Moses properly; not the Pharisees, Sadducees, Scribes, or Synagogue officials. Our Savior, Jesus Christ, kept and fulfilled the requirements of the Law perfectly. Christ kept ALL the Ceremonial, Moral, and Judicial Law in its entirety. Paul wrote,

> *There is therefore now no condemnation for those who are in Christ Jesus. For the law of the Spirit of life in Christ Jesus has set you free from the law of sin and of death. For what the Law could not do, weak as it was through the flesh, God did: sending His own Son in the likeness of sinful flesh and as an offering for sin, **He condemned sin in the flesh, in order that the requirement of the Law might be fulfilled in us**, who do not walk according to the flesh, but according to the Spirit. (Rom 8:1-4 NAS)*

The leaders of ancient Israel during the time of Christ only cared about their personal situation and their tradition.

b. Doing good on the Sabbath

The Fourth Commandment "to keep the Sabbath holy" does not imply neglecting life. The leaders of Israel during Christ's time had a radical interpretation of the Sabbath. They had the view that performing activities broke the Sabbath. Jesus Christ, the Author of the Law, said,

> *So then, **it is lawful to do good on the Sabbath**. (Mat 12:12 NAS see Luk 6:9, Mar 3:4)*

He did NOT say the Sabbath was abolished, changed, or established for specific time for worship. The Sabbath is for doing good for our neighbors and ourselves. Jesus said,

> ***The Sabbath was made for man**, and not man for the Sabbath. (Mar 2:27 NAS)*

Everybody is required to tend to their family and household obligations. The Apostle Paul said,

> ***But if anyone does not provide for his own**, and especially for those of his household, **he has denied the faith**, and is worse than an unbeliever. (1Ti 5:8 NAS)*

Neglecting your household is breaking the Sabbath. If your household is sick or in need, you are required to give them aid. Healing the sick is a requirement regardless if it is the Sabbath. The priests in ancient Israel were required to help the sick on the Sabbath. Christ upheld the requirement of a priest by healing on the Sabbath. He healed a man with a withered hand. Matthew wrote,

> *And departing from there, He went into their synagogue. And behold, there was a man with a withered hand. And they questioned Him, saying, "**Is it lawful to heal on the Sabbath?**"-- in order that they might accuse Him. And He said to them, "What man shall there be among you, who shall have one sheep, and if it falls into a pit on the Sabbath, will he not take hold of it, and lift it out? "Of how much more value then is a man than a sheep! So then, **it is lawful to do good on the Sabbath**." Then He said to the man, "Stretch out your hand!" And he stretched it out, and it was restored to normal, like the other. But the Pharisees went out, and counseled together against Him, as to how they might destroy Him. But Jesus, aware of this, withdrew from there. And many followed Him, and He healed them all. (Mat 12:9-15 NAS)*

He did not only heal the man with a withered hand. He healed a multitude of people. He healed a paralytic.

Chapter 6 - The Sabbath

> *He who made me well was the one who said to me, 'Take up your pallet and walk.'*
> *(Joh 5:11 NAS)*

He healed a blind man.

> *Now it was a Sabbath on the day when Jesus made the clay, and opened his eyes.*
> *(Joh 9:14 NAS)*

Giving aid to those in need is a requirement in the Law of Moses. When a synagogue official questioned Jesus after He healed a woman on the Sabbath, the synagogue official was humiliated because of Christ's response.

> *And the synagogue official, indignant because Jesus had healed on the Sabbath, began saying to the multitude in response, "There are six days in which work should be done; therefore come during them and get healed, and not on the Sabbath day." But the Lord answered him and said, "You hypocrites, does not each of you on the Sabbath untie his ox or his donkey from the stall, and lead him away to water him? "And this woman, a daughter of Abraham as she is, whom Satan has bound for eighteen long years, should she not have been released from this bond on the Sabbath day?" And* **as He said this, all His opponents were being humiliated; and the entire multitude was rejoicing over all the glorious things being done by Him**.
> *(Luk 13:14-17 NAS)*

Jesus scolded the synagogue officials for their years of dereliction of duty. The woman could have been healed eighteen years prior. Jesus makes the point that the synagogue officials had the ability to heal her. They thoroughly neglected their duty to God's Law. Saving a life cannot possibly be breaking the Sabbath. Jesus said,

> *Is it lawful on the Sabbath to do good or to do harm, to save a life or to kill?*
> *(Mar 3:4 NAS)*

Christ used the scenario of a son falling into a pit as an example. Jesus said,

> *Which one of you shall have a son or an ox fall into a well, and will not immediately pull him out on a Sabbath day? (Luk 14:5 NAS)*

It does not take much digging into the Word of God to see that the leadership of Israel during the time of Christ failed to keep the Law of Moses. The Sabbath is NOT merely a day to restrict activities or go to a worship service. The Fourth Commandment to "keep the Sabbath holy" is a Moral statutory law involving labor, land, commerce, debt relief, and helping the needy.

Civil and criminal judgments made for breaking the Sabbath Moral Law are Judicial Laws. The Judicial Laws are clear case applications of the statutes called the Moral Law. The Ceremonial Laws are statutes and judgments establishing feasts, sabbaths, new moons, sacrifices, and offerings to God. The Ceremonial Laws are also judgments made by the priests that encompassed healthcare duties for the people. Jesus Christ satisfied all the requirements for the Moral, Ceremonial, and Judicial Laws by living a sinless life and offering Himself as the sacrifice for the sins of His people once and for all. We receive the forgiveness of sins against God's Law. This does not remove the obligation to keep the Law. In fact, everyone is required to keep ALL of God's Law to this day. The Ceremonial Laws establishing the feasts, new moons, sabbaths, and sacrifices are fulfilled in Christ. Christ is our Priest who sacrificed Himself in our place and mediates between His people and God. Christ is our Prophet who teaches us His Law. Christ is our King who executes His Law at the right hand of God in heaven. He fulfilled all the requirements of the Law for us in His one act of being born of a virgin, living a sinless life, suffering, dying, raising from the dead, ascending to heaven, sitting at the right hand of God, and judging the living and the dead. He keeps the Law of God for us then, now, and forever more. The Law is not abolished. It is fulfilled.

Chapter 6 - The Sabbath

Chapter 7 - Modern Day Consequences

There are real consequences of breaking the Sabbath that can be seen today. This is seen in healthcare, sweatshops, bad debt, modern travel, deforestation, food waste, pollution, and countless other examples. These are mostly caused by greed. Breaking one commandment breaks the other commandments as well. An extreme example is the Wall of China where many laborers were literally worked to death. Their bodies were thrown into the wall as a tomb. The Chinese government would find a new laborer to work till death. This is when Sabbath breaking turns into murder. James wrote,

> *For whoever keeps the whole law and yet stumbles in one point, he has become guilty of all. (Jam 2:10 NAS)*

Understanding the relationship between each law is critical. Breaking the Fourth Commandment "to keep the Sabbath holy" leads to murder, slavery, starvation, waste, the destruction of the Earth's habitat, and more.

1. Workaholism

The most prevalent example of breaking the Sabbath in our modern time is workaholism.

> *The term workaholism originates from Oates, who described it as "the compulsion of the uncontrollable need to work excessively." [111]*

Fatigue, divorce, drug addiction, heart disease, alcoholism, and suicide are among a few outcomes of workaholism. The Fourth Commandment "to keep the Sabbath holy" is to be observed by each person within the family.

> *In it **you** shall not do any work, **you** or your **son** or your **daughter**. (Exo 20:10 NAS)*

Individual health and families are negatively affected by workaholic behaviors. Studies show that workaholic people experience worse physical and mental health.

> *Previous studies have shown that workaholism is associated with poor health. By definition, workaholic people spend an excessive amount of time on their work. This suggests that they have insufficient opportunity to recover from their excessive efforts…leaving them emotionally or cognitively exhausted over time…In addition, they persistently and frequently think about work when they are not at work…, which may result in sympathetic arousal and emotional distress. Consequently, workaholism is associated with poor health, such as psychosomatic complaints and disabling backpain…and diminished sleep quality such as longer sleep latency, impaired awakening, workplace sleepiness, and higher levels of daytime dysfunction…Workaholism is also associated with impaired psychological health such as psychological distress, depression, and burnout and sickness absence. [112]*

Workaholism does not only degrade the performance of the individual, workaholism also destroys families. The workaholic ultimately fails to meet the needs of their spouse and children.

For instance, Robinson (1989) defines workaholism as a progressive, potentially fatal disorder of work addiction, leading to family disintegration and an increased inability to manage work habits and life domains. [113]

The reason the workaholic lifestyle is such a failure for the family is because it breaks the Fourth Commandment "to keep the Sabbath holy." God clearly does not want workaholic behavior.

2. Servants and Animals

Another important part of the Fourth Commandment is the treatment of servants and animals. The following part of the verse clearly shows the duty is to our neighbor and not a worship service for God.

*Your male or your female **servant** or your **cattle**. (Exo 20:10 NAS)*

The word "servant" has several meanings. There are many duties that encompass the word "servant." *Strong's NASB Concordance* defines "servant" as,

<05650> עֶבֶד *(ebed) (713d)*
Meaning: *slave, servant*
Origin: *from 5647*
Usage: *attendants(1), bondage(m)(2), male servant(8), male servants(17), male slave(4), male slaves(8), officers(m)(1), official(m)(2), servant(331), servant*(1), Servant(6), servant's(4), servants(341), servants*(12), servants'(2), slave(21), slave*(4), slave's(1), slavery(m)(11), slaves(12), slaves*(8)* [114]

The word "servant" applies to anyone doing work in an occupation. The specific word for a female servant is "maidservant." *Strong's NASB Concordance* defines "maidservant" as,

<0519> אָמָה *(amah) (51a)*
Meaning: *a maid, handmaid*
Origin: *of unc. Der.*
Usage: *female servant(4), female servant*(1), female servants*(6), female slave (2), female slave*(4), female slaves*(4), handmaid(2), handmaids(1), maid(8), maids(5), maidservant(19).*
Notes: *¹ Lit., is in your gates ᵃ Neh 13:16-19* [115]

Many businesses in the United States are open 24 hours and/or 7 days a week. The United States has the 5-day work week. Most citizens in the United States work a 5-day week. Overtime laws discourage employers from overworking employees because they have to pay extra for working employees' overtime. Workaholics usually are salaried employees who do not get paid hourly. They can work 7 days a week with no legal recourse. Staggering employees across multiple days during the week enables businesses to be open 24 hours a day 7 days a week. God did not intend for the Sabbath to be observed like that. Employees may achieve rest; however, the purpose of the Sabbath is to rest everything to prevent resource exhaustion. After the ancient Israelites went from captivity in Babylon, they were so grateful to the Lord that they enforced the Sabbath to its proper stature. Nehemiah wrote,

> *I saw in Judah some who were treading wine presses on the sabbath, and bringing in sacks of grain and loading them on donkeys, as well as wine, grapes, figs, and all kinds of loads, and they brought them into Jerusalem on the sabbath day... What is this evil thing you are doing, by profaning the sabbath day? (Neh 13:15,17 NAS)*

Notice donkeys are included in profaning the Sabbath. The idea of ceasing all occupational activities of servants also applies to the animals as well. All animals are to cease their occupational duties. *The Strong's NASB Concordance* definition of the word "animal" is,

> **<0929>** בְּהֵמָה *(behemah) (96d)*
> **Meaning:** *a beast, animal, cattle*
> **Origin:** *from an unused word*
> **Usage:** *animal(32), animals(27), beast(45), beasts(31), cattle(49), cattle*(1), herd(1), kinds of cattle(1), mount(m)(1).*
> **Notes:** *[1] Lit., is in your gates ᵃ Neh 13:16-19 [116]*

The donkey was the "automobile" of that day. The donkey would be equivalent to modern day trucks delivering merchandise, cars driving to markets, air travel, farming tractors, and so forth. Breaking the Sabbath on a large global scale has significant negative effects especially on climate change. By climate change, I am not referring to the "Greenhouse Gas Effect." By climate change I am referring to the destruction, pollution, and contamination of the land causing it to become unusable. The Sabbath especially applies to livestock and land. The ancient Israelites were shepherds. Livestock and land management were at the core of the Israelite agricultural system. What applied to the Israelites then, still applies to us today.

a. Livestock and pollution

Factory farming is a type of farming that cages and keeps animals in unhealthy and unsanitary conditions. The problem with factory farming is that the animals are treated deplorably. These animals never get a rest let alone a weekly Sabbath. The factory farmed animals live in hazardous environments. Their only life is to be in captivity and harvested in the most abusive environmental conditions.

> *Intensive livestock production systems are characterized by a high stocking density, a high output of animal products per unit surface area, and a relatively large share of milk, beef, pork, and egg and poultry production worldwide. Cattle, pigs, and poultry are the dominant species. These systems rely extensively on imported animal feed and are known as landless systems. [117]*

A landless system contains the animals in a building their entire life. It is the opposite of a cage free chicken or a grass-fed cow. These factory farm producers cause major environmental health problems and are expanding all over the globe.

> Intensive livestock production systems are rapidly expanding, especially in East and Southeast Asia and Latin America. This expansion is characterized by the following; an agglomeration of livestock production near urban (market) centers; a shift from ruminants to pigs and poultry; a trend towards large, landless, highly specialized farms; a shift from litter-based housing to slurry-based systems, with insufficient manure storage, poor manure management, and little account of the crop-nutritive value of livestock manure. *[118]*

Air, water, and coastal ecosystems are significantly polluted by factory farming of animals.

> *Poor manure management has serious impacts on the environment. It contributes to pollution and eutrophication of surface waters, groundwater, and coastal marine ecosystems. It contributes to air pollution through emission of odor, ammonia, methane, and nitrous oxide, and it contributes to soil pollution through the accumulation of heavy metals. These pollution and eutrophication effects subsequently lead to loss of human health and biodiversity, to climate change and acidification, and to ecosystem degradation. [119]*

This destruction of the environment and poor food quality is caused by breaking the Sabbath in animal production. Animals should be able to rest in the way "Grass-Fed" and "Cage-Free" meat producers rest their animals. Animals are to be rested just like the land needs to be rested. The depletion of farmland and climate change are directly related to breaking the Sabbath.

3. Cultivating Land

Giving the land a Sabbath rest is equally as important. The Law of Moses has specific Laws regarding land management.

> *Speak to the sons of Israel, and say to them, 'When you come into the land which I shall give you, then the land shall have a sabbath to the LORD.* ***Six years you shall sow your field, and six years you shall prune your vineyard and gather in its crop, but during the seventh year the land shall have a sabbath rest, a sabbath to the LORD;*** *you shall not sow your field nor prune your vineyard. 'Your harvest's aftergrowth you shall not reap, and your grapes of untrimmed vines you shall not gather; the land shall have a sabbatical year. 'And all of you shall have the sabbath products of the land for food; yourself, and your male and female slaves, and your hired man and your foreign resident, those who live as aliens with you. 'Even your cattle and the animals that are in your land shall have all its crops to eat.' (Lev 25:2-7 NAS)*

A perfect example of breaking the Sabbath in regards to land management is the "Dust Bowl of the 1930's." Because of the scientific advancements in machine farming, the farmers in the early 1900's over cultivated and incorrectly cultivated large parts of the Great Plains in the United States. Over cultivation in conjunction with drought caused major climate change in the Midwest that lasted years.

The sources we reviewed suggest dust storms and eolian transport of soil are a natural geomorphological phenomenon on the Great Plains..., with shallow sandy deposits being highly sensitive to variations in climate.... Soil and dust are transported by low magnitude, frequent wind events as well as less common but high magnitude storms.... Based on written records of severe dust storms on the southern Great Plains dating back to the 1830s, before agricultural settlement took place, environmental historian James Malin... has argued that the high frequency of dust storms in the 1930s was partly a reflection of better reporting, although he did acknowledge the human contribution to the creation of dust storms through..." the initial exploitive stage of power farming, the period of the late 1920s [which] was analogous in a sense to pioneering" (1946c, p. 412). Social and natural scientists generally agree that farming practices contributed to soil erosion and dust storm occurrence, but there is a lively and ongoing debate as to the relative importance of that contribution... Several scholars have suggested that supporters of New Deal agricultural policies in the US played up the role of farming practices as a cause of erosion to advance political ends... while others such as Worster (1979) place much more blame on the farming system. [120]

The "Dust Bowl of the 1930's" in the United States was a direct result of breaking the Sabbath. Many people were displaced from their homes, farmers lost their land, workers lost their jobs, the stock market crashed, starvation, and large areas of the Great Plains were unfarmable and uninhabitable for years. The consequences of breaking the Sabbath are irrefutable. God has fixed in science, nature, and all creation the mandate of keeping the Sabbath. The Sabbath will always be relevant to society.

a. Deforestation

The deforestation of the Amazon Forest is another form of Sabbath breaking. Land management is a central part of the Sabbath. The combination of profits and the need to feed a growing global population has brought about a global crisis in regards to the overall sustainability of our global environment. The over production of land is causing a climate change problem.

The in-depth assessment presented in this document of the various significant impacts of the world's livestock sector on the environment is deliberately termed Livestock's long shadow so as to help raise the attention of both the technical and the general public to the very substantial contribution of animal agriculture to climate change and air pollution, to land, soil and water degradation and to the reduction of biodiversity. [121]

With the overproduction of the land and the disregard for "the Sabbath," the usability of the land is destroyed for long periods of time.

Expansion of livestock production is a key factor in deforestation, especially in Latin America where the greatest amount of deforestation is occurring – 70 percent of previous forested land in the Amazon is occupied by pastures, and feedcrops cover a large part of the remainder. About 20 percent of the world's pastures and rangelands, with 73 percent of rangelands in dry areas, have been degraded to some extent, mostly through overgrazing, compaction and erosion created by livestock action. The dry lands in particular are affected by these trends, as livestock are often the only source of livelihoods for the people living in these areas. [122]

The outcome of deforestation and overproducing the land is realized immediately.

Major forms of pollution, associated with manure management in intensive livestock production, were described in Chapter 4. They include (FAO, 2005e):

- *Eutrophication of surface water, killing fish and other aquatic life;*
- *Leaching of nitrates and pathogens into groundwater, threatening drinking-water supplies;*
- *Buildup of excess nutrients and heavy metals in the soil, damaging soil fertility;*
- *Contamination of soil and water resources with pathogens; and*
- *Release of ammonia, methane and other gases into the air. [123]*

Overproducing the land and the deforestation of enormous parts of South America will contribute to climate change problems. Similar to the "Dust Bowl of the 1930's," the overproduction and deforestation of the land will have devastating effects on the ability to recover farm land.

Livestock-induced degradation of the world's arid and semi-arid lands will continue, in particular in Africa and South and Central Asia, again contributing significantly to climate change, water depletion and biodiversity losses, and sometimes leading to irreversible loss of productivity. The poor who derive a living from livestock will continue to extract the little they can from dwindling common property resources while facing growing marginalization. [124]

Everyone on Earth will be affected by the destruction of the South American ecology caused by breaking the Sabbath Law.

b. Enslavement of farmers

Another problem with Sabbath breaking in regards to South America is the extortion, murder, and enslavement of the farmers. This is where murder, stealing, and breaking the Sabbath intersect. The Bible condemns those who afflict the needy.

There is a kind of man whose teeth are like swords, And his jaw teeth like knives, To devour the afflicted from the earth, And the needy from among men. (Pro 30:14 NAS)

Woe to those who enact evil statutes, And to those who constantly record unjust decisions, So as to deprive the needy of justice, And rob the poor of My people of their rights, In order that widows may be their spoil, And that they may plunder the orphans. Now what will you do in the day of punishment, And in the devastation which will come from afar? To whom will you flee for help? And where will you leave your wealth? Nothing remains but to crouch among the captives Or fall among the slain. In spite of all this His anger does not turn away, And His hand is still stretched out. (Isa 10:1-4 NAS)

Then I will draw near to you for judgment; and I will be a swift witness against the sorcerers and against the adulterers and against those who swear falsely, and against those who oppress the wage earner in his wages, the widow and the orphan, and those who turn aside the alien, and do not fear Me, says the LORD of hosts. (Mal 3:5 NAS)

The Sabbath is broken by the forced servitude, extortion, murder, and theft exacted upon the farmers in Mexico and South America. The "Los Caballeros Templarios" or "the Knights Templar" Cartel is a Mexican criminal organization that kidnaps, extorts, murders and in many cases steals the Mexican farmer's land. The Mexican farmers are forced into slavery for the purpose of draining as much money out of their farms.

For the Knights Templar, extortion is also a major income earner. One of their biggest victims have been avocado farms. The Mexican avocado export business has grown rapidly in the last decade going from $73 million in 2000 to $672 million in 2010 with most exports going to the U.S. With this growth trouble has also surfaced; with avocado farms being extorted first by the Michoacán Family and later the Knights Templar. [125]

Because of the boom in global avocado sales, the overproduction of avocado farms is steadily being forced by criminal organizations.

In Michoacán suborned public officials provided the Knights Templar with land records about the avocado growers and the size of their holdings. The cartel then 'taxed' the growers – about $100 a year for each hectare of orchard, plus a few cents for each kilogram of avocado production. Growers who refused to pay the tax were dealt with like government officials. (If they refused 'the silver', they were given 'the lead'.) Those who were deemed obstreperous had their orchards burned and their families terrorized. Growers who abandoned their orchards to escape the terror were forced to sign the land over to members of the Knights Templar. [126]

The exploitation of poor people and the enslavement of the farmers and farm workers in Mexico spills over into the United States through undocumented immigrant workers.

4. Immigrant exploitation

Sweatshops in the United States largely exploit undocumented immigrant workers who are residing in the United States illegally. Because no law enforcement can be performed in regards to labor laws on immigrants who are undocumented or illegal, these immigrants become abused, threatened physically, extorted, trafficked, and much more. Sweatshops are found in many industries such as garment making

Chapter 7 - Modern Day Consequences

and farming. A very important part of the Sabbath has to do with immigration. The Fourth Commandment states,

> *Nor thy **stranger** that is within thy gates. (Exo 20:10 KJV)*

The word "stranger" is specifically referring to immigrants. *Strong's NASB Concordance* defines "stranger" as,

> **1616** גֵּר ger {gare} or (fully) גֵּיר geyr (gare)
> **Meaning:** 1) sojourner 1a) a temporary inhabitant, a newcomer lacking inherited rights 1b) of foreigners in Israel, though conceded rights
> **Origin:** from 01481; TWOT – 330a; n m
> **Usage:** AV – stranger 87, alien 1, sojourner 1, stranger + 0376 1, stranger + 04480 1, strangers + 0582 1; 92 [127]

The treatment of immigrants is extremely important in observing the Sabbath.

> ***You shall not oppress a hired servant** who is poor and needy, whether he is one of your **countrymen** or one of your **aliens** who is in your land in your towns. (Deu 24:14 NAS)*

Undocumented Immigrants most often do not know the laws of the land. They are not monitored by law enforcement because they are not documented in the legal system. Undocumented immigrants in the United States become enslaved to Cartels and other criminals because they are outside the rule of law. Many of the undocumented immigrants were trying to escape the persecution of the drug Cartels in the first place. Sabbath breaking is almost guaranteed for most undocumented aliens.

> *The arduousness of farm labor has been well documented. The average migrant has a life expectancy of just forty-nine years. Twenty thousand farmworkers requite medical treatment for acute pesticide poisoning each year; at least that many more cases go unreported. Nationally, 50 percent of migrants-up from 12 percent in 1990- are without legal work papers. Their median annual income is somewhere around $7,500. [128]*

In Florida 2002, the case United States v. Juan Ramos shows the severity of the problem.

> *The defendants Ramiro and Juan Ramos, brothers, and both labor contractors, supplied undocumented migrant farm laborers to Florida citrus growers. After smuggling workers from Mexico to Florida, the defendants used physical violence and threats of physical violence to prevent the workers from leaving their positions until they had repaid their smuggling debt. The defendants rented housing units, which were dirty and poorly maintained, assigned as many as six workers to live together, and then deducted $30 a week from each laborer's earnings to pay for the lodging. The laborers worked approximately 12 hours a day, never had a day off, and received payment based on the number of tokens they had collected. Federal authorities*

began investigating the defendants after being contacted by a local workers' rights organization. [129]

This is just a small example. The slavery of undocumented workers is a large-scale tragedy. A couple more examples of Sabbath breaking is in the cases, *U.S. vs. Lee* 2001 and *U.S. vs. Ronald Evans* 2007. People who were recruited from homeless shelters with promises of a better future ended up as slaves in agriculture. The garment industry is another area where immigrants are forced into Sabbath breaking practices. An example of this is in 1995 where Thai immigrants were enslaved in a garment factory in El Monte California. The exploitation of undocumented immigrants in the United States is almost inevitable. The impact of the exploitation of undocumented immigrants has ramifications that reverberate through all of society and government.

> *Illegal aliens comprise a substantial portion of the sweatshop work force. These undocumented workers are easily exploited by unscrupulous employers and frequently labor for long hours at less than the minimum wage under unsafe and unhealthy conditions. In some cases, illegal aliens are held in sweatshops under conditions of involuntary servitude. Sweatshops exact both social and economic costs including lost wages and taxes and the fostering of organized criminal enterprises including alien smuggling, drug trafficking, money laundering, labor racketeering, and extortion. [130]*

Businesses that run sweatshops are breaking the Sabbath severely. Sweatshops are a form of involuntary servitude, immoral, and are contrary to God's Law.

> *Open your mouth, judge righteously, And defend the rights of the afflicted and needy. (Pro 31:9 NAS)*

The government has an obligation to enforce the Laws against such practices.

> *Woe to those who enact evil statutes, And to those who constantly record unjust decisions, So as to deprive the needy of justice, And rob the poor of My people of their rights, In order that widows may be their spoil, And that they may plunder the orphans. (Isa 10:1-2 NAS)*

5. Wasting food, water, and energy

The loss of food due to spoiling is a huge problem. The conservation and distribution of food is a key point in the Fourth Commandment.

> *This is what the LORD has commanded, "Gather of it every man as much as he should eat; you shall take an omer apiece according to the number of persons each of you has in his tent." And the sons of Israel did so, and some gathered much and some little. When they measured it with an omer, he who had gathered much had no excess, and he who had gathered little had no lack; every man gathered as much as he should eat. And Moses said to them, "Let no man leave any of it until morning."*

> *But they did not listen to Moses, and some left part of it until morning, and **it bred worms and became foul; and Moses was angry with them.** (Exo 16:16-20 NAS)*

Moses specifically interprets the waste of food from working on the Sabbath as the evidence of the Sabbath Law.

> *Then he said to them, "This is what the LORD meant: Tomorrow is a sabbath observance, a holy sabbath to the LORD. Bake what you will bake and boil what you will boil, and all that is left over put aside to be kept until morning." So they put it aside until morning, as Moses had ordered, and **it did not become foul, nor was there any worm in it**. (Exo 16:23-24 NAS)*

The food was to be efficiently distributed to the people. In modern times, the amount of food harvested versus the amount of food eaten in the global economy is astonishing.

> *The scale of the problem is staggering. Each year, 1.6 billion tons of food worth about $1.2 trillion are lost or go to waste—one-third of the total amount of food produced globally. To put the figure in perspective, that is ten times the mass of the Island of Manhattan. And the problem is only growing: BCG estimates that by 2030 annual food loss will hit 2.1 billion tons worth $1.5 trillion. [131]*

The Food and Agriculture Organization in 2011 (NRDC issue paper in August 2012 iP:12-06-B) shows the losses in fruits and vegetables is 52%, seafood 50%, grain 38%, meat 22%, and milk 20%. Large amounts of energy, water, and land that is required to produce and deliver the food is ultimately wasted.

> *Food is simply too good to waste. Even the most sustainably farmed food does us no good if the food is never eaten. Getting food to our tables eats up 10 percent of the total U.S. energy budget, uses 50 percent of U.S. land, and swallows 80 percent of freshwater consumed in the United States. Yet, 40 percent of food in the United States today goes uneaten. That is more than 20 pounds of food per person every month. Not only does this mean that Americans are throwing out the equivalent of $165 billion each year, but also 25 percent of all freshwater and huge amounts of unnecessary chemicals, energy, and land. Moreover, almost all of that uneaten food ends up rotting in landfills where it accounts for almost 25 percent of U.S. methane emissions. Nutrition is also lost in the mix—food saved by reducing losses by just 15 percent could feed more than 25 million Americans every year at a time when one in six Americans lack a secure supply of food to their tables. Given all the resources demanded for food production, it is critical to make sure that the least amount possible is needlessly squandered on its journey to our plates. [132]*

Over producing food for the purpose of making money at the expense of the land breaks the Sabbath. It should be a main priority for governments and farmers to keep the Sabbath in land maintenance, food production, and food distribution. Waste should be minimized to the smallest loss possible.

6. Effects of bad debt

Debt is another issue addressed in observing the Sabbath. Laws that prohibit students from claiming bankruptcy or receiving debt relief from these loans break the Sabbath. Student loans are a lifelong albatross around the student's neck. This is why student loans should cease from being issued. Most student loans given are a debt trap that enslave the citizens. Excessive debt is bad for people, businesses, and the entire Nation. The Law of Moses mandates debt forgiveness on the yearly Sabbath. Deuteronomy states,

> ***At the end of every seven years you shall grant a remission of debts.*** *And this is the manner of remission: every creditor shall release what he has loaned to his neighbor; he shall not exact it of his neighbor and his brother, because the LORD's remission has been proclaimed. (Deu 15:1-2 NAS)*

Nehemiah also shows the Law of God requires debt forgiveness.

> As for the peoples of the land who bring wares or any grain on the sabbath day to sell, we will not buy from them on the sabbath or a holy day; and **we will forego the crops the seventh year and the exaction of every debt.** (Neh 10:31 NAS*)*

The wisdom contained in the Law of Moses is undeniable. Economists that run research on debt come to the same conclusion that excessive debt stunts the growth of a Nation. When people are unable to recover from debt, they cannot invest their resources into the Nation as a whole. The government obtains its revenue through the success and wealth of its people.

> *Debt is a two-edged sword. Used wisely and in moderation, it clearly improves welfare. But, when it is used imprudently and in excess, the result can be disaster. For individual households and firms, overborrowing leads to bankruptcy and financial ruin. For a country, too much debt impairs the government's ability to deliver essential services to its citizens. [133]*

Debt is linked to the Gross domestic product (GDP) of the Nation. The excess of debt creates a poorer GDP and less growth.

> *Our examination of debt and economic activity in industrial countries leads us to conclude that there is a clear linkage: high debt is bad for growth. When public debt is in a range of 85% of GDP, further increases in debt may begin to have a significant impact on growth: specifically, a further 10 percentage point increase reduces trend growth by more than one tenth of 1 percentage point. [134]*

It is crystal clear that debt forgiveness is important to God. The Law of Moses is God's Law. True justice is found in God's Law. Jesus spoke out against people who do not forgive debts.

> *And the lord of that slave felt compassion and released him and forgave him the debt. But that slave went out and found one of his fellow slaves who owed him a hundred denarii; and he seized him and began to choke him, saying, "Pay back what you owe." So his fellow slave fell down and began to entreat him, saying, "Have*

patience with me and I will repay you." He was unwilling however, but went and threw him in prison until he should pay back what was owed. So when his fellow slaves saw what had happened, they were deeply grieved and came and reported to their lord all that had happened. Then summoning him, his lord said to him, "You wicked slave, I forgave you all that debt because you entreated me. Should you not also have had mercy on your fellow slave, even as I had mercy on you?" And his lord, moved with anger, handed him over to the torturers until he should repay all that was owed him. So shall My heavenly Father also do to you, if each of you does not forgive his brother from your heart. (Mat 18:27-35 NAS)

The teaching "to keep the Sabbath holy" is completely neglected by most Christian theologians. Teaching the Fourth Commandment properly is extremely important. To teach that the Sabbath is abolished or merely a worship day is an incredible injustice to the Fourth Commandment "to keep the Sabbath holy."

Chapter 8 - The Ceremonial Law fulfilled in Christ

It is impossible to ignore the sabbaths, feasts, new moons, and sacrifices in the Law of Moses. To fully understand the Fourth Commandment to "keep the Sabbath holy," it is necessary to explain how Christ fulfilled the ceremonies in the Law of Moses. The Apostle Paul explains briefly how Christ fulfilled the Ceremonial Law to the Colossians.

> *And when you were dead in your transgressions and the uncircumcision of your flesh, He made you alive together with Him, having forgiven us all our transgressions, having canceled out the certificate of debt consisting of decrees against us and which was hostile to us; and He has taken it out of the way, having nailed it to the cross. When He had disarmed the rulers and authorities, He made a public display of them, having triumphed over them through Him.* **Therefore let no one act as your judge in regard to food or drink or in respect to a festival or a new moon or a Sabbath day-** *- things which are a mere shadow of what is to come; but the substance belongs to Christ. (Col 2:13-17 NAS)*

Christ fulfilled the sabbaths, feasts, new moons, and sacrifices in His messianic work. This is clearly seen in His: crucifixion, death, resurrection, ascension, and judgment. Table 8.1, "A Comparison of the Festivals and the Messianic Work of Christ," shows the fulfillment of the Ceremonial Law in Christ.

It is disputed in the Church that Christ fulfilled ALL the feasts in the Old Testament. Those who hold the futurist" and historicist views of prophecy teach that the feasts in the Law of Moses are NOT all fulfilled in Christ's messianic work. Both futurists and historicists teach the Feast of Trumpets, the Day of Atonement, and the Feast of Booths, have a future fulfillment. The different "end times" or "eschatological" views are discussed in the chapter on "the Feasts and the end times." For now, it is necessary to explain how Christ fulfilled ALL the requirements for observing the sabbaths, new moons, feasts, and sacrifices. The Ceremonial Laws are not abolished. Jesus Christ fulfilled the Law once and for all as our high priest. According to the Apostle Paul, observing the Ceremonial Law is going backwards to "weak and beggarly elements." Paul wrote,

> *But now, after that ye have known God, or rather are known of God, how turn ye again to the weak and beggarly elements, whereunto ye desire again to be in bondage? Ye observe days, and months, and times, and years. I am afraid of you, lest I have bestowed upon you labour in vain. (Gal 4:9-11 KJV)*

Continuing to observe the earthly days, times, and years that foreshadowed Christ as the Messiah is a form of unbelief. It denies that Jesus Christ is the promised messiah. There is a big difference between abolishing and fulfilling the Law. Jesus Christ is our high priest, then, now, and forever more (Heb 4:14-15). Priests no longer need to be appointed to perform the sacrificial duties of the Ceremonial Law. Jesus Christ, once and for all, as our high priest fulfilled this requirement (Rom 6:10; Heb 7:27; 1Pe 3:18; Jud 1:3-5). The writer of Hebrews wrote,

Chapter 8 - The Ceremonial Law fulfilled in Christ

For the Law appoints men as high priests who are weak, but the word of the oath, which came after the Law, appoints a Son, made perfect forever. (Heb 7:28 NAS)

	Table 8.1 - A Comparison of Festivals and the Messianic Work of Christ	
	Festivals	**Messianic Work**
1	Sabbath (Lev 23:3)	Christ is our rest (Heb 4:8-11)
2	Passover (Lev 23:4-5)	Crucifixion of Christ (1Co 5:7)
3	Unleavened Bread (Lev 23:6)	Lord's Supper (Luk 22:19-20)
4	First Fruits (Lev 23:7-15)	Resurrection of Christ (Jam 1:18; 1Co 15:20-21)
5	Feast of Weeks (Lev 23:16-23)	Pentecost (Act 1:9; Act 2:1)
6	Feast of Trumpets (Lev 23:24)	Resurrection of the dead (1Co 15:52)
7	Day of Atonement (Lev 23:26-32)	Last Judgment (Rom 2:5-6)
8	Feast of Booths (Levs 23:34)	Heaven (Joh 14:2)

1. The Sabbath

Sacrifices were offered for the people daily and every weekly Sabbath. The weekly Sabbath is included with the festivals, new moons, feasts, and sacrifices. The Sabbath is clearly included as an appointed time in Leviticus 23.

*Speak to the sons of Israel, and say to them, 'The LORD's appointed times which you shall proclaim as holy convocations-- **My appointed times are these: For six days work may be done; but on the seventh day there is a sabbath of complete rest**, a holy convocation. You shall not do any work; **it is a sabbath to the LORD** in all your dwellings. (Lev 23:2-3 NAS)*

Some Rabbis argue that the weekly Sabbath is not part of the festivals in Leviticus 23. Rabbi Jonathan Sacks wrote,

In one respect in particular, the Leviticus account is quite strange – in its treatment of Shabbat. ... The problem is glaring and was noted by the commentators. Two terms are used here in connection with Shabbat that are not used elsewhere: mo'ed, *"appointed festival," and* mikra kodesh, *"sacred assembly." But neither fits Shabbat. It is not a* mo'ed *in the sense of a day with a date on the calendar. The Hebrew calendar is both lunar and solar, lunar in respect of months, solar in relation to the seasons of the year. Shabbat is neither. It creates its own unique rhythm, the seven-day week, which did noy exist in any other ancient system of counting time. The very institution of the seven-day week is now a global phenomenon, has its origins in the Hebrew Bible. So Shabbat is not a fixed date on the calendar. It is not* mo'ed.

Chapter 8 - The Ceremonial Law fulfilled in Christ

> *Nor is it a mikra kodesh. The commentators give two explanations. One is "sacred assembly," meaning a time when the nation gathered in a central sanctuary (Nahmanides). But this does not apply to Shabbat. It was celebrated locally, not centrally. The other is "a day proclaimed holy: (Rashi, Rashbam), referring to the fact that the calendar depended on the proclamation of the* Beit Din *as to which day or days were announced as Rosh Hodesh, the start of the new month. It is precisely in this respect that Shabbat differs from the festivals. It is not dependent on any human proclamation. Shabbat is holy because God Himself sanctified it on the seventh day of creation.*
>
> *So Shabbat does not belong in a list of the festivals.* [135]

The problem with the commentators Rabbi Jonathan Sacks quotes is that they are going by the modern Jewish lunisolar calendar. There is no evidence ancient Israel, during the time the Torah was written, used the lunisolar calendar at all. After the Jews were released from captivity, they most likely used the Babylonian lunisolar calendar. As mentioned in the chapter of "the Calendar," Bible expositors use modern calendars when interpreting ancient Biblical events. Applying modern calendar systems to scripture leads to misinterpretation. Also, the Sabbath being "locally" or "centrally" observed or being "proclaimed" is irrelevant to the fact that sacrifices were required to be done on the Sabbath. Since Leviticus lists the weekly Sabbath with the other festivals, it is evidence enough that the ancient Israelites did include the weekly Sabbath with the festivals. Negating a Bible verse because of a specific theological view is unacceptable. Monitoring the new moons to determine when the month starts appears to be directly related to the Sabbath. Circumstantial evidence from 2 Kings 4:23 shows that the Sabbath and the new moon are rest days.

> *And he said, "Why will you go to him today?* **It is neither new moon nor sabbath."**
> *And she said, "It will be well." (2Ki 4:23 NAS)*

The Sabbath is included with the festivals because the daily and weekly sacrifices were also appointed times. In 2 Chronicles 8, sabbaths are included with new moons, and the festivals.

> *Then Solomon offered burnt offerings to the LORD on the altar of the LORD which he had built before the porch; and did so according to the daily rule, offering them up* ***according to the commandment of Moses, for the sabbaths, the new moons, and the three annual feasts*--** *the Feast of Unleavened Bread, the Feast of Weeks, and the Feast of Booths. (2Ch 8:12-13 NAS)*

As shown in the chapter on "the Calendar," advocates of the Creator's calendar argue that the new moon is integral in calculating the Sabbath day. It is possible ancient Israel followed a calendar similar to the Creator's calendar.

A common argument is that, because the people were commanded to assemble on the Sabbath day, the seventh day is the designated day for worship. Worship is not the purpose of the weekly Sabbath. The purpose of the convocation on any day including the Sabbath day was to offer a sin sacrifice for the people.

Chapter 8 - The Ceremonial Law fulfilled in Christ

> *These are the appointed times of the LORD which you shall proclaim as holy convocations,* **to present offerings** *by fire to the LORD-- burnt offerings and grain offerings, sacrifices and libations, each day's matter on its own day. (Lev 23:37 NAS)*

The sin sacrifice performed by the ancient Israelite priests were not worship services. They were instituted for the purpose of foreshadowing the messianic work of Christ and a memorial of the Exodus from Egypt. The Sabbath is a perpetual "sign" between God and His people. Exodus says,

> *So the sons of Israel shall observe the sabbath,* **to celebrate the sabbath throughout their generations as a perpetual covenant. It is a sign** *between Me and the sons of Israel forever; for in six days the LORD made heaven and earth, but on the seventh day He ceased from labor, and was refreshed. (Exo 31:16-17 NAS)*

The Sabbath is a perpetual covenant because God requires the people to honor and have faith in Him continually forever. Entering the Lord's Sabbath rest is contingent on faith in Jesus Christ. The writer of Hebrews wrote,

> *For we who have believed enter that rest, just as He has said, "As I swore in My wrath, they shall not enter My rest," although His works were finished from the foundation of the world. (Heb 4:3 NAS)*

Only coming to Christ in faith can anyone enter the Sabbath rest. Jesus said,

> *Come to Me, all who are weary and heavy-laden, and* **I will give you rest**. *(Mat 11:28 NAS)*

We enter the Sabbath rest through Christ who raises us from the dead spiritually (causes us to be born again) and raises us from the dead at death. Only those who are "born again" will enter the Sabbath rest received in the heavenly dimension.

> *Jesus answered and said to him, "Truly, truly, I say to you,* **unless one is born again, he cannot see the kingdom of God.**"... *Jesus answered, "Truly, truly, I say to you, unless one is born of water and the Spirit, he cannot enter into the kingdom of God.* **That which is born of the flesh is flesh, and that which is born of the Spirit is spirit."** *(Joh 3:3,5-6 NAS)*

The Earthly dimension of the flesh and the Heavenly dimension of the spirit. God's people become citizens in the kingdom of God when they are born again or regenerated by the power of the Holy Spirit (Tit 3:5) while living on Earth. After death God's people are transformed into a body of Christ's glory.

> *For our* **citizenship is in heaven,** *from which also we eagerly wait for a Savior, the Lord Jesus Christ;* **who will transform the body of our humble state into conformity with the body of His glory,** *by the exertion of the power that He has even to subject all things to Himself. (Phi 3:20-21 NAS)*

When God's people are born again, they enter Christ's kingdom. This means we enter His Sabbath rest in this life. Paul wrote,

Chapter 8 - The Ceremonial Law fulfilled in Christ

> *For the kingdom of God is not eating and drinking, but righteousness and peace and joy in the Holy Spirit. (Rom 14:17 NAS)*

When believers in Christ persevere until death, they will enter the Sabbath rest in heaven. We are not to observe the Ceremonial Laws on the Sabbath as if the Messiah never came. Performing the Ceremonial Law on the Sabbath is abandoning the faith in Christ as the fulfillment of God's promises. This is why the writer of Hebrews said,

> *For if we go on sinning willfully after receiving the knowledge of the truth, there no longer remains a sacrifice for sins (Heb 10:26 NAS)*

The writer of Hebrews was referring to continuing to perform sacrifices instead of accepting Christ as our sacrifice (Heb 10:1-14). Obedience to Christ is required in order to enter His rest. The writer of Hebrews explains how the disobedient Israelites did not enter the promised rest.

> *Therefore, I was angry with this generation, And said, "They always go astray in their heart; And they did not know My ways'; As I swore in My wrath, 'They shall not enter My rest." (Heb 3:10-11 NAS)*

Those who believe in Christ, that is to say, obey His commandments (in this life) firm until the end (at death) will enter His rest (the Sabbath). Hebrews chapter three states,

> *For we have become partakers of Christ, if we hold fast the beginning of our assurance firm until the end. (Heb 3:14 NAS)*

Disobedience and unbelief prohibit people from entering the Sabbath rest in this life and at death. The writer of Hebrews wrote,

> *And to whom did He swear that they should not enter His rest, but to those who were disobedient? And so we see that they were not able to enter because of unbelief. (Heb 3:18-19 NAS)*

Therefore, we should fear of not entering His rest because of unbelief and be diligent to enter that rest, the final Sabbath. The writer of Hebrews wrote,

> *Therefore, let us fear lest, while a promise remains of entering His rest, any one of you should seem to have come short of it. (Heb 4:1 NAS)*

The earthly plot of land given to ancient Israel is NOT the object of the promised rest for the people of God. The writer of Hebrews tells us to, instead of looking to an earthly place, be diligent to enter the heavenly rest promised in Christ.

> *For if Joshua had given them rest, He would not have spoken of another day after that. There remains therefore a Sabbath rest for the people of God. For the one who has entered His rest has himself also rested from his works, as God did from His. Let us therefore be diligent to enter that rest, lest anyone fall through following the same example of disobedience. (Heb 4:8-11 NAS)*

We should no longer look to earth as our destination for God's promises. Our eyes should be on Christ in Heaven, a better world, the City of God. The final Sabbath rest is the heavenly rest God promised to His people. Those who are disobedient will not enter in. As our high priest, Jesus Christ fulfilled the Sabbath sacrifice for us permanently and mediates for us in heaven. The Apostles believed the Sabbath rest is ultimately fulfilled at death and NOT in a future establishment of an earthly Nation in the land of Israel (Mat 6:20-21, 8:11, Joh 14:2).

2. The Passover

When the Israelites were in slavery in Egypt, the Lord told Moses He was going to kill the first born across the land (Exo 12:12). The Israelites were commanded to sacrifice a lamb and apply its blood to the doorposts. If the people did not apply the blood to the doorposts, their first born would be killed. All those who obeyed and put the blood on their doorposts survived. This event is called the "Passover." The Passover sacrifice is an ordinance forever. The book of Exodus says,

> *Then Moses called for all the elders of Israel, and said to them, Go and take for yourselves lambs according to your families, and slay the Passover lamb. And you shall take a bunch of hyssop and dip it in the blood which is in the basin, and apply some of the blood that is in the basin to the lintel and the two doorposts; and none of you shall go outside the door of his house until morning. For the LORD will pass through to smite the Egyptians; and when He sees the blood on the lintel and on the two doorposts, the LORD will pass over the door and will not allow the destroyer to come in to your houses to smite you.* ***And you shall observe this event as an ordinance for you and your children forever****. (Exo 12:21-24 NAS see Exo 24:6-8)*

In Exodus 12, the lintel and doorposts were sprinkled with the blood as a covenant with Gods people that they were to be spared or "passed over." On the ceremony of Passover, also called Feast of Unleavened Bread, the ancient Israel priests were required to sprinkle the lamb's blood on the doorposts, the people, and the altar. This foreshadowed the messianic work of Christ dying for the sins of His people. Paul clearly wrote,

> *For Christ our Passover also has been sacrificed. (1Co 5:7 NAS)*

The Passover lamb was not to have any broken bones. The book of Numbers says,

> *They shall leave none of it until morning, nor break a bone of it; according to all the statute of the Passover they shall observe it. (Num 9:12 NAS)*

The Apostle John connected Jesus Christ as the Passover Lamb because He had no bone broken when He was crucified.

> *For these things came to pass, that the Scripture might be fulfilled, "Not a bone of Him shall be broken." (Joh 19:36 NAS)*

According to John, Passover was an event that prophetically foretold the atonement of Christ. John wrote that John the Baptist witnessed Jesus Christ as the Lamb of God.

> *The next day he saw Jesus coming to him, and said, Behold, the Lamb of God who takes away the sin of the world! (Joh 1:29 NAS)*

Table 8.2 compares the Passover or Feast of Unleavened Bread with the messianic work of Christ.

	Table 8.2 - Passover and the Messianic work of Christ comparison	
1	**Passover**	**Messianic work**
2	The male lamb (Exo 12:3)	Christ the Lamb (Joh 1:29)
3	Lamb without blemish (Exo 12:5)	Spotless unblemished lamb (2Co 5:21; 1Pe 1:19)
4	Passover sacrifice (Exo 12:26-27)	That night the Lord's Supper (Mar 14:12-24)
5	Not break any of its bones (Exo 12:46)	Crucified on Passover (Joh 19:14)
6	Not break any of its bones (Exo 12:46)	Not a bone of it will be broken. (Joh 19:36)
7	The blood applied to the post (Exo 12:7)	Sprinkling the blood of Jesus Christ (1Pe 1:2)

a. Christ's blood of the covenant

Jesus said His blood is the blood of the covenant. He shed His blood for our sins. In Matthew chapter 26 Jesus said,

> *This is My blood of the covenant, which is poured out for many for forgiveness of sins. (Mat 26:28 NAS see also Mar 14:24, 1Co 11:25)*

> *And in the same way He took the cup after they had eaten, saying, "This cup which is poured out for you is the new covenant in My blood." (Luk 22:20 NAS)*

Sprinkling the lintel and door posts with the lamb's blood was fulfilled when Christ died for our sins. While we were enemies and had not sought for God at all, Jesus died for our sins. Paul wrote,

> *But God demonstrates His own love toward us, in that while we were yet sinners, Christ died for us. Much more then, **having now been justified by His blood**, we shall be saved from the wrath of God through Him. **For if while we were enemies, we were reconciled to God through the death of His Son, much more, having been reconciled, we shall be saved by His life.** And not only this, but we also exult in God through our Lord Jesus Christ, through whom we have now received the reconciliation. Therefore, just as through one man sin entered into the world, and death through sin, and so death spread to all men, because all sinned. (Rom 5:8-12 NAS)*

Because Christ died for us, we shall be saved. Peter also uses the same language in regards to the Passover Lamb and Christ's blood. God's people are redeemed with the blood of Christ. Peter wrote,

> *Knowing that you were not redeemed with perishable things like silver or gold from your futile way of life inherited from your forefathers, but with precious blood, **as of a lamb unblemished and spotless, the blood of Christ**. For He was foreknown before the foundation of the world, but has appeared in these last times for the sake of you. (1Pe 1:18-20 NAS)*

Christ was destined before creation to die for our sins. Sprinkling the people with the blood of the lamb can be visualized in the book of Revelation. The robes of the saints are washed with the blood of Christ.

> *And I said to him, "My lord, you know." And he said to me, "These are the ones who come out of the great tribulation, and they have washed their robes and made them white **in the blood of the Lamb**." (Rev 7:14 NAS)*

The Passover is permanently observed forever by Christ offering Himself once and for all for the sins of God's people throughout all time. The sacrifice of Christ for the sins of the people is essential to the fulfillment of the Passover ceremony. There is no forgiveness of sin when there is no sacrifice for that sin.

> *And according to the Law, one may almost say, all things are cleansed with blood, and **without shedding of blood there is no forgiveness**. (Heb 9:22 NAS)*

Paul specifically connects the sin sacrifice required for God's people with the sacrifice of Christ for our sins.

> *For I delivered to you as of first importance what I also received, that Christ died for our sins according to the Scriptures. (1Co 15:3 NAS)*

If Christ did not fulfill the Passover requirement specifically for us, we would die in our sins. Only those who believe will be covered by the sacrifice of Christ.

> *I said therefore to you, that you shall die in your sins; for unless you believe that I am He, you shall die in your sins. (Joh 8:24 NAS)*

The Bible undeniably teaches Christ fulfilled the requirement for the Passover Ceremonial Law. The Passover is continually kept by Jesus Christ offering Himself as our Passover lamb once and for all and in Him as our mediator.

3. The Feast of Unleavened Bread

The Feast of Unleavened Bread and Passover are the same event (Luk 22:1). The Pharaoh kept hardening his heart by refusing to let the Israelites go (Exo 7:13,22; 8:15,19,32; 9:34-35; 10:1,20,27; 11:10; 14:8). God told Moses in advance when the Pharaoh would let the Israelites go.

> *Now the LORD said to Moses, "One more plague I will bring on Pharaoh and on Egypt; after that he will let you go from here. When he lets you go, he will surely drive you out from here completely." (Exo 11:1 NAS)*

Moses told the Israelites to eat unleavened bread to prepare for a rapid departure from Egypt. The Israelites ate unleavened bread as they waited for the first born to be killed in Egypt. When the first born of Egypt were struck at Passover, the pharaoh told the Israelites to leave (Exo 12). After the Pharaoh finally decided to let the Israelites go, the Israelites wasted no time to leave.

> *Now you shall eat it in this manner: with your loins girded, your sandals on your feet, and your staff in your hand; and you shall eat it in haste-- it is the LORD's Passover. (Exo 12:11 NAS)*

The Feast of Unleavened Bread is the memorial of the Passover and the release of the ancient Israelites from slavery in Egypt.

> *Now this day will be a memorial to you, and you shall celebrate it as a feast to the LORD; throughout your generations you are to celebrate it as a permanent ordinance. (Exo 12:14 NAS)*

The Feast of Unleavened Bread foreshadows the events of the Lord's Supper and the sacrifice of Christ as our Passover Lamb. Luke wrote,

> *Now the Feast of Unleavened Bread, which is called the Passover, was approaching…And He said to them, "I have earnestly desired to eat this Passover with you before I suffer; for I say to you, I shall never again eat it until it is fulfilled in the kingdom of God." (Luk 22:1,15-16 NAS Mar 14:12)*

The Lord's supper is a memorial looking back to what Christ did. Christ ate the Feast of Unleavened Bread before He was crucified. Christ clearly instituted the Lord's Supper as the memorial of the Passover of God's people in the new covenant. Luke wrote,

> *And when He had taken some bread and given thanks, He broke it, and gave it to them, saying,* **"This is My body which is given for you; do this in remembrance of Me."** *And in the same way He took the cup after they had eaten, saying,* **"This cup which is poured out for you is the new covenant in My blood."** *(Luk 22:19-20 NAS)*

The Feast of Unleavened Bread is the memorial of the old covenant of how God spared the Israelites from slavery in Egypt. It also established a ceremony that kept the promise that looked forward to the coming of the Messiah, Jesus Christ. The ancient Israelites were anticipating the coming of the Messiah during the time of Christ based on the Law of Moses and the Prophets.

> *Philip found Nathanael and said to him, "We have found Him of whom Moses in the Law and also the Prophets wrote, Jesus of Nazareth, the son of Joseph." (Joh 1:45 NAS)*

The Lord's Supper is a memorial of the new covenant pointing back to what Christ did for us. The Passover looked forward to Christ's sacrifice for us. Jesus said "do this in remembrance of Me." Paul connects Christ our Passover sacrifice with the continued celebration of the Feast of Unleavened Bread.

> *Clean out the old leaven, that you may be a new lump, just as you are in fact unleavened. For Christ our Passover also has been sacrificed. Let us therefore celebrate the feast, not with old leaven, nor with the leaven of malice and wickedness, but with the unleavened bread of sincerity and truth. (1Co 5:7-8 NAS)*

The Lord's Supper is celebrated with the unleavened bread of sincerity and truth. In other words, the leaven is sin in our lives and Christ is the sacrifice for our sins. This is what Jesus taught. Luke wrote,

> *Beware of the leaven of the Pharisees, which is hypocrisy. (Luk 12:1 NAS)*

Jesus clearly taught the leaven is not about bread but the sinfulness of people. The leaven is specifically referring to the false teachings and traditions of the Pharisees and Sadducees. Matthew wrote,

> *How is it that you do not understand that I did not speak to you concerning bread? But beware of the leaven of the Pharisees and Sadducees." Then they understood that He did not say to beware of the leaven of bread, but of the teaching of the Pharisees and Sadducees. (Mat 16:11-12 NAS)*

Jesus was not talking about bread. Christ referred to Himself as the bread of life.

> *I am the bread of life. (Joh 6:48 NAS)*

This is because Jesus Christ is our Passover Lamb and our unleavened bread. Following Christ's teaching is pure. Only in Him can we be saved.

> *Jesus said to him, "I am the way, and the truth, and the life; no one comes to the Father, but through Me." (Joh 14:6 NAS)*

The Feast of Unleavened Bread is the keeping of the promises foreshadowing the messianic work of Christ. The fulfillment is the pure truth of the Eternal Word Jesus Christ and memorialized in the institution of the Lord's Supper.

4. The Feast of First Fruits

The Feast of First Fruits is the celebration of the first fruits of the harvest. A sheaf from the first of the crop was given to the priest as an offering to dedicate the harvest to God. Leviticus says,

> *On the first day you shall have a holy convocation; you shall not do any laborious work…you shall bring in the sheaf of the first fruits of your harvest to the priest. (Lev 23:7,10 NAS)*

A one-year old male lamb was offered as a sacrifice along with flour mixed with oil and wine. Moses wrote,

> *Now on the day when you wave the sheaf, you shall offer a male lamb one year old without defect for a burnt offering to the LORD. Its grain offering shall then be two-tenths of an ephah of fine flour mixed with oil, an offering by fire to the LORD for a soothing aroma, with its libation, a fourth of a hin of wine. (Lev 23:12-13 NAS see Num 28:18-19)*

Chapter 8 - The Ceremonial Law fulfilled in Christ

The offering of the male lamb, the mixture of flour and oil, and the wine also foreshadows the sacrifice of Christ and the Lord's Supper. Jesus Christ fulfilled the requirement to observe the Feast of the First Fruits in His death and resurrection from the dead. He is the first to raise from the dead. Paul wrote,

> *He is also head of the body, the church; and He is the beginning, the first-born from the dead; so that He Himself might come to have first place in everything. (Col 1:18 NAS see Rom 8:29)*

The feast also foreshadows the resurrection of His people. God's people are spiritually and physically raised from the dead as the outcome of Christ's resurrection. Paul wrote,

> *But now Christ has been raised from the dead, the first fruits of those who are asleep. For since by a man came death, by a man also came the resurrection of the dead. (1Co 15:20-21 NAS)*

The resurrection of the dead happens in this life and at death. The resurrection that happens during this life is called being born again (1Pe 1:3) or regeneration (Tit 3:5). The Feast of First Fruits starts on the same day Christ rose from the dead. This is why the Church observes the Lord's Day on the first day of the week. We shall rise from the dead because He rose from the dead. Christ purchased His people as first fruits to God. The book of Revelation states,

> *These are the ones who have not been defiled with women, for they have kept themselves chaste. These are the ones who follow the Lamb wherever He goes. These **have been purchased from among men as first fruits** to God and to the Lamb. (Rev 14:4 NAS)*

All those who are purchased by the Christ are the first fruits offered to God. James wrote,

> *In the exercise of His will He brought us forth by the word of truth, so that we might be, as it were, the first fruits among His creatures. (Jam 1:18 NAS)*

When Jesus called the disciples, He said He was going to make them fishers of men.

> *And He said to them, "Follow Me, and I will make you fishers of men." (Mat 4:19 NAS)*

Christ was saying that He was going to turn the disciples from fishing to converting people to Christ. The Apostles were the workers of the harvest. God regenerating and gathering His elect is often compared to a harvest in the Bible. Christ says He sends out workers into the harvest.

> *Then He said to His disciples, "The harvest is plentiful, but the workers are few. Therefore beseech the Lord of the harvest to send out workers into His harvest." (Mat 9:37-38 NAS; Luk 10:2)*

Christ is referring to the disciples being sent to evangelize the world. Preaching the Word of God causes people to be born again. Peter wrote,

> *for you have been born again not of seed which is perishable but imperishable, that is, through the living and abiding word of God. (1Pe 1:23 NAS)*

The First Fruits of the harvest are God's elect. God gathers His elect from the world at the end of the age. Those who are not God's people are cast into the furnace.

> *Then He left the multitudes, and went into the house. And His disciples came to Him, saying, "Explain to us the parable of the tares of the field." And He answered and said, "The one who sows the good seed is the Son of Man, and the field is the world; and as for the good seed, these are the sons of the kingdom; and the tares are the sons of the evil one; and the enemy who sowed them is the devil, and the harvest is the end of the age; and the reapers are angels. Therefore just as the tares are gathered up and burned with fire, so shall it be at the end of the age. "The Son of Man will send forth His angels, and they will gather out of His kingdom all stumbling blocks, and those who commit lawlessness, and will cast them into the furnace of fire; in that place there shall be weeping and gnashing of teeth. (Mat 13:36-42 NAS)*

Christ is using the harvest metaphorically. The "end of the age" is the end of the harvest. *The NASB Concordance* defines the word "age" as,

> **<165> αἰών (aion)**
> **Meaning:** *a space of time, an age*
> **Origin:** *from a prim. root appar. mean. continued duration*
> **Usage:** *age(20), ages(6), ancient time(1), beginning of time(m)(1), course(m)(1), eternal(2),eternity(1), ever*(2), forever(27), forever and ever(20), forevermore(2), never*(8), old(2), time(1), world(m)(7),worlds(m)(1).*
> **Notes:** *¹ Lit., this time ᵃ Mat 12:32 [136]*

The "end of the age" is NOT the end of the world in the future. It only means "a space of time." The field is the world, the wheat are the people sown by God, the tares are the people sown by the devil, and the end of the age is at the end of the harvest. God continually harvests His people from the world when each generation dies. The gathering of God's people from the world is a continual event. This is depicted in the book of Revelation.

> *And another angel came out of the temple, crying out with a loud voice to Him who sat on the cloud, "Put in your sickle and reap, because the hour to reap has come, because the harvest of the earth is ripe." **And He who sat on the cloud swung His sickle over the earth; and the earth was reaped.** (Rev 14:15-16 NAS)*

Christ sends His angels to reap the earth throughout every age and generation. The Feast of First Fruits foreshadows the resurrection of Christ from the dead and the regeneration of God's people.

5. The Feast of Weeks

The counting of weeks from the beginning of the harvest till the fiftieth day is the Feast of Weeks. It is the continual harvesting of God's people. The fiftieth day is key to understand the fulfillment of the feast. The Law of Moses says,

> *You shall count seven weeks for yourself; you shall begin to count seven weeks from the time you begin to put the sickle to the standing grain. (Deu 16:9 NAS see Lev 23:16; Num 28:26)*

Jeremiah prophesied the fulfillment of the Feast of Weeks. Jeremiah prophesied that God would write the Law on the heart of His people.

> *But this is the covenant which I will make with the house of Israel after those days, declares the LORD, I will put My law within them, and on their heart I will write it; and I will be their God, and they shall be My people. (Jer 31:33 NAS)*

The writing of the Law on the heart was ultimately fulfilled on the day of Pentecost in the book of Acts. Fifty days after the resurrection of Christ, the apostles experienced the outpouring of the Holy Spirit. Joel prophesied the outpouring of the Spirit upon all mankind at the day of Pentecost in the book of Acts.

> *And it will come about after this That I will pour out My Spirit on all mankind; And your sons and daughters will prophesy, Your old men will dream dreams, Your young men will see visions. (Joe 2:28 NAS)*

The word "Pentecost" is Greek for "fiftieth" day. The *Strong's NASB Concordance* says,

> *<4005> πεντηκοστός (pentekostos)*
> ***Meaning**: fiftieth, Pentecost, the second of the three great Jewish feasts*
> ***Origin**: an ord. num. from 4004*
> ***Usage**: Pentecost(3).*
> ***Notes**: [1] Lit., was being fulfilled [a] Lev 23:15f.; Act 20:16; 1Co 16:8 [137]*

In Acts, Luke writes about the fulfillment of the Feast of Weeks on the day of Pentecost.

> *And when the day of Pentecost had come, they were all together in one place. And suddenly there came from heaven a noise like a violent, rushing wind, and it filled the whole house where they were sitting. (Act 2:1-2 NAS)*

Some of the people accused the Apostles of being drunk. The Apostle Peter said Joel 2:28 was fulfilled at that day. Peter said,

> *For these men are not drunk, as you suppose, for it is only the third hour of the day;* ***but this is what was spoken of through the prophet Joel: "And it shall be in the last days, God says, That I will pour forth of My Spirit upon all mankind;*** *And your sons and your daughters shall prophesy, And your young men shall see visions, And your old men shall dream dreams." (Act 2:15-17 NAS)*

The Holy Spirit was prophesied to be poured out in the "last days." The "last days" in Acts 2 clearly refers to the time of the Apostles. Joel wrote,

> *And it will come about **after this That I will pour out My Spirit on all mankind**; And your sons and daughters will prophesy, Your old men will dream dreams, Your young men will see visions (Joe 2:28 NAS)*

The Old Testament Hebrew is translated as "after this" where the New Testament Greek is translated as "last days." This undeniably places the phrase "last days" in the New Testament at the time of the Apostles. The Apostles were witness to the fulfillment of this prophesy on the day of Pentecost. God regenerates or causes to be born again ALL mankind, Jews and Gentiles alike, by the power of His Holy Spirit. The writer of Hebrews correlates Jeremiah's prophecy of the covenant with the house of Israel.

> *For this is **the covenant that I will make with the house of Israel After those days**, says the Lord: I will put My laws into their minds, And I will write them upon their hearts. And I will be their God, And they shall be My people. (Heb 8:10 NAS)*

The writer of Hebrews applies the covenant with the house of Israel to the Christian Church.

> *But you have come to Mount Zion and to the city of the living God, the heavenly Jerusalem, and to myriads of angels, **to the general assembly and church of the first-born who are enrolled in heaven**, and to God, the Judge of all, and to the spirits of righteous men made perfect, and **to Jesus, the mediator of a new covenant**, and to the sprinkled blood, which speaks better than the blood of Abel. (Heb 12:22-24 NAS)*

The epistle to the Hebrews undeniably applies the covenant with the house of Israel and the writing of the Law on their hearts to the Christian Church. The Apostle Paul taught the same doctrine to the Corinthians.

> *You are our letter, written in our hearts, known and read by all men; being manifested that you are a letter of Christ, cared for by us, **written not with ink, but with the Spirit of the living God, not on tablets of stone, but on tablets of human hearts.** (2Co 3:2-3 NAS)*

The day of Pentecost in the book of Acts is the fulfillment of the Feast of Weeks. It is the effectual call of all of God's people across all time. It is the salvation of all God's people, Jew or Greek.

> *There is neither Jew nor Greek, there is neither slave nor free man, there is neither male nor female; for you are all one in Christ Jesus. And **if you belong to Christ, then you are Abraham's offspring, heirs according to promise**. (Gal 3:28-29 NAS)*

No longer is there a specific location to worship the Lord. For God's people must worship in spirit and truth. Jesus said,

> *Our fathers worshiped in this mountain, and you people say that in Jerusalem is the place where men ought to worship. Jesus said to her, Woman, believe Me, an hour is coming when neither in this mountain, nor in Jerusalem, shall you worship the Father. "You worship that which you do not know; we worship that which we know, for salvation is from the Jews. **But an hour is coming, and now is, when the true worshipers shall worship the Father in spirit and truth; for such people the Father***

seeks to be His worshipers. *God is spirit, and those who worship Him must worship in spirit and truth. (Joh 4:20-24 NAS)*

The Feast of Weeks is fulfilled in the effectual call and the outpouring of His Spirit upon all of God's people.

6. The Feast of Trumpets

The Feast of Trumpets was celebrated as a reminder of the experience the ancient Israelites had at Mount Sinai in Exodus 19. God said in the Book of Leviticus,

> *Speak to the sons of Israel, saying, In the seventh month on the first of the month, you shall have a rest, a reminder by blowing of trumpets, a holy convocation. (Lev 23:24 NAS)*

After the third month of leaving the land of Egypt, the Lord called Moses to Mount Sinai. God commanded Moses to tell the Israelites to obey Him as His people.

> *Now then,* ***if you will indeed obey My voice and keep My covenant, then you shall be My own possession among all the peoples,*** *for all the earth is Mine; and you shall be to Me a kingdom of priests and a holy nation.' These are the words that you shall speak to the sons of Israel. (Exo 19:5-6 NAS)*

God commanded Moses to consecrate the people and have them wash their garments.

> *The LORD also said to Moses, Go to the people and consecrate them today and tomorrow, and let them wash their garments. (Exo 19:10 NAS)*

Nobody except Moses was allowed to go up the mountain. If someone touched the border or went up the mountain, they were put to death. The book of Exodus states,

> *Beware that you do not go up on the mountain or touch the border of it; whoever touches the mountain shall surely be put to death. No hand shall touch him, but he shall surely be stoned or shot through; whether beast or man, he shall not live. When the ram's horn sounds a long blast, they shall come up to the mountain. (Exo 19: 12-13 NAS)*

On the third day the Lord came in the clouds to the top of the mountain, Moses interceded for the people who were at the foot of the mountain.

> *So it came about on the third day, when it was morning, that there were thunder and lightning flashes and a thick cloud upon the mountain and a very loud trumpet sound, so that all the people who were in the camp trembled. And Moses brought the people out of the camp to meet God, and they stood at the foot of the mountain. (Exo 19:16-17 NAS)*

The Lord came down to the top of Mount Sinai and Moses interceded for the people.

> *And the LORD came down on Mount Sinai, to the top of the mountain; and the LORD called Moses to the top of the mountain, and Moses went up. (Exo 19:20 NAS)*

Afterwards, in Exodus 20, God gives the Moral Law in the Ten Commandments. The Feast of Trumpets foreshadows the resurrection of the dead and the coming of the Lord in the clouds.

a. The resurrection of the dead

At death, ALL will see Christ coming in the clouds. Jesus said YOU will see the Son of Man coming on the clouds. Matthew wrote,

> *Jesus said to him, "You have said it yourself; nevertheless I tell you, hereafter **you shall see the Son of Man sitting at the right hand of Power, and coming on the clouds of heaven.**" (Mat 26:64 NAS)*

Death is a continual historical event; therefore, the last trumpet and resurrection of the dead is a continual event. Paul taught the dead do not sleep but are raised from the dead first. The resurrection happens at the time of death. The dead do not wait in a temporary holding place until judgment day. Paul wrote,

> *In a moment, in the twinkling of an eye, at the last trumpet; for the trumpet will sound, and the dead will be raised imperishable, and we shall be changed. (1Co 15:52 NAS)*

The dead do not sleep but are changed at death. The dead rise first. Paul wrote,

> *For the Lord Himself will descend from heaven with a shout, with the voice of the archangel, and with the trumpet of God; and **the dead in Christ shall rise first**. (1Th 4:16 NAS)*

To interpret the resurrection as a single distant future event that is not connected to the time of death is unscriptural. All people are raised from the dead at death.

> *And inasmuch as it is appointed for men to die once and after this comes judgment. (Heb 9:27 NAS)*

Christ then, now, and forever more, will continue to gather His people from earth till the end of all things. The inheritance in heaven is the final Sabbath rest.

> *Blessed be the God and Father of our Lord Jesus Christ, who according to His great mercy has caused us to be born again to a living hope through the resurrection of Jesus Christ from the dead, to obtain an inheritance which is imperishable and undefiled and will not fade away, reserved in heaven for you, who are protected by the power of God through faith for a salvation ready to be revealed in the last time. (1Pe 1:3-5 NAS)*

Chapter 8 - The Ceremonial Law fulfilled in Christ

The Bible shows the "Last Trumpet" as a continual event and not a one-time event. Just like the tares and the wheat are gathered at the end of the harvest, so the Angels gather the wicked (tares) and the righteous (wheat) at their death. Matthew wrote,

> *And He will send forth His angels with a great trumpet and they will gather together His elect from the four winds, from one end of the sky to the other. (Mat 24:31 NAS)*

Just like the gathering of a harvest is done in stages over time, so is the resurrection of the dead. The sound of a trumpet is heard when transported to heaven. John wrote,

> *After these things I looked, and behold, a door standing open in heaven, and the first voice which I had heard, like **the sound of a trumpet speaking with me, said, "Come up here**, and I will show you what must take place after these things." **Immediately I was in the Spirit; and behold, a throne was standing in heaven**, and One sitting on the throne. (Rev 4:1-2 NAS)*

When the trumpet is sounded, the person is transported to the throne of God in heaven. The Feast of Trumpets is a general outline of the resurrection of the dead and the coming of Christ. Table 8.3, "A Comparison of the Feast of Weeks and the Resurrection," compares the Feast of Weeks and the resurrection of the dead.

	Table 8.3 - A Comparison of the Feast of Weeks and the Resurrection	
	Old Testament	**New Testament**
1	Obeying Gods Law (Exo 19:5-6)	Only the doers of the Law (Rom 2:13, Jam 1:22, Heb 10:23-24)
2	Washing the Garments (Exo 19:10)	Robes washed by the blood of Christ (Heb 10:22, Rev 7:14)
3	Mount Sinai (Exo 19:12)	Mount Zion (Heb 12:20-24)
4	Blowing of the trumpet and death (Exo 19:13)	The trumpet at the last day (1Co 15:52, 1Th 4:16)
5	Lord coming in the clouds (Exo 19:16-17)	Jesus coming in clouds (Mat 26:64, Rev 1:7)
6	Moses intercedes for the people (Exo 19:20)	Christ intercedes for the people (Rom 8:34, Heb 5:9)

b. The Sadducees denied the afterlife

When the Sadducees questioned Jesus about the resurrection from the dead, Jesus said, "God is not the God of the dead but of the living." Matthew wrote,

Chapter 8 - The Ceremonial Law fulfilled in Christ

> *On that day some Sadducees (who say there is no resurrection) came to Him and questioned Him...**But regarding the resurrection of the dead**, have you not read that which was spoken to you by God, saying, I am the God of Abraham, and the God of Isaac, and the God of Jacob? **He is not the God of the dead but of the living.** (Mat 22: 23,31-32 NAS)*

Matthew 22:31-32 can only be understood to mean Abraham, Isaac, and Jacob were raised from the dead at death. Both the righteous and the unrighteous will receive immortal physical bodies at death.

> ***And many of those who sleep in the dust of the ground will awake**, these to everlasting life, but the others to **disgrace and everlasting contempt**. (Dan 12:2 NAS)*

The phrase "sleep in the dust of the ground" simply means those who have died and were buried. The phrase "will awake" is actually incorrect. The word "will" is not in the original Hebrew text. The translation of the Hebrew word is "to awake" and is frequently translated as a past or present event. The interpreters of the Old Testament inserted the word "will" into the verse forcing the future tense. *The NASB concordance* defines the word "awake" as,

> *<07019a> קִיץ (qits) (884c)*
> **Meaning:** *to awake*
> **Origin:** *a prim. Root*
> **Usage:** *awake(13), awakened(2), awakens(2), awakes(1), awoke(2).*
> **Notes:** [1] *Lit., abhorrence [a] Isa 26:19; Eze 37:12-14 [b] Mat 25:46; Joh 5:28, Joh 5:29*
> *[138]*

If you look at the usage of the Hebrew word in other passages of the Bible, the same word is interpreted in different tenses depending on the context. The following examples show the word can be past tense.

> *Then **Jacob awoke from his sleep** and said, "Surely the LORD is in this place, and I did not know it." (Gen 28:16 NAS)*

> *So David took the spear and the jug of water from beside Saul's head, and they went away, but no one saw or knew it, **nor did any awake**, for they were all asleep, because a sound sleep from the LORD had fallen on them. (1Sa 26:12 NAS)*

Or as present or continual event,

> *The Lord God has given Me the tongue of disciples, That I may know how to sustain the weary one with a word. **He awakens Me** morning by morning, **He awakens My ear** to listen as a disciple. (Isa 50:4 NAS)*

Or as future,

> *As for me, I shall behold Thy face in righteousness; I will be satisfied with Thy likeness **when I awake**. (Psa 17:15 NAS)*

The verse literally should read "many sleeping dust ground awake." The fact is that ALL people who died, past, present, and future raise from the dead or "awake" in the resurrection of the dead. The Bible interpreters inserted the word "will" into the phrase in an attempt to interpret the sentence how they logically understand it. This is not because of malintent or some conspiracy to misinform. They interpreted "awake" as only a future event because the verse is referring to a future prophetic event. It is not necessary to insert the word "will" to understand the meaning of "awake." Simply put, a sleeping person awoke, is awakening, or will awake. "To awake" encompasses all three of those events. All people who die raise from the dead at death and then are judged by God. The statement, "He is not the God of the dead but of the living" in Matthew 22:32 clearly teaches that all people are raised from the dead at death. If the Old Testament believers were not raised from the dead, the transfiguration of Christ would make no sense.

> *And He was transfigured before them; and His face shone like the sun, and His garments became as white as light. And behold, **Moses and Elijah appeared to them**, talking with Him. (Mat 17:2-3 NAS Mar 9:2)*

The word "transfiguration" is defined in *the Oxford Advanced Learner's Dictionary* as

> *A complete change of form or appearance into something more beautiful or spiritual.*
> [139]

The transfiguration of Christ shows how both the heavenly dimension and the earthly dimension coexist with each other. We simply cannot perceive the heavenly dimension without being enabled by God to do so. Moses and Elijah were in the heavenly dimension and were made visible to the disciples on earth. Clearly Moses and Elijah were raised from the dead already, otherwise, they would not be present at the transfiguration of Christ. All people past, present, and future were raised to either everlasting life or everlasting contempt as a result of the messianic work of Christ. The resurrection of the dead only makes sense if it happens at death. It is hard for people to grasp because it is a time transcendent reality. Christ clearly taught the resurrection of the dead occurs at death. It is important to understand that Daniel is not teaching "Soul Sleep." He is teaching the resurrection of the dead as the result of the messianic work of Christ. Soul sleep is discussed further in the chapter on "the Feasts and the end times" in the section on "the Intermediate state."

7. The Day of Atonement

The Day of Atonement is the final judgment upon all people past, present, and future. At death everyone will stand before Christ at the "Day of Judgment." Only believers for whom Christ died will be found innocent; while, the wicked are pronounced unrighteous. In ancient Israel, the Day of Atonement was so important that those who did not observe this day were destroyed from the people. Leviticus says,

> *If there is any person who will not humble himself on this same day, he shall be cut off from his people. As for any person who does any work on this same day, that person I will destroy from among his people. (Lev 23:29-30 NAS Num 29:7-11)*

The concept of the "scapegoat" is critical to understand the Day of Atonement. In Leviticus, the scapegoat was released while the other was slain.

> *And Aaron shall cast lots for the two goats, one lot for the LORD and the other lot for the scapegoat. Then Aaron shall offer the goat on which the lot for the LORD fell, and make it a sin offering. But the goat on which the lot for the scapegoat fell, shall be presented alive before the LORD, to make atonement upon it, to send it into the wilderness as the scapegoat. Then Aaron shall offer the bull of the sin offering which is for himself, and make atonement for himself and for his household, and he shall slaughter the bull of the sin offering which is for himself. (Lev 16:8-11 NAS)*

The sacrifice performed on the Day of Atonement portrays the trial of Christ. The governor of Israel, Pontius Pilate, gave the people the option of releasing Jesus or Barabbas. The release of Barabbas as the scapegoat is a significant piece of the fulfillment of the Day of Atonement in the Law of Moses. Matthew wrote,

> *When therefore they were gathered together, Pilate said to them, "Whom do you want me to release for you? Barabbas, or Jesus who is called Christ?" For he knew that because of envy they had delivered Him up... But the governor answered and said to them, "Which of the two do you want me to release for you?" And they said, "Barabbas." (Mat 27:17-21 NAS)*

The priests were required to take the Sin offering outside of the city. Exodus says,

> *But the flesh of the bull and its hide and its refuse, you shall burn with fire outside the camp; it is a sin offering. (Exo 29:14 NAS)*

Taking the sacrifice outside the camp was fulfilled in the trial and crucifixion of Christ. The writer of Hebrews explains the fulfillment of the Day of Atonement with Christ's sacrifice.

> *For the bodies of those animals whose blood is brought into the holy place by the high priest as an offering for sin, are burned outside the camp. Therefore Jesus also, that He might sanctify the people through His own blood, suffered outside the gate. (Heb 13:11-12 NAS)*

The crucifixion of Christ is central to the fulfillment of the Day of Atonement. Christ's atonement is absolutely necessary for God's people on Judgment Day. If Christ did not die for the sins of His people, everyone will be held accountable for the deeds they did during their life.

a. The day of Judgment

After Christ offered Himself as a sacrifice and ascended to heaven, He sat down at the right hand of God. He will continue at the right hand of God until His enemies are vanquished. Hebrews says,

> *But He, having offered one sacrifice for sins for all time, sat down at the right hand of God, waiting from that time onward until His enemies be made a footstool for His feet. (Heb 10:12-13 NAS)*

It is important to point out that the verse does NOT say Christ sits at the right hand of God until the Nation of Israel is restored on earth. Christ sits at the right hand of God to judge the world. Christ will continue to judge the world during this life and at death. God appointed Christ as Judge of the living and the dead. Luke says,

> *And He ordered us to preach to the people, and solemnly to testify that this is the One who has been appointed by God as Judge of the living and the dead. (Act 10:42 NAS see 1Pe 4:5)*

Everyone will stand before the judgment seat of Christ after death. Nobody will be exempt from being judged according to their deeds. Paul wrote,

> *For to this end Christ died and lived again, that He might be Lord both of the dead and of the living. But you, why do you judge your brother? Or you again, why do you regard your brother with contempt?* ***For we shall all stand before the judgment seat of God.*** *For it is written, "As I live, says the Lord, every knee shall bow to Me, And every tongue shall give praise to God."* ***So then each one of us shall give account of himself to God.*** *(Rom 14:9-12 NAS see 2Ti 4:1)*

Paul is warning people to heed God's commandments NOW in this life. Nobody gets a second chance after death. Because we are judged at death. Judgment is imminent.

> *For we must all appear before the judgment seat of Christ, that each one may be recompensed for his deeds in the body, according to what he has done, whether good or bad. (2Co 5:10 NAS)*

Every deed of every individual person is recorded in books. John saw the books opened and used as a basis for the judgment of the dead.

> *And I saw the dead, the great and the small, standing before the throne, and books were opened; and another book was opened, which is the book of life; and the dead were judged from the things which were written in the books, according to their deeds. And the sea gave up the dead which were in it, and death and Hades gave up the dead which were in them; and they were judged, every one of them according to their deeds. (Rev 20:12-13 NAS)*

The Day of Atonement is fulfilled by Christ sacrificing Himself for His people and sitting at the right hand of God in heaven. Christ exonerates His people at the great Day of Judgment. All the nations will be judged at death.

> *And **all the nations will be gathered before Him; and He will separate them from one another, as the shepherd separates the sheep from the goats**; But when the Son of Man comes in His glory, and all the angels with Him, then He will sit on His glorious throne. "And all the nations will be gathered before Him; and He will separate them from one another, as the shepherd separates the sheep from the goats; and He will put the sheep on His right, and the goats on the left. "Then the King will say to those on His right, 'Come, you who are blessed of My Father, inherit the kingdom prepared for you from the foundation of the world. (Mat 25:31-34 NAS)*

Christ judges the living and the dead from all nations from the beginning of time and will continue to judge till the end of time.

8. The Feast of Booths

The Feast of Booths foreshadows our final Sabbath rest in heaven. The feast originates from the same event the Israelites experienced while in the wilderness with Moses at Mount Sinai. The Israelites were told to live in booths for seven days according to the Law of Moses. This was a ceremonial reminder of what God did for the people in the wilderness. This event foreshadows the place Christ reserved for us in heaven after we die. The "Booths" are replicas of the dwelling places God prepared for us in heaven. This is the heavenly rest we receive at death. The foreshadowing of our heavenly rest is depicted in the Feast of Booths. In the Law of Moses, the Feast of Booths is a perpetual statute throughout your generations.

> *Speak to the sons of Israel, saying, "On the fifteenth of this seventh month is the Feast of Booths for seven days to the LORD. 'On the first day is a holy convocation; you shall do no laborious work of any kind. 'For seven days you shall present an offering by fire to the LORD. On the eighth day you shall have a holy convocation and present an offering by fire to the LORD; it is an assembly. You shall do no laborious work. 'These are the appointed times of the LORD which you shall proclaim as holy convocations, to present offerings by fire to the LORD-- burnt offerings and grain offerings, sacrifices and libations, each day's matter on its own day--'You shall thus celebrate it as a feast to the LORD for seven days in the year.* **It shall be a perpetual statute throughout your generations;** *you shall celebrate it in the seventh month. 'You shall live in booths for seven days; all the native-born in Israel shall live in booths, so that your generations may know that I had the sons of Israel live in booths when I brought them out from the land of Egypt. I am the LORD your God." (Lev 23: 34-37 ,41-43 NAS see Num 29:12-13, Deu 16:13-16)*

Jesus Christ, our high priest, Himself entered the temple "not made with hands." The writer of Hebrews says,

> *But when Christ appeared as a high priest of the good things to come,* ***He entered through the greater and more perfect tabernacle****, not made with hands, that is to say,* ***not of this creation****; and not through the blood of goats and calves, but through His own blood, He entered the holy place* ***once for all****, having obtained eternal redemption. (Heb 9:11-12 NAS)*

This is discussed further in the chapter on "the Feasts and the end times" in the section on "the throne of God." The fulfillment of the sacrifices in the Law of Moses is clearly seen in the messianic work of Christ. The sin offering was burned outside the camp. Exodus says,

> *But the flesh of the bull and its hide and its refuse, you shall burn with fire outside the camp; it is a sin offering. (Exo 29:14 NAS)*

Chapter 8 - The Ceremonial Law fulfilled in Christ

The offering of fire is fulfilled in Christ. The Apostles clearly taught the Ceremonial Laws foreshadowed the work of Christ in His atoning for our sins.

> For the bodies of those animals whose blood is brought into the holy place by the high priest as an offering for sin, are burned outside the camp. Therefore **Jesus also, that He might sanctify the people through His own blood, suffered outside the gate**. Hence, let us go out to Him outside the camp, bearing His reproach. For here we do not have a lasting city, but we are seeking the city which is to come. (Heb 13:11-14 NAS)

Notice the connection between the offering for sin, burning the offering outside the camp, and the seeking the city which is to come. All these events are critical to understand the salvation we have in Christ.

a. Mount Sinai and Mount Zion

The heavenly Mount Zion, the New Jerusalem, is contrasted to the earthly Mount Sinai. Paul allegorically compares Mount Sinai, the present Jerusalem, to Hagar and the New Jerusalem to Sarah.

> **This is allegorically speaking**: for these women are two covenants, one proceeding from Mount Sinai bearing children who are to be slaves; she is Hagar. Now this Hagar is **Mount Sinai in Arabia, and corresponds to the present Jerusalem**, for she is in slavery with her children. But **the Jerusalem above is free; she is our mother**. (Gal 4:24-26 NAS)

The writer of Hebrews allegorically shows how the earthly Mount Sinai is slavery and Mount Zion is freedom. The writer of Hebrews explains,

> For you have not come to a mountain that may be touched and to a blazing fire, and to darkness and gloom and whirlwind... But you have come to Mount Zion and to the city of the living God, the heavenly Jerusalem, and to myriads of angels, to the general assembly and church of the first-born who are enrolled in heaven, and to God, the Judge of all, and to the spirits of righteous men made perfect, and to Jesus, the mediator of a new covenant, and to the sprinkled blood, which speaks better than the blood of Abel. (Heb 12: 18,22-24 NAS)

The Feast of Booths finds its fulfillment in Christ as our Prophet, Priest, and King. Mount Zion, the New Jerusalem is the final Sabbath rest for Gods people. It is freedom from sin and abolishment of death.

b. The City of God

The Feast of Booths foreshadows the City of God in heaven. The New Jerusalem, the City of God, is physically in the dimension of heaven. At death, our final Sabbath rest will be in the sanctuary of the Lord Himself. God the Father has many dwelling places for His people in heaven. Jesus said,

> **In My Father's house are many dwelling places**; if it were not so, I would have told you; **for I go to prepare a place for you**. "And if I go and prepare a place for you, I

> *will come again, and receive you to Myself; that where I am, there you may be also. (Joh 14:2-3 NAS)*

The Apostle Paul makes the connection that when our earthly tent or booth is torn down, we have a house prepared for us in the eternal heavens. Paul wrote,

> *For we know that if the earthly tent which is our house is torn down, **we have a building from God, a house not made with hands, eternal in the heavens**. For indeed in this house we groan, longing to be clothed with our dwelling from heaven; inasmuch as we, having put it on, shall not be found naked. (2Co 5:1-3 NAS)*

The Sabbath rest we receive at death is not simply a future event. The Sabbath rest was, is, and will always be received by all of God's people at death in the past, present, and future. For Jesus Christ was gathering, is gathering, and will continue to gather His elect unto Himself. Jesus Christ, the Eternal Word, created all things past, present, and future to display the glory of His salvation. All things came into being by Christ. John wrote,

> *In the beginning was the Word, and the Word was with God, and the Word was God. He was in the beginning with God. **All things came into being by Him, and apart from Him nothing came into being that has come into being**. (Joh 1:1-3 NAS)*

Jesus said,

> *I am the Alpha and the Omega, says the Lord God, **who is and who was and who is to come**, the Almighty. (Rev 1:8 NAS)*

The phrase "who is and who was and who is to come" shows that Christ is continually coming in the clouds. Christ already came, is coming as we speak, and will continue to come in the future to gather His people from the earth. Only those who overcome until death will be allowed in the City of God. John said,

> ***He who overcomes, I will make him a pillar in the temple of My God**, and he will not go out from it anymore; and I will write upon him the name of My God, and the name of the city of My God, the new Jerusalem, which comes down out of heaven from My God, and My new name (Rev 3:12 NAS)*

The New Jerusalem is described as a bride traveling down the aisle towards her husband. John wrote,

> *And I saw the holy city, new Jerusalem, coming down out of heaven from God, **made ready as a bride adorned for her husband**. And I heard a loud voice from the throne, saying, "Behold, the tabernacle of God is among men, and He shall dwell among them, and they shall be His people, and God Himself shall be among them." (Rev 21:2-3 NAS)*

John saw the city coming down out of heaven. John said,

> *And he carried me away in the Spirit to a great and high mountain, and showed me the holy city, Jerusalem, coming down out of heaven from God. (Rev 21:10 NAS)*

There was no temple in the city because God and the Lamb are the temple. John wrote,

> *And I saw no temple in it, for the Lord God, the Almighty, and the Lamb, are its temple. (Rev 21:22 NAS)*

The New Jerusalem is continually coming down out of heaven. Nowhere does the Bible teach the New Jerusalem lands on earth like a UFO. This is discussed further in the chapter on "the Feasts and the end times." All those who die in Christ go to the New Jerusalem, the City of God. The Feast of Booths foreshadows the dwelling place prepared by God in heaven for His people.

> *For the grace of God has appeared, bringing salvation to all men, instructing us to deny ungodliness and worldly desires and to live sensibly, righteously and godly in the present age, looking for the blessed hope and the appearing of the glory of our great God and Savior, Christ Jesus; who gave Himself for us, that He might redeem us from every lawless deed and purify for Himself a people for His own possession, zealous for good deeds. (Tit 2:11-14 NAS)*

Chapter 9 - The Feasts and the end times

Jesus taught that no one will worship on the mountain or in Jerusalem. True worship will be "in spirit and truth" and not at the temple (Joh 4:24). Jesus told the disciples that ALL the Law of Moses, Prophets, and Psalms were fulfilled by Him. Luke wrote,

> Now He said to them, "These are My words which I spoke to you while I was still with you, that **all things which are written about Me in the Law of Moses and the Prophets and the Psalms must be fulfilled.**" (Luk 24:44 NAS)

According to Christ, "now" is the time when true worship of God began. John wrote,

> Jesus said to her, "Woman, believe Me, an hour is coming when neither in this mountain, nor in Jerusalem, shall you worship the Father. You worship that which you do not know; we worship that which we know, for salvation is from the Jews. **But an hour is coming, and now is, when the true worshipers shall worship the Father in spirit and truth**; for such people the Father seeks to be His worshipers." (Joh 4:21-23 NAS)

When the Feasts are compared to the gospel found in *the Apostles Creed*, it is clear that the last three feasts are an integral part of the gospel. *The Apostles Creed* teaches "the resurrection of the body" occurs at death. The resurrection of the body is directly related to the Feast of Trumpets. Likewise, the judgement of the "living and the dead" is a clear warning that we are judged in this life and after we die. The Day of Atonement is fulfilled in Christ judging the living and the dead. The statement in *the Apostles Creed* "life everlasting" expresses the direct fulfilment of the Feast of Booths. *The Apostles Creed* was written for the purpose of explaining the gospel timeline in an easy to remember format.

The events in *the Apostles Creed* depict the direct fulfillment of the Feasts in Leviticus 23. Table 9.1, "the comparison of the Feasts and *the Apostles Creed*," shows how the feasts correlate to the messianic work of Christ delineated in *the Apostles Creed*. The Day of Atonement has an asterisk because it correlates to two sections in *the Apostles Creed*: "He shall come to judge the living and the dead" and "the resurrection of the body." The Day of Atonement is placed at "He shall come to judge the living and the dead" because all people will be judged according to their deeds they did during their life. The Day of Atonement is also placed after "the resurrection of the body" because the final judgment or the Day of Atonement occurs when we are raised from the dead and judged. The reason the Day of Atonement is split into two sections of *the Apostles Creed* is because *the Apostles Creed* is sectioned into three sections: Father, Son, and Holy Spirit. The Day of Atonement is referring specifically to the work of Christ as judge. *The Apostles creed* places the final judgment in the section about Christ, which is in the middle of the creed. To compensate for the triune structure of *the Apostles creed*, the Day of Atonement is split into two sections in Table 9.1.

Chapter 9 - The Feasts and the end times

Table 9.1 - The comparison of the Feasts and the Apostles Creed		
The Feasts	**The Creed**	**Fulfillment**
1. Sabbath (Lev 23:3)	I believe in God the Father, Almighty, Maker of heaven and earth. (Gen 2:1-4, Heb 4:4)	For if Joshua had given them rest, He would not have spoken of another day after that. There remains therefore a Sabbath rest for the people of God. For the one who has entered His rest has himself also rested from his works, as God did from His. (Heb 4:8-11 NAS)
2. Passover (Lev 23:4-5)	And in Jesus Christ, His only begotten Son, our Lord; Who was conceived by the Holy Spirit, born of the virgin Mary; Suffered under Pontius Pilate; was crucified, (Mat 1:23-24, Mat 26:2, Joh 1:29)	The next day he saw Jesus coming to him, and said, "Behold, the Lamb of God who takes away the sin of the world! (Joh 1:29 NAS)
3. Unleavened Bread (Lev 23:6)	Dead, and buried; He descended into hell; (1 Co 15:3-4)	And when He had taken some bread and given thanks, He broke it, and gave it to them, saying, "This is My body which is given for you; do this in remembrance of Me." ... "This cup which is poured out for you is the new covenant in My blood. (Luk 22:19-20 NAS)
4. First Fruits (Lev 23:7-15)	The third day He rose again from the dead; He ascended into heaven, and sitteth at the right hand of God the Father Almighty (Mar 16:19, Luk 22:69, Act 2:33-34)	In the exercise of His will He brought us forth by the word of truth, so that we might be, as it were, the first fruits among His creatures. (Jam 1:18 NAS Rev 14:4)
* 7. Day of Atonement (Lev 23:26-32)	[Judgment of the living] From thence He shall come to judge the living and the dead. (2 Ti 4:1, 1 Pe 4:5)	For we must all appear before the judgment seat of Christ, that each one may be recompensed for his deeds in the body, according to what he has done, whether good or bad. (2Co 5:10 NAS)
5. Feast of Weeks (Lev 23:16-23)	I believe in the Holy Spirit. I believe a holy catholic Church, the communion of saints; The forgiveness of sins; (Act 2, 1 Ti 3:15, Heb 10:25, Col 1:4)	And it shall be in the last days,' God says, 'That I will pour forth of My Spirit upon all mankind; And your sons and your daughters shall prophesy, And your young men shall see visions, And your old men shall dream dreams; (Act 2:17 NAS)
6. Feast of Trumpets (Lev 23:24)	The resurrection of the body; (Mat 26:64, Joh 11:24-25, 1 Co 15)	in a moment, in the twinkling of an eye, at the last trumpet; for the trumpet will sound, and the dead will be raised imperishable, and we shall be changed. (1Co 15:52 NAS)
* 7. Day of Atonement (Lev 23:26-32)	[Judgment of the dead] From thence He shall come to judge the living and the dead. (2 Ti 4:1, 1 Pe 4:5)	For we must all appear before the judgment seat of Christ, that each one may be recompensed for his deeds in the body, according to what he has done, whether good or bad. (2Co 5:10 NAS)
8. Feast of Booths (Levs 23:34)	And the life everlasting. AMEN. (Mat 25:46, Joh 3:16, Rom 6:23)	For we know that if the earthly tent which is our house is torn down, we have a building from God, a house not made with hands, eternal in the heavens. (2Co 5:1 NAS)

Chapter 9 - The Feasts and the end times

1. The fulfillment of the Law for all time

The messianic work of Christ applies to all of God's people throughout time. His sacrifice on the cross applies to His people past, present, and future for all time. The expression "all time" conveys the concept of all "ages" from the past, present, unto the future. Jude wrote,

> To the only God our Savior, through Jesus Christ our Lord, be glory, majesty, dominion and authority, **before all time and now and forever**. Amen. (Jud 1:25 NAS)

"Before all time and now and forever" means Christ is Lord and Savior from the beginning of creation continually into the future forever. In Jude 1:25, the word "all" is defined as,

> *<3956> πᾶς (pas)*
> **Meaning**: all, every
> **Origin**: a prim. Word
> **Usage**: all(735), all*(1), all kinds(1), all men(21), all respects(3), all things(133),always*(3), any(17), anyone(3), anything*(1), anything(3), constantly*(1), continually*(6), entire(4), every(129), every form(1),every kind(9), every man(2), every respect(1), every way(2), everyone(63), everyone*(1), everyone's(1), everything(43), forever*(1), full(2), great(2), however*(1), no*(11), no one*(5), nothing*(m)(1),nothing(1), perfectly(m)(1), quite(1), whatever(2), whatever*(2), whoever(7), whole(17).
> **Notes**:[1] *Lit., to all the ages* [a] Joh 5:44; 1Ti 1:17 [b] Luk 1:47 [c] Rom 11:36 [d] Heb 13:8 [140]

The expression "all time" in Jude 1:25 is referring to the continuation from the past, through the present, unto the future. The word for "time" in Jude 1:25 is the same as the word "age." *Strong's NASB concordance* defines "age" as "continued duration."

> *<165> αἰών (aion)*
> **Meaning**: a space of time, an age
> **Origin**: from a prim. root appar. mean. continued duration
> **Usage**: age(20), ages(6), ancient time(1), beginning of time(m)(1), course(m)(1), eternal(2),eternity(1), ever*(2), forever(27), forever and ever(20), forevermore(2), never*(8), old(2), time(1), world(m)(7),worlds(m)(1).
> **Notes**: [1] *Lit., to all the ages* [a] Joh 5:44; 1Ti 1:17 [b] Luk 1:47 [c] Rom 11:36 [d] Heb 13:8 [141]

The "futurist" interpretation that the Feast of Trumpets, the Day of Atonement, and the Feast of Booths are to be fulfilled in the earthly Nation of Israel is contrary to all that God has revealed in His scriptures. It nearly denies that Jesus fulfilled the messianic promises in the Old Testament at all. The Atonement of Christ applies to ALL of Gods people, Jews and Gentiles, throughout time. His atonement applies to all the past generations before Christ, to the generations of today, and to all future generations. Salvation in Christ is perfected for all time.

> For by one offering He has perfected **for all time** those who are sanctified. (Heb 10:14 NAS)

God's people in the Old Testament were saved by faith through grace, just like God's people are in the New Testament (Heb 11). The writer of Hebrews wrote,

> Now faith is the assurance of things hoped for, the conviction of things not seen. **For by it the men of old gained approval.** (Heb 11:1-2 NAS)

Faith in the Lord has always been the criteria for salvation. The Bible does not teach a separation between the "dispensation of Law" and the "dispensation of Grace" or "Old Covenant Law" and "New Covenant Law."

a. Christ was "slain from the foundation of the world"

Even though Christ was crucified at a particular time in history, His crucifixion applies throughout eternity. Christ is from eternity where there is no time (2Ti 1:9). In Revelation 13, *the King James Bible* says the lamb was "slain from the foundation of the world." In newer Bible translations, the word order is rearranged to say something different. Because the modern Bible translators do not understand the logic of how Christ was slain from the foundation of the world, they reworded the passage. *The New American Standard Bible* says,

> *All the inhabitants of the earth will worship it, all whose names were not **written from the foundation of the world** in the book of life, which belongs to the Lamb who was slain. (Rev 13:8 NAB)*

The King James version says,

> *And all that dwell upon the earth shall worship him, whose names are not written in the book of life of **the Lamb slain from the foundation of the world**. (Rev 13:8 KJV)*

The King James version is correct. Bible verses that show paradoxes between Christ being eternal and Christ being a man born at a specific time cause confusion in the mind of Bible translators and interpreters. Bible translators reordered the verse to rationalize the text from expressing a paradox. Similarly, people dispute how Christ is begotten from eternity because they can't grasp paradoxes. Christ's atonement for people in the past, present, and future is paradoxical. This is why, in the book of Revelation, John says Christ was "slain from the foundation of the world." Christ's birth, death, resurrection, ascension, and sitting at the right hand of God are applied to all people throughout all time. In other words, Christ's crucifixion happened at a specific time in history and at the same time is from eternity. The phrase "the Lamb slain from the foundation of the world" holds the same meaning that Christ is begotten from eternity. Many object to the doctrine that Christ was begotten from eternity. Likewise, the doctrine of predestination is an eternal reality. God predestined the actions of all creation by creating it and governing it by His providence. Yet, at the same time, all of creation works according to its own free will. This discussion is extensive and is reserved for another book. For now, it is important to understand that Christ is from eternity; therefore, all His actions apply equally to eternity. This is an interdimensional reality. Interdimensional theology is discussed further in this chapter. The purpose of mentioning this now is to show that ALL people are saved by the messianic work of Christ throughout all ages. This is purely Christocentric theology.

b. Old Testament Saints were saved by faith in Christ

Living by faith in Gods promises of redemption is how the saints of old obtained salvation. Habakkuk wrote,

> Behold, as for the proud one, His soul is not right within him; **But the righteous will live by his faith**. (Hab 2:4 NAS)

The righteous have always lived by faith. Paul quoted Habakkuk saying,

> For in it the righteousness of God is revealed from faith to faith; as it is written, "**But the righteous man shall live by faith**." (Rom 1:17 NAS)

The writer of Hebrews explains this by showing that the Old Testament believers lived by faith in Christ. They did not receive the earthly promises because they received the heavenly promises in Christ. All of God's people in the Old Testament died having faith in the promises of God. Hebrews says,

> All these died in faith, without receiving the promises, but having seen them and having welcomed them from a distance, and having confessed that they were strangers and exiles on the earth. For those who say such things make it clear that they are seeking a country of their own. And indeed if they had been thinking of that country from which they went out, they would have had opportunity to return. **But as it is, they desire a better country, that is a heavenly one. Therefore God is not ashamed to be called their God; for He has prepared a city for them.** (Heb 11:13-16 NAS)

Their faith was not in earthly promises, but in the promises of a better place, the City of God. This is vastly different than teaching the promises of God are for the restoration of the earthly Nation of Israel. Hebrews says,

> And all these, having gained approval through their faith, did not receive what was promised, **because God had provided something better for us**, so that apart from us they should not be made perfect. (Heb 11:39-40 NAS)

> But you have come to Mount Zion and to the city of the living God, the heavenly Jerusalem, and to myriads of angels. (Heb 12:22 NAS)

The promises are received at death when Christ raises us from the dead. This can be clearly seen in the transfiguration of Christ. Moses and Elijah were not asleep in the grave waiting for the future resurrection. They received the promises of God when they were resurrected from the dead at death. Moses and Elijah appeared to Christ and the Apostles (Mat 17:2-3; Mar 9:4). Prior to the historical event of the crucifixion of Christ, the promises of heaven, the New Jerusalem, and judgment was clearly received by Moses and Elijah at death. Christ's explanation of the rich man and Lazarus proves the resurrection of the dead happens at death. The angels carried Lazarus to heaven where he was embraced by Abraham.

> Now it came about that **the poor man died and he was carried away by the angels to Abraham's bosom; and the rich man also died and was buried. And in Hades he**

> *lifted up his eyes, being in torment, and saw Abraham far away, and Lazarus in his bosom. (Luk 16:22-23 NAS)*

The language Christ used about Lazarus being carried away by angels is similar to the language He used about the angels gathering God's elect from the earth.

> *And **He will send forth His angels** with a great trumpet and **they will gather together His elect** from the four winds, from one end of the sky to the other. (Mat 24:31 NAS Mar 13:27)*

The fulfillment of the Law is a time transcendent reality. The messianic work of Christ does not only apply to those after the crucifixion. Christ dying for the sins of His people applies to all of God's people throughout all history.

2. Differing views on the fulfillment of the feasts

It is necessary to mention different views to fully understand just exactly how the final Sabbath rest applies to our world. As seen in the chapters on Sabbatarian and Antinomian theology, how the Law of God is taught effects how the Christian applies the Sabbath to their life. How the Law of God is interpreted effects Christian end times doctrines. The main end times or "eschatological" views are the Futurist, Historicist, Preterist, and Idealist. The Idealist view will not be discussed in this book because it is a nonliteral interpretation of the Bible. I will only consider literal interpretations of the Bible. Nonliteral interpretations are purely allegorical and do not use proper deductive reasoning. Allegorical interpretations can lead to any interpretation that has no foundation in reason.

Comparing the Futurist, Historicist, and Preterist views with the view proposed in this book will show how the Sabbath applies to Christ's kingdom. Comparing these views will help the reader to understand the concept in this book. The different views represented here are general view points and not an exhaustive list. I have no intent to perfectly represent every theological viewpoint. These are included as a brief overview. The purpose for comparing these views is to explain Interdimensional theology in relation to the fulfillment of the feasts. The weekly Sabbath is not included as a feast in the Futurist, Historicist, and Preterist views. The views are graphically compared in Appendix III "Comparison of End Times Doctrines."

a. The Futurist

The main proponents of Futurist theology are the Dispensationalists referred to in the chapter on "Antinomian Non-Sabbatarian." Futurist theology is the Biblical hermeneutic that interprets prophecies in the Bible as being fulfilled in future events. The Dispensationalist Futurist view teaches the feasts of Passover, Unleavened Bread, First Fruits, and Weeks are fulfilled but the feasts of Trumpets, Atonement, and Booths have a future fulfilment. Clarence Larkin wrote,

> *The First Four Feasts foreshadow truths connected with this present Gospel Dispensation and those who form the "heavenly" people of the Lord, the Church; while **the Last Three Feasts foreshadow the blessings in store for God's "earthly" people, the Jews**. [142]*

Chapter 9 - The Feasts and the end times

Dispensationalists believe the feasts are fulfilled in the earthly Nation of Israel only and not the Church. This teaching makes the prophecies about the kingdom of Christ and the Law not applicable to the Church. Dispensationalists like Clarence Larkin taught the earthly kingdom was postponed due to the Jews rejecting Christ. This means Dispensationalists believe that the Nation of Israel is a separate entity from the Church. This makes the fulfillment of the promises of God realized only in the earthly restoration of the Nation of Israel. According to this view, the coming of Christ and the resurrection of the dead are a onetime future event. Dispensationalists believe the soul goes to heaven while the body stays in the ground till the second coming of Christ. *The Niagara Creed* states,

> *We believe that **the souls of those who have trusted in the Lord Jesus Christ for salvation do at death immediately pass into His presence, and there remain in conscious bliss until the resurrection of the body at His coming, when soul and body reunited shall be associated with Him forever in the glory**; but the souls of unbelievers remain after death in conscious misery until the final judgment of the great white throne at the close of the millennium, when soul and body reunited shall be cast into the lake of fire, not to be annihilated, but to be punished with everlasting destruction from the presence of the Lord, and from the glory of His power. [143]*

The "Rapture" doctrine that the Church is taken to heaven before the "second coming of Christ" is a central theme in Dispensational Futurist theology. Futurists believe the Feast of Trumpets, the Day of Atonement, and the Feast of Booths are fulfilled at the restoration of the Nation of Israel in the future.

b. The Historicist

There are many different Christian groups that ascribe to Historicist interpretation of the end times. Historicist theology is the Biblical hermeneutic that interprets prophecies in the Bible as being fulfilled in stages through historical events. The Reformed churches (See the chapter on "First Day Sabbatarian") like the Presbyterian Church of Scotland and the Reformed Baptist church teach Historicist theology. An example of the Historicist point of view is in *the Reformed Baptist Confession of 1689*. The *Reformed Baptist Confession of 1689* teaches the Pope is the historical fulfillment of the "antichrist."

> *The Lord Jesus Christ is the Head of the church, in whom, by the appointment of the Father, all power for the calling, institution, order or government of the church, is invested in a supreme and sovereign manner; neither can **the Pope of Rome** in any sense be head thereof, but **is that antichrist, that man of sin, and son of perdition, that exalteth himself in the church against Christ**, and all that is called God; whom the Lord shall destroy with the brightness of his coming. [144]*

The Seventh Day Adventist church also teaches Historicist theology.

> *We affirm that the apocalyptic books of Daniel and Revelation are foundational for the understanding of biblical eschatology and **that the historicist method is the proper approach to interpreting them**. [145]*

Chapter 9 - The Feasts and the end times

The Historicist view that the fulfillment of prophecy occurs through historic events can be confused as a Futurist view. In general, the difference between the Historicist and Futurist view is in the separation of Israel and the Church. Historicists typically believe that the Church is the continuance of Israel or that Israel is the Old Testament church. Historicists, similar to Futurists, also believe Passover, the Feast of Unleavened Bread, the Feast of First Fruits, and the Feast of Weeks are fulfilled in the messianic work of Christ. They typically teach that the Feast of Trumpets, the Day of Atonement, and the Feast of Booths are to be fulfilled in the future. They believe that prophecies are fulfilled through historical events and that some Bible prophecies still have a future fulfillment. This is why the SDA Church places the Sabbath as a central issue in the fulfillment of prophecy in history. Historicists typically teach the souls of the dead wait until the resurrection of the dead at the coming of Christ in judgment at the last day. According to most Historicists, this is when the Feast of Trumpets, the Day of Atonement, and the Feast of Booths are fulfilled.

c. The Preterist

Preterist theology is the Biblical hermeneutic that interprets prophecies in the Bible as being fulfilled in past historical events. There are different types of Preterists. There are "full" and "partial" Preterists. Even though Preterist theology is ascribed to Roman Catholic Jesuit Luis de Alcasar, most Preterists are not Roman Catholic. Preterist theologians come from many different backgrounds. John Gill (Baptist), Kenneth Gentry (Reformed), and Nicholas Thomas Wright (Anglican) are Preterist theologians. Reformed Preterists typically teach all the feasts are fulfilled in Christ on earth and finished at the destruction of Jerusalem in AD 70. In general, Preterists see the Nation of Israel as the physical kingdom and the church is the spiritual kingdom. While it is true not all Preterists are Roman Catholic, the Preterist teaching goes hand in hand with the Roman Catholic teaching of the Mass. The Roman Catholic view is a partial Preterist view. Roman Catholics teach the church is the continuing of the sacrifices and feasts of Israel in the bread and the wine on earth or the "Eucharist." The assembly of the people to receive the sacrament of the Eucharist is an ongoing earthly fulfillment of the feasts in the Law of Moses. The Roman Catechism states,

> *The Holy Sacrifice, because it makes present the one sacrifice of Christ the Savior and includes the Church's offering.* **The terms holy sacrifice of the Mass,** *"sacrifice of praise," spiritual sacrifice, pure and holy sacrifice are also used,* **since it completes and surpasses all the sacrifices of the Old Covenant**. *[146]*

The official Roman Catholic end times view would fit into a partial Preterist view because they believe in a second coming and an earthly reign of Christ at the end of the world. *The Roman Catholic Catechism* states,

> *Though already present in his Church, Christ's reign is nevertheless yet to be fulfilled "with power and great glory" by the King's return to earth. [147]*

Full Preterists typically teach that the "second coming of Christ," the resurrection of the dead, and the last judgment happened at the destruction of Jerusalem in AD 70. This view typically teaches all the feasts were ultimately fulfilled historically in AD 70. According to full Preterist theology, the Feast of Trumpets was fulfilled at the destruction of Jerusalem in AD 70.

> *Almost four months after the Pentecost, though not at a precise interval, the feast of Trumpets was a day of rest celebrated with trumpet blasts and sacrifices when the nation was presented before God. This prefigured the time when the Lord came down from heaven with the trumpet call of God. This was fulfilled in 70 AD.* [148]

Preterists also teach that the Feast of Booths was fulfilled in AD 70.

> *The feast of tabernacles commemorated their wandering forty years in the wilderness, but foreshadowed when they were given a judgment period of 40 years to repent before the destruction of Jerusalem.* [149]

In general, the Preterist view interprets the feasts as either being fulfilled in the destruction of Jerusalem in AD 70 or continued in the Sacraments and feasts of the Church on earth.

d. The Interdimensional

"Interdimensional theology" is particular to the theology presented in this book. Interdimensional theology is the Biblical hermeneutic that interprets the feasts of Leviticus 23 as being fulfilled in heaven and on earth. In other words, some prophecies are fulfilled in the earthly realm and some are fulfilled in the heavenly realm. These realms are different dimensions of space. The dimensions discussed are referring to spatial dimensions. These dimensions are "extra dimensions." Think of the earthly realm as a third dimension (3D) and the heavenly realm as a fourth dimension (4D). The idea that creatures from one dimension being unable to perceive creatures from another dimension is explained in the book *Flatland: A Romance of Many Dimensions (by a Square)* [150]. In the book, Edwin Abbott describes the relationship between a flat square (2D) from "Flatland" and a sphere (3D) from "Spaceland." The square could not perceive the sphere in 3D and could only see the sphere as flat until the sphere brough the square to "Spaceland." In the same way, people in the earthly dimension cannot perceive the heavenly dimension unless someone from heaven brings them there. The dimensions of heaven and earth are distinct yet correlative spatial dimensions. *The Oxford Advanced Learner's Dictionary* defines "spatial" as,

> *Relating to space and the position, size, shape, etc. of things in it.* [151]

The theology in this book is Interdimensional theology because it teaches that the earthly and heavenly dimensions coincide with each other yet are separate from each other. The Interdimensional view teaches that Christ fulfilled the feasts of Passover, Unleavened Bread, First Fruits, and Weeks in the earthly dimension and the feasts of Trumpets, Atonement, and Booths and the weekly Sabbath in the heavenly dimension; yet, all the feasts are of the heavenly dimension, which is eternity. Interdimensional theology is purely "Christocentric." Interdimensional theology focuses on Christ as the center of all the Old Testament promises. "Christocentric" is defined as,

> *Of systems of theology which maintain that God has never revealed Himself to humanity except in the Incarnate Christ.* [152]

The Interdimensional view maintains that all Scripture is specifically magnifying the Eternal Word of God, Jesus Christ. For example, in Genesis, the Lord Jesus Christ walked in the garden with Adam.

> *And they heard the sound of the LORD God walking in the garden in the cool of the day, and the man and his wife hid themselves from the presence of the LORD God among the trees of the garden. (Gen 3:8 NAS)*

The Lord who walked in the garden is Jesus Christ, the Eternal Word of God. He was, is and will always be the Lord.

> *I am the Alpha and the Omega, says the Lord God, who is and who was and who is to come, the Almighty. (Rev 1:8 NAS)*

Jesus Christ physically existed before eternity. This is also known as being "begotten from eternity." He revealed Himself physically from the beginning before He was born of the virgin in our historical timeline. Our present earthly dimension coincides with the heavenly dimension. For now, it is only necessary to understand that the heavenly dimension occupies the same location as the earthly dimension but a different space and time. Those in the earthly dimension cannot physically perceive the heavenly dimension. The earthly and heavenly dimensions are depicted in the graphic "Interdimensional Theology – The Christocentric Kingdom of God" in Appendix IV.

3. The Intermediate State

Many Christian theologians teach that there is a temporary holding place where the souls of the righteous and/or unrighteous wait until the "second coming of Christ." These teachings are manifested in the doctrines of soul sleep, purgatory, and Abraham's bosom. The fulfillment of our Sabbath rest in Christ is NOT received in any Intermediate State. The SDA Church teaches that all souls who die sleep in the grave till the second coming of Christ at the last day. *The 28 Fundamental Beliefs of the Seventh Day Adventist Church* states,

> *The wages of sin is death. But God, who alone is immortal, will grant eternal life to His redeemed.* **Until that day death is an unconscious state for all people.** *When Christ, who is our life, appears, the resurrected righteous and the living righteous will be glorified and caught up to meet their Lord.* [153]

The Westminster Confession of Faith teaches the souls of the righteous wait in heaven while the unrighteous wait in hell until the second coming of Christ. This is similar to the Dispensationalist view. *The Westminster Confession of Faith* states,

> *The bodies of men, after death, return to dust, and see corruption: but their souls, which neither die nor sleep, having an immortal subsistence, immediately return to God who gave them:* **the souls of the righteous, being then made perfect in holiness, are received into the highest heavens,** *where they behold the face of God, in light and glory,* **waiting for the full redemption of their bodies**. *And the* **souls of the wicked are cast into hell**, *where they remain in torments and utter darkness,*

> ***reserved to the judgment of the great day.*** *Beside these two places, for souls separated from their bodies, the Scripture acknowledges none. [154]*

Many Reformed Theologians teach there is a heavenly waiting place for believers called "Abraham's Bosom" while the unrighteous wait in "Hades." This is similar to the Roman Catholic teaching of Abraham's Bosom. *The Roman Catholic Catechism* states,

> *Scripture calls the abode of the dead, to which the dead Christ went down, "hell" - Sheol in Hebrew or Hades in Greek - because those who are there are deprived of the vision of God. Such is the case for all the dead, whether evil or righteous, while they await the Redeemer: which does not mean that their lot is identical, as Jesus shows through the parable of the poor man Lazarus who was received into "Abraham's bosom":* ***"It is precisely these holy souls, who awaited their Savior in Abraham's bosom, whom Christ the Lord delivered when he descended into hell."*** *Jesus did not descend into hell to deliver the damned, nor to destroy the hell of damnation, but to free the just who had gone before him. [155]*

The Roman Catholic church also teaches that there is a final "purification for sins" for God's elect in purgatory before entering heaven. *The Roman Catholic Catechism* states,

> *All who die in God's grace and friendship, but still imperfectly purified, are indeed assured of their eternal salvation; but* ***after death they undergo purification,*** *so as to achieve the holiness necessary to enter the joy of heaven. [156]*

The teaching of purgatory also has its roots in the "Prayer for the Dead." Mormons or the Church of Latter-Day Saints (LDS) also practice "Baptism for the Dead" in a similar way that the Roman Catholic Church teaches Prayers for the Dead. The LDS church is a non-Christian cult so they are not addressed in this book. The Roman Catholic Church teaches to pray for the dead who are in purgatory for the hope they may be delivered from the intermediate state.

> *This teaching is also based on the practice of prayer for the dead, already mentioned in Sacred Scripture: "Therefore Judas [Maccabeus] made atonement for the dead, that they might be delivered from their sin." [157]*

The Bible teaches nothing about any intermediate State. The writer of Hebrews articulates the view of the Apostles clearly stating,

> *And inasmuch as it is appointed* ***for men to die once and after this comes judgment****, so Christ also, having been offered once to bear the sins of many, shall appear a second time for salvation without reference to sin, to those who eagerly await Him. (Heb 9:27-28 NAS)*

After death comes judgment. There is no waiting period for the dead for a future distant judgment. This means that the Sabbath rest for God's people is received at death. The passage where theologians derive the Abraham's bosom doctrine is in Luke 16. Luke 16 says nothing about waiting for a future judgment. On the contrary, the judgment is shown to occur at death.

> *Now it came about that the poor **man died and he was carried away** by the angels to Abraham's bosom; and **the rich man also died and was buried**. And in Hades he lifted up his eyes, **being in torment**, and saw Abraham far away, and Lazarus in his bosom. (Luk 16:22-23 NAS)*

The statement "he was carried to Abraham's bosom" is merely showing that Lazarus was embraced by Abraham and welcomed into heaven immediately after death. Likewise, the rich man was immediately sent to hell. All those who are sent to hell will be in the presence of the angels and God for eternity.

> *He also will drink of the wine of the wrath of God, which is mixed in full strength in the cup of His anger; and **he will be tormented with fire and brimstone in the presence of the holy angels and in the presence of the Lamb**. And the smoke of their torment goes up forever and ever; and they have no rest day and night, those who worship the beast and his image, and whoever receives the mark of his name. (Rev 14:10-11 NAS)*

Clearly the resurrection of the dead occurs at death. Luke clearly taught that all those who are sent to hell will see God's people in heaven.

> *There will be weeping and gnashing of teeth there when **you see Abraham and Isaac and Jacob and all the prophets in the kingdom of God, but yourselves being cast out**. (Luk 13:28 NAS)*

Our Sabbath rest in Christ is received at death. There is no waiting period for the righteous or the unrighteous for a future judgment after death found anywhere in the Bible.

4. The Seventy Weeks of Daniel

The Seventy Weeks prophecy of Daniel 9 is pivotal to the fulfillment of the feasts, festivals, new moons, sabbaths, and sacrifices of the Ceremonial Law. This is graphically represented in Appendix IV "Interdimensional Theology - The Christocentric Kingdom of God." The fulfillment of the Ceremonial Law is crucial in understanding the Fourth Commandment "to keep the Sabbath holy." Jesus warned the people that the prophecy of Daniel was being fulfilled as Jesus spoke to the disciples (Mat 24:15; Mar 13:14). The prophesy of Daniel clearly teaches that the sacrifices were to cease forever with the establishment of Christ's eternal kingdom. Daniel wrote,

> *Seventy weeks have been decreed for your people and your holy city, to finish the transgression, to make an end of sin, to make atonement for iniquity, to bring in everlasting righteousness, to seal up vision and prophecy, and to anoint the most holy place. (Dan 9:24 NAS)*

The "regular sacrifice" was "abolished" (Dan 12:11) with the coming of the Messiah and ultimately realized with the destruction of the ancient Nation of Israel at the Battle of Masada. The Seventy Weeks prophecy of Daniel starts with the decree of the Persian king Cyrus' to restore the temple.

Chapter 9 - The Feasts and the end times

> *So you are to know and discern that **from the issuing of a decree to restore and rebuild Jerusalem** until Messiah the Prince there will be seven weeks and sixty-two weeks; it will be built again, with plaza and moat, even in times of distress. (Dan 9:25 NAS)*

As discussed in the chapter on "the Calendar," the historical timeline of the Persian Empire is incalculable. No one knows exactly what the date was when Cyrus made the decree. Cyrus issued the decree when he released the Israelites from captivity in Babylon.

> *However, in the first year of Cyrus king of Babylon, **King Cyrus issued a decree to rebuild this house of God**. (Ezr 5:13 NAS)*

The word "week" is an incorrect translation of the Hebrew text. The correct definition of the original Hebrew text is "a period of seven." *The NASB Concordance* states,

<07620> שָׁבוּעַ *(shabua) (988d)*
Meaning: *a period of seven (days, years), heptad, week*
Origin: *from 7651*
Usage: *seven(1), week(4), weeks(10), Weeks(5) [158]*

The Hebrew word is translated as "week" in Genesis when it actually means a period of seven years. An example of this is when Jacob swore to serve Laban for seven years in order to marry Rachel.

> *Now Laban had two daughters; the name of the older was Leah, and the name of the younger was Rachel. And Leah's eyes were weak, but Rachel was beautiful of form and face. Now Jacob loved Rachel, so he said, "**I will serve you seven years** for your younger daughter Rachel." (Gen 29:16-18 NAS)*

Laban's response to Jacob in serving "seven years" is translated as completing "the week" which in the same context is counted as seven years.

> *But Laban said, "It is not the practice in our place, to marry off the younger before the first-born. "**Complete the week of this one**, and we will give you the other also for the service which **you shall serve with me for another seven years**." And Jacob did so and completed her week, and he gave him his daughter Rachel as his wife. (Gen 29:26-28 NAS)*

The definition of the Hebrew word is not "week" or "weeks" but "a period of seven." The "weeks" spoken of in Daniel is a period of seven years and not seven days. The reason why the duration of the "week" is not counted in days is because the date the Israelites were released from captivity was sometime between 516 BC and 416 BC depending on how the calendar is interpreted. The inaccuracy of dates is discussed earlier in the chapter on "the Calendar." If the duration is counted in days, the seventy weeks would be 490 days and not 490 years. 490 days is approximately 1.3 years. That would mean the messiah was "cut off" or crucified 1.2 years after Cyrus' decree. That would place the crucifixion of Christ approximately between 514 BC and 414 BC. The interpretation of weeks as days is completely incompatible with Biblical facts. First, the ancient Israelites did not occupy the land of Israel in that time frame. The second and most obvious fact is that Jesus' crucifixion was approximately between AD 18 and AD 36 which is hundreds of years after the decree from Cyrus.

The word "week" is used solely for the purpose of counting by the numeric value of 7. After the decree of Cyrus, sixty-two weeks or 62 times 7 years for a total of 434 years is counted to the crucifixion of Christ (Dan 9:25; Ezr 5:13). Daniel foretells the crucifixion of Christ in the phrase "Messiah will be cut off."

> *Then after the **sixty-two weeks the Messiah will be cut off** and have nothing, and the people of the prince who is to come will destroy the city and the sanctuary. And its end will come with a flood; even to the end there will be war; desolations are determined. (Dan 9:26 NAS)*

The final 8 weeks or 56 years after the "Messiah is cut off" is a total of 490 years. During the last week or last 7 years, "in the middle of the week," 486 ½ years after the decree of Cyrus, the sacrifices were to stop forever.

> *And he will make a firm covenant with the many for one week, but **in the middle of the week he will put a stop to sacrifice** and grain offering; and on the wing **of abominations will come one who makes desolate**, even until a complete destruction, one that is decreed, is poured out on the one who makes desolate. (Dan 9:27 NAS)*

Sacrifices stopped when the Romans destroyed Jerusalem in AD 70 also known as the "abomination that makes desolate" (Dan 9:27). Three and a half years after the destruction of the temple in AD 70 the ancient Nation of Israel was ended at the Battle of Masada in AD 74. This was the end of the Seventy Weeks prophecy for a total of 490 years from the decree of Cyrus (Dan 12:11; Ezr 5:13). Because Josephus chronicled the destruction of Jerusalem by the Romans, he established the date of AD 70 as the reference point for the destruction of Jerusalem based on the Julian calendar. The desolation of the Jewish temple and the demise of the ancient Nation of Israel is the final outcome of the fulfillment of the Seventy Weeks prophesy.

a. This generation will not pass till all is fulfilled

Jesus clearly taught that Daniels seventy weeks occurred during the generation of those whom He was speaking. Jesus told the people during His time that they will witness the abomination of desolation spoken by Daniel. In Matthew 24, Luke 21, and Mark 13, Christ specifically told everyone Daniels prophesy was to be fulfilled with "this generation."

> *Therefore when **you see** the abomination of desolation which was spoken of through Daniel the prophet, standing in the holy place (let the reader understand). (Mat 24:15 NAS See Mar 13 and Luk 21)*

> *"Truly I say to you, **this generation will not pass away** until all these things take place. (Mat 24:34 NAS See Mar 13 and Luk 21)*

Chapter 9 - The Feasts and the end times

Jerusalem's destruction occurred during the generation of the time of Christ. This is an indisputable fact. The fact that Jesus said, "this generation will not pass away until all these things take place" is completely ignored or rationalized by Futurist and Historicist theologians. For example, Clarence Larkin interprets the word "generation" to mean the "Jewish race." Clarence Larkin wrote,

> *Now learn a Parable of the 'FIG-TREE.' When his branch is yet tender, and putteth forth LEAVES, ye know that summer is nigh: so likewise ye, when ye shall see all these things, know that it (He, R.V.), is near, even at the doors. Verily I say unto you,* **This GENERATION (the word means 'Race'-JEWISH RACE)** *shall not pass, till all these things be fulfilled. Heaven and earth shall pass away, but my words shall not pass away. Matt. 24:32-34.* [159]

Rationalizing the phrase "this generation" as referring to some faraway group of people and not those during the time of Christ is unacceptable. The word generation in the Old Testament never means "Jewish race." A generation is specifically the period of time a specific group of people exists. Ecclesiastes shows this clearly.

> *A generation goes and a generation comes, But the earth remains forever. (Ecc 1:4 NAS)*

The NASB Concordance defines the Hebrew word for "generation" as,

> **<01755>** דּוֹר *or* דֹּר *(dor or dor) (189c)*
> **Meaning:** *period, generation, dwelling*
> **Origin:** *from 1752*
> **Usage:** *age-old(1), all generations(20), another(1), dwelling(1), every generation(1), forever(m)(1), generation(53), generations(52), kind(m)(4), many generations(3), time(m)(2)* [160]

Never does the word "generation" mean the "Jewish race" in the Old Testament. In the New Testament, there is no reason we should believe the word "generation" would change from the Old Testament. While the Greek word can be used to mean "race," there is no possible way to equate the word "race" with "Jewish race." The word "race" is generic for any race. *The NASB concordance* defines the Greek word for "generation" as,

> **<1074>** γενεά *(genea)*
> **Meaning:** *race, family, generation*
> **Origin:** *from 1096*
> **Usage:** *generation(32), generations(10), kind(m)(1)* [161]

The fact that the word "generation" is preceded by the word "this" clearly qualifies the word "generation" as relating to the people whom Christ was speaking. *The NASB Concordance* defines the word "this" as,

> **<3778>** οὗτος *or* αὕτη *or* τοῦτο *(houtos, haute, touto)*
> **Meaning:** *this (demonstrative pron.)*
> **Origin:** *from 3588 and 846*

> ***Usage:*** *afterward*(3), consequently*(2), especially(1), follow*(1), here*(1), hereafter*(1),now*(1), one(1), one whom(1), partly*(1), present(m)(1), same(1), so(1), so*(1), some(2), such(m)(2), that man(1), the fact that(2), then*(1), therefore*(17), these(178), these men(12), these things(193), this(735), this man(52), this Man(3), this man's(1), this Man's(1), this one(3), this One(1), this thing(3), this way(1), this woman(4), those(2), those things(1), thus(1), very(3), very thing(2), who(2), whom(m)(1) [162]*

The word "this" is always referring to a near event. *The Oxford Advanced Learner's Dictionary* defines the word "this" as,

> *Used to refer to a particular person, thing or event that is close to you, especially compared with another. [163]*

Clarence Larkin is clearly manipulating the definition of the word "generation" in order to support his Futurist theology. The Futurist argument is a semantic ambiguity that destroys the literal meaning of Christ's statement. The Futurist interpretation is unacceptable and leads to many false prophecies. One only need to watch the plethora of "end times" movies like the *Left Behind series*, the *Mark*, or the *Thief in the Night* that espouse hysterical interpretations of the Bible. Even worse, people's lives have been ruined and many have apostatized from the faith because of Futurist and Historicist interpretations. An example of this is the Millerite movement in 1844. The Baptist preacher William Miller proclaimed Jesus Christ was coming back to earth (called the "Advent" of Christ) in 1844. Many of the followers of Miller sold their possessions and waited for Christ to come back. When Christ did not return as promised by Miller, many apostatized from Christianity completely. This became known as "the Great Disappointment." Miller completely wrecked the faith of many with his second coming of Christ theology. The Seventh Day Adventist church came out of the ashes of the Millerite movement. Historicist and Futurist end times interpretations have produced many false prophecies and have wrecked the faith of many. Examples of false predictions are found in Isaac Newton's *Observations upon the Prophecies of Daniel, and the Apocalypse of St. John*, Ed Dobson's *The End: Why Jesus Could Return by A.D. 2000*, Harold Camping's *1994?*, and Edgar C. Whisenant's *89 Reasons Why the Rapture will be in 1989*. There are many hysterical Futurist and Historicist interpretations of the second coming of Christ throughout history. Christ clearly taught to not believe anyone who claims to predict the coming of Christ.

> Then ***if anyone says to you, 'Behold, here is the Christ,' or 'There He is,' do not believe him.*** *For false Christs and false prophets will arise and will show great signs and wonders, so as to mislead, if possible, even the elect. Behold,* ***I have told you in advance****. If therefore they say to you, 'Behold, He is in the wilderness,' do not go forth, or, 'Behold, He is in the inner rooms,'* ***do not believe them****. (Mat 24:23-26 NAS)*

As discussed in the chapter on "the Calendar," it is impossible to set any date accurately. The abomination of desolation officially took place at the destruction of Jerusalem in AD 70. This does not mean the "second coming of Christ" is a single event that took place at AD 70. The Seventy Weeks prophecy of Daniel unlocks the entire fulfillment of the Ceremonial Laws, especially the sacrifices. To change Christ's interpretation of Daniels prophesy as not occurring during His time, makes Christ a liar.

> *May it never be! Rather, let God be found true, though every man be found a liar, as it is written, "That Thou mightest be justified in Thy words, And mightest prevail when Thou art judged." (Rom 3:4 NAS)*

Christ told the absolute truth about the timing of the abomination of desolation. The end of the Jewish war and the demise of the ancient Nation of Israel is ultimately realized in the Battle of Masada circa AD 74. This was the absolute finality of all the Old Testament prophecies concerning the sabbaths, new moons, and sacrifices in the Old Testament. The fulfillment of Daniels seventy weeks prophecy in the destruction of Jerusalem in AD 70 is historically and Biblically accurate.

b. The daily sacrifices were prophesied to cease

Moses set up the Ceremonial Laws according to specific times for the remembrance of the promises of God. God ordained the ancient Nation of Israel as the keepers of the promise of the Messiah, Jesus Christ. This is because Christ was to come from the genealogy of David (Mat 1; Luk 1; Act 2:25-35). Once Christ fulfilled the promises in sacrificing Himself for the people, there is no necessity to keep the festivals, new moons, and sabbaths anymore. They are fulfilled in Christ. In Daniel chapter 8, the regular sacrifice and the sanctuary is prophesied to be thrown down. Daniel wrote,

> *It even magnified itself to be equal with the Commander of the host; and **it removed the regular sacrifice from Him, and the place of His sanctuary was thrown down**. And on account of transgression the host will be given over to the horn along with the regular sacrifice; and it will fling truth to the ground and perform its will and prosper. (Dan 8:11-12 NAS)*

Daniel prophesied that the sacrifices and offerings will stop and complete destruction will come. Daniel wrote,

> *And he will make a firm covenant with the many for one week, but in the middle of the week **he will put a stop to sacrifice and grain offering**; and on the wing of abominations will come one who makes desolate, **even until a complete destruction**, one that is decreed, is poured out on the one who makes desolate. (Dan 9:27 NAS)*

Daniel prophesied again in chapter 11 saying the regular sacrifice will stop. Daniel said,

> *And forces from him will arise, desecrate the sanctuary fortress, and **do away with the regular sacrifice**. And they will set up the abomination of desolation. (Dan 11:31 NAS)*

Daniel further says in chapter 12 that the sacrifice is "abolished" (NASB) or "taken away" (KJV) and the land is desolated. Daniel wrote,

> *And from the time that the regular sacrifice is **abolished**, and the abomination of desolation is set up, **there will be 1,290 days**. (Dan 12:11 NAS)*
>
> *And from the time that the daily sacrifice shall be **taken away**, and the abomination that maketh desolate set up, **there shall be a thousand two hundred and ninety days**. (Dan 12:11 KJV)*

The word "abolished" is not a good translation. "Turned aside" is the correct translation. *The NASB concordance* translates the Hebrew word as,

> *<05493> סוּר or שׂוּר (sur or sur) (693b)*
> ***Meaning:*** *to turn aside*
> ***Origin:*** *a prim. Root*
> ***Usage:*** *abolished(1), avoid(1), beheaded*(1), cut off(m)(1), degenerate(1), depart(46), departed(7), deposed(1), deprives(2), do away with(1), escape(m)(1), get out(1), go away(1), gone(1), keep away(1), keeps away(1), lacks(1), leave*(2), left(1), left undone*(1), move(1), pardoning(m)(1), pass away(m)(1), past(1), put away(12), relieved(m)(1), remove(45), removed(43), removing(1), retract(1), return(1), separated(1), strip away(1), swerve(1), take(2), take away(7), take off(1), taken(14), takes away(1), took(3), took away(2), took off(2), turn aside(26), turn away(11), turned aside(24), turned away(3), turned in(2), turning aside(1), turning away(3), turns aside(1), turns away(3), wanderer(1), withdrawn(1).*
> ***Notes:***[1] *Or, horrible abomination* [a] *Dan 9:27; Dan 11:31; Mat 24:15; Mar 13:14 [164]*

The sacrifice in the earthly temple is turned aside, removed, or taken away because Christ is our sacrifice once and for all forever. No longer will there be a sacrifice required in the earthly temple. The 1,290 days is referring to the last 3 ½ years between the destruction of Jerusalem and the Battle of Masada. The end of the ancient Nation of Israel and the sacrifices were also prophesied by Hosea.

> **I will also put an end to all** her gaiety, Her feasts, her new moons, *her* Sabbaths, And all her festal assemblies. (Hos 2:11 NAS)

Isaiah also prophesied saying Israel's offerings, feasts, and new moon festivals were an abomination to God. Isaiah wrote,

> ***Bring your worthless offerings no longer, Incense is an abomination to Me.*** *New moon and sabbath, the calling of assemblies-- I cannot endure iniquity and the solemn assembly.* ***I hate your new moon festivals and your appointed feasts***, *They have become a burden to Me. I am weary of bearing them. (Isa 1:13-14 NAS)*

In Amos, God was so angry with Israel that He only wanted justice upon them. Amos wrote,

> ***I hate, I reject your festivals, Nor do I delight in your solemn assemblies***. *"Even though you offer up to Me burnt offerings and your grain offerings, I will not accept them; And I will not even look at the peace offerings of your fatlings. Take away from Me the noise of your songs; I will not even listen to the sound of your harps. "But let*

justice roll down like waters And righteousness like an ever-flowing stream. (Amo 5:21-24 NAS)

Notice the feasts, sabbaths, sacrifices, and new moons were to cease and not to be continued in the Church. The feasts, sabbaths, sacrifices, and new moons were established not only as memorials of what God did for Israel when they left Egypt but also to foreshadow the salvation in Jesus Christ through His messianic work.

5. Heaven and Earth

The kingdom of God and the kingdom of Heaven are the same thing. God's kingdom is a spiritual dimension separate from earth. The kingdom of God is not of the earthly dimension. The word "spiritual" is not referring to nonphysical beings. Paul makes a distinction between the natural and the spiritual body.

> *It is sown a natural body, it is raised a spiritual body. If there is a **natural body**, there is also a **spiritual body**. (1Co 15:44 NAS)*

The spiritual body is also a physical body. The properties of a spiritual body are different than that of the natural body. One is a body of flesh and the other is a body of spirit. The spiritual body is transported to the heavenly dimension at death. The heavenly and earthly dimensions are key to how the feasts are fulfilled in Christ. The ultimate reception of the Sabbath rest by God's people is in the heavenly dimension. In Appendix IV, the "Interdimensional Theology – The Christocentric Kingdom of God" illustration shows how the feasts are fulfilled and how the promises of God are received in the heavenly dimension.

Even though the Bible does not use the word "dimension," the word "dimension" describes the relationship between the earthly world and heavenly world. The heavenly dimension is "not of this world." The distinction between the earthly dimension and the heavenly dimension is seen in the Lord's Prayer.

> *Thy kingdom come. Thy will be done, **On earth as it is in heaven**. (Mat 6:10 NAS)*

Jesus clearly distinguishes between heaven and earth in teaching that God is Lord of heaven and earth.

> *At that time Jesus answered and said, "I praise Thee, O Father, **Lord of heaven and earth**, that Thou didst hide these things from the wise and intelligent and didst reveal them to babes." (Mat 11:25 NAS)*

Jesus Christ, who is the Eternal Word of God, has always existed. He created all things and came into the earthly dimension from the heavenly dimension.

> ***In the beginning was the Word**, and the Word was with God, and the Word was God. He was in the beginning with God. All things came into being by Him, and apart from Him nothing came into being that has come into being.... And **the Word became flesh, and dwelt among us**, and we beheld His glory, glory as of the only begotten from the Father, full of grace and truth. (Joh 1: 1-3,14 NAS)*

Jesus metaphorically describes Himself as "bread" that comes from heaven. Jesus said,

> For **the bread of God is that which comes down out of heaven**, and gives life to the world….For **I have come down from heaven**, not to do My own will, but the will of Him who sent Me….The Jews therefore were grumbling about Him, because He said, "I am the bread that came down out of heaven." And they were saying, "Is not this Jesus, the son of Joseph, whose father and mother we know? How does He now say, 'I have come down out of heaven'?...I am the bread of life. Your fathers ate the manna in the wilderness, and they died. **This is the bread which comes down out of heaven,** so that one may eat of it and not die. **I am the living bread that came down out of heaven**; if anyone eats of this bread, he shall live forever; and the bread also which I shall give for the life of the world is My flesh….**This is the bread which came down out of heaven**; not as the fathers ate, and died, he who eats this bread shall live forever. (Joh 6:33,38, 41-42,48-51,58 NAS)

Jesus is referring to Numbers 11 that describes the manna as falling from the sky.

> And when the dew fell on the camp at night, the manna would fall with it. (Num 11:9 NAS)

When Jesus refers to the manna in the wilderness, He said it came from heaven.

> Our fathers ate the manna in the wilderness; as it is written, He gave them bread out of heaven to eat. (Joh 6:31 NAS)

The Jews who complained "Is not this Jesus, the son of Joseph, whose father and mother we know?" were partially correct. Christ did not come down out of heaven like a UFO or an angel. He was born of the Virgin. Jesus came from eternity and manifested Himself in the flesh from the heavenly dimension through the miraculous incarnation of the Holy Spirit of the Virgin Mary.

a. Heavenly dimension

Sometimes the word "heaven" simply means "the sky." Jesus metaphorically references the manna in the wilderness to describe Himself as coming from heaven. The word "heaven" has multiple meanings depending on the context it is used. *The NASB Concordance* defines word for "heaven" as,

> **<08064>** שָׁמַיִם *(shamayim) (1029c)*
> **Meaning:** *heaven, sky*
> **Origin:** *from an unused word*
> **Usage:** *astrologers*(1), compass(m)(1), earth(m)(1), heaven(195), heavenly(3), heavens(152), heavens to the other*(1), highest heaven(2), highest heavens(4), horizons(1), sky(50).*
> **Notes:** [1] *Lit., heavens* [a] *Gen 3:22; Gen 11:7* [b] *Gen 5:1; Gen 9:6; 1Co 11:7; Eph 4:24; Jam 3:9* [c] *Psa 8:6-8* [165]

Greek word for "heaven" in *the NASB Concordance* is,

> **<3772>** οὐρανός *(ouranos)*
> **Meaning:** heaven
> **Origin:** a prim. word
> **Usage:** air(9), heaven(217), heavenly*(1), heavens(24), sky(22).
> **Notes:** ¹ Lit., face ᵃ Luk 12:56 [166]

During the Apostles time, many had a view of heaven that is found in *the Second Book of Enoch*. *The Second Book of Enoch* describes heaven as having ten heavens. The Apostle Paul references the third heaven which is paradise in *the Second book of Enoch* (2 Enoch 8:1-10, 9:1, 10:1-3). Paul wrote,

> *I know a man in Christ who fourteen years ago-- whether in the body I do not know, or out of the body I do not know, God knows--* **such a man was caught up to the third heaven.** *And I know how such a man-- whether in the body or apart from the body I do not know, God knows--* **was caught up into Paradise,** *and heard inexpressible words, which a man is not permitted to speak. (2Co 12:2-4 NAS)*

The Paradise in heaven is of the heavenly dimension, not of the earthly dimension. Christ Himself is not of this world or earthly dimension. John wrote,

> *And He was saying to them, You are from below, I am from above; you are of this world,* **I am not of this world.** *(Joh 8:23 NAS)*

The NASB Concordance defines the Greek word for "world" as,

> **<2889>** κόσμος *(kosmos)*
> **Meaning:** order, the world
> **Origin:** a prim. Word
> **Usage:** adornment(1), world(184), world's(1).
> **Notes:** ¹ Or, is not derived from ² Lit., from here ᵃ Mat 26:53; Luk 17:21; Joh 6:15 [167]

Christ is not of this cosmos. In John 18:36, the *NASB Bible* translators used the phrase "not of this realm" where the *KJV Bible* translators used the phrase "not from hence."

> *Jesus answered, My kingdom is* **not of this world.** *If My kingdom were of this world, then My servants would be fighting, that I might not be delivered up to the Jews; but as it is,* **My kingdom is not of this realm.** *(Joh 18:36 NAS)*

> *Jesus answered,* **My kingdom is not of this world**: *if my kingdom were of this world, then would my servants fight, that I should not be delivered to the Jews: but now is* **my kingdom not from hence.** *(Joh 18:36 KJV)*

The word "realm" is not an accurate translation of the Greek word. The interpreters of the KJV Bible translated the Greek correctly. *The NASB Concordance* shows the Greek word for "realm" as,

> **<1782>** ἐντεῦθεν *(enteuthen)*
> **Meaning:** hence, on each side, thereupon
> **Origin:** from 1759b

Usage: either side(2), here(4), source(m)(1), this realm(1).
Notes: [1] Or, is not derived from [2] Lit., from here [a] Mat 26:53; Luk 17:21; Joh 6:15 [168]

"Not of this realm" simply means not from here. God's kingdom in heaven is not of the earthly cosmos. The heavenly and earthly dimensions are different "realms" or "worlds." Some may object to this interpretation claiming that God's people are "not of the world" yet they are in the earthly cosmos. Some may say the phrase "not of this world" simply means not a worldly person. The deduction that the phrase "not from the world" means not "worldly" is partially true. John wrote,

> *If you were of the world, the world would love its own;* ***but because you are not of the world, but I chose you out of the world****, therefore the world hates you. (Joh 15:19 NAS)*

A conclusion can be deduced from John 15:19 that "the world" is only referring to the "worldly" unbelievers. John wrote for believers to not love the world.

> *Do not love the world, nor the things in the world. If anyone loves the world, the love of the Father is not in him. For **all that is in the world, the lust of the flesh and the lust of the eyes and the boastful pride of life, is not from the Father, but is from the world***. *And the world is passing away, and also its lusts; but the one who does the will of God abides forever. (1Jo 2:15-17 NAS)*

It is true the statement in 1 John 2, "all that is in the world," is referring to the "worldly" life of unbelievers on earth. This does not mean every time the word "world" is used, it is solely referring to the lusts of the world. Jesus also said His people are not of the world just as Christ is not of the world.

> *I have given them Thy word; and the world has hated them,* ***because they are not of the world, even as I am not of the world****. I do not ask Thee to take them out of the world, but to keep them from the evil one.* ***They are not of the world, even as I am not of the world****. (Joh 17:14-16 NAS)*

Some could conclude from John 17 that the "world" is not a separate dimension but simply the "worldly" unbelieving people. If that were true, then Christ would not be from heaven. He would just not be a "worldly" person. Not being "from the world" means we are not of the fleshly world (earthly dimension) and we are from the spiritual world (heavenly dimension). Both are true.

b. Children of God

God's people are from the heavenly dimension because God regenerates or causes them to be born again. First, they are born of the flesh (earthly dimension) and secondly from the Spirit (heavenly dimension). God's people are reborn of the Holy Spirit, God Himself.

> *But as many as received Him, to them* ***He gave the right to become children of God****, even to those who believe in His name,* ***who were born*** *not of blood, nor of the will of the flesh, nor of the will of man,* ***but of God****. (Joh 1:12-13 NAS)*

Chapter 9 - The Feasts and the end times

This is why God's people are called "children of God." Jesus specifically taught that God's people are born of the flesh (earthly dimension) and then born again of the Spirit (heavenly dimension).

> *Jesus answered and said to him, "Truly, truly, I say to you, **unless one is born again**, he cannot see the kingdom of God." Nicodemus said to Him, "How can a man be born when he is old? He cannot enter a second time into his mother's womb and be born, can he?" Jesus answered, "Truly, truly, I say to you, unless one is born of water and the Spirit, he cannot enter into the kingdom of God. **"That which is born of the flesh is flesh, and that which is born of the Spirit is spirit.**" (Joh 3:3-6 NAS)*

Jesus was explaining to Nicodemus that being born from the mother's womb was not sufficient to enter into the kingdom of God. People first are born of the water from their mother (fleshly or earthly dimension) and then must be born of the Holy Spirit, God Himself (spiritually or heavenly dimension). This means that God's people are born again as children of God.

> *See how great a love the Father has bestowed upon us, that **we should be called children of God**; and such we are. For this reason the world does not know us, because it did not know Him. Beloved, **now we are children of God**, and it has not appeared as yet what we shall be. **We know that, when He appears, we shall be like Him**, because we shall see Him just as He is. (1Jo 3:1-2 NAS)*

This does not mean we are equal to Christ as the Son of God. We are God's children by adoption.

> *He **predestined us to adoption as sons** through Jesus Christ to Himself, according to the kind intention of His will. (Eph 1:5 NAS; Gal 4:5; Rom 8:15,23; 9:4)*

God's people are citizens in the kingdom of God in the heavenly dimension. While God's people are citizens in heaven, they do not enter into the heavenly dimension until death.

> *For our **citizenship is in heaven**, from which also we eagerly wait for a Savior, the Lord Jesus Christ. (Phi 3:20 NAS)*

> *But you have come to Mount Zion and to the city of the living God, the heavenly Jerusalem, and to myriads of angels, to the general assembly and church of the first-born who are **enrolled in heaven**, and to God, the Judge of all, and to the spirits of righteous men made perfect. (Heb 12:22-23 NAS)*

God's people are waiting to receive their inheritance in heaven.

> *Blessed be the God and Father of our Lord Jesus Christ, who according to His great mercy **has caused us to be born again to a living hope** through the resurrection of Jesus Christ from the dead, **to obtain an inheritance which is imperishable** and undefiled and will not fade away, **reserved in heaven for you**. (1Pe 1:3-4 NAS)*

This inheritance is the Sabbath rest promised to God's people. It is an eternal rest in the heavenly dimension.

c. Children of wrath

Those who are born again are the children of God. Those who are not born again are the "children of Wrath." The children of Wrath are those who are disobedient and follow the "prince of the power of the air."

> *And you were dead in your trespasses and sins, in which you formerly walked according to the course of this world, **according to the prince of the power of the air, of the spirit that is now working in the sons of disobedience**. Among them we too all formerly lived in the lusts of our flesh, indulging the desires of the flesh and of the mind, and were by nature children of wrath, even as the rest. (Eph 2:1-3 NAS)*

The phrase "this world" is talking about the earthly dimension. Christ redeemed us with His blood and purchased us, transferring us from the earthly dimension and bringing us into the heavenly dimension.

> *For **He delivered us from the domain of darkness, and transferred us to the kingdom of His beloved Son**, in whom we have redemption, the forgiveness of sins. (Col 1:13-14 NAS)*

Those who are born again by the Holy Spirit have turned from the dominion of Satan to the kingdom of God.

> *To open their eyes so that they may **turn from darkness to light and from the dominion of Satan to God, in order that they may receive forgiveness of sins and an inheritance** among those who have been sanctified by faith in Me. (Act 26:18 NAS)*

The prince of the power of the air is Satan. Jesus said He saw Satan fall from heaven.

> *And He said to them, "I was watching **Satan fall from heaven** like lightning." (Luk 10:18 NAS)*

Even though Satan is a fallen angel from the heavenly dimension, he is said to be the "ruler" or "god" of this world.

> *In whose case **the god of this world** has blinded the minds of the unbelieving, that they might not see the light of the gospel of the glory of Christ, who is the image of God. (2Co 4:4 NAS)*

Satan is the god of those who follow him and his commands on earth. This does not mean God has no control of the earthly dimension. Jesus Christ is God, the judge of the world and the angels.

> *Now judgment is upon this world; now **the ruler of this world** shall be cast out. (Joh 12:31 NAS; Joh 14:30)*

> *And concerning judgment, because **the ruler of this world** has been judged. (Joh 16:11 NAS)*

Satan has been judged and cast out of the presence of God in the heavenly dimension. In Job chapters 1 and 2, Satan makes demands in the presence of the Lord.

> *Now there was a day when the sons of God came to present themselves before the LORD, and Satan also came among them. (Job 1:6 NAS)*

> *Then Satan went out from the presence of the LORD, and smote Job with sore boils from the sole of his foot to the crown of his head. (Job 2:7 NAS)*

The "sons of God" are those who died and were raised from the dead and are in the presence of God (Luk 20:36). Satan can no longer come in the presence of the Lord to ask for anything. Satan is the ruler of the sons of disobedience. "The forces of darkness" are spiritual beings from the heavenly dimension who follow Satan.

> *For our struggle is not against flesh and blood, but against the rulers, against the powers, against **the world forces of this darkness,** against **the spiritual forces of wickedness in the heavenly places.** (Eph 6:12 NAS)*

The "the spiritual forces of wickedness in the heavenly places" are the evil spirits in the heavenly dimension that influence the wicked in the earthly dimension. The earthly and heavenly dimensions occupy the same locations; yet, the spirits in the heavenly dimension cannot be naturally perceived from the earthly dimension.

d. Traversing heaven and earth

The heavenly dimension can only be seen when someone is enabled to see it or when they die. Beings can traverse between the earthly and heavenly dimensions. *The Merriam-Webster Dictionary* defines "traverse" as,

> ***1a:*** *to go or travel across or over* ***b:*** *to move or pass along or through.* [169]

This interdimensional reality is seen with Balaam in Numbers 22. Balaam's donkey saw an angel that Balaam could not see.

> *When the donkey saw the angel of the LORD, she lay down under Balaam. (Num 22:27 NAS)*

Balaam was physically incapable of seeing the angel. The Lord had to physically enable Balaam to see the angel of the Lord.

> *Then the LORD opened the eyes of Balaam, and he saw the angel of the LORD. (Num 22:31 NAS)*

The angel of the Lord would have killed Balaam if the donkey did not turn aside.

> *And the angel of the LORD said to him, "Why have you struck your donkey these three times? Behold, I have come out as an adversary, because your way was contrary to me. "But the donkey saw me and turned aside from me these three times.*

If she had not turned aside from me, I would surely have killed you just now, and let her live." (Num 22:32-33 NAS)

The angel of the Lord had the physical capability to interact with Balaam, yet the angel of the Lord is from the heavenly dimension. In fact, the angel of the Lord is Jesus Christ who is begotten from eternity. Christ appeared to Moses (Exo 3), Gideon (Jdg 6), Elijah (2Ki 1), David (1 Chr 21, Psa 35), Zechariah (Zec 1) and many other instances in the Old Testament. Christ wrote His Law with His finger (Exo 31:18). The angel of the Lord is a topic for another book. Regardless, people in the earthly dimension must be enabled to see the heavenly dimension. John was enabled to see the heavenly dimension.

The Revelation of Jesus Christ, which God gave Him to show to His bond-servants, the things which must shortly take place; and He sent and communicated it by His angel to His bond-servant John… ***I was in the Spirit on the Lord's day, and I heard behind me a loud voice like the sound of a trumpet.*** *(Rev 1:1,10 NAS)*

The voice of an angel like the sound of the trumpet is heard when someone is enabled or transferred from the earthly dimension to the heavenly dimension. The Apostle John was called up to heaven with a voice like the sound of a trumpet.

The first voice *which I had heard,* ***like the sound of a trumpet*** *speaking with me, said,* ***"Come up here, and I will show you*** *what must take place after these things."* ***Immediately I was*** *in the Spirit; and behold, a throne was standing* ***in heaven****, and One sitting on the throne. (Rev 4:1-2 NAS)*

John was able to see what was happening in heaven when he was transported to the heavenly dimension. John saw the City of God, the New Jerusalem in the heavenly dimension. John wrote,

And ***he carried me away in the Spirit*** *to a great and high mountain,* ***and showed me the holy city, Jerusalem, coming down out of heaven from God****. (Rev 21:10 NAS)*

It is clear that the heavenly dimension is a physical entity we cannot perceive from the earthly dimension. Humans and angels both travel between the earthly and heavenly dimensions. How beings traverse between the heavenly and earthly dimension is unknown; nevertheless, the Bible clearly teaches that there is a heavenly and earthly dimension.

e. The heavens open up

In Genesis, Jacob dreamt of angels going to and from heaven to earth.

And he had a dream, and behold, ***a ladder was set on the earth with its top reaching to heaven****; and behold, the angels of God were ascending and descending on it. (Gen 28:12 NAS)*

When the Bible states the heavens opened up, it is always talking about the heavenly dimension.

Now it came about in the thirtieth year, on the fifth day of the fourth month, while I was by the river Chebar among the exiles, the ***heavens were opened and I saw visions of God****. (Eze 1:1 NAS)*

The Psalmist said the doors of heaven opened raining manna from the heavenly dimension. The manna is called "the bread of angels."

> *Yet He commanded the clouds above, And **opened the doors of heaven**; And He rained down manna upon them to eat, And gave them food from heaven. **Man did eat the bread of angels;** He sent them food in abundance. (Psa 78:23-25 NAS)*

The description of heaven opening always refers to the heavenly dimension which is distinct from the earthly dimension. The heavens opening is similar to what Jesus told Nathanael. Nathanael was told that he would see angels ascending and descending from heaven upon Christ.

> *And He said to him, "Truly, truly, I say to you, **you shall see the heavens opened**, and the **angels of God ascending and descending** on the Son of Man." (Joh 1:51 NAS)*

The Bible consistently shows that, when angels come from heaven, the heavens open up. The same event occurs when the Holy Spirit descended upon Jesus when He was baptized.

> *And after being baptized, Jesus went up immediately from the water; and behold, **the heavens were opened**, and he saw the Spirit of God descending as a dove, and coming upon Him, and behold, **a voice out of the heavens**, saying, "This is My beloved Son, in whom I am well-pleased." (Mat 3:16-17 NAS Luk 3:21-22)*

The Apostle Peter gives similar description. Peter was hungry and while he was waiting for the food to be prepared, he went to the rooftop to pray. When Peter went to the rooftop, he saw the heavens open up. Peter said,

> *and **he beheld the sky opened up**, and a certain object like a great sheet coming down, lowered by four corners to the ground. (Act 10:11 NAS Act 11:5)*

John saw the heavens open up and Christ on a white horse in heaven.

> *And **I saw heaven opened**; and behold, a white horse, and He who sat upon it is called Faithful and True; and in righteousness He judges and wages war. (Rev 19:11 NAS)*

Stephen saw the heavens open up and Christ standing at the right hand of God.

> *Behold, I see the **heavens opened up and the Son of Man standing at the right hand of God**. (Act 7:56 NAS)*

The heavens opening up is referring to the heavenly dimension being revealed. The heavens opening up is directly connected with the coming of Christ

6. The coming of Christ

The coming of Christ is not a onetime event that occurs in the far distant future. Christ is, was, and will continue to come for His people. The Bible clearly shows that people see the heavens open up and Christ coming in the heavenly dimension. This is why everyone will see Christ in the heavenly dimension at death. Christ is coming in the clouds sitting at the right hand of God.

Chapter 9 - The Feasts and the end times

> *And Jesus said, "I am; **and you shall see the Son of Man sitting at the right hand of Power, and coming with the clouds of heaven.**" (Mar 14:62 NAS)*

Christ coming in the clouds in heaven and sitting at the right hand of God happen at the same time. While Christ is coming in the clouds and sitting at the right hand of God, He sends His angels to gather His elect. This is the resurrection of the dead. The resurrection of the dead is an event that occurs when people die. When people die, Christ sends His angels to gather them to be judged in heaven (Mat 13:24-41). The elect receive an inheritance and enter into the final Sabbath rest in heaven (Mat 25:34), while the rest are cast out into eternal torment (Mat 25:41,46). Paul expressly taught that those who die are raised from the dead at death. Christ comes for those who die first.

> *But we do not want you to be uninformed, brethren, about those who are asleep, that you may not grieve, as do the rest who have no hope. For if we believe that Jesus died and rose again, even so **God will bring with Him those who have fallen asleep in Jesus**. For this we say to you by the word of the Lord, that **we who are alive**, and remain until the coming of the Lord, **shall not precede those who have fallen asleep**. (1Th 4:13-15 NAS)*

This means that Jesus personally comes for His people at death. Paul uses the word "sleep" in place of the word "death." The word "alive" in 1 Thessalonians 4:15 is confused by those who hold the Dispensationalist view of the "Rapture." Paul says,

> *Then **we who are alive and remain shall be caught up** together with them in the clouds to meet the Lord in the air, and thus we shall always be with the Lord. (1Th 4:17 NAS)*

Paul is talking about the order of operations. This is made clear by reading Paul's explanation of the resurrection of the dead in 1 Corinthians 15.

> ***For as in Adam all die, so also in Christ all shall be made alive. But each in his own order**: Christ the first fruits, after that those who are Christ's at His coming. (1Co 15:22-23 NAS)*

1 Thessalonians 4:17 is not teaching a separate event from the resurrection of the dead and the coming of Christ called the "Rapture." Paul is only explaining that those who die will be raised from the dead before those who are still living. Whether some believers will be translated to heaven without dying like Enoch (Gen 5:24) or Elijah (2Ki 2:11) remains to be seen. There are no Bible verses showing any evidence that believers will be translated to heaven without dying first. 1 Thessalonians 4:17 is too ambiguous to build an entire "Rapture" doctrine from it. Paul clearly is referring to those who die will be raised from the dead at death. Teachings like the "Rapture" are irrelevant, pure speculation, and not taught in Interdimensional Theology. Nevertheless, the coming of Christ at death can be seen in the martyrdom of Saint Stephen.

Chapter 9 - The Feasts and the end times

When Saint Stephen rebuked the leaders of ancient Israel, the leaders murdered Stephen. When Stephen was about to die, he witnessed Christ coming in the clouds, standing at the right hand of God. Christ came for Stephen when he fell "asleep" or died. Stephen spoke to Christ before he died saying "receive my spirit."

> Now when they heard this, they were cut to the quick, and they began gnashing their teeth at him. **But being full of the Holy Spirit, he gazed intently into heaven and saw the glory of God, and Jesus standing at the right hand of God; and he said, "Behold, I see the heavens opened up and the Son of Man standing at the right hand of God."** But they cried out with a loud voice, and covered their ears, and they rushed upon him with one impulse. And when they had driven him out of the city, they began stoning him, and the witnesses laid aside their robes at the feet of a young man named Saul. And they went on stoning **Stephen as he called upon the Lord and said, "Lord Jesus, receive my spirit!"** And falling on his knees, he cried out with a loud voice, "Lord, do not hold this sin against them!" And having said this, **he fell asleep.** (Act 7:54-60 NAS)

The martyrdom of Saint Stephen is the same as what is described in Revelation. Every eye will see Christ coming in the clouds.

> Behold, **He is coming with the clouds, and every eye will see Him, even those who pierced Him**; and all the tribes of the earth will mourn over Him. Even so. Amen. (Rev 1:7 NAS)

a. Coming in the clouds

Christ is continually coming in the clouds. The coming of Christ is inseparable from the resurrection from the dead and Christ reigning as King from heaven. Teaching that the resurrection of the dead occurs in the distant future diminishes the urgency of the gospel significantly. Teaching that there is a waiting place for those who die can lead to the assumption that there is a second chance of salvation after death or that someone can repent sometime in the future at their convenience. His coming in the clouds is an ongoing event from our perspective in the earthly dimension. Every person on earth throughout every age will see Christ in the clouds. This is why John says Christ is, was, and is to come.

> John to the seven churches that are in Asia: Grace to you and peace, from Him who **is and who was and who is to come**; and from the seven Spirits who are before His throne. (Rev 1:4 NAS)

The NASB concordance defines the word "come" as,

> **<2064>** ἔρχομαι *(erchomai)*
> **Meaning:** *to come, go*
> **Origin:** *a prim. vb.*
> **Usage:** *arrival(1), arrived(1), brought(1), came(219), come(234), comes(62), coming(88), Expected(m)(3), fall(2), falls(m)(1), go(1), going(2), grown(1), next(1),*

Chapter 9 - The Feasts and the end times

> *turned(1), went(18).*
> **Notes:** *Dan 7:13; 1Th 4:17; Zec 12:10-14; Joh 19:37; Luk 23:28 [170]*

When the Gospels are matched together, it becomes evident that the coming of Christ is His appearance in the sky, heavens, or clouds.

> *But immediately after the tribulation of those days the sun will be darkened, and the moon will not give its light, and the **stars will fall from the sky**, and **the powers of the heavens will be shaken**, and then the sign of **the Son of Man will appear in the sky**, and then all the tribes of the earth will mourn, and they will see the Son of Man coming on the clouds of the sky with power and great glory. (Mat 24:29-30 NAS)*

> *But in those days, after that tribulation, the sun will be darkened, and the moon will not give its light, and the **stars will be falling from heaven**, and **the powers that are in the heavens will be shaken**. "And then they will see **the Son of Man coming in clouds** with great power and glory. And then He will send forth the angels, and will gather together His elect from the four winds, from the farthest end of the earth, to the farthest end of heaven. (Mar 13:24-27 NAS)*

> *And there will be signs in sun and moon and stars, and upon the earth dismay among nations, in perplexity at the roaring of the sea and the waves, men fainting from fear and the expectation of the things which are coming upon the world; for **the powers of the heavens will be shaken**. And then they will see **the Son of Man coming in a cloud** with power and great glory. (Luk 21:25-27 NAS)*

Even the soldier who pierced the side of Christ while He was on the cross will see Christ coming in the clouds.

> *Behold, **He is coming with the clouds**, and every eye will see Him, **even those who pierced Him;** and all the tribes of the earth will mourn over Him. Even so. Amen. "I am the Alpha and the Omega," says the Lord God, "who is and who was and who is to **come**, the Almighty." (Rev 1:7-8 NAS)*

The translation could be "came," "come," or "comes." The word "coming" is an accurate translation in the context of the verse. The word "coming" is what is called the "gerund" form of the word. *The Merriam-Webster Dictionary* defines "gerund" as,

> *a verbal noun in Latin that expresses generalized or uncompleted action. [171]*

This is similar to saying a choir is singing or the farmer is farming. Placing the suffix "ing" after the verb makes the verb an action that is an ongoing process. The phrase "He is coming in the clouds" is stating that the coming of Christ is an ongoing process of the resurrection of the dead.

b. The resurrection at death

Those whom Christ raises from the dead are like angels in heaven. They are called "sons of God" because they are sons of the resurrection from the dead.

> *And Jesus said to them, "The sons of this age marry and are given in marriage, but those who are considered worthy to attain to that age and the resurrection from the dead, neither marry, nor are given in marriage; **for neither can they die anymore, for they are like angels, and are sons of God, being sons of the resurrection**. (Luk 20:34-36 NAS)*

The resurrection of God's people at death is explained by Paul to the Corinthians. Paul clearly stated that if Christ did not raise from the dead, those who have "fallen asleep" or died did not raise from the dead.

> *For if the dead are not raised, not even Christ has been raised; and **if Christ has not been raised**, your faith is worthless; you are still in your sins. Then **those also who have fallen asleep in Christ have perished**. If we have hoped in Christ in this life only, we are of all men most to be pitied. (1Co 15:16-19 NAS)*

Paul continues by explaining that because Christ rose from the dead, all those who die are "made alive" or raised from the dead. Paul is specifically referring to those who died "are asleep." Christ, being the first to raise from the dead, raised all people from the dead. Believers in Christ are raised "at His coming" which occurs in the order of each person's death. Paul wrote,

> ***For if the dead are not raised**, not even Christ has been raised; and if Christ has not been raised, your faith is worthless; you are still in your sins. **Then those also who have fallen asleep in Christ have perished**. If we have hoped in Christ in this life only, we are of all men most to be pitied. But now Christ has been raised from the dead, the first fruits of those who are asleep. **For since by a man came death, by a man also came the resurrection of the dead**. For as in Adam all die, so also in Christ all shall be made alive. **But each in his own order**: Christ the first fruits, after that those who are Christ's at His coming. (1Co 15:16-23 NAS)*

Christ comes for His people in the order of their death throughout all history. Christ must reign until His enemies are all in subjection to Him; therefore, His coming is a continual event. Christ coming at death is an imminent event. Nobody knows when they are going to die; therefore, it is imperative to repent and follow Christ NOW.

c. Coming quickly

The fact that Christ will come at any moment is why we should always be ready. Death is an imminent reality. We do not know what day or hour.

> *Be on the alert then, for you do not know the day nor the hour. (Mat 25:13 NAS)*

During the days of Noah, the people were warned that the flood was coming and they did not listen. They mocked Noah. Yet when the flood came, they realized they were going to die, but it was too late to change their behavior. They all died in their sin. It is the same with the coming of Christ. Jesus said,

> *For the coming of the Son of Man will be just like the days of Noah. For as in those days which were before the flood they were eating and drinking, they were marrying*

*and giving in marriage, until the day that Noah entered the ark, **and they did not understand until the flood came and took them all away**; so shall the coming of the Son of Man be. (Mat 24:37-39 NAS)*

Believing in Christ and obeying God's commands is a lifelong endeavor. Many people think they will believe, get baptized, or repent at the end of their life. The fact is when death is at your door, you have no choice in the matter. This is what Jesus meant when He said,

But if that evil slave says in his heart, 'My master is not coming for a long time,' and shall begin to beat his fellow slaves and eat and drink with drunkards; the master of that slave will come on a day when he does not expect him and at an hour which he does not know, and shall cut him in pieces and assign him a place with the hypocrites; weeping shall be there and the gnashing of teeth. (Mat 24:48-51 NAS)

It's just like when a person is sleeping in their house and a thief comes in, kills them, and plunders their possessions. Jesus said,

And be sure of this, that if the head of the house had known at what hour the thief was coming, he would not have allowed his house to be broken into. You too, be ready; for the Son of Man is coming at an hour that you do not expect. (Luk 12:39-40 NAS)

Nobody knows when death will occur. It is unexpected. While people are thinking all is well, suddenly destruction comes.

For you yourselves know full well that the day of the Lord will come just like a thief in the night. While they are saying, "Peace and safety!" then destruction will come upon them suddenly like birth pangs upon a woman with child; and they shall not escape. (1Th 5:2-3 NAS)

This is just like when a country goes to war or the government power changes and the people immediately and unexpectedly suffer. An example of this is during World War 2 when people were sleeping in their beds and all of a sudden, their whole city was bombed in mass destruction. Thousands of people died in a matter of minutes. In the atomic bombings of Hiroshima and Nagasaki in Japan, between 140,000 to 200,000 people were killed [172]. The people of Japan most assuredly did not know that was coming. Nowhere does the Bible suggest that people can ignore God's commands till they are ready to follow Him. The book of Revelation clearly shows that all must repent now and that all will be judged according to the deeds they did during their life. The theme throughout the book of Revelation is that Christ is coming quickly.

*Repent therefore; or else **I am coming to you quickly**, and I will make war against them with the sword of My mouth. (Rev 2:16 NAS)*

***I am coming quickly**; hold fast what you have, in order that no one take your crown. (Rev 3:11 NAS)*

> *And behold, **I am coming quickly**. Blessed is he who heeds the words of the prophecy of this book. (Rev 22:7 NAS)*
>
> *Behold, **I am coming quickly**, and My reward is with Me, to render to every man according to what he has done. I am the Alpha and the Omega, the first and the last, the beginning and the end. (Rev 22:12-13 NAS)*
>
> *He who testifies to these things says, "Yes, **I am coming quickly**." Amen. Come, Lord Jesus. (Rev 22:20 NAS)*

The NASB Concordance translates the Greek word for "quickly" as,

> **<5035> ταχύ (tachu)**
> **Meaning:** *quickly*
> **Origin:** *neut. of 5036*
> **Usage:** *before long(1), possible(1), quickly(11), soon afterward(1).*
> **Notes:** *¹ Or, keeps ᵃ Rev 1:3; Rev 3:3, Rev 3:11; Rev 16:15; Rev 22:12, Rev 22:20 ᵇ Rev 1:3; Rev 16:15 ᶜ Rev 1:11; Rev 22:9, Rev 22:10, 18f [173]*

This is similar to the word "speedily." God executes His justice speedily.

> *I tell you that He will bring about justice for them **speedily**. However, when the Son of Man comes, will He find faith on the earth? (Luk 18:8 NAS)*

The Greek word for "speedily" in Luke 18:8 is,

> **<5034> τάχος (tachos)**
> **Meaning:** *speed*
> **Origin:** *from 5036*
> **Usage:** *quickly(2), shortly(3), soon(1), speedily(1).*
> **Notes:** *¹ Lit., the faith ᵃ Luk 17:26ff [174]*

The book of Acts gives us an idea of the duration of time for the word τάχος (tachos).

> *Festus then answered that Paul was being kept in custody at Caesarea and that he himself was about to leave **shortly**. "Therefore," he said, "let the influential men among you go there with me, and if there is anything wrong about the man, let them prosecute him." And **after he had spent not more than eight or ten days** among them, he went down to Caesarea; and on the next day he took his seat on the tribunal and ordered Paul to be brought. (Act 25:4-6 NAS)*

The word τάχος (tachos) is equated to eight to ten days. The word origin for ταχύ (tachu) and τάχος (tachos) comes from *Strong's NASB Concordance* #5036 ταχύς (tachus).

> **<5036> ταχύς (tachus)**
> **Meaning:** *quick, swift*
> **Origin:** *a prim. word*

Usage: *faster(1), quick(1), quickly(1), soon(2), sooner(1).*
Notes: *None [175]*

The same word "quick" is used by James as how a person is to behave with everyone in real time.

> *This you know, my beloved brethren. But let everyone be **quick** to hear, slow to speak and slow to anger. (Jam 1:19 NAS)*

James did not mean to listen far off in the future. He is saying to listen quick when you are having dialogue with someone. Quickly means at any moment. The coming of Christ happens quickly. Futurists teach that Christ is not coming quickly for God's people individually but at a single event far into the distant future from the time of the Apostles. Dispensationalist Clarence Larkin argues that Christ coming quickly is not an immediate concern of a person during the lifetime of those who listened to Him; but, referred to a class of people far into the future.

> *One of the objections to the Doctrine of the "Second Coming of Christ" is the claim that He may come back at any time. Post-millennialists tell us that the writers of the New Testament looked for Him to come back in their day, and that He did not do so, is proof that they were mistaken, and that Paul in his later writings modified his statements as to the imminency of Christ's return. It is a fact that while Jesus said: "Watch therefore: for ye know not what hour your Lord doth come. ... Therefore be ye also ready: for in such an hour as ye think not the Son of man cometh" (Matt. 24:42-44), **He did not in these passages teach that He would return during the lifetime of those who listened to Him**. In fact, in His Parables He intimated that His return would be delayed, as in the Parable of The Talents, where it is said: "After a long time the Lord of those servants cometh. Matt. 25:19. What Jesus wanted to teach was the sudden and unexpected character of His return. As to the Apostles, while they exhorted their followers to be ready, for the "night is far spent, the day is at hand, " and the "coming of the Lord draweth nigh, " their language simply implied "imminency, " but not necessarily "IMMEDIATENESS." **And the use of the word "WE" in 1Cor. 15:5 1Cor. 15:1, "WE" shall not all sleep, but WE shall all be changed, " is not a declaration that the Lord would return in Paul's day and some would not die but be translated, for the Apostle is talking about the Rapture and he means by "WE" a certain class of persons**, the saints that shall be alive when that event occurs, whether in his day or at some later time. [176]*

Clarence Larkin horribly destroys the meaning of the Biblical text. Clarence Larkin's argument that the word "We" is only talking about a certain class of people is absolutely unacceptable. Christ did not say He was coming for a certain class of people. Christ specifically said He was coming for those who eagerly await Him.

> *So Christ also, having been offered once to bear the sins of many, **shall appear a second time for salvation without reference to sin, to those who eagerly await Him**. (Heb 9:28 NAS)*

Christ specifically said for all to come to Him and He will give them rest.

> *Come to Me, all who are weary and heavy-laden, and I will give you rest. (Mat 11:28 NAS)*

Christ will appear a second time personally for His people individually.

> ***And if I go and prepare a place for you, I will come again, and receive you to Myself;*** *that where I am, there you may be also. "And you know the way where I am going." (Joh 14:3-4 NAS)*

There are no references to a single future event called the "Second Coming" in the Bible. Christ simply says He will come again for His people. Christ returns for His people to take them to a place He prepared for them beforehand. This fulfills the Feast of Trumpets. The place prepared is the City of God, the New Jerusalem. This fulfills the Feast of Booths, the final Sabbath rest for God's people.

7. The New Jerusalem, the City of God

Our final Sabbath rest is fulfilled in the coming of Christ and in the New Jerusalem from the heavenly dimension. The City of God is not a future earthly place. It is an actual place in the physical dimension of heaven that exists in the past, present, and future. The angel's dwell in the New Jerusalem, the City of God. The writer of Hebrews wrote,

> *But you have come to Mount Zion and to the city of the living God, the heavenly Jerusalem, and **to myriads of angels**. (Heb 12:22 NAS)*

a. The throne of God

When Christ ascended to heaven, He sat at the right hand of God.

> *So then, when the Lord Jesus had spoken to them, He was received up into heaven, and sat down at the right hand of God. (Mar 16:19 NAS Luk 22:69; Act 2:33; 5:31; 7:55-56; Col 3:1)*

Sitting at the right hand of God is sitting on the throne of God.

> *But when the Son of Man comes in His glory, and all the angels with Him, then **He will sit on His glorious throne**. (Mat 25:31 NAS)*

> *fixing our eyes on Jesus, the author and perfecter of faith, who for the joy set before Him endured the cross, despising the shame, **and has sat down at the right hand of the throne of God**. (Heb 12:2 NAS)*

God's throne is in heaven. Jesus said heaven is the throne of God.

> *But I say to you, make no oath at all, either by **heaven, for it is the throne of God**. (Mat 5:34 NAS)*

The New Jerusalem, the City of God, and the heavenly dimension is not made with human hands. It is a heavenly dimension unlike the earthly dimension.

> *The God who made the world and all things in it, since **He is Lord of heaven and earth, does not dwell in temples made with hands;** neither is He served by human hands, as though He needed anything, since He Himself gives to all life and breath and all things. (Act 17:24-25 NAS)*

> *However, the Most High does not dwell in houses made by human hands; as the prophet says: **Heaven is My throne,** And earth is the footstool of My feet; What kind of house will you build for Me? says the Lord; Or what place is there for My repose? (Act 7:48-49 NAS)*

The book of Revelation shows how Christ is on the throne at the right hand of God.

> *After these things I looked, and behold, a door standing open in heaven, and the first voice which I had heard, like the sound of a trumpet speaking with me, said, Come up here, and I will show you what must take place after these things." Immediately I was in the Spirit; and behold, **a throne was standing in heaven, and One sitting on the throne.** (Rev 4:1-2 NAS)*

We are not waiting for Christ to become King on a throne on earth. Christ is our King NOW. Christ does not merely reign spiritually in the heart of believers. He reigns over all people on earth NOW. Every nation on earth must submit to His rule or they will be destroyed. Christ physically rose from the dead and is physically reigning from the dimension of heaven. Any Nation on earth who fails to keep His commands will utterly be destroyed from the face of the earth. Psalm 2 states,

> *I will surely tell of the decree of the LORD: He said to Me, Thou art My Son, Today I have begotten Thee. Ask of Me, and I will surely give the nations as Thine inheritance, And the very ends of the earth as Thy possession. Thou shalt break them with a rod of iron, Thou shalt shatter them like earthenware. (Psa 2:7-9 NAS)*

Psalms 2 is speaking of the reality that Christ is King then, now, and forever more. The writer of Hebrews wrote,

> *But to which of the angels has He ever said, "Sit at My right hand, Until I make Thine enemies A footstool for Thy feet "? (Heb 1:13 NAS)*

> *but He, having offered one sacrifice for sins for all time, sat down at the right hand of God, waiting from that time onward until His enemies be made a footstool for His feet (Heb 10:12-13 NAS)*

All nations will bow and confess Jesus Christ as Lord. Paul wrote,

> *Therefore also God highly exalted Him, and bestowed on Him the name which is above every name, that at the name of Jesus every knee should bow, of those who are in heaven, and on earth, and under the earth, and that every tongue should confess that Jesus Christ is Lord, to the glory of God the Father. (Phi 2:9-11 NAS)*

All angels and powers are His subjects.

> *Who is at the right hand of God, having gone into heaven, after angels and authorities and powers had been subjected to Him. (1Pe 3:22 NAS)*

Christ is ruling as King from the New Jerusalem in the heavenly dimension.

b. The Fathers house

The fulfillment of the Feast of Booths is clearly seen in the New Jerusalem. The tabernacle of God is in heaven. The Ark of the covenant is in the temple of the tabernacle in heaven in the New Jerusalem.

> *And **the temple of God which is in heaven was opened**; and **the ark of His covenant appeared in His temple**, and there were flashes of lightning and sounds and peals of thunder and an earthquake and a great hailstorm. (Rev 11:19 NAS)*

The tabernacle is in heaven. It can be opened and angels come out from it.

> *After these things I looked, and the temple of **the tabernacle of testimony in heaven was opened**, and the seven angels who had the seven plagues came out of the temple, clothed in linen, clean and bright, and girded around their breasts with golden girdles. And one of the four living creatures gave to the seven angels seven golden bowls full of the wrath of God, who lives forever and ever. And **the temple was filled with smoke from the glory of God and from His power**; and no one was able to enter the temple until the seven plagues of the seven angels were finished. (Rev 15:5-8 NAS)*

The tabernacle of God is said to dwell with His people.

> *And I heard a great voice out of heaven saying, **Behold, the tabernacle of God is with men, and he will dwell with them**, and they shall be his people, and God himself shall be with them, and be their God. (Rev 21:3 KJV)*

The Hebrew word for "tabernacle" is,

> **<04908>** מִשְׁכָּן *(mishkan) (1015c)*
> **Meaning:** dwelling place, tabernacle
> **Origin:** from 7931
> **Usage:** dwelling(1), dwelling place(8), dwelling places(9), dwellings(9), resting place(1), tabernacle(109), tents(1), where it dwells(1).
> **Notes:** [a] Exo 25:40; Exo 26:30; Act 7:44; Heb 8:2, Heb 8:5 [177]

The Greek word for "tabernacle" is,

> **<4633>** σκηνή *(skene)*
> **Meaning:** a tent
> **Origin:** a prim. word
> **Usage:** dwellings(1), tabernacle(15), tabernacles(3), tents(1).
> **Notes:** [1] Or, tabernacle [2] Some ancient mss. add, and be their God [a] Lev 26:11f.; Eze 37:27; Eze 48:35; Heb 8:2; Rev 7:15 [b] Joh 14:23; 2Co 6:16 [178]

Chapter 9 - The Feasts and the end times

The fulfillment of the Feast of Booths becomes clearer when reading the Greek and Hebrew words. Tabernacle simply means a dwelling place. The word "Booth" is the same as dwelling place.

> **<05521>** סֻכָּה *(sukkah) (697c)*
> **Meaning:** *a thicket, booth*
> **Origin:** *from 5526b*
> **Usage:** *booth(1), booths(8), Booths(9), canopies(m)(1), canopy(m)(1), hut(1), lair(1), pavilion(m)(1), shelter(4), temporary shelters(m)(3).*
> **Notes:** *ᵃ Exo 23:14-17; Exo 34:23, Exo 34:24 ᵇ Exo 34:20 [179]*

The tabernacle in heaven is the direct fulfillment of and the foreshadowing in the Feast of Booths.

> *You shall live in booths for seven days; all the native-born in Israel shall live in booths, so that your generations may know that I had the sons of Israel live in booths when I brought them out from the land of Egypt. I am the LORD your God. (Lev 23:42-43 NAS)*

> *In the third month after the sons of Israel had gone out of the land of Egypt, on that very day they came into the wilderness of Sinai. When they set out from Rephidim, they came to the wilderness of Sinai, and camped in the wilderness; and there Israel camped in front of the mountain. (Exo 19:1-2 NAS)*

Our dwelling place is in heaven.

> *For indeed in this house we groan, longing to be clothed with **our dwelling from heaven**. (2Co 5:2 NAS)*

He is describing an actual place that exists in a specific location in heaven. Jesus said in His Father's house are many dwelling places.

> ***In My Father's house are many dwelling places***; *if it were not so, I would have told you; for **I go to prepare a place for you**. And if I go and prepare a place for you, I will come again, and receive you to Myself; that where I am, there you may be also. (Joh 14:2-3 NAS)*

Believers in Christ have a reward in heaven.

> *Be glad in that day, and leap for joy, for behold, **your reward is great in heaven**; for in the same way their fathers used to treat the prophets. (Luk 6:23 NAS)*

Clearly Heaven is another world from the earthly world. Jesus said to not store your treasure on earth but to store your treasure in heaven.

> *Do not lay up for yourselves treasures upon earth, where moth and rust destroy, and where thieves break in and steal. **But lay up for yourselves treasures in heaven**, where neither moth nor rust destroys, and where thieves do not break in or steal. (Mat 6:19-20 NAS)*

Chapter 9 - The Feasts and the end times

Christ will come for His people at death and bring them to heaven. This is the final Sabbath rest. Paul wrote,

> *Blessed be the God and Father of our Lord Jesus Christ, who according to His great mercy has caused us to be born again to a living hope through the resurrection of Jesus Christ from the dead,* **to obtain an inheritance which is imperishable and undefiled and will not fade away, reserved in heaven for you,** *who are protected by the power of God through faith for a salvation ready to be revealed in the last time. (1Pe 1:3-5 NAS)*

The New Jerusalem is in heaven. The New Jerusalem is not an earthly city but the heavenly City of God.

c. The bride

There will be those who read this and object because they were taught the Church is the bride of Christ. A common teaching in the church is that the New Jerusalem is not a literal city. Many Christians teach that the New Jerusalem is the Church or the people of God. Herman Hoeksema wrote,

> *Now **the bride of the lamb surely is not a city in the literal sense of the word**. Against this literalism is also the development of Jerusalem in Scripture. As we have pointed out before, Jerusalem is manifested in a three-fold form. First of all, it was the capital of the old land of Canaan. Secondly, it is also the church of the New Testament in the broadest sense of the word. This is also very plain from Scripture, and I do not have to corroborate this idea. But, in the third place, **Jerusalem is also the perfected church, the bride of the Lamb in glory**. This, therefore, is the idea of the text. **Jerusalem here is not a literal city, but it is the church triumphant in perfect glory**.* [180]

Herman Hoeksema is interpreting the book of Revelation as symbolism. Many attempt to build a doctrine that the Church is the "wife of the Lamb." Hendriksen makes the argument that the New Jerusalem coming down from heaven is the transformation of believers by the work of the Holy Spirit. William Hendriksen wrote,

> *Now,* **this new and holy Jerusalem is very clearly the church of the Lord Jesus Christ,** *as is also plainly evident from the fact that it is here and elsewhere* **called the bride, the wife of the Lamb**, *Is 54:1; Eph 5:32, etc. Even in the O.T. the church is represented under the symbolism of a city, Is. 26:1; 40:9; Ps. 48; etc. A city calls to our mind the concepts of permanent residence, a great number of inhabitants, safety and security, fellowship, beauty. With respect to all of these characteristics the church—in principle, even today, in perfection by and by—is like a city. We read that John saw this Holy City coming down out of heaven from God.* **This, too, is true with respect to both the ideal church of the present and the church of the future. It is ever born from above. It is ever the result of the transforming work of the Holy Spirit, Rev. 3:12; 21:9 ff.; cf. Gal. 4:26; Heb. 11:10, 16; 12:22.** *The words "made ready as a bride adorned for her husband" find their commentary in Rev. 19:7.* [181]

Chapter 9 - The Feasts and the end times

I would like to point out that, the Church is far from "perfection." The church is being sanctified which is a process of becoming more holy. This sanctification is actualized at death when the Church enters the Sabbath rest. Interpreting the New Jerusalem as symbolism or the transforming work of the Holy Spirit in the believer is completely false. Scripture should not be "allegorically" or "symbolically" interpreted unless there is warrant for such an interpretation. For example, Paul compares Hagar, the bondwoman, with the earthly Jerusalem and Sarah, the free woman, with the New Jerusalem in heaven.

> *But the son by the bondwoman was born according to the flesh, and the son by the free woman through the promise.* **This is allegorically speaking:** *for these women are two covenants, one proceeding from Mount Sinai bearing children who are to be slaves; she is Hagar.* **Now this Hagar is Mount Sinai in Arabia, and corresponds to the present Jerusalem, for she is in slavery with her children. But the Jerusalem above is free; she is our mother.** *(Gal 4:23-26 NAS)*

We know Paul is speaking allegorically because he told us. Ironically, Galatians 4:23-26 is used as proof the Church is the bride of Christ. Galatians says the New Jerusalem is our "mother" not bride. The Bible does not teach the Church is the bride of Christ. Jesus calls the Church "attendants" of the bridegroom.

> *And Jesus said to them,* **"The attendants of the bridegroom** *cannot mourn as long as the bridegroom is with them, can they? But the* **days will come when the bridegroom is taken away from them***, and then they will fast." (Mat 9:15 NAS)*

In the parable of the wedding feast, Christ says those who were invited to the feast paid no attention so He invited other people.

> *Then he said to his slaves, The wedding is ready, but those who were invited were not worthy. Go therefore to the main highways, and* **as many as you find there, invite to the wedding feast***. (Mat 22:8-9 NAS)*

Clearly, the Church is invited to the wedding and not in the wedding. This is clear in the book of Revelation.

> *And he said to me, Write,* **'Blessed are those who are invited to the marriage supper of the Lamb.'** *And he said to me, These are true words of God. (Rev 19:9 NAS)*

The Church is invited to the wedding and not the bride in the wedding. The Church are the children of God, not brides of God. Some use Matthew 25:1 as proof that the Church is the bride.

> *Then the kingdom of heaven will be* **comparable** *to ten virgins, who took their lamps, and went out to meet the bridegroom. (Mat 25:1 NAS)*

Jesus says the kingdom of heaven is "comparable" to virgins and not "are" virgins who went out to meet the bridegroom. Comparing an object is not the same as defining the object. This is also seen in Ephesians 5:22-33. Paul compares the relationship of a husband and wife to the relationship between the Church and Christ.

> *Wives, be subject to your own husbands, as to the Lord. For the husband is the head of the wife, as Christ also is the head of the church, He Himself being the Savior of the body. But as the church is subject to Christ, so also the wives ought to be to their husbands in everything. Husbands, love your wives, just as Christ also loved the church and gave Himself up for her; that He might sanctify her, having cleansed her by the washing of water with the word, that He might present to Himself the church in all her glory, having no spot or wrinkle or any such thing; but that she should be holy and blameless. So husbands ought also to love their own wives as their own bodies. He who loves his own wife loves himself; for no one ever hated his own flesh, but nourishes and cherishes it, just as Christ also does the church, because we are members of His body. For this cause a man shall leave his father and mother, and shall cleave to his wife; and the two shall become one flesh. This mystery is great; but **I am speaking with reference to Christ and the church**. Nevertheless let each individual among you also love his own wife even as himself; and let the wife see to it that she respect her husband. (Eph 5:22-33 NAS)*

Paul expressly says he is speaking in "reference" to Christ and the Church. He is using the relationship as an example of how husbands are to behave with their wife and vice versa. Paul is not teaching the Church is the bride of Christ. He is only making a comparison. The writer of Hebrews compares the event in Exodus 19 to the New Jerusalem in heaven. The writer of Hebrews say we "have come to Mount Zion and to the city of the living God."

> *For they could not bear the command, "If even a beast touches the mountain, it will be stoned." And so terrible was the sight, that Moses said, "I am full of fear and trembling." But you **have come to Mount Zion and to the city of the living God**, the heavenly Jerusalem, **and** to myriads of **angels**, to the general assembly and **church** of the first-born who are enrolled in heaven, and to **God**, the Judge of all, and to the **spirits** of righteous men made perfect, and to **Jesus**, the mediator of a new covenant, and to the sprinkled blood, which speaks better than the blood of Abel. (Heb 12:20-24 NAS)*

The writer of Hebrews does NOT say we ARE the city of the living God. Those who are in the city are angels, the Church, God, spirits, and Jesus. The Church are only occupants of the city and not the city itself. The New Jerusalem does not come down to earth and inhabit believers. The New Jerusalem is not a symbolic or allegorical riddle. The New Jerusalem does not come down out of heaven and land on earth in the future. The New Jerusalem is the bride, a literal city in heaven.

d. Descending from heaven

The New Jerusalem is described as a bride meeting her groom. John wrote,

> *And I saw the holy city, new Jerusalem, **coming down out of heaven** from God, made ready **as a bride adorned for her husband**. (Rev 21:2 NAS)*

The imagery used to describe the New Jerusalem depicts a bride's dress that flows down the aisle as she travels to meet the groom. The description of the New Jerusalem does not depict a city descending from the sky and landing on earth, nor is it talking about a spiritual descent to believers. It would be strange to describe a bride descending from the sky and landing on the ground before her groom. Brides do not come out of heaven they travel down an aisle. *The NASB Concordance* translates the Greek "coming down" as,

> *<2597> καταβαίνω (katabaino)*
> **Meaning:** *to go down*
> **Origin:** *from 2596 and the same root as 939*
> **Usage:** *brought down(1), came down(10), come down(16), comes down(4), coming(1), coming down(9), descend(3), descended(9), descending(5), descends(1), falling down(1), go down(4), go downstairs(1), going down(3), got out of(1), steps(1), steps down(1), went down(12).*
> **Notes:** *Act 13:13* [182]

The word is used to mean descend. For example,

> *And **the rain descended**, and the floods came, and the winds blew, and burst **against that house**; and yet it did not fall, for it had been founded upon the rock. (Mat 7:25 NAS)*

In Matthew 7:25, the rain came out of the sky down to earth; however, the location of where the rain landed is qualified with a preposition. The rain descended against that house. The word requires a preposition to qualify the direction of travel. *The Oxford Advanced Learner's Dictionary* defines a "preposition" as,

> *A word or group of words, such as in, from, to, out of and on behalf of, used before a noun or pronoun to show place, position, time or method* [183]

The following verses show how the word "καταβαίνω" (katabaino) is used in conjunction with a preposition. The word is used to describe going from one city to another.

> *And when they had spoken the word in Perga, **they went down to Attalia**. (Act 14:25 NAS)*

> *and passing by Mysia, they **came down to Troas**. (Act 16:8 NAS)*

> *And He **went down** with them, and came **to Nazareth**; and He continued in subjection to them; and His mother treasured all these things in her heart. (Luk 2:51 NAS)*

Going from one city to another does not mean descending from the sky. It is the motion from one location to another. The word is also used to describe travelling on a road.

> *And by chance a certain priest **was going down on that road**, and when he saw him, he passed by on the other side. (Luk 10:31 NAS)*

> *Jesus replied and said, "A certain man was going down from Jerusalem to Jericho; and he fell among robbers, and they stripped him and beat him, and went off leaving him half dead And by chance a certain priest was **going down on that road**, and when he saw him, he passed by on the other side." (Luk 10:30-31 NAS)*

The word also is used to describe from where the person came from previously.

> *And when **He had come down from the mountain**, great multitudes followed Him. (Mat 8:1 NAS)*

James said all good things come from the Father from above.

> *Every good thing bestowed and every perfect gift is from above, **coming down from the Father** of lights, with whom there is no variation, or shifting shadow. (Jam 1:17 NAS)*

This does not mean the gift itself descended from heaven and travelled down to earth and landed on us. It simply means God gave it to us. When Christ comes in heaven, He is descending from heaven.

> *For the Lord Himself **will descend from heaven** with a shout, with the voice of the archangel, and with the trumpet of God; and the dead in Christ shall rise first. Then we who are alive and remain shall be caught up together with them **in the clouds** to meet the Lord **in the air**, and thus we shall always be with the Lord. (1Th 4:16-17 NAS)*

This does not say He descends and lands on earth. Paul literally said "in the clouds" and "in the air." Descending in heaven simply means, He is traveling in heaven. The Bible never says that the New Jerusalem comes down out of heaven and lands on earth or to believers. If the City of God was coming down to land on earth like a UFO, it would seem that the proper Greek word would be καθίημι (kathiemi). *The NASB Concordance* defines καθίημι (kathiemi) as,

> *<2524> καθίημι (kathiemi)*
> *Meaning: to let down*
> *Origin: from 2596 and hiemi (to send)*
> *Usage: down(1), let down(2), lowered(2), lowering*(1).*
> *Notes: ¹ Or, heaven ² Or, vessel ᵃ Joh 1:51 [184]*

The vision of Peter is an example of an object coming from heaven and landing on earth. Peter had a vision of a great sheet coming down from heaven and landing on the ground. Acts 10:11 states,

> *And he behold the sky opened up, and a certain object like a great sheet **coming down** [καταβαίνω (katabaino)], **lowered** [καθίημι (kathiemi)] by four corners **to the ground**, (Act 10:11 NAS)*

The same account of Peters vision was explained again in Acts 11:5.

> *I was in the city of Joppa praying; and in a trance I saw a vision, a certain object **coming down** [καταβαίνω (katabaino)] like a great sheet **lowered** [καθίημι*

*(kathiemi)] by four corners from the sky; and it came [ἔρχομαι (erchomai)] right [ἄχρι (achri)] down **to me.** (Act 11:5 NAS)*

The phrase "down to me" in Acts 11:5 is not in the Greek. The word "right" is expressing the position in front of him. *The NASB Concordance* defines the word "right" as,

> **<891>** ἄχρι *(achri)*
> **Meaning:** *until, as far as*
> **Origin:** *a prim. particle, prep.*
> **Usage:** *as far as(5), as high as(1), as long as(1), even to(1), right(1), thus far(1), until(29), within(1).*
> **Notes:**¹ *Or, vessel* ² *Or, heaven* ᵃ *Act 10:9-32; Act 11:5-14* ᵇ *Act 9:10 [185]*

The "great sheet" came "right" before Peter. If John, in Revelation 21:2, wanted to say the New Jerusalem came down to earth or inhabited believers, it seems he would have said, I saw the New Jerusalem coming down, lowering on to believers or something to that effect. The Bible says nothing of the sort. When believers die, they are raised from the dead and receive their inheritance in heaven which is located in the New Jerusalem, the City of God. Christ reigns over heaven and earth from the New Jerusalem. Christ will continue to reign over the earthly dimension from the heavenly dimension, the City of God, until all His enemies including death is abolished. All Nations must submit to the rule of Christ NOW and not in some future event.

> *The last enemy that will be abolished is death. For He has put all things in subjection under His feet. But when He says, "All things are put in subjection," it is evident that He is excepted who put all things in subjection to Him. And when all things are subjected to Him, then the Son Himself also will be subjected to the One who subjected all things to Him, that God may be all in all. (1Co 15:26-28 NAS)*

All nations are subject to Christ as King in heaven as an ongoing event.

Chapter 9 - The Feasts and the end times

Chapter 10 - The Christian Day of Worship

As we learned from the beginning of this book, the day of worship is a point of division in the church. Some demand Christian worship to be observed on Saturday and some on Sunday. The arguments are hinged upon the relationship between Christian worship and the Sabbath. The fact is, there is no specific day designated for worship. The ceremonies in the Law of Moses were scheduled on many different days of the week not just the seventh day. Likewise, Jesus and the Apostles were at the temple every day. The Scriptural evidence is overwhelming that Christian worship is not constrained to the seventh day or the Sabbath. The Ceremonial Laws in the Old Testament were not worship services. Also, the worship services performed by the Christian Church are not instituted in the Old Testament. The Old Testament Ceremonial Laws looked forward to the coming of the Messiah and the New Testament Christians looked back to the fulfillment of the Ceremonial Laws in Christ's messianic work. The Ceremonial Law in the Old Testament was always differentiated from the Church service by the early Church Fathers.

1. The designated day for worship in the Old Testament

Ceremonies, feasts, festivals, new moons, and the sacrifices were all scheduled on many different days during the week. The purpose of this section is to show the seventh day is NOT the sole day for worship ceremonies. Actually, worship services should be very limited on the Sabbath. Seventh Day Adventist church members argue that the seventh day is the day for worship because Leviticus 23:3 says to have a "holy convocation" on the seventh day. There are many instances in the Old Testament where God's people were commanded to assemble on the first or eighth day. This fact is largely overlooked by most Christians. The circumcision ceremony is an example of a ceremony not being constrained to the seventh day. Circumcision on the eighth day after the child is born (Lev 12:3) can cause circumcision to be performed any day of the week including the Sabbath. Sacrifices are not constrained to the seventh day either. Lambs and grain were offered on the eighth day (Lev 14:10, 23, Lev 15:14). A Seventh Day Adventist friend of mine argued that Leviticus 23 verse 3 says to have a convocation on the seventh day; therefore, God commanded him to go to church on Saturday. Leviticus says,

> *For six days work may be done; but on **the seventh day there is a sabbath of complete rest**, a holy convocation. You shall not do any work; it is a sabbath to the LORD in all your dwellings. (Lev 23:3 NAS)*

This Seventh Day Adventist argument lacks any serious study of Scripture. God's people assembled (or had a convocation) and did no work on the first day also.

a. The assembly and the first day

There are Ceremonial Laws in the Old Testament requiring the people to do no work and to assemble on the first day (Num 28:18, 29:1). The Feast of Unleavened Bread, Feast of Trumpets, and Feast of Booths all required no work on the first day. In the book of Exodus, the people were to assemble and do no work on the Feast of Unleavened Bread.

> *And on **the first day you shall have a holy assembly, and another holy assembly on the seventh day; no work at all shall be done on them**, except what must be eaten by every person, that alone may be prepared by you. (Exo 12:16 NAS see Exo 13:6)*

The books of Leviticus and Numbers also commanded the people to do no work and assemble on the first day for the Feast of Unleavened Bread.

> ***On the first day you shall have a holy convocation**; you shall not do any laborious work. (Lev 23:7 NAS see also Num 28:18)*

In the book of Numbers, the people were to assemble and do no work on the first day on the Feast of Trumpets.

> *Now in the seventh month, **on the first day of the month, you shall also have a holy convocation; you shall do no laborious work.** It will be to you a day for blowing trumpets. (Num 29:1 NAS see also Num 10:10)*

On the Feast of Booths, ancient Israel also assembled on the first day and the eighth day. The book of Leviticus states,

> *On **the first day is a holy convocation; you shall do no laborious work of any kind**...On exactly the fifteenth day of the seventh month, when you have gathered in the crops of the land, you shall celebrate the feast of the LORD for seven days, **with a rest on the first day and a rest on the eighth day**. (Lev 23:23,39 NAS)*

The people assembled on the first and eighth day for the Feast of Booths. The book of Nehemiah states,

> *And they found written in the law how the LORD had commanded through Moses that the sons of Israel should live in booths during the feast of the seventh month....And he read from the book of the law of God daily, **from the first day to the last day**. And they celebrated the feast seven days, and **on the eighth day there was a solemn assembly** according to the ordinance. (Neh 8:14,18 NAS)*

The Law required God's people to do no work on the eighth day. In second Chronicles, the people assembled on the eighth day for dedicating the altar.

> *And **on the eighth day they held a solemn assembly**, for the dedication of the altar they observed seven days, and the feast seven days. (2Ch 7:9 NAS)*

In Ezekiel, sacrifices were offered on the eight day and throughout the week.

> *And when they have completed the days, it shall be that **on the eighth day and onward**, the priests shall offer your burnt offerings on the altar, and your peace offerings; and I will accept you, declares the Lord God. (Eze 43:27 NAS)*

The Consecration of the Temple began on the first and ended on the eighth day. Second Chronicles states,

> *Now **they began the consecration on the first day of the first month, and on the eighth day of the month** they entered the porch of the LORD. Then they consecrated the house of the LORD in eight days, and finished on the sixteenth day of the first month. (2Ch 29:17 NAS)*

Clearly the seventh day is not the only day the Israelites were commanded to assemble, do no work, and perform ceremonies. To argue the holy convocation was ONLY on the seventh day requires a considerable amount of ignorance. Only providing evidence that supports the argument while ignoring all the counter evidence is the "fallacy of exclusion" or "cherry picking."

Some may argue we are required to go to church on Sunday from these Bible passages. These feasts are not teaching a Sunday Sabbath either. The requirement to assemble and do no labor on the first day is not the Fourth Commandment to "keep the Sabbath holy." The command to assemble and do no labor on these days was for the purpose of performing sacrifices for the people. This was to keep the promises that the Messiah was to come from the Jewish genealogy.

> *Paul, a bond-servant of Christ Jesus, called as an apostle, set apart for the gospel of God, which He promised beforehand through His prophets in the holy Scriptures, **concerning His Son, who was born of a descendant of David according to the flesh**, who was declared the Son of God with power by the resurrection from the dead, according to the Spirit of holiness, Jesus Christ our Lord. (Rom 1:1-4 NAS)*

Jesus Christ is the fulfillment of the sacrifices Himself. Christ ended all the feasts, festivals, new moons and sacrifices forever by offering Himself as the sacrifice. The writer of Hebrews wrote,

> *After saying above, "Sacrifices and offerings and whole burnt offerings and sacrifices for sin Thou hast not desired, nor hast Thou taken pleasure in them" (which are offered according to the Law), then He said, "Behold, I have come to do Thy will." He takes away the first in order to establish the second. By this will we have been sanctified through the offering of the body of Jesus Christ once for all. And every priest stands daily ministering and offering time after time the same sacrifices, which can never take away sins; but He, having offered one sacrifice for sins for all time, sat down at the right hand of God, waiting from that time onward until His enemies be made a footstool for His feet. **For by one offering He has perfected for all time those who are sanctified.** (Heb 10:8-14 NAS)*

b. Daily offerings in the Old Testament

The seventh day was NOT the day for performing the Ceremonial Laws. The Ceremonial Laws were performed every day of the week. Sacrifices and offerings were a daily activity in the Old Testament. They not only would have feasts and festivals on various days, the Israelites would be able to go to the temple, offer sacrifices, and worship any day of the week. Offerings were to be done continually. The Book of Numbers says,

> *This is the offering by fire which you shall offer to the LORD; two male lambs one year old without defect as **a continual burnt offering every day**. (Num 28:3 NAS Num 28:24; 29:6)*

Solomon continued the daily practice of the Ceremonial Laws. Solomon called the feasts, new moons, sabbaths and duties the priest performed "the daily rule."

> *Then Solomon offered burnt offerings to the LORD on the altar of the LORD which he had built before the porch; and did so according to the daily rule, offering them up according to the commandment of Moses, for the Sabbaths, the new moons, and the three annual feasts-- the Feast of Unleavened Bread, the Feast of Weeks, and the Feast of Booths. Now according to the ordinance of his father David, he appointed the divisions of the priests for their service, and the Levites for **their duties of praise and ministering before the priests according to the daily rule**, and the gatekeepers by their divisions at every gate; for David the man of God had so commanded. (2Ch 8:12-14 NAS)*

During the ancient Israelites captivity in Babylon, Ezekiel prophesied of the restoration of the daily offering in Israel. Ezekiel wrote,

> *Thus they shall provide the lamb, the grain offering, and the oil, morning by morning, for **a continual burnt offering**. (Eze 46:15 NAS)*

After the ancient Israelites were released from the Babylonian captivity, the daily offerings were reinstituted in Jerusalem at the beginning of the rebuilding of the second temple. Ezra wrote,

> *And whatever is needed, both young bulls, rams, and lambs for a burnt offering to the God of heaven, and wheat, salt, wine, and anointing oil, as the priests in Jerusalem request, **it is to be given to them daily without fail**, that they may offer acceptable sacrifices to the God of heaven and pray for the life of the king and his sons. (Ezr 6:9-10 NAS)*

There is no sole designated day in the week for ceremonies. The Bible clearly teaches ceremonies in the Law of Moses were performed every day of the week.

2. The designated day for worship in the New Testament

The Christian Church has always gathered together on the first day of the week which was always called the "Lord's Day." The Lord's Day is not the Sabbath or the Christian Sabbath. Christ rose from the dead and visited the disciples on the first day of the week. Starting the main service on the first day of the week is easily established in the Bible. On the first day of the week, Jesus came to the disciples and stood with them. John wrote,

> *When therefore it was evening, on that day, **the first day of the week**, and when the doors were shut where the disciples were, for fear of the Jews, Jesus came and stood in their midst, and said to them, "Peace be with you." And when He had said this, He*

> *showed them both His hands and His side. The disciples therefore rejoiced when they saw the Lord. Jesus therefore said to them again, "**Peace be with you; as the Father has sent Me, I also send you**." (Joh 20:19-21 NAS)*

On that same day, Christ "breathed" on the disciples to "receive the Holy Spirit" and preached faith in His resurrection from the dead. John continues,

> *And when He had said this, He breathed on them, and said to them, "**Receive the Holy Spirit. If you forgive the sins of any, their sins have been forgiven them; if you retain the sins of any, they have been retained**." But Thomas, one of the twelve, called Didymus, was not with them when Jesus came. The other disciples therefore were saying to him, "We have seen the Lord!" But he said to them, "Unless I shall see in His hands the imprint of the nails, and put my finger into the place of the nails, and put my hand into His side, I will not believe." (Joh 20:22-25 NAS)*

Christ met with the disciples to remove any doubts about His resurrection from the dead and to preach faith in Him as Christ. Christ promised He would come again after His crucifixion. Jesus visited the disciples again after eight days or on the eighth day which is the first day of the week. This similarly aligns with the Feast of Booths "with a rest on the first day and a rest on the eighth day" (Lev 23:39 NAS). The Apostles continued to assemble and preach faith in Christ in a weekly cycle starting on the first day. John wrote,

> *And **after eight days** again His disciples were inside, and Thomas with them. Jesus came, the doors having been shut, and stood in their midst, and said, "Peace be with you." Then He said to Thomas, "Reach here your finger, and see My hands; and reach here your hand, and put it into My side; and be not unbelieving, but believing." Thomas answered and said to Him, "My Lord and my God!" Jesus said to him, "Because you have seen Me, have you believed? Blessed are they who did not see, and yet believed." (Joh 20:26-29 NAS)*

John 20 is showing the disciples gathering together in a weekly cycle starting on the first day. Jesus gave the "Great Commission" on the first day when Christ rose from the dead. Mark wrote,

> *Now after He had risen early **on the first day of the week**, He first appeared to Mary Magdalene, from whom He had cast out seven demons...And afterward He appeared to the eleven themselves as they were reclining at the table; and He reproached them for their unbelief and hardness of heart, because they had not believed those who had seen Him after He had risen. And He said to them, "**Go into all the world and preach the gospel to all creation**. "He who has believed and has been baptized shall be saved; but he who has disbelieved shall be condemned. (Mar 16: 9,14-16 NAS)*

The Apostles assembled to teach, fellowship, eat, pray, and give gifts to those in need. Luke shows how much work is required to collect gifts.

> *And they were continually devoting themselves to the apostles' teaching and to fellowship, to the breaking of bread and to prayer. And everyone kept feeling a sense of awe; and many wonders and signs were taking place through the apostles. And all those who had believed were together, and had all things in common; and **they began selling their property and possessions, and were sharing them with all, as anyone might have need**. (Act 2:42-45 NAS)*

Selling property breaks the Sabbath. This is one reason why the first day is the designated day to gather "the collection for the saints." This example is shown by the Apostles in Acts. The Apostle Paul explains to the Corinthians the same thing he explained to Galatia and all the churches. Paul wrote,

> *Now concerning the collection for the saints, as I directed the churches of Galatia, so do you also. **On the first day of every week let each one of you put aside and save**, as he may prosper, that no collections be made when I come. (1Co 16:1-2 NAS)*

It is efficient and maintains the anonymity of the giver to give gifts for the saints on the first day when the church assembles. Those who give to the saints are not to put themselves into the spotlight, but give in secret. When gifts are distributed throughout the week, those who receive the gifts should not see who donated the gifts. Also, those who give gifts should not seek to be publicly recognized. Jesus said,

> *But when you give alms, do not let your left hand know what your right hand is doing. (Mat 6:3 NAS)*

The first day of the week is also the proper day to assemble because it does not conflict with the Fourth Commandment to "keep the Sabbath holy." Collecting and distributing gifts, teaching and studying, cooking and serving, travelling, etc. are all works that break the Sabbath especially if there are profits. It stands to reason why these activities would not be done on the Sabbath.

a. Christ and the Apostles worshiped daily

Jesus was in the temple every day. He did not designate the Sabbath or the first day to be the sole day to worship God. Luke wrote,

> *And **He was teaching daily in the temple**; but the chief priests and the scribes and the leading men among the people were trying to destroy Him. (Luk 19:47 NAS)*

Jesus marveled at the leaders of Israel for arresting Him like a thief or robber. He sat with the leaders of Israel in the temple every day. Christ was not hiding from the law like a criminal. Matthew wrote,

> *At that time Jesus said to the multitudes, "Have you come out with swords and clubs to arrest Me as against a robber? **Every day I used to sit in the temple** teaching and you did not seize Me." (Mat 26:55 NAS see Mar 14:49, Luk 22:53)*

As a matter of fact, the leaders of Israel arrested Jesus in a secluded location at night where no one could see (Mat 26). Clearly, Jesus was in the temple every day and not specifically on the Sabbath. The Apostles did not designate a sole day for worship. The Apostles were also in the temple daily. In the book of Acts, Luke wrote,

> ***And day by day continuing with one mind in the temple,*** *and breaking bread from house to house, they were taking their meals together with gladness and sincerity of heart, praising God, and having favor with all the people. And* ***the Lord was adding to their number day by day*** *those who were being saved. (Act 2:46-47 NAS)*

Disciples were added to the church daily and not on every Sabbath. Luke wrote,

> *So the churches were being strengthened in the faith, and were* ***increasing in number daily****. (Act 16:5 NAS)*

Paul noted how the Bereans examined the Scriptures daily. In the book of Acts, Luke wrote,

> *Now these were more noble-minded than those in Thessalonica, for they received the word with great eagerness,* ***examining the Scriptures daily****, to see whether these things were so. (Act 17:11 NAS)*

Paul knew the Bereans were studying every day because Paul himself was at the synagogue every day. Luke wrote in Acts,

> *So he was reasoning* ***in the synagogue*** *with the Jews and the God-fearing Gentiles,* ***and in the market place every day*** *with those who happened to be present. (Act 17:17 NAS)*

When they could not be at the synagogue, they were at schools, homes, and many different locations. Luke says,

> *But when some were becoming hardened and disobedient, speaking evil of the Way before the multitude, he withdrew from them and took away the disciples,* ***reasoning daily*** *in the school of Tyrannus. (Act 19:9 NAS)*

The temple is no longer the designated location for God's people to worship. God's people will worship Him in spirit and truth. Jesus said,

> *But an hour is coming, and now is, when the true worshipers shall worship the Father in spirit and truth; for such people the Father seeks to be His worshipers. "****God is spirit, and those who worship Him must worship in spirit and truth.****" (Joh 4:23-24 NAS)*

The most important mission Christians have is the "Great Commission." We are to make disciples, baptizing them, teaching them God's commandments even to the end of the age. Matthew wrote,

> *And Jesus came up and spoke to them, saying, "All authority has been given to Me in heaven and on earth. Go therefore and make disciples of all the nations, baptizing them in the name of the Father and the Son and the Holy Spirit, teaching them to observe all that I commanded you; and lo,* ***I am with you always, even to the end of the age.****" (Mat 28:18-1 NAS)*

The Christian focus is on the gospel and the needs of the people. The Christian Church is not a social club, haven for criminals, source of entertainment, for profit business, marketing campaign, or anything of the sort. Many Churches in modern times operate more like a for profit business. They have posted business hours. The mission of the Church is not to show up at Church one day a week and then go home. It is a constant preaching of the Word of God every day.

3. Communion breaks the Sabbath

The Church is united as one in Christ regardless of the denomination (Rom 12:5; 1Co 8:6). If Christians do not partake or have communion with other Christians, they will spiritually starve, and wither like a plant without water (Joh 6:33-351, 15:5; Pet 2:2). The word "communion" has all but lost its meaning in the modern church. The average Christian defines the word "communion" as the "Lord's Supper" or the "Eucharist." The Lord's Supper or the Eucharist are not communion in and of themselves. Communion is all of the church activities combined. The doctrine of "the Communion of Saints" is critical to Christian worship and life. The sole day for worship should NOT be on the Sabbath because of the Communion of the Saints.

The doctrine of the Communion of the Saints has fallen to the wayside in modern Christianity. It is difficult for some to accept that communion is actually doing good works in the Church as opposed to a ritual ceremony of bread and wine. The Communion of the Saints is rejected largely due to antinomian theologians teaching that good works are not necessary for salvation. Church members are obligated to help each other who are in need. *The Westminster Confession of Faith* states this perfectly.

> *All saints, that are united to Jesus Christ their Head, by his Spirit, ... and, being united to one another in love, they have communion in each other's gifts and graces, and are obliged to the performance of such duties, public and private, as do conduce to their mutual good, both in the inward and outward man. [186]*

The Church is required to perform services to help other Christians with their spiritual and physical necessities. *The Westminster Confession of Faith* states,

> *Saints by profession are bound to maintain an holy fellowship and communion in the worship of God, and in performing such other spiritual services as tend to their mutual edification; as also in relieving each other in outward things, according to their several abilities and necessities. Which communion, as God offereth opportunity, is to be extended unto all those who, in every place, call upon the name of the Lord Jesus. [187]*

The core duties performed on the Lord's Day are the Lord's Supper, Baptism, Prayer, preaching the Word, teaching, and giving thanks to our Lord. Those are not the only duties required by Christians. The Christian Church is also required to support food banks, give cloths, educate people, heal those who are sick, offer psychological help, help with drug addiction and alcoholism, shelter the homeless, and much more. The Great Commission of the Church is a missionary outreach to the world. This does not mean the Christian Church is a "communist" or "socialist" ideology.

a. Socialism or Communism

Some Christians confuse communion with socialism or communism. The Bible does not teach socialism or communism. Communion is nothing like socialism or communism. It is important to clarify the difference between communion and communism in order to prevent some from becoming confused with the communion doctrine. The Church has no right to deprive people of their property as if the Church is Christ Himself. The Bible nowhere teaches any kind of socialism or communism. Those who teach the "redistribution of wealth" are false teachers and are to be rejected. *The Westminster Confession of Faith* states,

> *This communion which the saints have with Christ, doth not make them in any wise partakers of the substance of his Godhead; or to be equal with Christ in any respect: either of which to affirm is impious and blasphemous.* **Nor doth their communion one with another, as saints, take away, or infringe the title or propriety which each man hath in his goods and possessions.** *[188]*

There are some who believe Christ and the Apostles were teaching a socialist or communist type of redistribution of the wealth. They believe that the Church is required to redistribute the wealth to the poor in the world. A common Scripture that is quoted for this is in Matthew.

> *Then the righteous will answer Him, saying, "Lord, when did we see You hungry, and feed You, or thirsty, and give You drink? And when did we see You a stranger, and invite You in, or naked, and clothe You? And when did we see You sick, or in prison, and come to You?" And the King will answer and say to them, "Truly I say to you, to the extent that you did it to one of these brothers of Mine, even the least of them, you did it to Me." (Mat 25:37-40 NAS)*

They believe Jesus is teaching that He required food, clothes, and housing to be supplied to everyone. Claiming Christ taught socialism is far from the truth. It does not take much digging into the Bible to show how erroneous socialism is. In the same chapter of Matthew 25, Jesus taught the parable of the ten virgins. Jesus said,

> *Then the kingdom of heaven will be comparable to ten virgins, who took their lamps, and went out to meet the bridegroom.* **And five of them were foolish, and five were prudent.** *For when the foolish took their lamps, they took no oil with them, but the prudent took oil in flasks along with their lamps. Now while the bridegroom was delaying, they all got drowsy and began to sleep. But at midnight there was a shout, 'Behold, the bridegroom! Come out to meet him.' Then all those virgins rose, and trimmed their lamps.* **And the foolish said to the prudent, 'Give us some of your oil, for our lamps are going out.' But the prudent answered, saying, 'No, there will not be enough for us and you too; go instead to the dealers and buy some for yourselves.'** *And while they were going away to make the purchase, the bridegroom came, and those who were ready went in with him to the wedding feast; and the door was shut. And later the other virgins also came, saying, 'Lord, lord, open up for us.' But he answered and said,* **"Truly I say to you, I do not know you."** *(Mat 25:1-12 NAS)*

The "foolish" virgins' lamps were not given oil by the "prudent" virgins to help them meet the bridegroom. The Lord said, "I do not know you" to the foolish virgins. Likewise, in the same chapter of Matthew 25, Jesus taught the parable of the talents. The parable of the talents clearly shows God promotes the capitalistic use of money. Jesus said,

> *For it is just like a man about to go on a journey, who called his own slaves, and entrusted his possessions to them.* **And to one he gave five talents, to another, two, and to another, one, each according to his own ability**; *and he went on his journey. Immediately the one who had received the five talents went and* **traded with them, and gained five more talents.** *In the same manner the one who had received the* **two talents gained two more.** *But he who received the one talent went away and dug in the ground, and* **hid his master's money.** *(Mat 25:14-18 NAS)*

When the master came back, He castigated the slave who buried the talent. He gave the talent to the slave with ten talents and cast out the slave who had the one talent.

> *But his master answered and said to him, You wicked, lazy slave, you knew that I reap where I did not sow, and gather where I scattered no seed.* **Then you ought to have put my money in the bank, and on my arrival I would have received my money back with interest. Therefore take away the talent from him, and give it to the one who has the ten talents.** *For to everyone who has shall more be given, and he shall have an abundance; but from the one who does not have, even what he does have shall be taken away.* **And cast out the worthless slave into the outer darkness; in that place there shall be weeping and gnashing of teeth.** *(Mat 25:26-30 NAS)*

Jesus taught the opposite of the redistribution of wealth. The parable of the talents clearly does not promote the idea of taking talents from the wealthier person and giving it to the poorer person. Those who worked to increase their financial gain are not condemned but praised by Jesus. The Bible verse claimed to support socialism is talking about the judgment at the last day.

> *But when the Son of Man comes in His glory, and all the angels with Him, then He will sit on His glorious throne. (Mat 25:31 NAS)*

Christ is dividing the sheep, those who inherit the kingdom prepared from the foundation of the world, (Mat 25:34) and the goats, those who inherit eternal fire which has been prepared for the devil and his angels (Mat 25:41). Jesus said of the sheep,

> *For I was hungry, and you gave Me something to eat; I was thirsty, and you gave Me drink; I was a stranger, and you invited Me in; naked, and you clothed Me; I was sick, and you visited Me; I was in prison, and you came to Me. (Mat 25:35-36 NAS)*

Helping someone who is hungry, thirsty, a stranger, naked, sick, and in prison is not necessarily referring to poor people. You do not need to be poor to experience any of these things. Christ is talking about caring about His "brothers" the sheep. Those who claimed to be righteous persecuted Christ's sheep. Christ takes it personally how His sheep are treated.

> *Truly I say to you, to the extent that you did it to one of **these brothers of Mine**, even the least of them, you did it to Me....Then He will answer them, saying, Truly I say to you, to the extent that you did not do it to one of the least of these, you did not do it to Me. (Mat 25:40,45 NAS)*

God's people are to be cared for. This does not mean that those who do no work or who have no regard for Christ or His commandments are to be given special treatment. Nowhere does the Bible teach to give food or anything to those who refuse to work or who lead an undisciplined life. The Apostle Paul wrote,

> *For even when we were with you, we used to give you this order: **if anyone will not work, neither let him eat.** For we hear that some among you are leading an undisciplined life, doing no work at all, but acting like busybodies. (2Th 3:10-11 NAS)*

When the Church feeds the poor and provides services for those in need, it is for the purpose of reforming their life or because they are incapable of helping themselves. For example, widows, the blind, or the crippled. Christianity is missionary work and not a socialistic society for people who do not love Christ. The Christian Church should provide food, clothing, volunteer work and more for those in need as a part of their service. The people are not to have their wealth stolen by the Church to redistribute it to the poor. Paul said to willingly put aside gifts according to the determination of the individual.

> *Let each one of you put aside and save, as he may prosper. (1Co 16:2 NAS)*

The Apostles set the example of helping the needy in the ministry after Pentecost. Luke wrote in the book of Acts,

> *And with great power the apostles were giving witness to the resurrection of the Lord Jesus, and abundant grace was upon them all. For there was not a needy person among them, **for all who were owners of land or houses would sell them and bring the proceeds of the sales, and lay them at the apostles' feet**; and they would be distributed to each, as any had need. (Act 4:33-35 NAS)*

The Apostles helped those among the Christian Church. They did not go out and help God hating lazy people. Taking money from anyone is called stealing. Redistribution of the wealth is stealing. Implementing a socialist or communist government actually causes starvation and the imprisonment of God's people. God requires each individual person to help their neighbor in need. Pushing an individual's responsibility on to a socialistic government does not negate that individua's responsibility.

b. Helping the needy

Helping the needy is an integral part of the Christian mission. The Law of God commands us to help the needy individually. The leaders of Israel during Christ's time did not help God's people at all. The Law of God required the people to provide help for the poor and the alien. Not that long ago, the doctrine of the Communion of the Saints was taught throughout Christianity. This is why the "Old Denominations" have hospitals, schools, thrift stores, mental health services, and food distribution ministries. This is why the Apostles collected gifts on the first day or the Lord's Day (1Co 16:1-2). There will always be people in need (Mat 26:11; Mar 14:7; Luk 12:8). For this reason, helping the poor is an integral part of the mission of the Church. God commands us to open our hand to the needy. The book of Deuteronomy says,

> *For the poor will never cease to be in the land; therefore I command you, saying, You shall freely open your hand to your brother, to your needy and poor in your land. (Deu 15:11 NAS)*

God does not forget the poor. He has compassion on the poor. The Psalmist wrote,

> *He will have compassion on the poor and needy, And the lives of the needy he will save. (Psa 72:13 NAS)*

He desires for the poor to be lifted up and not suppressed.

> *Vindicate the weak and fatherless; Do justice to the afflicted and destitute. Rescue the weak and needy; Deliver them out of the hand of the wicked. (Psa 82:3-4 NAS)*

God desires for the needy to be lifted up from poverty. The Psalmist wrote,

> *He raises the poor from the dust, And lifts the needy from the ash heap, To make them sit with princes, With the princes of His people. (Psa 113:7-8 NAS)*

God takes it personally when the poor are abused. Proverbs says,

> *He who oppresses the poor reproaches his Maker, But he who is gracious to the needy honors Him. (Pro 14:31 NAS)*

Oppressing people and destroying lives for dishonest gain is particularly abhorrent to the Lord. Ezekiel wrote,

> *Her princes within her are like wolves tearing the prey, by shedding blood and destroying lives in order to get dishonest gain. And her prophets have smeared whitewash for them, seeing false visions and divining lies for them, saying, 'Thus says the Lord God,' when the LORD has not spoken.* **The people of the land have practiced oppression and committed robbery, and they have wronged the poor and needy and have oppressed the sojourner without justice.** *And I searched for a man among them who should build up the wall and stand in the gap before Me for the land, that I should not destroy it; but I found no one. (Eze 22:27-30 NAS)*

> *Behold, this was the guilt of your sister Sodom: she and her daughters had arrogance, abundant food, and careless ease,* **but she did not help the poor and needy.** *(Eze 16:49 NAS)*

The gospel is not for specific social classes. Jesus said for all to come to Him.

> *Come to Me, all who are weary and heavy-laden, and I will give you rest. Take My yoke upon you, and learn from Me, for I am gentle and humble in heart; and you*

shall find rest for your souls. For My yoke is easy, and My load is light. (Mat 11:28-30 NAS)

There should be no partiality in the Christian church or in the government legal system towards poor people. Showing partiality and neglecting the needy is sinning against Gods Law.

But if you show partiality, you are committing sin and are convicted by the law as transgressors...If a brother or sister is without clothing and in need of daily food, and one of you says to them, "Go in peace, be warmed and be filled," and yet you do not give them what is necessary for their body, what use is that? Even so faith, if it has no works, is dead, being by itself. (Jam 2:9,15-17 NAS)

The reality is that Churches who do not help and neglect those in need will be held accountable in the judgment at the last day which is at death.

Now it came about that the poor man died and he was carried away by the angels to Abraham's bosom; and the rich man also died and was buried. And in Hades he lifted up his eyes, being in torment, and saw Abraham far away, and Lazarus in his bosom. And he cried out and said, Father Abraham, have mercy on me, and send Lazarus, that he may dip the tip of his finger in water and cool off my tongue; for I am in agony in this flame. (Luk 16:22-24 NAS)

The day of worship is not the Sabbath. Clearly, the mission of the church is a lot of work. For this reason, the Apostles continued the tradition of meeting on the first day as the starting day for the church to assemble. This does not mean it is the only day to worship God. Christians should be able to go to church and worship any day of the week, as long as they do no work on the Sabbath. Helping the sick, feeding those who are in need, helping those in an emergency, giving cloths, and so forth is not breaking the Sabbath. Collecting money, cooking food, collecting cloths, paying musicians to play instruments, selling property, paying church government, or anything that has to do with an occupation is breaking the Sabbath.

Chapter 10 - The Christian Day of Worship

Chapter 11 - Conclusion

The divisions in the Church over the Sabbath are trivial and meaningless. Why is the day of worship a point of division? We can worship God any day of the week; however, when it comes to the Sabbath day, there should be no work done at Church. Worship, sacrifices, ceremonies, and festivals were clearly done every day of the week. Yet, observing a Saturday or Sunday worship service has become such a central point for division that churches split over it. Dividing over First Day Sabbatarian, Seventh Day Sabbatarian, and Antinomian doctrines is completely absurd. All of these arguments are poorly constructed and lack support from Scripture. The First Day Sabbatarian has no evidence the Sabbath was changed to Sunday or called the "Christian Sabbath." The Seventh Day Sabbatarian insists the Sabbath is the designated day for Christian worship on Saturday. The Bible clearly does not teach this. Jesus clearly said the priest broke the Sabbath,

> *Or have you not read in the Law, that on the Sabbath the priests in the temple break the Sabbath, and are innocent? (Mat 12:5 NAS)*

Performing ceremonies on the Sabbath breaks the Fourth Commandment. The First Day Sabbatarian and Seventh Day Sabbatarian doctrines both fail tremendously in this regard. The Antinomian says we are under grace; therefore, we no longer are required to keep ANY of God's Law. Teaching Christians to not keep God's Law destroys the gospel. How do we repent from our sin if we have no Law?

> *Do not think that I came to abolish the Law or the Prophets; I did not come to abolish, but to fulfill. For truly I say to you, until heaven and earth pass away, not the smallest letter or stroke shall pass away from the Law, until all is accomplished.* ***Whoever then annuls one of the least of these commandments, and so teaches others, shall be called least in the kingdom of heaven; but whoever keeps and teaches them, he shall be called great in the kingdom of heaven.*** *(Mat 5:17-19 NAS)*

Antinomian doctrine is bewildering to figure out. What is the Christian supposed to follow according to this view? They turn the sermon on the Mount or any verse on the Law into an irrelevant teaching for Christians. The Law of Moses must be taught in its entirety in order for the gospel message to be preached. Leaving out the Law negates the need for repentance and acknowledgment of our sin. The three prevalent views of the Sabbath are undeniably unscriptural and divisive.

The Law of Moses should be acknowledged as having a three-part structure: The Moral, Judicial, and Ceremonial law. All law has divisions within it. In order to properly understand the gospel, it is crucial to divide the Law of Moses into three parts. The feasts, festivals, new moons, sabbaths, and sacrifices are Ceremonial Laws that foreshadow the messianic work of Christ. The fulfillment of the Ceremonial Law does not abolish the requirement for the Law to be enforced. Jesus Christ fulfilled all the requirements of the entire Law for us on our behalf once and for all, past, present, and future. This does not mean we are no longer required to observe the law. It simply means that our sins are forgiven for transgressing the Law. The Ceremonial Law can only be performed by the high priest. Jesus forever satisfied the requirement of the Ceremonial Law for us as our high priest. Christians do not need to appoint a high priest or carry out the sacrifices because Christ has, is, and will continue to satisfy the requirement for us on our behalf. If Christ is not our high priest and He did not satisfy the requirement of the sacrifices, then we are still obligated to perform sacrifices. The Moral Laws summary found in the Ten Commandments, are forever binding, and permanently in force to this day. The Judicial Laws are based on decisions made by judges from specific cases. The Moral and Judicial Laws are to be enforced by the government and kept by the people. The Moral statutory and the Judicial civil laws are legal standards in Law to this day.

The Fourth Commandment to "keep the Sabbath holy" was never established by God to be a day for worship. It is the law regulating labor, land, and commerce. Breaking the Sabbath is an actual problem in our modern world. The key aspect of the Sabbath is labor, land, and commerce. The people of any Nation must enforce a day of rest. Individuals are required to take a day for rest. Breaking the Sabbath produces workaholic behaviors that ruin families. Workers who are "undocumented" immigrants are treated as slaves getting no day off with poor working conditions and inadequate pay. Abusing immigrants and laborers breaks the Sabbath. The deforestation of land and the overproduction of the land causes the climate to become uninhabitable in those areas. Breaking the Sabbath has large ripple effects that are not noticed until they arrive. The Dust Bowl of the 1930's is a perfect example.

The feasts, festivals, new moons, sabbaths, and sacrifices prophetically foreshadow the work Christ accomplished for us as our messiah. The feasts of Leviticus 23 are all fulfilled in Christ's messianic work. For example, Christ promised to come again for His disciples. John wrote,

> *And if I go and prepare a place for you, I will come again, and receive you to Myself; that where I am, there you may be also. (Joh 14:3 NAS)*

The place Christ prepared for His people in heaven fulfills the Feast of Booths. It is our heavenly dwelling place, our final Sabbath rest. It is not the "second coming of Christ" taught by Futurist theologians. Christ personally comes for His people at death; therefore, His coming, from our perspective, occurs throughout history. In fact, His coming would be an event that occurs in the past, present, and future. When Christ gave the Great Commission to baptize and teach, He did not put a time limit on it. Matthew wrote,

> *Observe all that I commanded you; and lo, **I am with you always, even to the end of the age.** (Mat 28:20 NAS)*

We are to continue to observe the Great Commission always till the end of the age. There is no time we are to stop teaching and baptizing. As a matter of fact, Christ is reassuring the disciples that He will be with them till death. Christ coming again is part of the resurrection of the dead. This is starkly contrasted to the Futurist teaching that Christ postponed the kingdom of Heaven until the Nation of Israel is restored in the future. God's kingdom is not earthly.

> *Jesus answered, My kingdom is not of this world. If My kingdom were of this world, then My servants would be fighting, that I might not be delivered up to the Jews; but as it is, My kingdom is not of this realm. (Joh 18:36 NAS)*

Chapter 11 - Conclusion

Sound Bible exegesis leads to the conclusion that Christian worship is done every day of the week. The first day is the "Lord's Day" when the church assembles to collects gifts for the needy, the saints, and missionaries. The rest of the week is regular worship. The Bible does not designate a sole day of the week for Christian worship. The Ceremonies of the priests in the Old Testament and duties of the Apostles in the New Testament are all performed on every day of the week. The "Lord's Day" is the day the Lord rose from the dead. The first day starts the weekly communion in the Church. The institution of the Lord's supper was not the first or seventh day, but on the day He was betrayed by Judas.

> *For I received from the Lord that which I also delivered to you, that the Lord Jesus in the night in which He was betrayed took bread; and when He had given thanks, He broke it, and said, "This is My body, which is for you; do this in remembrance of Me." In the same way He took the cup also, after supper, saying, "This cup is the new covenant in My blood; do this, as often as you drink it, in remembrance of Me." (1Co 11:23-25 NAS)*

The Lord's Supper can be done any day of the week. After Christ rose from the dead, He gave the Great Commission on the first day as a fulfillment of the Feast of First Fruits.

> *Go therefore and make disciples of all the nations, baptizing them in the name of the Father and the Son and the Holy Spirit, teaching them to observe all that I commanded you; and lo, I am with you always, even to the end of the age. (Mat 28:19-20 NAS)*

Christians are to make disciples and baptize every day of the week. For Christians to divide over which day to worship by definition is "heresy." Heresy is the act of dividing the church. The word "heretick" comes from *the King James Bible*. "Heretick" is an untranslated word from the Greek word αἱρετικός (hairetikos). When comparing the *New American Standard Bible* with the *King James Bible*, it is clear that the word "heretick" is an untranslated Greek word. The NASB translators used the word "factious" instead of "heretick."

> *A man that is an **heretick** after the first and second admonition reject. (Tit 3:10 KJV)*

> *Reject a **factious** man after a first and second warning. (Tit 3:10 NAS)*

The word "factious" is an acceptable translation as opposed to the word "heretick." The context of the passage necessitates the definition of αἱρετικός (hairetikos) to be defined as "factious." The *NASB Concordance* defines the Greek word for "heretick" as,

> ***<141> αἱρετικός (hairetikos)***
> **Meaning:** *causing division*
> **Origin:** *from 138*
> **Usage:** *factious (1).*
> **Notes:** *2Jo 1:10, Rom 16:17, Mat 18:15f [189]*

Arguing and creating controversies over the Law and causing division between Christians is heresy. Foolish disputes over the Law are to be rejected. Paul wrote,

> *But shun foolish controversies and genealogies and strife and disputes about the Law; for they are unprofitable and worthless. Reject a factious man after a first and second warning, knowing that **such a man is perverted and is sinning, being self-condemned**. (Tit 3:9-11 NAS)*

Those who divide the Church and stigmatize those who disagree with their specialized interpretation of the Law are heretics. The SDA Church members who enforce Ellen White's divisive interpretation are excellent examples of causing division in the church. The SDA members who teach Sunday Christians are followers of Satan or harass SDA members for associating with Sunday Christians are condemning themselves. Labelling Christians as followers of Satan because they don't obey the Sabbath worship doctrine of the SDA church is heresy at its finest. It is truly sad because there are many God-fearing believers in the SDA church who could be more effective at preaching the Word of God if the SDA leadership did not promote Ellen White's end times Sabbath teaching. Divisive Sabbath doctrines must be rejected. Christians should never divide over which day to worship.

So, what are Christians supposed to do? What is the message? Is the Law abolished because we have grace? Are we to attend church on Saturday to obtain salvation? Are we obedient to God because we attend church on Sunday? The primary responsibility of the Christian is to preach repentance, faith, and good works. Faith, repentance, and good works are irrelevant to which day Christians attend church. God wants compassion and mercy and not sacrifices or offerings at church.

> *But go and learn what this means, I desire compassion, and not sacrifice, for I did not come to call the righteous, but sinners. (Mat 9:13 NAS)*

Christ came to save sinners and not righteous people.

> *It is a trustworthy statement, deserving full acceptance, that Christ Jesus came into the world to save sinners, among whom I am foremost of all. (1Ti 1:15 NAS)*

Only those who acknowledge themselves as sinners in repentance will be saved.

> *I tell you that in the same way, there will be more joy in heaven over one sinner who repents, than over ninety-nine righteous persons who need no repentance. (Luk 15:7 NAS)*

Christians are required to explain the entire Law of God to everyone not just Jews. ALL people are called to repent from transgressing the Law of God.

> *Or is God the God of Jews only? Is He not the God of Gentiles also? Yes, of Gentiles also, since indeed God who will justify the circumcised by faith and the uncircumcised through faith is one. Do we then nullify the Law through faith? May it never be! On the contrary, we establish the Law. (Rom 3:29-31 NAS)*

Teaching that the Law of God is only for the Nation of Israel or that it is abolished is contrary to the gospel of Christ. God is offended that ALL of humanity throughout ALL ages do not obey His Law. God's relationship with humanity is broken.

Chapter 11 - Conclusion

> *But your iniquities have made a separation between you and your God, And your sins have hidden His face from you, so that He does not hear. (Isa 59:2 NAS)*

Everyone is a sinner and will continue to be a sinner. All humanity has sinned against God. We recognize our sin because of God's Law being witnessed by the Holy Spirit within us.

> *Therefore, just as through one man sin entered into the world, and death through sin, and so death spread to all men, because all sinned--for until the Law sin was in the world; but sin is not imputed when there is no law. (Rom 5:12-13 NAS)*

> *When the Helper comes, whom I will send to you from the Father, that is the Spirit of truth, who proceeds from the Father, He will bear witness of Me. (Joh 15:26 NAS)*

> *And it is the Spirit who bears witness, because the Spirit is the truth. (1Jo 5:7 NAS)*

We are to preach and teach that the crucifixion of Christ is the ONLY sacrifice for our sins. The only way our relationship with God can be repaired is by Jesus Christ fulfilling the requirement of the Law for us.

> *For if while we were enemies, we were reconciled to God through the death of His Son, much more, having been reconciled, we shall be saved by His life. (Rom 5:10 NAS)*

Keeping the feasts, festivals, new moons, sabbaths, and sacrifices has no redemptive value.

> *For it is impossible for the blood of bulls and goats to take away sins. (Heb 10:4 NAS)*

The sacrifices in the Old Testament were only foreshadowing what Christ did for us on the cross. We are to study, teach, and obey God's commandments.

> *But one who looks intently at the perfect law, the law of liberty, and abides by it, not having become a forgetful hearer but an effectual doer, this man shall be blessed in what he does. (Jam 1:25 NAS)*

Only in studying God's Law can we see who we really are, sinners. God's Law leads us to repentance. Repentance is the change of mind about yourself. It is the knowledge and awareness that you are a sinner and in need of a savior. Repentance is acknowledging that you are incapable of saving yourself. It is the realization that you cannot stop sinning. Repentance is the acknowledgment that you are a sinner and are incapable of pleasing God. The Apostles preached,

> *That they should repent and turn to God, performing deeds appropriate to repentance. (Act 26:20 NAS)*

With repentance, one can turn to God in faith for their salvation and begin to perform good works out of sincerity of heart. Without repentance there is no salvation.

> *I tell you, no, but unless you repent, you will all likewise perish. (Luk 13:3 NAS)*

Christians are required to openly acknowledge their sin. Refusing to acknowledge your sinfulness is denying your need for Christ.

Chapter 11 - Conclusion

> *If we confess our sins, He is faithful and righteous to forgive us our sins and to cleanse us from all unrighteousness. If we say that we have not sinned, we make Him a liar, and His word is not in us. (1Jo 1:9-10 NAS)*

Confessing your sin is not something that is done privately to a priest. After receiving forgiveness, they commit the same sin again knowing they can just return to the priest and ask for forgiveness again. This type of confession is abhorrent to God. True confession is an open acknowledgment to all that you are a sinner and in need of Jesus Christ as your savior. Christ is the only way to receive the forgiveness of sins and be reconciled to God.

> *Everyone therefore who shall confess Me before men, I will also confess him before My Father who is in heaven. But whoever shall deny Me before men, I will also deny him before My Father who is in heaven. (Mat 10:32-33 NAS)*

Faith and Repentance is how we seek to keep God's commandments. God's commandments are how we live life as God intended. God's Law is the measure for which we use to determine whether we are living to God or to ourselves.

> *For we are His workmanship, created in Christ Jesus for good works, which God prepared beforehand, that we should walk in them. (Eph 2:10 NAS)*

Following God's commandments pleases God. Abandon all useless arguments over Saturday or Sunday worship. Abandon arguments of which laws are abolished and which laws are not abolished. Follow Christ and not theologians and their doctrinal schemes.

> *Let love be without hypocrisy. Abhor what is evil; cling to what is good. (Rom 12:9 NAS)*

Give up on date setting and the endless end times predictions that only prove to be false. Stop dividing over observing festivals like Christmas, Easter, Sabbath, Passover, and new moons which are mere representations of the true salvation we have in heaven. Do not hide in a Christian cult who hates other Christians for the purpose of showing how wise they are in their own doctrines. As Paul told Timothy,

> *Fight the good fight of faith; take hold of the eternal life to which you were called, and you made the good confession in the presence of many witnesses. I charge you in the presence of God, who gives life to all things, and of Christ Jesus, who testified the good confession before Pontius Pilate, that you keep the commandment without stain or reproach until the appearing of our Lord Jesus Christ, which He will bring about at the proper time-- He who is the blessed and only Sovereign, the King of kings and Lord of lords; who alone possesses immortality and dwells in unapproachable light; whom no man has seen or can see. To Him be honor and eternal dominion! Amen.*
>
> *Instruct those who are rich in this present world not to be conceited or to fix their hope on the uncertainty of riches, but on God, who richly supplies us with all things to enjoy. Instruct them to do good, to be rich in good works, to be generous and ready*

to share, storing up for themselves the treasure of a good foundation for the future, so that they may take hold of that which is life indeed. O Timothy, guard what has been entrusted to you, **avoiding worldly and empty chatter and the opposing arguments of what is falsely called "knowledge "--which some have professed and thus gone astray from the faith. Grace be with you.** *(1Ti 6:12-21 NAS)*

Chapter 11 - Conclusion

Appendix I

Early Church Fathers on the Sabbath and Lord's Day

Excerpts from
The Early Church Fathers **by Philip Schaff**

Appendix I

The Didache

But every Lord's day do ye gather yourselves together, and break bread, and give thanksgiving after having confessed your transgressions, that your sacrifice may be pure. [190]

The Letter of Barnabas

Since, therefore, the days are evil, and Satan possesses the power of this world, we ought to give heed to ourselves, and diligently inquire into the ordinances of the Lord. Fear and patience, then, are helpers of our faith; and long-suffering and continence are things which fight on our side. While these remain pure in what respects the Lord, Wisdom, Understanding, Science, and Knowledge rejoice along with them. For He hath revealed to us by all the prophets that He needs neither sacrifices, nor burnt-offerings, nor oblations, saying thus, "What is the multitude of your sacrifices unto Me, saith the Lord? I am full of burnt-offerings, and desire not the fat of lambs, and the blood of bulls and goats, not when ye come to appear before Me: for who hath required these things at your hands? Tread no more My courts, not though ye bring with you fine flour. Incense is a vain abomination unto Me, and your new moons and sabbaths I cannot endure." He has therefore abolished these things, that the new law of our Lord Jesus Christ, which is without the yoke of necessity, might have a human oblation. [191]

Further, He says to them, "Your new moons and your Sabbath I cannot endure." Ye perceive how He speaks: Your present Sabbaths are not acceptable to Me, but that is which I have made, [namely this,] when, giving rest to all things, I shall make a beginning of the eighth day, that is, a beginning of another world. Wherefore, also, we keep the eighth day with joyfulness, the day also on which Jesus rose again from the dead. And when He had manifested Himself, He ascended into the heavens. [192]

Ignatius of Antioch

If, therefore, those who were brought up in the ancient order of things have come to the possession of a new hope, no longer observing the Sabbath, but living in the observance of the Lord's Day, on which also our life has sprung up again by Him and by His death—whom some deny, by which mystery we have obtained faith, and therefore endure, that we may be found the disciples of Jesus Christ, our only Master. [193]

During the Sabbath He continued under the earth in the tomb in which Joseph of Arimathæa had laid Him. At the dawning of the Lord's day He arose from the dead, according to what was spoken by Himself, "As Jonah was three days and three nights in the whale's belly, so shall the Son of man also be three days and three nights in the heart of the earth." The day of the preparation, then, comprises the passion; the Sabbath embraces the burial; the Lord's Day contains the resurrection [194]

Justin Martyr

The Lawgiver is present, yet you do not see Him; to the poor the Gospel is preached, the blind see, yet you do not understand. You have now need of a second circumcision, though you glory greatly in the flesh. The new law requires you to keep perpetual sabbath, and you, because you are idle for one day, suppose you are pious, not discerning why this has been commanded you: and if you eat unleavened bread, you say the will of God has been fulfilled. The Lord our God does not take pleasure in such observances: if there is any perjured person or a thief among you, let him cease to be so; if any adulterer, let him repent; then he has kept the sweet and true sabbaths of God. If anyone has impure hands, let him wash and be pure. [195]

For we too would observe the fleshly circumcision, and the Sabbaths, and in short, all the feasts, if we did not know for what reason they were enjoined you, —namely, on account of your transgressions and the hardness of your hearts. For if we patiently endure all things contrived against us by wicked men and demons, so that even amid cruelties unutterable, death and torments, we pray for mercy to those who inflict such things upon us, and do not wish to give the least retort to anyone, even as the new Lawgiver commanded us: how is it, Trypho, that we would not observe those rites which do not harm us, —I speak of fleshly circumcision, and Sabbaths, and feasts? [196]

And we afterwards continually remind each other of these things. And the wealthy among us help the needy; and we always keep together; and for all things wherewith we are supplied, we bless the Maker of all through His Son Jesus Christ, and through the Holy Ghost. And on the day called Sunday, all who live in cities or in the country gather together to one place, and the memoirs of the apostles or the writings of the prophets are read, as long as time permits; then, when the reader has ceased, the president verbally instructs, and exhorts to the imitation of these good things. Then we all rise together and pray, and, as we before said, when our prayer is ended, bread and wine and water are brought, and the president in like manner offers prayers and thanksgivings, according to his ability, and the people assent, saying Amen; and there is a distribution to each, and a participation of that over which thanks have been given, and to those who are absent a portion is sent by the deacons. And they who are well to do, and willing, give what each thinks fit; and what is collected is deposited with the president, who succours the orphans and widows and those who, through sickness or any other cause, are in want, and those who are in bonds and the strangers sojourning among us, and in a word takes care of all who are in need. But Sunday is the day on which we all hold our common assembly, because it is the first day on which God, having wrought a change in the darkness and matter, made the world; and Jesus Christ our Saviour on the same day rose from the dead. For He was crucified on the day before that of Saturn (Saturday); and on the day after that of Saturn, which is the day of the Sun, having appeared to His apostles and disciples, He taught them these things, which we have submitted to you also for your consideration. [197]

Wherefore, Trypho, I will proclaim to you, and to those who wish to become proselytes, the divine message which I heard from that man. Do you see that the elements are not idle, and keep no Sabbaths? Remain as you were born. For if there was no need of circumcision before Abraham, or of the observance of Sabbaths, of feasts and sacrifices, before Moses; no more need is there of them now, after that, according to the will of God, Jesus Christ the Son of God has been born without sin, of a virgin sprung from the stock of Abraham. For when Abraham himself was in uncircumcision, he was justified and blessed by reason of the faith which he reposed in God, as the Scripture tells. Moreover, the

Scriptures and the facts themselves compel us to admit that He received circumcision for a sign, and not for righteousness. [198]

As, then, circumcision began with Abraham, and the Sabbath and sacrifices and offerings and feasts with Moses, and it has been proved they were enjoined on account of the hardness of your people's heart, so it was necessary, in accordance with the Father's will, that they should have an end in Him who was born of a virgin, of the family of Abraham and tribe of Judah, and of David; in Christ the Son of God, who was proclaimed as about to come to all the world, to be the everlasting law and the everlasting covenant, even as the forementioned prophecies show. [199]

Tertullian

[L]et him who contends that the Sabbath is still to be observed as a balm of salvation, and circumcision on the eighth day . . . teach us that, for the time past, righteous men kept the Sabbath or practiced circumcision, and were thus rendered 'friends of God.' For if circumcision purges a man, since God made Adam uncircumcised, why did he not circumcise him, even after his sinning, if circumcision purges? . . . Therefore, since God originated Adam uncircumcised and unobservant of the Sabbath, consequently his offspring also, Abel, offering him sacrifices, uncircumcised and unobservant of the Sabbath, was by him [God] commended [Gen. 4:1–7, Heb. 11:4].... Noah also, uncircumcised—yes, and unobservant of the Sabbath—God freed from the deluge. For Enoch too, most righteous man, uncircumcised and unobservant of the Sabbath, he translated from this world, who did not first taste death in order that, being a candidate for eternal life, he might show us that we also may, without the burden of the law of Moses, please God." [200]

It follows, accordingly, that, in so far as the abolition of carnal circumcision and of the old law is demonstrated as having been consummated at its specific times, so also the observance of the Sabbath is demonstrated to have been temporary. For the Jews say, that from the beginning God sanctified the seventh day, by resting on it from all His works which He made; and that thence it was, likewise, that Moses said to the People: "Remember the day of the sabbaths, to sanctify it: every servile work ye shall not do therein, except what pertaineth unto life." Whence we (Christians) understand that we still more ought to observe a sabbath from all "servile work" always, and not only every seventh day, but through all time. And through this arises the question for us, what sabbath God willed us to keep? For the Scriptures point to a sabbath eternal and a sabbath temporal. For Isaiah the prophet says, "Your sabbaths my soul hateth;" and in another place he says, "My sabbaths ye have profaned." Whence we discern that the temporal sabbath is human, and the eternal sabbath is accounted divine; concerning which He predicts through Isaiah: "And there shall be," He says, "month after month, and day after day, and sabbath after sabbath; and all flesh shall come to adore in Jerusalem, saith the Lord;" which we understand to have been fulfilled in the times of Christ, when "all flesh"—that is, every nation—"came to adore in Jerusalem" God the Father, through Jesus Christ His Son, as was predicted through the prophet: "Behold, proselytes through me shall go unto Thee." Thus, therefore, before this temporal sabbath, there was withal an eternal sabbath foreshown and foretold; just as before the carnal circumcision there was withal a spiritual circumcision foreshown. In short, let them teach us, as we have already premised, that Adam observed the sabbath; or that Abel, when offering to God a holy victim, pleased Him by a religious reverence for the sabbath; or that Enoch, when translated, had been a keeper of the sabbath; or that Noah the ark-builder observed, on account of the deluge, an immense sabbath; or that Abraham, in observance of the sabbath, offered Isaac his son; or that Melchizedek in his priesthood received the law of the sabbath

But the Jews are sure to say, that ever since this precept was given through Moses, the observance has been binding. Manifest accordingly it is, that the precept was not eternal nor spiritual, but temporary, which would one day cease. In short, so true is it that it is not in the exemption from work of the sabbath—that is, of the seventh day—that the celebration of this solemnity is to consist, that Joshua the son of Nun, at the time that he was reducing the city Jericho by war, stated that he had received from God a precept to order the People that priests should carry the ark of the testament of God seven days, making the circuit of the city; and thus, when the seventh day's circuit had been performed, the walls of the city would spontaneously fall. Which was so done; and when the space of the seventh day was finished, just as was predicted, down fell the walls of the city. Whence it is manifestly shown, that in the number of the seven days there intervened a sabbath-day. For seven days, whencesoever they may have commenced, must necessarily include within them a sabbath-day; on which day not only must the priests have worked, but the city must have been made a prey by the edge of the sword by all the people of Israel. Nor is it doubtful that they "wrought servile work," when, in obedience to God's precept, they drave the preys of war. For in the times of the Maccabees, too, they did bravely in fighting on the sabbaths, and routed their foreign foes, and recalled the law of their fathers to the primitive style of life by fighting on the sabbaths. Nor should I think it was any other law which they thus vindicated, than the one in which they remembered the existence of the prescript touching "the day of the sabbaths." Whence it is manifest that the force of such precepts was temporary, and respected the necessity of present circumstances; and that it was not with a view to its observance in perpetuity that God formerly gave them such a law. [201]

Therefore, since it is manifest that a sabbath temporal was shown, and a sabbath eternal foretold; a circumcision carnal foretold, and a circumcision spiritual pre-indicated; a law temporal and a law eternal formally declared; sacrifices carnal and sacrifices spiritual foreshown; it follows that, after all these precepts had been given carnally, in time preceding, to the people Israel, there was to supervene a time whereat the precepts of the ancient Law and of the old ceremonies would cease, and the promise of the new law, and the recognition of spiritual sacrifices, and the promise of the New Testament, supervene; while the light from on high would beam upon us who were sitting in darkness, and were being detained in the shadow of death. And so there is incumbent on us a necessity binding us, since we have premised that a new law was predicted by the prophets, and that not such as had been already given to their fathers at the time when He led them forth from the land of Egypt, to show and prove, on the one hand, that that old Law has ceased, and on the other, that the promised new law is now in operation.

And, indeed, first we must inquire whether there be expected a giver of the new law, and an heir of the new testament, and a priest of the new sacrifices, and a purger of the new circumcision, and an observer of the eternal sabbath, to suppress the old law, and institute the new testament, and offer the new sacrifices, and repress the ancient ceremonies, and suppress the old circumcision together with its own sabbath, and announce the new kingdom which is not corruptible. Inquire, I say, we must, whether this giver of the new law, observer of the spiritual sabbath, priest of the eternal sacrifices, eternal ruler of the eternal kingdom, become or no: that, if he is already come, service may have to be rendered him; if he is not yet come, he may have to be awaited, until by his advent it be manifest that the old Law's precepts are suppressed, and that the beginnings of the new law ought to arise. And, primarily, we must lay it down that the ancient Law and the prophets could not have ceased, unless He were come who was constantly announced, through the same Law and through the same prophets, as to come. [202]

But you, many of you, also under pretense sometimes of worshipping the heavenly bodies, move your lips in the direction of the sunrise. In the same way, if we devote Sun-day to rejoicing, from a far different reason than Sun-worship, we have some resemblance to those of you who devote the day of Saturn to ease and luxury, though they too go far away from Jewish ways, of which indeed they are ignorant. [203]

Constitutions of the holy apostles

But from the eve of the fifth day till cock-crowing break your fast when it is daybreak of the first day of the week, which is the Lord's day. [204]

But assemble yourselves together every day, morning and evening, singing psalms and praying in the Lord's house: in the morning saying the sixty-second Psalm, and in the evening the hundred and fortieth, but principally on the Sabbath-day. And on the day of our Lord's resurrection, which is the Lord's day, meet more diligently, sending praise to God that made the universe by Jesus, and sent Him to us, and condescended to let Him suffer, and raised Him from the dead. [205]

Origen

If it be objected to us on this subject that we ourselves are accustomed to observe certain days, as for example the Lord's day, the Preparation, the Passover, or Pentecost, I have to answer, that to the perfect Christian, who is ever in his thoughts, words, and deeds serving his natural Lord, God the Word, all his days are the Lord's, and he is always keeping the Lord's day. [206]

Peter, Archbishop of Alexandria

No one shall find fault with us for observing the fourth day of the week, and the preparation, on which it is reasonably enjoined us to fast according to the tradition. On the fourth day, indeed, because on it the Jews took counsel for the betrayal of the Lord; and on the sixth, because on it He himself suffered for us. But the Lord's day we celebrate as a day of joy, because on it He rose again, on which day we have received it for a custom not even to bow the knee. [207]

Appendix I

Cyprian

For because the eighth day, that is, the first day after the Sabbath, was to be that on which the Lord should rise again, and should quicken us, and give us circumcision of the spirit, the eighth day, that is, the first day after the Sabbath, and the Lord's day, went before in the figure; which figure ceased when by and by the truth came, and spiritual circumcision was given to us. [208]

Victorinus

The sixth day [Friday] is called parasceve, that is to say, the preparation of the kingdom.... On this day also, on account of the passion of the Lord Jesus Christ, we make either a station to God or a fast. On the seventh day he rested from all his works, and blessed it, and sanctified it. On the former day we are accustomed to fast rigorously, that on the Lord's day we may go forth to our bread with giving of thanks. And let the parasceve become a rigorous fast, lest we should appear to observe any Sabbath with the Jews . . . which Sabbath he [Christ] in his body abolished." [209]

This sixth day is called parasceve, that is to say, the preparation of the kingdom. For He perfected Adam, whom He made after His image and likeness. But for this reason, He completed His works before He created angels and fashioned man, lest perchance they should falsely assert that they had been His helpers. On this day also, on account of the passion of the Lord Jesus Christ, we make either a station to God, or a fast. On the seventh day He rested from all His works, and blessed it, and sanctified it. On the former day we are accustomed to fast rigorously, that on the Lord's day we may go forth to our bread with giving of thanks. And let the parasceve become a rigorous fast, lest we should appear to observe any Sabbath with the Jews, which Christ Himself, the Lord of the Sabbath, says by His prophets that "His soul hateth;" which Sabbath He in His body abolished, although, nevertheless, He had formerly Himself commanded Moses that circumcision should not pass over the eighth day, which day very frequently happens on the Sabbath, as we read written in the Gospel. [210]

Eusebius of Caesarea

They [the early saints of the Old Testament] did not care about circumcision of the body, neither do we [Christians]. They did not care about observing Sabbaths, nor do we. They did not avoid certain kinds of food, neither did they regard the other distinctions which Moses first delivered to their posterity to be observed as symbols; nor do Christians of the present day do such things." [211]

[T]he day of his [Christ's] light... was the day of his resurrection from the dead, which they say, as being the one and only truly holy day and the Lord's day, is better than any number of days as we ordinarily understand them, and better than the days set apart by the Mosaic law for feasts, new moons, and Sabbaths, which the apostle [Paul] teaches are the shadow of days and not days in reality." [212]

For as the name Christians is intended to indicate this very idea, that a man, by the knowledge and doctrine of Christ, is distinguished by modesty and justice, by patience and a virtuous fortitude, and by a profession of piety towards the one and only true and supreme God; all this no less studiously cultivated by them than by us. They did not, therefore, regard circumcision, nor observe the Sabbath, neither do we; neither do we abstain from certain foods, nor regard other injunctions, which Moses subsequently delivered to be observed in types and symbols, because such things as these do not belong to Christians." [213]

The Ebionites cherished low and mean opinions of Christ. For they considered Him a plain and common man, and justified only by His advances in virtue, and that He was born of the Virgin Mary, by natural generation. With them the observance of the law was altogether necessary, as if they could not be saved, only by faith in Christ and a corresponding life. These, indeed, thought on the one hand that all of the epistles of the apostles ought to be rejected, calling him an apostate from the law, but on the other, only using the gospel according to the Hebrews, they esteem the others as of little value. They also observe the Sabbath and other disciplines of the Jews, just like them, but on the other hand, they also celebrate the Lord's days very much like us, in commemoration of His resurrection." [214]

The Sabbath and the rest of the discipline of the Jews they observed just like them, but at the same time, like us, they celebrated the Lord's days as a memorial of the resurrection of the Saviour. Wherefore, in consequence of such a course they received the name of Ebionites, which signified the poverty of their understanding. For this is the name by which a poor man is called among the Hebrews. [215]

Council of Laodicea

Christians must not judaize by resting on the Sabbath, but must work on that day, rather honouring the Lord's Day; and, if they can, resting then as Christians. But if any shall be found to be judaizers, let them be anathema from Christ. [216]

John Chrysostom

For though few are now circumcised, yet, by fasting and observing the sabbath with the Jews, they equally exclude themselves from grace. If Christ avails not to those who are only circumcised, much more is peril to be feared where fasting and sabbatizing are observed, and thus two commandments of the Law are kept in the place of one. And this is aggravated by a consideration of time: for they so acted at first while the city and temple and other institutions yet existed; but these who with the punishment of the Jews, and the destruction of the city before their eyes, observe more precepts of the Law than the others did, what apology can they find for such observance, at the very time when the Jews themselves, in spite of their strong desire, cannot keep it? Thou hast put on Christ, thou hast become a member of the Lord, and been enrolled in the heavenly city, and dost thou still grovel in the Law? How is it possible for thee to obtain the kingdom? Listen to Paul's words, that the observance of the Law overthrows the Gospel, and learn, if thou wilt, how this comes to pass, and tremble, and shun this pitfall. Wherefore dost thou keep the sabbath, and fast with the Jews? Is it that thou fearest the Law and abandonment of its letter? But thou wouldest not entertain this fear, didst thou not disparage faith as weak, and by itself powerless to save. A fear to omit the sabbath plainly shows that you fear the Law as still in force; and if the Law is needful, it is so as a whole, not in part, nor in one commandment only; and if as a whole, the righteousness which is by faith is little by little shut out. If thou keep the sabbath, why not also be circumcised? and if circumcised, why not also offer sacrifices? If the Law is to be observed, it must be observed as a whole, or not at all." [217]

Augustine of Hippo

Well, now, I should like to be told what there is in these ten commandments, except the observance of the Sabbath, which ought not to be kept by a Christian. . . .. Which of these commandments would anyone say that the Christian ought not to keep? It is possible to contend that it is not the law which was written on those two tables that the apostle [Paul] describes as 'the letter that kills' [2 Cor. 3:6], but the law of circumcision and the other sacred rites which are now abolished" [218]

So he says elsewhere, "Let no man judge you in meat, or in drink, or in respect of an holy day, or of the new moon or of the sabbath-days, which are a shadow of things to come." Here also, when he says, "Let no one judge you" in these things, he shows that we are no longer bound to observe them. And when he says, "which are a shadow of things to come," he explains how these observances were binding at the time when the things fully disclosed to us were symbolized by these shadows of future things. [219]

He brought it about that His body rested from all its works on Sabbath in the tomb, and that His resurrection on the third day, which we call the Lord's day, the day after the Sabbath, and therefore the eighth, proved the circumcision of the eighth day to be also prophetical of Him. [220]

So, when you ask why a Christian does not keep the Sabbath, if Christ came not to destroy the law, but to fulfill it, my reply is, that a Christian does not keep the Sabbath precisely because what was prefigured in the Sabbath is fulfilled in Christ. For we have our Sabbath in Him who said, "Come unto me, all ye that labor and are heavy laden, and I will give you rest. Take my yoke upon you, and learn of me; for I am meek and lowly in heart, and ye shall find rest unto your souls." [221]

And by this I am persuaded that exemption from fasting on the seventh day is more suitable, not indeed to obtain, but to foreshadow, that eternal rest in which the true Sabbath is realized, and which is obtained only by faith, and by that righteousness whereby the daughter of the King is all glorious within. [222]

Wherefore, although the sacramental import of the 8th number, as signifying the resurrection, was by no means concealed from the holy men of old who were filled with the spirit of prophecy (for in the title of Psalms [vi. and xii.] we find the words "for the eighth," and infants were circumcised on the eighth day; and in Ecclesiastes it is said, with allusion to the two covenants, "Give a portion to seven, and also to eight"); nevertheless before the resurrection of the Lord, it was reserved and hidden, and

Appendix I

the Sabbath alone was appointed to be observed, because before that event there was indeed the repose of the dead (of which the Sabbath rest was a type), but there was not any instance of the resurrection of one who, rising from the dead, was no more to die, and over whom death should no longer have dominion; this being done in order that, from the time when such a resurrection did take place in the Lord's own body (the Head of the Church being the first to experience that which His body, the Church, expects at the end of time), the day upon which He rose, the eighth day namely (which is the same with the first of the week), should begin to be observed as the Lord's day. The same reason enables us to understand why, in regard to the day of keeping the Passover, on which the Jews were commanded to kill and eat a lamb, which was most clearly a foreshadowing of the Lord's Passion, there was no injunction given to them that they should take the day of the week into account, waiting until the Sabbath was past, and making the beginning of the third week of the moon coincide with the beginning of the third week of the first month; the reason being, that the Lord might rather in His own Passion declare the significance of that day, as He had come also to declare the mystery of the day now known as the Lord's day, the eighth namely, which is also the first of the week. [223]

Appendix II

Comparison of
Solar, Lunar, and Lunisolar Calendars

The Gregorian Calendar

The Creator's Calendar

The Jewish Calendar

Lunar Sabbath & Gregorian Calendar Compared AD 31

Lunar to Solar

Lunar Days

Months	1	2	3	4	5	6	7	8	9	10	11	12	13	14	15
1 Nissan	Wed Mar 28	Thur Mar 29	Fri Mar 30	Sat Mar 31	Sun Apr 1	Mon Apr 2	Tues Apr 3	Wed Apr 4	Thur Apr 5	Fri Apr 6	Sat Apr 7	Sun Apr 8	Mon Apr 9	Tues Apr 10	Wed Apr 11
2 Ziv	Thur Apr 26	Fri Apr 27	Sat Apr 28	Sun Apr 29	Mon Apr 30	Tues May 1	Wed May 2	Thur May 3	Fri May 4	Sat May 5	Sun May 6	Mon May 7	Tues May 8	Wed May 9	Thur May 10
3 Sivan	Sat May 26	Sun May 27	Mon May 28	Tues May 29	Wed May 30	Thur May 31	Fri June 1	Sat June 2	Sun June 3	Mon June 4	Tues June 5	Wed June 6	Thur June 7	Fri June 8	Sat June 9
4	Fri June 24	Sat June 25	Sun June 26	Mon June 27	Tues June 28	Wed June 29	Thur June 30	Fri July 1	Sat July 2	Sun July 3	Mon July 4	Tues July 5	Wed July 6	Thur July 7	Fri July 8
5	Sat July 23	Sun July 24	Mon July 25	Tues July 26	Wed July 27	Thur July 28	Fri July 29	Sat July 30	Sun July 31	Mon Aug 1	Tues Aug 2	Wed Aug 3	Thur Aug 4	Fri Aug 5	Sat Aug 6
6 Elul	Mon Aug 22	Tues Aug 23	Wed Aug 24	Thur Aug 25	Fri Aug 26	Sat Aug 27	Sun Aug 28	Mon Aug 29	Tues Aug 30	Wed Aug 31	Thur Sep 1	Fri Sep 2	Sat Sep 3	Sun Sep 4	Mon Sep 5
7 Ethanim	Tues Sep 20	Wed Sep 21	Thur Sep 22	Fri Sep 23	Sat Sep 24	Sun Sep 25	Mon Sep 26	Tues Sep 27	Wed Sep 28	Thur Sep 29	Fri Sep 30	Sat Oct 1	Sun Oct 2	Mon Oct 3	Tues Oct 4
8 Bul	Thur Oct 20	Fri Oct 21	Sat Oct 22	Sun Oct 23	Mon Oct 24	Tues Oct 25	Wed Oct 26	Thur Oct 27	Fri Oct 28	Sat Oct 29	Sun Oct 30	Mon Oct 31	Tues Nov 1	Wed Nov 2	Thur Nov 3
9 Chisleu	Fri Nov 18	Sat Nov 19	Sun Nov 20	Mon Nov 21	Tues Nov 22	Wed Nov 23	Thur Nov 24	Fri Nov 25	Sat Nov 26	Sun Nov 27	Mon Nov 28	Tues Nov 29	Wed Nov 30	Thur Dec 1	Fri Dec 2
10 Teheth	Sun Dec 18	Mon Dec 19	Tues Dec 20	Wed Dec 21	Thur Dec 22	Fri Dec 23	Sat Dec 24	Sun Dec 25	Mon Dec 26	Tues Dec 27	Wed Dec 28	Thur Dec 29	Fri Dec 30	Sat Dec 31	Sun Jan 1
11 Shebat	Tues Jan 17	Wed Jan 18	Thur Jan 19	Fri Jan 20	Sat Jan 21	Sun Jan 22	Mon Jan 23	Tues Jan 24	Wed Jan 25	Thur Jan 26	Fri Jan 27	Sat Jan 28	Sun Jan 29	Mon Jan 30	Tues Jan 31
12 Adar	Thur Feb 16	Fri Feb 17	Sat Feb 18	Sun Feb 19	Mon Feb 20	Tues Feb 21	Wed Feb 22	Thur Feb 23	Fri Feb 24	Sat Feb 25	Sun Feb 26	Mon Feb 27	Tues Feb 28	Wed Feb 29	Thur Mar 1
13 Adar II	Fri Mar 16	Sat Mar 17	Sun Mar 18	Mon Mar 19	Tues Mar 20	Wed Mar 21	Thur Mar 22	Fri Mar 23	Sat Mar 24	Sun Mar 25	Mon Mar 26	Tues Mar 27	Wed Mar 28	Thur Mar 29	Fri Mar 30

Lunar Days

Months	16	17	18	19	20	21	22	23	24	25	26	27	28	29	30
1 Nissan	Thur Apr 12	Fri Apr 13	Sat Apr 14	Sun Apr 15	Mon Apr 16	Tues Apr 17	Wed Apr 18	Thur Apr 19	Fri Apr 20	Sat Apr 21	Sun Apr 22	Mon Apr 23	Tues Apr 24	Wed Apr 25	
2 Ziv	Fri May 11	Sat May 12	Sun May 13	Mon May 14	Tues May 15	Wed May 16	Thur May 17	Fri May 18	Sat May 19	Sun May 20	Mon May 21	Tues May 22	Wed May 23	Thur May 24	Fri May 25
3 Sivan	Sun June 10	Mon June 11	Tues June 12	Wed June 13	Thur June 14	Fri June 15	Sat June 16	Sun June 17	Mon June 18	Tues June 19	Wed June 20	Thur June 21	Fri June 22	Thur June 23	
4	Sat July 9	Sun July 10	Mon July 11	Tues July 12	Wed July 13	Thur July 14	Fri July 15	Sat July 16	Sun July 17	Mon July 18	Tues July 19	Wed July 20	Thur July 21	Fri July 22	
5	Sun Aug 7	Mon Aug 8	Tues Aug 9	Wed Aug 10	Thur Aug 11	Fri Aug 12	Sat Aug 13	Sun Aug 14	Mon Aug 15	Tues Aug 16	Wed Aug 17	Thur Aug 18	Fri Aug 19	Sat Aug 20	Sun Aug 21
6 Elul	Tues Sep 6	Wed Sep 7	Thur Sep 8	Fri Sep 9	Sat Sep 10	Sun Sep 11	Mon Sep 12	Tues Sep 13	Wed Sep 14	Thur Sep 15	Fri Sep 16	Sat Sep 17	Sun Sep 18	Mon Sep 19	
7 Ethanim	Wed Oct 5	Thur Oct 6	Fri Oct 7	Sat Oct 8	Sun Oct 9	Mon Oct 10	Tues Oct 11	Wed Oct 12	Thur Oct 13	Fri Oct 14	Sat Oct 15	Sun Oct 16	Mon Oct 17	Tues Oct 18	Wed Oct 19
8 Bul	Fri Nov 4	Sat Nov 5	Sun Nov 6	Mon Nov 7	Tues Nov 8	Wed Nov 9	Thur Nov 10	Fri Nov 11	Sat Nov 12	Sun Nov 13	Mon Nov 14	Tues Nov 15	Wed Nov 16	Thur Nov 17	
9 Chisleu	Sat Dec 3	Sun Dec 4	Mon Dec 5	Tues Dec 6	Wed Dec 7	Thur Dec 8	Fri Dec 9	Sat Dec 10	Sun Dec 11	Mon Dec 12	Tues Dec 13	Wed Dec 14	Thur Dec 15	Fri Dec 16	Sat Dec 17
10 Teheth	Mon Jan 2	Tues Jan 3	Wed Jan 4	Thur Jan 5	Fri Jan 6	Sat Jan 7	Sun Jan 8	Mon Jan 9	Tues Jan 10	Wed Jan 11	Thur Jan 12	Fri Jan 13	Sat Jan 14	Sun Jan 15	Mon Jan 16
11 Shebat	Wed Jan 1	Thur Feb 2	Fri Feb 3	Sat Feb 4	Sun Feb 5	Mon Feb 6	Tues Feb 7	Wed Feb 8	Thur Feb 9	Fri Feb 10	Sat Feb 11	Sun Feb 12	Mon Feb 13	Tues Feb 14	Wed Feb 15
12 Adar	Fri Mar 2	Sat Mar 3	Sun Mar 4	Mon Mar 5	Tues Mar 6	Wed Mar 7	Thur Mar 8	Fri Mar 9	Sat Mar 10	Sun Mar 11	Mon Mar 12	Tues Mar 13	Wed Mar 14	Thur Mar 15	
13 Adar II	Sat Mar 31	Sun Apr 1	Mon Apr 2	Tues Apr 3	Wed Apr 4	Thur Apr 5	Fri Apr 6	Sat Apr 7	Sun Apr 8	Mon Apr 9	Tues Apr 10	Wed Apr 11	Thur Apr 12	Fri Apr 13	Sat Apr 14

New Years
Passover
Unleavened Bread
First Fruits
Feast of Weeks
Feast of Trumpets
Day of Atonement
Feast of Booths
Sabbath
New Moons

The Days of the lunar Sabbath calendar are at the top of the graph.
The dates within the chart are the corresponding Gregorian calendar days.

All dates come from:
https://www.thecreatorscalendar.com/ad-31-calendar/

Lunar Sabbath & Gregorian Calendar Compared AD 2020-2021

A full-page calendar chart comparing the Lunar Sabbath calendar to the Gregorian calendar for AD 2020-2021. The chart is organized with lunar months listed down the left side and lunar days (1-30) across the top, with corresponding Gregorian calendar dates filled in each cell.

Months (rows, top to bottom):
1. Nissan
2. Ziv
3. Sivan
4. (unnamed)
5. (unnamed)
6. Elul
7. Ethanim
8. Bul
9. Chisleu
10. Teheth
11. Shebat
12. Adar
13. Adar II

Lunar Days (columns): 1 through 30, labeled "Lunar to Solar"

Legend:
- Yellow: New Years
- Pink/Rose: Passover
- Green: Unleavened Bread
- Light gray/cream: First Fruits
- Peach/salmon: Feast of Weeks
- Yellow (gold): Feast of Trumpets
- Light blue: Sabbath
- Orange: Feast of Booths
- Dark cream: Day of Atonement
- Dotted/stippled: New Moon

Key dates highlighted:
- 1 Nissan Day 1: Wed Apr 8 (New Year)
- 1 Nissan Day 14: Tues Apr 14 (Passover)
- 1 Nissan Day 15: Wed Apr 15 (Unleavened Bread)
- 1 Nissan Day 16: Thur Apr 16 (First Fruits)
- 3 Sivan Day 8: Sun Jun 14 (Feast of Weeks)
- 7 Ethanim Day 1: *Fri Oct 2 (Feast of Trumpets)
- 7 Ethanim Day 10: *Sat Oct 10 (Day of Atonement)
- 7 Ethanim Day 15-22: Oct 15-22 (Feast of Booths)

Notes at bottom:
- The Days of the lunar Sabbath calendar are at the top of the graph.
- The dates within the chart are the corresponding Gregorian calendar days.
- *The feast of trumpets and Day of Atonement dates were adjusted from the source because they appear to be incorrect
- All dates come from: www.thecreatorscalendar.com/spring-2020-2021/

Months	1	2	3	4	5	6	7	8	9	10	11	12	13	14	15	16	17	18	19	20	21	22	23	24	25	26	27	28	29	30
1 Nissan	Wed Apr 8	Thur Apr 9	Fri Apr 10	Sat Apr 11	Sun Apr 12	Mon Apr 13	Tues Apr 14	Wed Apr 15	Thur Apr 16	Fri Apr 17	Sat Apr 18	Sun Apr 19	Mon Apr 20	Tues Apr 21	Wed Apr 22	Thur Apr 23	Fri Apr 24	Sat Apr 25	Sun Apr 26	Mon Apr 27	Tues Apr 28	Wed Apr 29	Thur Apr 30	Fri May 1	Sat May 2	Sun May 3	Mon May 4	Tues May 5	Wed May 6	
2 Ziv	Thur May 7	Fri May 8	Sat May 9	Sun May 10	Mon May 11	Tues May 12	Wed May 13	Thur May 14	Fri May 15	Sat May 16	Sun May 17	Mon May 18	Tues May 19	Wed May 20	Thur May 21	Fri May 22	Sat May 23	Sun May 24	Mon May 25	Tues May 26	Wed May 27	Thur May 28	Fri May 29	Sat May 30	Sun May 31	Mon Jun 1	Tues Jun 2	Wed Jun 3	Thur Jun 4	Fri Jun 5
3 Sivan	Sat Jun 6	Sun Jun 7	Mon Jun 8	Tues Jun 9	Wed Jun 10	Thur Jun 11	Fri Jun 12	Sun Jun 14	Mon Jun 15	Tues Jun 16	Wed Jun 17	Thur Jun 18	Fri Jun 19	Sat Jun 20	Sun Jun 21	Mon Jun 22	Tues Jun 23	Wed Jun 24	Thur Jun 25	Fri Jun 26	Sat Jun 27	Sun Jun 28	Mon Jun 29	Tues Jun 30	Wed Jul 1	Thur Jul 2	Fri Jul 3	Sat Jul 4	Sun Jul 5	
4	Mon Jul 6	Tues Jul 7	Wed Jul 8	Thur Jul 9	Fri Jul 10	Sat Jul 11	Sun Jul 12	Mon Jul 13	Tues Jul 14	Wed Jul 15	Thur Jul 16	Fri Jul 17	Sat Jul 18	Sun Jul 19	Mon Jul 20	Tues Jul 21	Wed Jul 22	Thur Jul 23	Fri Jul 24	Sat Jul 25	Sun Jul 26	Mon Jul 27	Tues Jul 28	Wed Jul 29	Thur Jul 30	Fri Jul 31	Sat Aug 1	Sun Aug 2	Mon Aug 3	
5	Tues Aug 4	Wed Aug 5	Thur Aug 6	Fri Aug 7	Sat Aug 8	Sun Aug 9	Mon Aug 10	Tues Aug 11	Wed Aug 12	Thur Aug 13	Fri Aug 14	Sat Aug 15	Sun Aug 16	Mon Aug 17	Tues Aug 18	Wed Aug 19	Thur Aug 20	Fri Aug 21	Sat Aug 22	Sun Aug 23	Mon Aug 24	Tues Aug 25	Wed Aug 26	Thur Aug 27	Fri Aug 28	Sat Aug 29	Sun Aug 30	Mon Aug 31	Tues Sep 1	
6 Elul	Wed Sep 2	Thur Sep 3	Fri Sep 4	Sat Sep 5	Sun Sep 6	Mon Sep 7	Tues Sep 8	Wed Sep 9	Thur Sep 10	Fri Sep 11	Sat Sep 12	Sun Sep 13	Mon Sep 14	Tues Sep 15	Wed Sep 16	Thur Sep 17	Fri Sep 18	Sat Sep 19	Sun Sep 20	Mon Sep 21	Tues Sep 22	Wed Sep 23	Thur Sep 24	Fri Sep 25	Sat Sep 26	Sun Sep 27	Mon Sep 28	Tues Sep 29	Wed Sep 30	Thur Oct 1
7 Ethanim	*Fri Oct 2	Sat Oct 3	Sun Oct 4	Mon Oct 5	Tues Oct 6	Wed Oct 7	Thur Oct 8	Fri Oct 9	*Sat Oct 10	Sun Oct 11	Mon Oct 12	Tues Oct 13	Wed Oct 14	Thur Oct 15	Fri Oct 16	Sat Oct 17	Sun Oct 18	Mon Oct 19	Tues Oct 20	Wed Oct 21	Thur Oct 22	Fri Oct 23	Sat Oct 24	Sun Oct 25	Mon Oct 26	Tues Oct 27	Wed Oct 28	Thur Oct 29	Fri Oct 30	
8 Bul	Sat Oct 31	Sun Nov 1	Mon Nov 2	Tues Nov 3	Wed Nov 4	Thur Nov 5	Fri Nov 6	Sat Nov 7	Sun Nov 8	Mon Nov 9	Tues Nov 10	Wed Nov 11	Thur Nov 12	Fri Nov 13	Sat Nov 14	Sun Nov 15	Mon Nov 16	Tues Nov 17	Wed Nov 18	Thur Nov 19	Fri Nov 20	Sat Nov 21	Sun Nov 22	Mon Nov 23	Tues Nov 24	Wed Nov 25	Thur Nov 26	Fri Nov 27	Sat Nov 28	Sun Nov 29
9 Chisleu	Mon Nov 30	Tues Dec 1	Wed Dec 2	Thur Dec 3	Fri Dec 4	Sat Dec 5	Sun Dec 6	Mon Dec 7	Tues Dec 8	Wed Dec 9	Thur Dec 10	Fri Dec 11	Sat Dec 12	Sun Dec 13	Mon Dec 14	Tues Dec 15	Wed Dec 16	Thur Dec 17	Fri Dec 18	Sat Dec 19	Sun Dec 20	Mon Dec 21	Tues Dec 22	Wed Dec 23	Thur Dec 24	Fri Dec 25	Sat Dec 26	Sun Dec 27	Mon Dec 28	Tues Dec 29
10 Teheth	Wed Dec 30	Thur Dec 31	Fri Jan 1	Sat Jan 2	Sun Jan 3	Mon Jan 4	Tues Jan 5	Wed Jan 6	Thur Jan 7	Fri Jan 8	Sat Jan 9	Sun Jan 10	Mon Jan 11	Tues Jan 12	Wed Jan 13	Thur Jan 14	Fri Jan 15	Sat Jan 16	Sun Jan 17	Mon Jan 18	Tues Jan 19	Wed Jan 20	Thur Jan 21	Fri Jan 22	Sat Jan 23	Sun Jan 24	Mon Jan 25	Tues Jan 26	Wed Jan 27	
11 Shebat	Thur Jan 28	Fri Jan 29	Sat Jan 30	Sun Jan 31	Mon Feb 1	Tues Feb 2	Wed Feb 3	Thur Feb 4	Fri Feb 5	Sat Feb 6	Sun Feb 7	Mon Feb 8	Tues Feb 9	Wed Feb 10	Thur Feb 11	Fri Feb 12	Sat Feb 13	Sun Feb 14	Mon Feb 15	Tues Feb 16	Wed Feb 17	Thur Feb 18	Fri Feb 19	Sat Feb 20	Sun Feb 21	Mon Feb 22	Tues Feb 23	Wed Feb 24	Thur Feb 25	
12 Adar	Fri Feb 26	Sat Feb 27	Sun Feb 28	Mon Mar 1	Tues Mar 2	Wed Mar 3	Thur Mar 4	Fri Mar 5	Sat Mar 6	Sun Mar 7	Mon Mar 8	Tues Mar 9	Wed Mar 10	Thur Mar 11	Fri Mar 12	Sat Mar 13	Sun Mar 14	Mon Mar 15	Tues Mar 16	Wed Mar 17	Thur Mar 18	Fri Mar 19	Sat Mar 20	Sun Mar 21	Mon Mar 22	Tues Mar 23	Wed Mar 24	Thur Mar 25	Fri Mar 26	Sat Mar 27
13 Adar II	Leap Year																													

Jewish & Gregorian Calendar Compared AD 2020-2021

Lunisolar to Solar

Lunar Days

Months	1	2	3	4	5	6	7	8	9	10	11	12	13	14	15
1 Nissan 5780	Thur Mar 26	Fri Mar 27	Sat Mar 28	Sun Mar 29	Mon Mar 30	Tues Mar 31	Wed Apr 1	Thur Apr 2	Fri Apr 3	Sat Apr 4	Sun Apr 5	Mon Apr 6	Tues Apr 7	Wed Apr 8	Thur Apr 9
2 Iyar	Sat Apr 25	Sun Apr 26	Mon Apr 27	Tues Apr 28	Wed Apr 29	Thur Apr 30	Fri May 1	Sat May 2	Sun May 3	Mon May 4	Tues May 5	Wed May 6	Thur May 7	Fri May 8	Sat May 9
3 Sivan	Sun May 24	Mon May 25	Tues May 26	Wed May 27	Thur May 28	Fri May 29	Sat May 30	Sun May 31	Mon Jun 1	Tues Jun 2	Wed Jun 3	Thur Jun 4	Fri Jun 5	Sat Jun 6	Sun Jun 7
4 Tammuz	Tues Jun 23	Wed Jun 24	Thur Jun 25	Fri Jun 26	Sat Jun 27	Sun Jun 28	Mon Jun 29	Tues Jun 30	Wed Jul 1	Thur Jul 2	Fri Jul 3	Sat Jul 4	Sun Jul 5	Mon Jul 6	Tues Jul 7
5 Av	Wed Jul 22	Thur Jul 23	Fri Jul 24	Sat Jul 25	Sun Jul 26	Mon Jul 27	Tues Jul 28	Wed Jul 29	Thur Jul 30	Fri Jul 31	Sat Aug 1	Sun Aug 2	Mon Aug 3	Tues Aug 4	Wed Aug 5
6 Elul	Fri Aug 21	Sat Aug 22	Sun Aug 23	Mon Aug 24	Tues Aug 25	Wed Aug 26	Thur Aug 27	Fri Aug 28	Sat Aug 29	Sun Aug 30	Mon Aug 31	Tues Sep 1	Wed Sep 2	Thur Sep 3	Fri Sep 4
7 Tishrei 5781	*Sat Sep 19	Sun Sep 20	Mon Sep 21	Tues Sep 22	Wed Sep 23	Thur Sep 24	Fri Sep 25	Sat Sep 26	Sun Sep 27	Mon Sep 28	Tues Sep 29	Wed Sep 30	Thur Oct 1	Fri Oct 2	Sat Oct 3
8 Cheshvan	Mon Oct 19	Tues Oct 20	Wed Oct 21	Thur Oct 22	Fri Oct 23	Sat Oct 24	Sun Oct 25	Mon Oct 26	Tues Oct 27	Wed Oct 28	Thur Oct 29	Fri Oct 30	Sat Oct 31	Sun Nov 1	Mon Nov 2
9 Kislev	Tues Nov 17	Wed Nov 18	Thur Nov 19	Fri Nov 20	Sat Nov 21	Sun Nov 22	Mon Nov 23	Tues Nov 24	Wed Nov 25	Thur Nov 26	Fri Nov 27	Sat Nov 28	Sun Nov 29	Mon Nov 30	Tues Dec 1
10 Tevet	Wed Dec 16	Thur Dec 17	Fri Dec 18	Sat Dec 19	Sun Dec 20	Mon Dec 21	Tues Dec 22	Wed Dec 23	Thur Dec 24	Fri Dec 25	Sat Dec 26	Sun Dec 27	Mon Dec 28	Tues Dec 29	Wed Dec 30
11 Shevat	Thur Jan 14	Fri Jan 15	Sat Jan 16	Sun Jan 17	Mon Jan 18	Tues Jan 19	Wed Jan 20	Thur Jan 21	Fri Jan 22	Sat Jan 23	Sun Jan 24	Mon Jan 25	Tues Jan 26	Wed Jan 27	Thur Jan 28
12 Adar	Sat Feb 13	Sun Feb 14	Mon Feb 15	Tues Feb 16	Wed Feb 17	Thur Feb 18	Fri Feb 19	Sat Feb 20	Sun Feb 21	Mon Feb 22	Tues Feb 23	Wed Feb 24	Thur Feb 25	Fri Feb 26	Sat Feb 27
13 Adar II				Leap	Year						Leap	Year			

Lunar Days

Months	16	17	18	19	20	21	22	23	24	25	26	27	28	29	30
1 Nissan 5780	Fri Apr 10	Sat Apr 11	Sun Apr 12	Mon Apr 13	Tues Apr 14	Wed Apr 15	Thur Apr 16	Fri Apr 17	Sat Apr 18	Sun Apr 19	Mon Apr 20	Tues Apr 21	Wed Apr 22	Thur Apr 23	Fri Apr 24
2 Iyar	Sun May 10	Mon May 11	Tues May 12	Wed May 13	Thur May 14	Fri May 15	Sat May 16	Sun May 17	Mon May 18	Tues May 19	Wed May 20	Thur May 21	Fri May 22	Sat May 23	
3 Sivan	Mon Jun 8	Tues Jun 9	Wed Jun 10	Thur Jun 11	Fri Jun 12	Sat Jun 13	Sun Jun 14	Mon Jun 15	Tues Jun 16	Wed Jun 17	Thur Jun 18	Fri Jun 19	Sat Jun 20	Sun Jun 21	Mon Jun 22
4 Tammuz	Wed Jul 8	Thur Jul 9	Fri Jul 10	Sat Jul 11	Sun Jul 12	Mon Jul 13	Tues Jul 14	Wed Jul 15	Thur Jul 16	Fri Jul 17	Sat Jul 18	Sun Jul 19	Mon Jul 20	Tues Jul 21	
5 Av	Thur Aug 6	Fri Aug 7	Sat Aug 8	Sun Aug 9	Mon Aug 10	Tues Aug 11	Wed Aug 12	Thur Aug 13	Fri Aug 14	Sat Aug 15	Sun Aug 16	Mon Aug 17	Tues Aug 18	Wed Aug 19	Thur Aug 20
6 Elul	Sat Sep 5	Sun Sep 6	Mon Sep 7	Tues Sep 8	Wed Sep 9	Thur Sep 10	Fri Sep 11	Sat Sep 12	Sun Sep 13	Mon Sep 14	Tues Sep 15	Wed Sep 16	Thur Sep 17	Fri Sep 18	
7 Tishrei 5781	Sun Oct 4	Mon Oct 5	Tues Oct 6	Wed Oct 7	Thur Oct 8	Fri Oct 9	Sat Oct 10	Sun Oct 11	Mon Oct 12	Tues Oct 13	Wed Oct 14	Thur Oct 15	Fri Oct 16	Sat Oct 17	Sun Oct 18
8 Cheshvan	Tues Nov 3	Wed Nov 4	Thur Nov 5	Fri Nov 6	Sat Nov 7	Sun Nov 8	Mon Nov 9	Tues Nov 10	Wed Nov 11	Thur Nov 12	Fri Nov 13	Sat Nov 14	Sun Nov 15	Mon Nov 16	
9 Kislev	Wed Dec 2	Thur Dec 3	Fri Dec 4	Sat Dec 5	Sun Dec 6	Mon Dec 7	Tues Dec 8	Wed Dec 9	Thur Dec 10	Fri Dec 11	Sat Dec 12	Sun Dec 13	Mon Dec 14	Tues Dec 15	
10 Tevet	Thur Dec 31	Fri Jan 1	Sat Jan 2	Sun Jan 3	Mon Jan 4	Tues Jan 5	Wed Jan 6	Thur Jan 7	Fri Jan 8	Sat Jan 9	Sun Jan 10	Mon Jan 11	Tues Jan 12	Wed Jan 13	
11 Shevat	Fri Jan 29	Sat Jan 30	Sun Jan 31	Mon Feb 1	Tues Feb 2	Wed Feb 3	Thur Feb 4	Fri Feb 5	Sat Feb 6	Sun Feb 7	Mon Feb 8	Tues Feb 9	Wed Feb 10	Thur Feb 11	Fri Feb 12
12 Adar	Sun Feb 28	Mon Mar 1	Tues Mar 2	Wed Mar 3	Thur Mar 4	Fri Mar 5	Sat Mar 6	Sun Mar 7	Mon Mar 8	Tues Mar 9	Wed Mar 10	Thur Mar 11	Fri Mar 12	Sat Mar 13	
13 Adar II			Leap	Year						Leap	Year				

- New Year
- Passover
- Unleavened Bread
- First Fruits
- Feast of Weeks
- Feast of Trumpets
- Day of Atonement
- Feast of Booths
- Sabbath
- New Moon

*The Feast of Trumpets and the New Year are the same day

The Days of the Jewish calendar are at the top of the graph.
The dates within the chart are the corresponding Gregorian calendar days.

All dates come from:
https://www.chabad.org/calendar/view/month_cdo/jewish/Jewish-Calendar.htm

Appendix III

Comparison of
End Times Doctrines

Futurist

Historicist

Preterist

Interdimensional

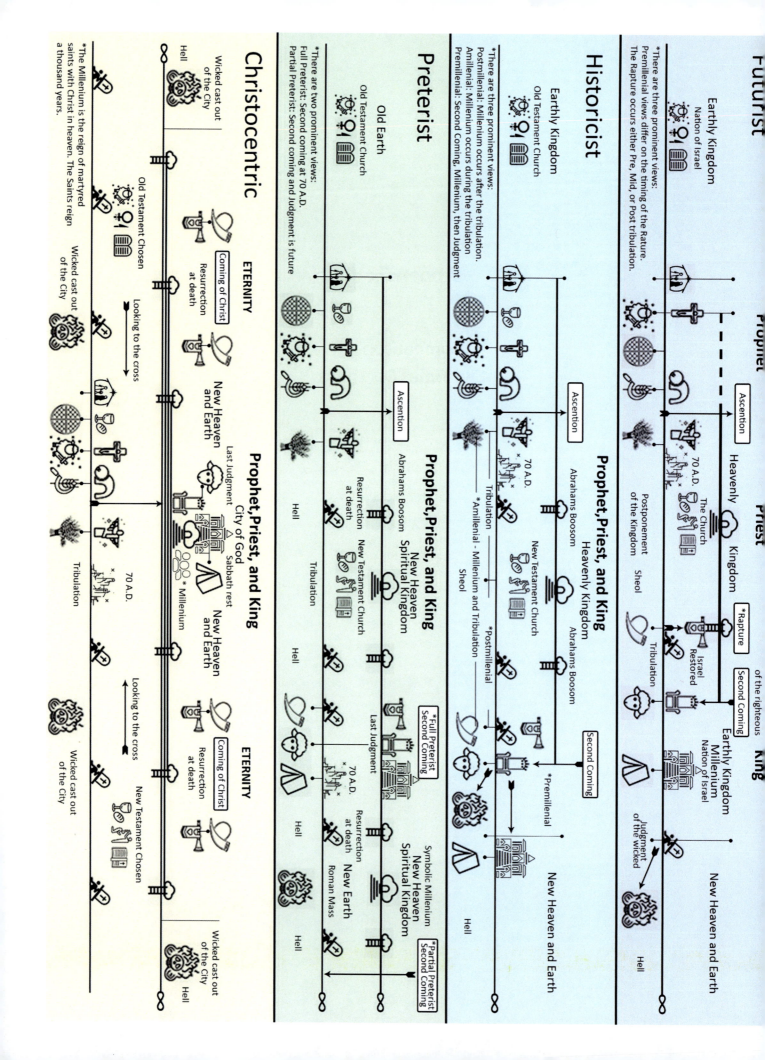

The Fulfillment of the Feasts of Leviticus 23
A comparison of different Eschatalogical views

> Therefore also God highly exalted Him, and bestowed on Him the name which is above every name, that at the name of Jesus every knee should bow, of those who are in heaven, and on earth, and under the earth, and that every tongue should confess that Jesus Christ is Lord, to the glory of God the Father. (Phi 2:9-11 NAS)

Futurist

The first 4 Feast are fulfilled in Christs first coming. The last 3 Feasts will be fulfilled in the future. The first 4 Feasts have an imminent fulfillment that will happen in our immediate future. The Futurist view typically includes the restoration of the Nation of Israel. The Feast are only fulfilled by the Nation of Israel. The Church is an interim period in between the destruction and restoration of the Nation of Israel. Christ is only King of Israel.

Historicist

The Feasts are fulfilled throughout Christian history. The first 4 Feasts are fulfilled up to Pentecost. The last 3 Feasts will be fulfilled through historical events. The Church replaced the Nation of Israel. Israel and the Church are the same entity in Historicist view. Christ is Prophet, Priest, and King for all. Prophecies can be interpreted as symbolic fulfillments of real events in history and not a literal fulfillment.

Preterist

All the Feasts are fulfilled in the first coming of Christ. The "second coming" and the last judgment occurred at the destruction of Jerusalem in 70 A.D. The first 4 Feasts are fulfilled in Christ's first coming. The last 3 Feasts are fulfilled in the Destruction of Jerusalem in 70 A.D. The resurrection of the dead, judgment, and the final state happens at death. Christ is Prophet, Priest, and King for all. Prophecy has literal and spiritual fulfillment.

Christocentric

The Christocentric view is an "interdimensional" view. This is the view of this book. All the Feasts are fulfilled in Christ coming, ascending to the Right Hand of God, and judging the living and the dead. The Heavenly Kingdom is a literal physical place that coincides with our physical dimension. Christs reign is over ALL time: past, present, and future. Christ is Prophet, Priest, and King for all. All prophecy has a literal interpretation not including figures of speech.

Relevant Events

 — Christ Birth

 — Destruction of Jerusalem 70 A.D.

 — Transport to Heaven "Rapture"

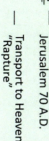 — Resurrection

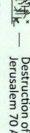 — Tribulation Saints

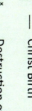 — Heaven or "Abrahams Bosom"

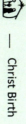 — Hell or "Lake of Fire"

Prophet, Priest and King

It pleased God, in his eternal purpose, to choose and ordain the Lord Jesus, his only begotten Son, to be the Mediator between God and man, the Prophet, Priest, and King, the Head and Savior of his church, the Heir of all things, and Judge of the world: unto whom he did from all eternity give a people, to be his seed, and to be by him in time redeemed, called, justified, sanctified, and glorified. WCF C8.1

The Millenium

The Millennium must be mentioned because it is relevant to the Feasts in Leviticus in regards to most end times doctrines. Christians differ in the interpretation.

The **Premillennial** view teaches the "second coming" of Christ occurs before Christ reigns for a thousand-year on Earth.

The **Postmillennial** view teaches that Christ reigns over Earth from heaven for a literal thousand years and then comes back to Earth.

The **Amillennial** view teaches that there is no literal Millennium but a symbolic representation of the Church Age.

The **Christocentric** view of this book teaches that all those who are martyred for the faith reign with Christ in heaven for a thousand years.

Feasts of Leviticus 23

- Passover Sacrifice
- Feast of Unleavened Bread
- Feast of First Fruits
- Feast of Weeks
- Feast of Trumpets
- Day of Atonement
- Feast of Booths

Old Testament

- Circumcision
- Passover Sacrifice
- Law and Prophets

New Testament

- Baptism
- Lords Supper
- Word of God

Fulfillment in Christ

- Resurrection
- Crucifixion
- Lords Supper
- Pentecost
- Last Trumpet
- Judgment Day "Second Coming"
- City of God

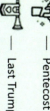
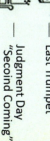

Appendix IV

Interdimensional Theology

The Christocentric Kingdom of God

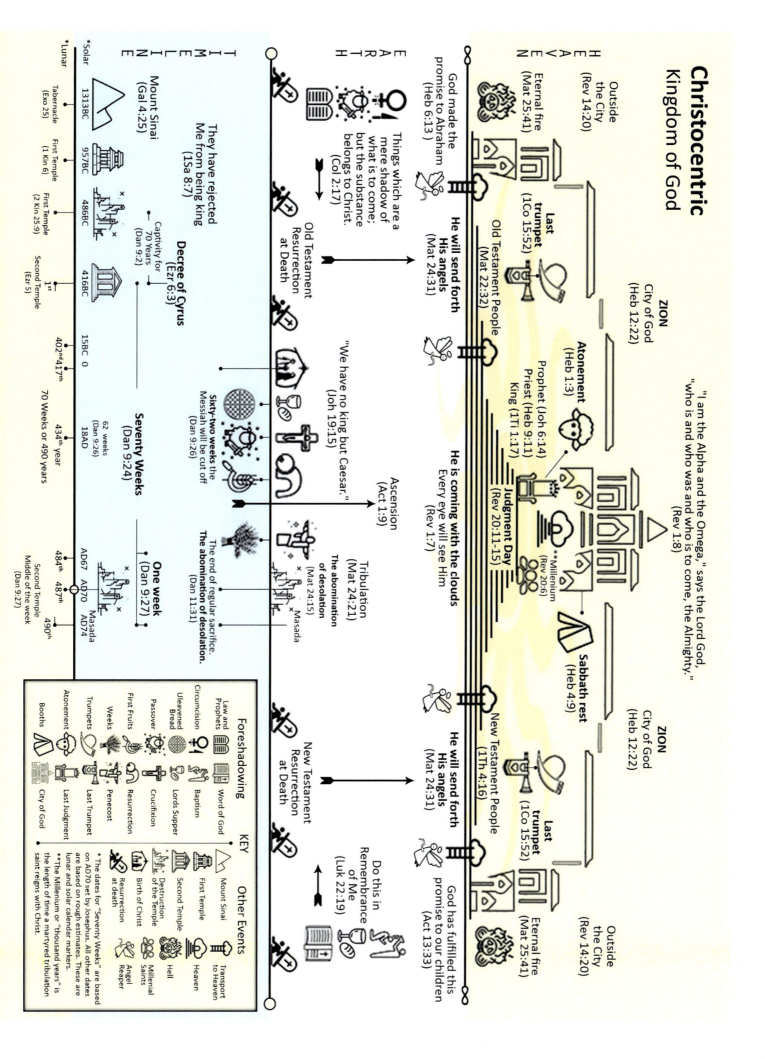

Index

Abomination of desolation, 20, 143–47
    This generation, 143
Advent, 145
All time, 132
    Call of people across, 118
    Creation of, iv
    Fulfillment of the Law, 131–35, 135
    Past, present, and future, 132
    Sacrifice for sins, 55, 56, 112, 124, 165, 177
Amazon Forest, 97
Angel
    Bread of angels, 156
    City of God, 118, 164
    Eternal punishment, 141
    Hell, 141
    Interdimensional being, 154–56
    Judgment of, 153
    Lazarus, 134, 187
    Lions den, 43
    Reapers, 116, 120, 157
    Sons of God, 159
    Subject to Christ, 165
    The beast, 18
Angel of the Lord, 155
Antinomian, 25–28, 43–44, 135, 189
    Communion of the Saints, 182
    Definition, 4, 25
    Futurist, 135
    Rejected, 34, 189
Apostles Creed, i, 4, 5, 130
    Father, Son, Holy Spirit, 130
Ark of the covenant, 166
Astrological readings, 61
Athanasius, 11
Augustine, 11
Avocado farmers, 99
Babylon, 80, 95, 178
Bad debt, 103
Balaam, 154
Barabbas, 124

Begotten from eternity, iii
Begotten from Eternity, 139, 155
Belgic Confession of Faith, v
Bible
    The Living Torah, 3
    Word of God, 90
Bible chronology, 71–75
Bible translation
    Abolished, 147
    Awake, 122
    Coming, 159
    Differences, 81
    Heretick, 191
    Literal translations, 3–4
    Ordinance, 36
    Realm, 150
    Slain from foundation of the world, 133
    Symbolism, 168
    Tenses, 122
    Week, 142
    Will, 123
Body
    Natural and the spiritual, 148
Born again, 108, 115, 118
    Of the Spirit, 152
    Resurrection, 120
    Sabbath rest, 108
Bride, 168
    Parable of the ten virgins, 169
    Parable of the wedding feast, 169
    Wife of the Lamb, 168
Calendar
    Disputes, 68
    Equinoxes and solstices, 60
    Fixed, 70
    Gregorian, 60, 64, 68, 79
    Inaccuracy, 70, 71, 145
    Intercalary, 71
    Jewish, 64, 70
    Jewish New Year, 65

Julian, 67, 68, 70
Lunar, 61
Lunisolar, 63, 107
Markers, 69
Pagan, 70
Passover, 68
Precession, 60
Seven day week, 79
Solar, 59
Talmudic, 64
Tropical, 60

Calvinism, iv

Cartel, 99–100
Knights Templar, 99

Case, 84, 85

Catechism
Roman Catholic Catechism, 137, 140
Saint Thomas Aquinas, 12
Westminster Larger, v, 49

Ceremonial Law, 30
Conflict, 81, 86
Daily offering, 177
Feasts, new moons, sabbaths, 4, 45, 105
Fulfillment, 54, 105, 141, 146, 175, 189
Judgments, 87
On the first day, 175
Sabbath, 85
Weak and beggarly, 105

Children of God, 151
Adoption, 152
First fruits, 115

Children of wrath, 153

Christian Sabbath, 9–14, 87

Christocentric, ii, 133, 138

Church
Bride of Christ, 169
Enters Sabbath rest, 169
Israel and the Church, 25, 28, 136

Church division, 1, 189–92
Calendar dates, 69, 74
Fourth Commandment, 1
Heresy, 191
Observance of holidays, 6
Sabbath, 1

Saturday, 7, 16, 175, 189
Scare tactics, 17
Sunday, 7, 189
Worship day, 175

Church Fathers, 10, 11
Christian Sabbath, 12

City of God, 164–66
A place prepared, 129
Literal city, 164
New Jerusalem, 127, 134, 155, 164–71
The bride, 168
The promises of God, 134

Climate change, 5
Deforestation, 97
Destruction of land, 96
Milankovitch Cycle, 61
Polution, 95

Coming of Christ, 156–60
At death, 157, 163
Every eye will see, 158
Imminent, 160
In heaven, 172
In the clouds, 157, 158
Judgment, 161
Ongoing event, 159
Quick, 160
Soldier who pierced, 159
Stephen, 158

Comparison of Bible Timelines, 74

Confessionalism, i

Constantine
Edict of Milan AD 313, 66

Controversy, 35–36

Convocations, 175
For offerings, 81

Cosmos, v, 33, 150

Creation, ii–v
All to worship God, 22
By the Word of God, 12, 22, 128, 148
Christ Lord of, 132
Fixed in nature, 97
Moral Law in, 47
Sabbath, 77
Tabernacle not of, 126

217

The first creation, 11–12
  Victorinus on, 203
  We are His, 194
Creator's Calendar, 61, 107
Cyrus, 141
Daily rule, 178
Daniel
  Lions den, 43
  Seventy Weeks, 141
Darius, 42
Date setting, 74
Day of Atonement, 123–26, 130
Death
  Abolished, 173
  Coming of Christ, 160
  Final Sabbath rest, 128, 141, 168
  Imminent, 160
  Immortal bodies, 122
  Sleep, 122, 134, 139
Death penalty, 84, 119
Definition
  Ad Hoc Rescue fallacy, 13
  Antinomian, 25
  Appeal to authority, 10
  Christocentric, ii, 138
  Confessionalism, i
  Desuetude, 52
  Dispensationalism, 25
  Equity, 44
  Factious, 191
  Gerund, 159
  Judicial, 36
  Means, 40
  Milankovitch Cycle, 61
  Naturalism, iv
  Ordinance, 36
  Paradox, 7
  Precession, 60
  Preposition, 171
  Rationalizing, 10
  Spatial, 138
  Statute, 38
  Subjective, 68
  Supernaturalism, iv
  This, 145
  Tort, 51
  Transfiguration, 123
  Traverse, 154
Deforestation, 97
Dimension, 138–39, 148–58
  Born again, 108
  Children of wrath, 153
  Christ reigns from, 165, 173
  City of God, 127, 164
  Coming of Christ, 156, 158
  Earth, 139
  Extra dimensions, 138
  Heaven, 149
  Heaven and Earth, iii, 108, 123, 133, 148, 164
  Heaven opened, 155, 166
  Not of this realm, 151
  Not of this world, 150
  Spatial, 138
  Transferred to, 155
  Transfiguration, 123
  Traversing, 154
  Worldy people, 151
Dispensationalism, 25–31
  Israel and the Church, 136
  Law and Grace, 133
Dispensationalist
  Coming of Christ, 163
  Futurist, 135
  Intermediate state, 139
  Old and New covenant Law, 46
  The Law abolished, 31, 51, 52
  Three-part structure of the Law, 44
Dust Bowl, 96
Easter, 13, 66
Ecumenical Church, 67
Egypt, 119
Elect
  Gathering, 115, 121, 128, 135, 157, 159
  Infralapsarian, v
  Inheritance, 157
  Mislead the, 145
  Purgatory, 140
  Supralapsarian, iv

Environmental polution, 95
Eucharist, 137
Factory farming, 95
Faith, 193
   Old Testament saints, 133
Fallacy
   Ad Hoc Rescue, 13
   Appeal to authority, 10
   Cherry picking, 177
   False dichotomy, 31
   Rationalization, 10, 133, 144
   Semantic ambiguity, 21, 145
False prophecies, 74, 145
Feast of Booths, 126–29, 176
   Fulfillment, 167
Feast of First Fruits, 114
Feast of Trumpets, 176
   Futurist, 132
Feast of Unleavened Bread, 175
Feast of Weeks, 116–19
Feasts
   An abomination, 147
   End times, 130, 135
   Fulfillment, 105, 135
   To cease, 148
First Council of Nicaea, 66
Flatland, 138
Fourth Commandment
   Abolishment, 25, 104
   Ancient Israel, 77
   Animals, 94
   Assembly, 177
   Breaking the, 84, 93
   Ceremonial Law, 87
   Core concept, 5
   Dispensationalist, 30
   Duty to neighbor, 44, 50
   Enforcement, 22
   False doctrine, 4
   First day, 180
   First Day Sabbatarian, 9
   Food conservation, 101
   Forever blessed, 80
   Fulfillment of, 105, 141
   Immigrants, 100
   In creation, 33
   Judicial Law, 85
   Labor, 86
   Lord's Day, 22
   Moral Law, 82, 90
   Priestly conflict, 23, 86
   Sabbath, 69, 77–82, 89
   Sacrifices, 55, 78, 81
   Seventh Day Sabbatarian, 15
   The Law, 35
   Three-part structure, 80
   Workaholism, 93
   Worship, 23, 55, 189, 190
Futurist, 105
   Interpretation of feasts, 132
Gospel
   Timeline, 130
Great Commission, 190
Great Disappointment, 145
   Millerite, 145
Greek definition
   Age, 116, 132
   All, 132
   Come, 158
   Coming down, 171
   Fiftieth, 117
   Generation, 144
   Heaven, 149
   Heretick, 191
   Quick, 162
   Quickly, 162
   Race, 144
   Realm, 150
   Right, 173
   Sabbath, 79
   Seventh, 79
   Shortly, 20
   Speedily, 162
   Tabernacle, 166
   This, 144
   To let down, 172
   World, 150
Greenhouse Gas Effect, 95

Hagar, 127, 169
Harvest
   Counting of weeks, 116
   First fruits, 114
   Tares and wheat, 115
Healthcare, 87
Heaven
   A house prepared, 128, 129
   Final Sabbath rest, 110, 127, 148, 157, 190
   Inheritance, 152
   Paradise, 150
   Reward in, 167
   Tabernacle, 166
Hebrew definition
   Abolished, 147
   Animal, 95
   Appointed time, 38
   Assembly, 38
   Awake, 122
   Booth, 167
   Charge, 48
   Convocation, 38
   Dispute, 35
   Generation, 144
   Heaven, 149
   Judge, 36
   Judgment, 36
   Maidservant, 94
   Sabbath, 78
   Sabbaths, 39
   Servant, 94
   Seventh, 78
   Statute, 37
   Stranger, 100
   Tabernacle, 166
   Torah, 37
   Week, 142
Hell, v, 141
   Roman Catholic Catechism, 140
   Westminster Confession of Faith, 139
Heretick, 191
Hillel, 64
Hiroshima and Nagasaki, 161
Historicist, 105, 136

holy Spirit
   Jesus baptism, 156
Holy Spirit
   Apostles Creed, 130
   Baptizing, 181, 191
   Born again, 108, 151
   Conception of Christ, 149
   Outpouring, 117
   Pentecost, 117
   Received, 179
   Stephen filled with, 158
   The work of, 168
   Witness of, 193
Homeless, 101
Immigrants
   Definition, 100
   Sweatshops, 99
   Thai, 101
   Undocumented illegal, 99
Intercalation, 61
Interdimensional theology, 6–7, 138–39
Intermediate state
   Abraham's Bosom, 140
   Purgatory, 140
   Soul Sleep, 123
Jacob, 142
Jacob's ladder, 155
Jerusalem, 200
   Commerce on the Sabbath, 83, 95
   Decree to rebuild, 142
   Destruction, 20, 137, 141, 143–48
   New Jerusalem, 127–29, 134
   New Jerusalem bride, 168
   Worship location, 118, 130
Jesus Christ
   Architect of the Law, 22
   Atonement, 132
   Begotten from eternity, iii, 139
   Begotten from God, ii
   Blood of the covenant, 111–12
   Bread of life, 114
   Christocentric, ii
   Coming of, 113, 128, 179, 190
   Crucifixion, 124

    Faith in, 108
    First-born of all creation, iii
    From eternity, 132
    Fulfilled promises, 4, 55, 59, 69, 146
    Fulfilled the Law, 105, 115, 189, 193
    Garden of Eden, 139
    High Priest, 46, 105, 126
    Is Lord, 57, 165
    Jewish geneology, 177
    Judge, 153
    Judgment seat, 125
    King, 165
    Messianic work, 132
    Obeyed the Law, 57, 88, 90
    Preaching, 1
    Prophet, Priest, King, 46, 91
    Propitiation for sin, 86
    Reconciliation, 194
    Reigns, 160, 173
    Right hand of God, 86, 91, 124, 156, 164
    Sacrifice, 27, 55, 110, 177
    The Lamb, 110, 112, 114, 129
    The Word of God, ii
    Transfiguration, 123
    Trial before Pilate, 124
    Unity in, 4
    Word of God, 128
Jewish
    Calendar, 13, 39, 55, 59
    Calendar day for Easter, 67
    Calendar specifications, 63–65
    Days, 64
    Dispensation, 26
    Leap year, 65
    Months, 64
    New Year, 65
    Pagan calendar conflict, 70
    Passover in Egypt, 57
    Race, 144
    Sabbath, 9–10
    Temple, 143
    Tradition, 3, 67
    War, 146
Jewish Chronology
    Missing years, 71
    Jews and Gentiles, 32
    Joseph, 149
    Josephus, 72, 143
    Judgement Day
        Living and dead, 130
    Judgment, 36–37, 39–40
        According to deeds, 161
        Based on Statutes, 80
        Breaking the Law, 35
        Case, 85
        Ceremonial Law, 39
        Civil and Criminal, 90
        Holding place till, 120
        Identifying, 39
        Judge, 36
        Priests, 87
        Remedy, 45
    Judgment Day, 124–26
        At death, 130, 140
        Day of Atonement, 123
        Futurist, 137
        Helping the needy, 187
        Intermediate state, 140
        Niagara Creed, 136
        Parable of talents, 184
        Preterist, 137
    Judicial Law, 30, 50–54
        Civil and Criminal, 87
        Dietary Law, 50
        Judgment, 36–37
        Judicial system, 36
    Kingdom of God
        Born again, 108, 153
        Citizens, 152
        Eternal, iii
        From the foundation of the world, 125, 184
        Has no end, 46
        In heaven, 46
        Least in, 31
        Not of this world, 190
        Passover fulfilled, 113
        Postponment theory, 136
        Preterist, 137

Priesthood of believers, 119
Tares and wheat, 116
Ten virgins, 169, 183
The least in, 189
The Sabbath, 135
Transferred to, 13
Laban, 142
Last day
Pentecost, 117
Last Day
End of the world, 116
Lazarus, 134
Leaven
Sin, 114
Lord's Day
Collection of gifts, 186, 191
Constantine, 67
Duties of, 182
First Day Sabbatarian, 9–13
Resurrection of Christ, 11, 191
Seventh Day Sabbatarian, 15, 21–22
Traditional day of worship, 178
Lord's Prayer, 148
Lord's Supper, 114, 191
Feast of First Fruits, 115
Feast of Unleavened Bread, 113
Lunar Sabbath calendar, 61
Manna, 149
Memorial
Athanasius Lord's day, 11
Athanasius on Sabbath, 11
Ceremonial Law, 5
Lord's Supper, 113
Passover, 57
SDA of creation, 15
SDA resurrection, 17
Slavery in Egypt, 39, 148
Unleavened bread, 113
Monopolies, 84
Moral Law, 43–51
Adultery, 45
Bearing false witness, 45
Breaking the law, 90
Difference from judicial law, 51, 54
Dispensationalism, 25
Genesis, 32, 48
Government, 41
Leviticus 19, 45
Sabbath, 82
Statutory, 38, 39, 47, 81
Ten Commandments, 4, 30, 35, 49, 120
Three-part structure, 4
Unchangeable, 47, 190
Mormons
Baptism for the dead, 140
Mount Sinai, 119–20, 126, 169
Mount Zion, 127, 170
Nation of Israel
Battle of Masada, 141, 143, 146, 147
Calendar, 66
Dispensationalism, 25–30, 136
Fulfillment of feasts, 132, 136
Futurist, 136
Government, 41
Jews and Gentiles, 27, 48
Judicial Law expired, 53
Keepers of the promise, 146
Preterist, 137
Restoration, 6, 26, 124, 134, 136, 190
Sacrifices ended, 147
The Law of God, 192
New Jerusalem, 164–66
Coming down from heaven, 128
Descending from heaven, 170
Final Sabbath rest, 164
In heaven, 169
Not earthly promise, 109
Symbolism, 169
The bride, 168
New moon
A rest day, 107
Niagara Creed, 136
Nicene Creed, i
Paradox, 133
Passover, 110–12
First born killed, 110
Lamb, 110
Unleavened bread, 112

Pentecost, 117
Persian Empire, 71, 142
Persian kings, 72
    Cyrus, 142
    Cyrus is Darius, 73
    Darius, 42
Peters vision, 172
Pharaoh, 112
Pharisees, 85, 88, 114
Pontius Pilate, 124
Pope, 136
Pope Gregory XIII, 70
Predestination, v, 152
    Christ sacrificed, 112
    Hell, v
Priest
    Duties, 87
Promises of God
    Christocentric, 138
    Faith in, 134–35
    Faith in Christ, 109
    Final Sabbath rest, 109, 152
    From Jewish geneology, 177
    Fulfilled in Christ, 132, 136
    Heirs of the promise, 32
    Israel keeping the, 39, 54–57
    New Covenant, 28
    Not earthly, 110
    Received at death, 134
    Received by the Church, 118
    Received in heaven, 134, 148
    Sacrifices, 80, 146
    Son of free woman, 169
    Tertullian, 201
    The Messiah, 5, 59, 86, 113
    Unbelief, 105
Ptolemy, 71
Purgatory, 140
Puritans, 9–10, 12
Rabbis, 3, 64, 71, 72, 106
Rachel, 142
Rapture, 136, 157
Realm, iv, 138, 150
    Not of this realm, 151

Reformed
    Abraham's Bosom, 140
    First Day Sabbitarian, 9
    Historicist, 136
    Preterist, 137
Reformed Baptist Confession, 136
Repentance, 193
Resurrection of the dead, 120–23
    At death, 115, 123, 130, 134, 141, 157
    Awake, 122
    Coming of Christ, 121, 159, 190
    Feast of Trumpets, 120
    Final judgment, 130
    Futurist, 136
    Made alive, 160
    Moses and Elijah, 123
    Preterist, 137
    Sadducees, 121
    The last trumpet, 120
    Urgency, 158
Roman Caesars, 19–20
Roman Catholic
    Abraham's bosom, 140
    Catholic, 7
    Changed Sabbath to Sunday, 68
    Jesuit Luis de Alcasar, 137
    Mass, 137
    Partial Preterist, 137
    Prayer for the dead, 140
    Purgatory, 140
Roman Empire, 66
Sabbatarian, 4, 135, 189
    First Day Sabbatarian, 9, 11, 13, 136
    Non-Sabbatarian, 25, 135
    Seventh Day Sabbatarian, 15
Sabbath
    Abolished, 30, 52, 54, 87, 89
    An appointed time, 106
    Animals, 33, 94, 95
    Breaking the, 23, 81, 83, 85, 89, 93
    Calendar day, 4, 61, 86
    Capitalization, 2
    Ceremonial Law, 85
    Changed to first day, 10

Christ dead, 11
Christ Lord of, 12, 13
Church activities, 23
Climate change, 95
Debt forgiveness, 103
Definition, 39, 54, 78–79
Different views, 4
Dispensationalism, 26
Do not leave home, 78
Doing good, 89
Duty to neighbor, 22, 49
Enforcement, 31, 84, 85
Exodus 16, 77
Feasts, new moons, sabbaths, 5, 39
First day, 9–14
First Day Sabbatarian, 9
Forever statute, 80
Fourth Commandment, 2, 39
Healing, 88, 89
Healthcare, 87
Helping the Needy, 85
Immigrants, 33
Jewish, 10
Jewish calendar, 64, 79
Judicial Law, 84
Labor, 5, 80, 86
Land management, 96–98
Lord of Sabbath, 10
Lord's Day, 11, 15
Lunisolar calendar, 63
Markets, 83
Monopolies, 84
My holy day, 21
Nation of Israel, 30
Neglecting household, 89
Not for the Church, 30
Restoration of Israel, 26
Sacrifices, 55, 106, 107
Slaves, 84
Statutory, 80
Three-part structure, 4, 80
Work week, 94
Workaholism, 93
Worship, 4, 89

Sacrifices
    Abolished, 141
    Ceased, 146
    Daily, 177
    God hated, 80
    Outside the camp, 127
Sadducees, 88, 114, 121
Sanhedrin, 64
Sarah, 127, 169
Satan, 16
Saturday, 70, 87
    Creator's calendar, 63
    Lunisolar calendar, 64
    Mistranslation, 3
    Not in the Bible, 83, 175
    Not the Sabbath, 68, 79
    Pagan day, 68
    Sabbath changed to Sunday, 68–70
    Seventh Day Sabbatarian, 15–17
    Solar calendar, 59
    Worship, 5, 21, 23
Scapegoat, 123
Scheduled
    Ceremonial Law, 59, 69
    Markers, 78
Scribes, 88
Second Book of Enoch
    Third heaven, 150
Second coming, 6, 136, 137, 190
    Dispensationalist, 25, 163
    False prophecies, 145
    Intermediate state, 139
    Single event, 164
    The Great Disappointment, 145
Seder Olam Rabbah, 72
Seven Hills of Rome, 18
Seventh Day Adventist
    28 Fundamental Beliefs, 15, 139
    Church division, 22
    Creation, 15
    Ellen White, 15–18, 68, 192
    Fourth Commandment, 68
    Great disappointment, 145
    Historicist, 136

Image of the beast, 16
Mark of the beast, 16–17, 22
Persecution, 17
Sabbath End times, 16
Sabbath worship, 15
Second coming, 139
Soul sleep, 139
Sunday worship, 16–18
Test of loyalty, 16
The Great Controversy, 17
Seventy weeks
Missing years, 71
Seventy Weeks, 141–43, 145
Calculation, 142
Destruction of Israel, 143
Sacrifices stop, 141
This generation, 143
Sheaf, 114
Slave, 84
Israel in Egypt, 113
Servant, 94
Solomon, 178
South America
Extortion, 98
Stephen, 156, 157
Student loans, 103
Sunday, 2, 12–13
Pagan, 68
Worship, 5
Supernaturalism and Naturalism, iv
Temple
Consecration, 176
First Temple, 71
Rebuilding, 141, 178
Tabernacle in heaven, 126
Ten Commandments, 190
The City of God
Final Sabbath rest, 164
The Law, 80
Abolished, 26
Application, 90
Daily, 178
End times, 135
Fulfilled for all time, 135
Fulfilled in Christ, 130
Nation of Israel, 26
Repentance, 27
Three-part structure, 4, 35, 43–46, 80, 189
Written on the heart, 117
This generation, 143–46
Thomas Aquinas
Sabbath, 12
Throne of God, 164
Right hand of God, 164
Transfiguration
Moses and Elijah, 123, 134
Unbelief, 105
Denies Christ, 132
Performing the Ceremonial Law, 109
United States, 52
Animal law, 41
Blue laws, 16
Cruel and unusual punishment, 52
Dust Bowl, 97
El Monte California, 101
FDA, 50
Food waste, 102
Great Plains, 96
Immigrants, 99–101
Judicial Law, 50–53
Labor laws, 22
Land managment, 96–97
Legal system, 35
Mark of the beast, 16–20
Moral law, 47
Not theocratic, 46
Self defence, 51
Statutes, 38
Work week, 94
Unjust gain, 83
Unleavened Bread, 110, 112
Virgin Mary, iii, 139, 149
Christ born of, ii
Wasting food, 101
Westminster Confession of Faith, i, 9
Ceremonial Law abrogated, 54
Communion of the Saints, 182
Duty to God and Neighbor, 44

    General equity therof, 53
    Hell, 139
    Judgment day, 139
    Moral Law, 47
    Ownership of possesions, 183
    Predestination, v
    Second coming, 139
    The Sabbath, 9, 50
    Three-part structure, 43
Westminster Larger Catechism, i, v, 49
Westminster Standard, i
Wilderness of Sin, 77, 84–85
    Dietary laws, 50
    Forty years, i, 138
    God spared Israel, 31
    Jail system, 84
    Manna, 149
    Mount Sinai, 126, 167
Word of God, i–iii, 139
    Eternal, iii, 139, 148
    Jesus Christ, ii
    Preaching, 115, 192
Worship, 175
    Breaks the Sabbath, 23, 82
    Ceremonial Law, 55
    Church division, 74, 189
    Communion, 182
    Constantine, 67
    Designated day, 107, 175, 178
    Every day, 22, 177, 191
    Fourth Commandment, 5, 15, 78, 190
    Heresy, 191
    Jewish Feasts, 13
    Location, 118
    Lord of Sabbath, 13
    Lord's Day, 9
    Mark of the beast, 16, 22
    Sabbatarian, 4, 15
    Sabbath, 23, 50, 86
    Seventh Day Adventist, 15
    Spirit and truth, 130, 181
    Thomas Aquinas, 12
Zionism, 6

Works Cited

Bible Versions

The New American Standard Bible (NASB) (NAS [1977] and NAU [1995]). Copyright © 1960, 1962, 1963, 1968, 1971, 1972, 1973, 1975, 1977, 1988, 1995, and La Biblia de Las Americas. Copyright © 1986, both by The Lockman Foundation. All rights reserved.

KJA, KJG Authorized Version (KJV) - 1769 Blayney Edition of the 1611 King James Version of the English Bible - with Larry Pierce's Englishman's-Strong's Numbering System, ASCII version. Copyright © 1988-1997 by the Online Bible Foundation and Woodside Fellowship of Ontario, Canada.

Preface

[1] Collins English Dictionary – Complete and Unabridged, 12th Edition 2014 © HarperCollins Publishers 1991, 1994, 1998, 2000, 2003, 2006, 2007, 2009, 2011, 2014.

[2] "Christocentric." The Concise Oxford Dictionary of the Christian Church (2 rev. ed.), Oxford University Press, 2006.
[3] "Supernaturalism." Merriam-Webster.com Dictionary, Merriam-Webster, https://www.merriam-webster.com/dictionary/supernaturalism. Accessed 14 Sep. 2020.
[4] "Naturalism." Merriam-Webster.com Dictionary, Merriam-Webster, https://www.merriam-webster.com/dictionary/naturalism. Accessed 14 Sep. 2020.
[5] The Belgic Confession, Article 16, About Divine Predestination.
[6] The Westminster Confession of Faith of 1689, Chapter 3 "Of God's Eternal Decree" Section 1.
[7] The Westminster Larger Catechism, Question 14.

Introduction

[8] The Religion Stylebook, Diversity Style Guide © 2020 https://www.diversitystyleguide.com/glossary/sabbath/
[9] The Living Torah, The five books of Moses and the Haftorot, Leviticus 23:3, by Rabbi Aryeh Kaplan 1981
[10] The Living Torah, The five books of Moses and the Haftorot, by Rabbi Aryeh Kaplan, Translator's Introduction, pg. v 1981
[11] "Paradox." Merriam-Webster.com Dictionary, Merriam-Webster, https://www.merriam-webster.com/dictionary/paradox. Accessed 16 Sep. 2020.

Chapter 1 - First Day Sabbatarian

[12] The Westminster Confession of Faith of 1689, Chapter 21 "Of Religious Worship and the Sabbath Day" Section 7.
[13] The Westminster Confession of Faith of 1689, Chapter 21 "Of Religious Worship and the Sabbath Day" Section 7.
[14] The Ten Commandments, Thomas Watson Chapter 2.4 The Fourth Commandment pg. 95.

[15] The Ten Commandments, Thomas Watson Chapter 2.4 The Fourth Commandment pg. 95.
[16] "Appeal to Authority," Logically Fallacious: The Ultimate Collection of Over 300 Logical Fallacies (Academic Edition), by Bo Bennett.
[17] "Rationalization," Logically Fallacious: The Ultimate Collection of Over 300 Logical Fallacies (Academic Edition), by Bo Bennett.
[18] Augustine, Reply to Faustus the Manichæan. Book XVI.-29.
[19] Athanasius, On Sabbath and Circumcision 3 from https://www.catholic.com/tract/sabbath-or-sunday. Original text not found.
[20] Thomas Aquinas, The Aquinas Catechism, Part 3 Section 3A.1.b. pg. 188.
[21] Eusebius Caesariensis, Vita Constantini, Book III Chapter XVIII. — He speaks of their Unanimity respecting the Feast of Easter, and against the Practice of the Jews. pg. 1005.
[22] "Ad Hoc Rescue "Logically Fallacious: The Ultimate Collection of Over 300 Logical Fallacies (Academic Edition), by Bo Bennett.

Chapter 2 - Seventh Day Sabbatarian
[23] Seventh Day Adventist, 28 Fundamental Beliefs, section 20, The Sabbath.
[24] Seventh-day Adventists Believe ...A Biblical Exposition of 27 Fundamental Doctrines, Chapter 19 p. 249. The Sabbath.
[25] Ellen White, The Great Controversy. 25. God's Law Immutable, pg. 442 -443.
[26] Ellen White, The Great Controversy. 25. God's Law Immutable, pg. 448.
[27] Ellen White, The Great Controversy. 38. The Final Warning pg. 605.
[28] The Adventist Review Week of Prayer Issue | Adventist Review October 14, 2015 1525 pg. 9 Worship and the Second Coming.
[29] The Adventist Review Week of Prayer Issue | Adventist Review October 14, 2015 1525 pg. 5 Power to Finish the Work by Ted N. C. Wilson.
[30] The Adventist Review Week of Prayer Issue | Adventist Review October 14, 2015 1525 Power to Finish the Work by Ted N. C. Wilson.
[31] The Editors of Encyclopaedia Britannica, Seven Hills of Rome, Encyclopædia Britannica, Encyclopædia Britannica, inc. July 20, 1998 https://www.britannica.com/place/Seven-Hills-of-Rome. Accessed 16 Sep. 2020
[32] The Editors of Encyclopaedia Britannica, List of Roman emperors, Encyclopædia Britannica, Encyclopædia Britannica, inc. November 11, 2015n https://www.britannica.com/topic/list-of-Roman-emperors-2043294. Accessed 16 Sep. 2020
[33] Titus Flavius Josephus, The Works of Josephus Book III Chapter 9 Section 2.
[34] "shortly." <5034> τάχος (tachos), Strong's Exhaustive Concordance: New American Standard Bible, updated ed., Lockman Foundation, 1995.

Chapter 3 - Antinomian Non-Sabbatarian
[35] "Dispensationalism" American Heritage® Dictionary of the English Language, Fifth Edition. Copyright © 2016 by Houghton Mifflin Harcourt Publishing Company. Published by Houghton Mifflin Harcourt Publishing Company. All rights reserved. Accessed 16 Sep. 2020
[36] "Antinomian." Merriam-Webster.com Dictionary, Merriam-Webster, https://www.merriam-webster.com/dictionary/antinomian. Accessed 16 Sep. 2020.
[37] Clarence Larkin, The Dispensational Truth, The Sabbath pg. 65.

[38] Clarence Larkin, The Dispensational Truth, The Sabbath pg. 65.
[39] Craig A. Blaising and Darrell L. Bock, Progressive Dispensationalism, "Jesus and the Mosaic Covenant" pg. 194.
[40] Craig A. Blaising and Darrell L. Bock, Progressive Dispensationalism, "Fulfillment of the Biblical Covenants" pg. 199.
[41] Journal of Dispensational Theology, March 2007 pg.77, The Sabbath and Dispensationalism by Joel T. Williamson Jr.
[42] Journal of Dispensational Theology, March 2007 pg.77-78, The Sabbath and Dispensationalism by Joel T. Williamson Jr.
[43] Journal of Dispensational Theology, March 2007 pg.79, The Sabbath and Dispensationalism by Joel T. Williamson Jr.
[44] Journal of Dispensational Theology, March 2007 pg.83, The Sabbath and Dispensationalism by Joel T. Williamson Jr.
[45] "False Dilemma" Logically Fallacious: The Ultimate Collection of Over 300 Logical Fallacies (Academic Edition), by Bo Bennett.

Chapter 4 - The Law

[46] "dispute." <07379> רִיב or רִב (rib or rib) (936d)' Strong's Exhaustive Concordance: New American Standard Bible, updated ed., Lockman Foundation, 1995.
[47] "judge." <08199> שָׁפַט (shaphat) (1047a), Strong's Exhaustive Concordance: New American Standard Bible, updated ed., Lockman Foundation, 1995.
[48] "judicial." The Oxford Advanced Learner's Dictionary, Oxford University Press, https://www.oxfordlearnersdictionaries.com/us/definition/english/judicial. Accessed 16 Sep. 2020.
[49] "ordinance." The Oxford Advanced Learner's Dictionary, Oxford University Press, https://www.oxfordlearnersdictionaries.com/us/definition/english/ordinance. Accessed 16 Sep. 2020.
[50] "judgement." <04941> מִשְׁפָּט (mishpat) (1048b), Strong's Exhaustive Concordance: New American Standard Bible, updated ed., Lockman Foundation, 1995.
[51] "laws." <08451> תּוֹרָה (torah) (435d), Strong's Exhaustive Concordance: New American Standard Bible, updated ed., Lockman Foundation, 1995.
[52] "statute." <02708> חֻקָּה (chuqqah) (349d), Strong's Exhaustive Concordance: New American Standard Bible, updated ed., Lockman Foundation, 1995.
[53] "statute." The Oxford Advanced Learner's Dictionary, Oxford University Press, https://www.oxfordlearnersdictionaries.com/us/definition/english/statute. Accessed 16 Sep. 2020.
[54] "appointed time." <04150> מוֹעֵד or מֹעֵד or מוֹעָדָה (moed or moed or moadah) (417b), Strong's Exhaustive Concordance: New American Standard Bible, updated ed., Lockman Foundation, 1995.
[55] "convocation." <04744> מִקְרָא (miqra) (896d), Strong's Exhaustive Concordance: New American Standard Bible, updated ed., Lockman Foundation, 1995.
[56] "assembly." <06951> קָהָל (qahal) (874c), Strong's Exhaustive Concordance: New American Standard Bible, updated ed., Lockman Foundation, 1995.
[57] "sabbath." <07676> שַׁבָּת (shabbath) (992a), Strong's Exhaustive Concordance: New American Standard Bible, updated ed., Lockman Foundation, 1995.
[58] "means." The Oxford Advanced Learner's Dictionary, Oxford University Press, https://www.oxfordlearnersdictionaries.com/us/definition/english/means. Accessed 16 Sep. 2020.

[59] Code of Virginia Title 3.2 Subtitle V. Chapter 65. Article 6 3.2-6540. Control of dangerous dogs; penalties.
60 The Westminster Confession of Faith of 1689, Chapter 19, "Of the Law of God" Section 2 – 4.
[61] "equity." Merriam-Webster.com Dictionary, Merriam-Webster, https://www.merriam-webster.com/dictionary/equity. Accessed 16 Sep. 2020.
[62] The Westminster Confession of Faith of 1689, Chapter 19, "Of the Law of God" Section 2.
[63] Journal of Dispensational Theology, March 2007 pg.84 The Sabbath and Dispensationalism by Joel T. Williamson Jr.
[64] The Westminster Confession of Faith of 1689, Chapter 19, "Of the Law of God" Section 2 – 3.
[65] "charge." <04931> מִשְׁמֶרֶת (mishmereth) (1038b), Strong's Exhaustive Concordance: New American Standard Bible, updated ed., Lockman Foundation, 1995.
[66] The Westminster Larger Catechism, Question 98.
[67] "tort." The Cambridge Academic Content Dictionary, Cambridge University Press. https://dictionary.cambridge.org/us/dictionary/english/tort. Accessed 16 Sep. 2020.
[68] Moses's restatement of torts: Modern principles of justice and efficiency in the Mishpatim, Louis W. Hensler III, pg. 70. Vermont Law Review [Vol. 44:069)
[69] Moses's restatement of torts: Modern principles of justice and efficiency in the Mishpatim, Louis W. Hensler III, pg. 70. Vermont Law Review [Vol. 44:069)
[70] Moses's restatement of torts: Modern principles of justice and efficiency in the Mishpatim, Louis W. Hensler III* pg. 107 Vermont Law Review [Vol. 44:069)
[71] "Desuetude." (n.d.) West's Encyclopedia of American Law, edition 2. (2008). Retrieved February 21 2020 from https://legal-dictionary.thefreedictionary.com/Desuetude. Accessed 16 Sep. 2020.
[72] Death, Desuetude, and Original Meaning Death, Desuetude, and Original Meaning, John F. Stinneford, William & Mary Law Review Volume 56 (2014-2015) Issue 2 Article 5 pg. 537-538
[73] Rockville, Maryland - Code of Ordinances Chapter 13 - MISCELLANEOUS PROVISIONS AND OFFENSES ARTICLE III. - OTHER OFFENSES Sec. 13-53. - Profanity; violation of section declared S violation of section declared misdemeanor.
[74] "Duty to Rescue." USLegal.com airSlate Legal Forms, inc. d/b/s USLegal, 1997-2019 Law and Legal Definition https://definitions.uslegal.com/d/duty-to-rescue/. Accessed 16 Sep. 2020.
[75] The Westminster Confession of Faith of 1689, Chapter 19, "Of the Law of God" Section 3.

Chapter 5 - The Calendar

[76] "precession." The Dictionary of Geophysics, Astrophysics, and Astronomy By Richard A. Matzner 2001
[77] "precession." The Dictionary of Geophysics, Astrophysics, and Astronomy By Richard A. Matzner 2001
[78] "Milankovitch Cycle." The Dictionary of Geophysics, Astrophysics, and Astronomy By Richard A. Matzner 2001
[79] "What is my sidereal sign?" by Athen Chimenti, masteringthezodiac.com/what-is-my-sidereal-sign.
[80] Biblical Calendar for This Month, SabbathHerald.com, http://www.sabbathherald.com/biblical-calendar-for-this-month/ 2020.
[81] Judaism 101 jewfaq.org, Jewish Calendar, Tracey R Rich http://www.jewfaq.org/calendar.htm 1995-2020.

[82] Judaism 101 jewfaq.org, Jewish Calendar, Tracey R Rich http://www.jewfaq.org/calendar.htm 1995-2020.

[83] Judaism 101 jewfaq.org, Jewish Calendar, Tracey R Rich http://www.jewfaq.org/calendar.htm 1995-2020.

[84] Eusebius Caesariensis, Vita Constantini, Book III Chapter V. "Of the Disagreement respecting the Celebration of Easter." pg. 998.

[85] Eusebius Caesariensis, Vita Constantini, Book III Chapter XVII. "Constantine's Letter to the Churches respecting the Council at Nicæa." pg. 1004.

[86] Eusebius Caesariensis, Vita Constantini, Book III Chapter XIX. "Exhortation to follow the Example of the Greater Part of the World." pg. 1006.

[87] Eusebius Caesariensis, Vita Constantini, Book III Chapter XIX. "Exhortation to follow the Example of the Greater Part of the World." pg. 1006.

[88] Eusebius Caesariensis, Vita Constantini, Book III Chapter XVIII. "He enjoins the General Observance of the Lord's Day, and the Day of Preparation." pg. 1039.

[89] The Great Controversy, By Ellen G White, p. 448-449, 1888.

[90] "subjective." The Oxford Advanced Learner's Dictionary, Oxford University Press, https://www.oxfordlearnersdictionaries.com/us/definition/english/subjective. Accessed 16 Sep. 2020.

[91] An Introduction to Error Analysis, by John R Taylor, Chapter 2.3 Discrepancy pg.18.

[92] The Romance of Bible Chronology, by Rev. Martin Anstey, BA, MA Chapter 1: Scope, Method, Standpoint and Sources pg. 4.

[93] The Romance of Bible Chronology, by Rev. Martin Anstey, BA, MA Chapter 1: Scope, Method, Standpoint and Sources pg. 20.

[94] The Romance of Bible Chronology, by Rev. Martin Anstey, Chapter 1 pg. 19

[95] Seder Olam Rabbah, Chapter 30: Nehemiah to Roman Destruction of Jerusalem 112.

[96] The Romance of Bible Chronology, by Rev. Martin Anstey, Chapter 1 pg. 23;

[97] The Works of Josephus, the Antiquities of the Jews Book XI Ch 1-7

[98] The Romance of Bible Chronology, by Rev. Martin Anstey, Chapter 1 pg. 24.

[99] The Romance of Bible Chronology, by Rev. Martin Anstey, Chapter 1 pg. 25.

[100] Bible Timeline © 2010 by Rich Valkanet, Discovery Bible and Biblos.com.

[101] The Romance of Bible Chronology, by Rev. Martin Anstey, Chapter 1 pg. 19.

[102] The Wonders of Bible Chronology, Phillip Mauro, Grace Abounding Ministries, GAM Printers 1987.

[103] The Romance of Bible Chronology, by Rev. Martin Anstey, Chapter 1 pg. 23.

[104] Hebrew Nations a Britam Website, Rabbinical Chronology hebrewnations.com/articles/16/chronology/rabbinical.html 2012

[105] Chabad.org, Chabad-Lubavitch Media Center, Excerpt from Miraculous Journey by Yosef Eisen chabad.org/library/article_cdo/aid/2836156/jewish/The-Discrepancy-Between-the-Rabbinic-and-Secular-Dates.htm 1993-2020

[106] The Romance of Bible Chronology, by Rev. Martin Anstey, Chapter 1 pg. 24.

Chapter 6 - The Sabbath

[107] "sabbath." <07676> שַׁבָּת (shabbath) (992a), Strong's Exhaustive Concordance: New American Standard Bible, updated ed., Lockman Foundation, 1995.

[108] "seventh." <07637> שְׁבִיעִי or שְׁבִיעִית (shebii or shebiith) (988c), Strong's Exhaustive Concordance: New American Standard Bible, updated ed., Lockman Foundation, 1995.
[109] "sabbath." <4521> σάββατον (sabbaton), Strong's Exhaustive Concordance: New American Standard Bible, updated ed., Lockman Foundation, 1995.
[110] "seventh." <1442> ἕβδομος (hebdomos), Strong's Exhaustive Concordance: New American Standard Bible, updated ed., Lockman Foundation, 1995.

Chapter 7 - Modern Day Consequences

[111] Oates, 1971. Heavy Work Investment: Its Nature, Sources, Outcomes, and Future Directions Itzhak Harpaz, Raphael Snir pg. 171.
[112] Heavy Work Investment: Its Nature, Sources, Outcomes, and Future Directions Itzhak Harpaz, Raphael Snir pg. 173-174.
[113] Heavy Work Investment: Its Nature, Sources, Outcomes, and Future Directions Itzhak Harpaz, Raphael Snir pg. 3-4.
[114] "servant." <05650> עֶבֶד (ebed) (713d), Strong's Exhaustive Concordance: New American Standard Bible, updated ed., Lockman Foundation, 1995.
[115] "maidservant." <0519> אָמָה (amah) (51a), Strong's Exhaustive Concordance: New American Standard Bible, updated ed., Lockman Foundation, 1995.
[116] "animal." <0929> בְּהֵמָה (behemah) (96d), Strong's Exhaustive Concordance: New American Standard Bible, updated ed., Lockman Foundation, 1995.
[117] Livestock in a Changing Landscape, Volume 1: Drivers, Consequences, and Responses by Henning Steinfeld, Harold A. Mooney, et al. | Jan 29, 2010 pg. 39.
[118] Livestock in a Changing Landscape, Volume 1: Drivers, Consequences, and Responses by Henning Steinfeld, Harold A. Mooney, et al. | Jan 29, 2010 pg. 39.
[119] Livestock in a Changing Landscape, Volume 1: Drivers, Consequences, and Responses by Henning Steinfeld, Harold A. Mooney, et al. | Jan 29, 2010 pg. 39.
[120] McLeman, R. A.; Dupre, J.; Berrang Ford, L.; Ford, J.; Gajewski, K.; Marchildon, G. (2014). "What we learned from the Dust Bowl: lessons in science, policy, and adaptation". Population and Environment. 35 (4): 417–440. doi:10.1007/s11111-013-0190-z. PMC 4015056. PMID 24829518.
[121] Livestock's Long Shadow: Environmental Issues and Options By Henning Steinfeld, Pierre Gerber, T. D. LIVESTOCK'S LONG SHADOW environmental issues and options P. iii.
[122] Livestock's Long Shadow: Environmental Issues and Options By Henning Steinfeld, Pierre Gerber, T. D. LIVESTOCK'S LONG SHADOW environmental issues and options P. xxi.
[123] Livestock's Long Shadow: Environmental Issues and Options By Henning Steinfeld, Pierre Gerber, T. D. LIVESTOCK'S LONG SHADOW environmental issues and options P 262.
[124] Livestock's Long Shadow: Environmental Issues and Options By Henning Steinfeld, Pierre Gerber, T. D. LIVESTOCK'S LONG SHADOW environmental issues and options P 276.
[125] Drug Cartel Wars, by Manuel Martinez. Extortion 2012.
[126] Avocado: A Global History, by Jeff Miller, Reaktion Books, Apr 13, 2020.
[127] "stranger." 1616 גֵּר ger {gare} or (fully) גֵּיר geyr (gare), Strong's Exhaustive Concordance: New American Standard Bible, updated ed., Lockman Foundation, 1995.
[128] Nobodies: Modern American Slave Labor and the Dark Side of the New Global Economy– August 12, 2008 John Bowe pg.8.
[129] United States v. Juan Ramos, Criminal Case No. 01-14019 Fact Summary 2002-11-202.

[130] "Inspections Report." Inspections Report. US Department of Justice, 1996. INS e9608 i9608p1 Web.
[131] TACKLING THE 1.6-BILLION-TON FOOD LOSS AND WASTE CRISIS AUGUST 20, 2018 By Esben Hegnsholt, Shalini Unnikrishnan, Matias Pollmann-Larsen, Bjorg Askelsdottir, and Marine Gerard.
[132] NRDC August 2012 iP:12-06-B Wasted: How America Is Losing More Than 30 Percent of Its Food from Farm to Fork to Landfill Dana Gunders.
[133] BIS Working Papers No 352 The real effects of debt by Stephen G Cecchetti, M S Mohanty and Fabrizio Zampolli 2011 pg. 1.
[134] BIS Working Papers No 352 The real effects of debt by Stephen G Cecchetti, M S Mohanty and Fabrizio Zampolli 2011 pg. 21.

Chapter 8 - The Ceremonial Law fulfilled in Christ

[135] Rabbi Jonathan Sacks, Covenant and Conversation, A weekly reading of the Jewish Bible. The Calendar pg. 324-325
[136] "age." <165> αἰών (aion), Strong's Exhaustive Concordance: New American Standard Bible, updated ed., Lockman Foundation, 1995.
[137] "Pentecost." <4005> πεντηκοστός (pentekostos), Strong's Exhaustive Concordance: New American Standard Bible, updated ed., Lockman Foundation, 1995.
[138] "awake." <07019a> קִיץ (qits) (884c), Strong's Exhaustive Concordance: New American Standard Bible, updated ed., Lockman Foundation, 1995.
[139] "transfiguration." The Oxford Advanced Learner's Dictionary, Oxford University Press, https://www.oxfordlearnersdictionaries.com/us/definition/english/transfiguration. Accessed 16 Sep. 2020.

Chapter 9 - The Feasts and the end times

[140] "all." <3956> πᾶς (pas), Strong's Exhaustive Concordance: New American Standard Bible, updated ed., Lockman Foundation, 1995.
[141] "age." <165> αἰών (aion), Strong's Exhaustive Concordance: New American Standard Bible, updated ed., Lockman Foundation, 1995.
[142] The Dispensational Truth, Clarence Larkin Chapter 30 the Feasts of the Lord pg. 347.
[143] The Niagara Creed, Article 13 Eschatology.
[144] London Baptist Confession of Faith 1689, Chapter 26 "Of the Church" Section 4.
[145] Fourth International Bible Conference Consensus Statement June 20, 2018.
[146] Catechism of the Catholic Church P2 S2 C1 A3 1330.
[147] Catechism of the Catholic Church P1 S2 C2 A7 671.
[148] How the Jewish Feasts were Fulfilled, curated by Richard Anthony, ecclesia.org/TRUTH/feasts.html.
[149] How the Jewish Feasts were Fulfilled, curated by Richard Anthony, ecclesia.org/TRUTH/feasts.html.
[150] Flatland: A Romance of Many Dimensions (by a Square) written by Edwin Abbott.
[151] "spatial." The Oxford Advanced Learner's Dictionary, Oxford University Press, https://www.oxfordlearnersdictionaries.com/us/definition/english/spatial. Accessed 16 Sep. 2020.
[152] "Christocentric." The Concise Oxford Dictionary of the Christian Church (2 rev. ed.), Oxford University Press, 2006.

[153] 28 Fundamental Beliefs of the Seventh Day Adventist Church, 26. Death and Resurrection.
[154] Westminster Confession Chapter 32 "Of the State of Men after Death, and of the Resurrection of the Dead" Section 1.
[155] The Roman Catholic Catechism P1 S2 C2 A5 633.
[156] Catechism of the Catholic Church P1 S 2 C3 A12 III. The Final Purification, or Purgatory 1030.
[157] Catechism of the Catholic Church P1 S 2 C3 A12 III. The Final Purification, or Purgatory 1032.
[158] "weeks." <07620> שָׁבוּעַ (shabua) (988d), Strong's Exhaustive Concordance: New American Standard Bible, updated ed., Lockman Foundation, 1995.
[159] The Dispensational Truth, Clarence Larkin, XXIX, Three Trees to Which Israel is compared - The vine – The Fig Tree – The Olive pg. 342.
[160] "generation." <01755> דּוֹר or דֹּר (dor or dor) (189c), Strong's Exhaustive Concordance: New American Standard Bible, updated ed., Lockman Foundation, 1995.
[161] "generation." <1074> γενεά (genea), Strong's Exhaustive Concordance: New American Standard Bible, updated ed., Lockman Foundation, 1995.
[162] "this." <3778> οὗτος or αὕτη or τοῦτο (houtos, haute, touto), Strong's Exhaustive Concordance: New American Standard Bible, updated ed., Lockman Foundation, 1995.
[163] "this." The Oxford Advanced Learner's Dictionary, Oxford University Press, https://www.oxfordlearnersdictionaries.com/us/definition/english/this. Accessed 16 Sep. 2020.
[164] "abolished." <05493> סוּר or שׂוּר (sur or sur) (693b), Strong's Exhaustive Concordance: New American Standard Bible, updated ed., Lockman Foundation, 1995.
[165] "heaven." <08064> שָׁמַיִם (shamayim) (1029c), Strong's Exhaustive Concordance: New American Standard Bible, updated ed., Lockman Foundation, 1995.
[166] "heaven." <3772> οὐρανός (ouranos), Strong's Exhaustive Concordance: New American Standard Bible, updated ed., Lockman Foundation, 1995.
[167] "world." <2889> κόσμος (kosmos), Strong's Exhaustive Concordance: New American Standard Bible, updated ed., Lockman Foundation, 1995.
[168] "world." <1782> ἐντεῦθεν (enteuthen), Strong's Exhaustive Concordance: New American Standard Bible, updated ed., Lockman Foundation, 1995.
[169] "traverse." Merriam-Webster.com Dictionary, Merriam-Webster, https://www.merriam-webster.com/dictionary/traverse. Accessed 14 Sep. 2020.
[170] "come." <2064> ἔρχομαι (erchomai), Strong's Exhaustive Concordance: New American Standard Bible, updated ed., Lockman Foundation, 1995
[171] "Gerund." Merriam-Webster.com Dictionary, Merriam-Webster, https://www.merriam-webster.com/dictionary/gerund. Accessed 16 Sep. 2020.
[172] Dr. James N. Yamazaki, M.D., Children of the Atomic Bomb, UCLA Asian American Studies Center Hiroshima and Nagasaki Death Toll http://www.aasc.ucla.edu/cab/200708230009.html updated: August 31, 2017
[173] "quickly." <3772> <5035> ταχύ, Strong's Exhaustive Concordance: New American Standard Bible, updated ed., Lockman Foundation, 1995.
[174] "speed." <5034> τάχος, Strong's Exhaustive Concordance: New American Standard Bible, updated ed., Lockman Foundation, 1995.
[175] "quick." <5036> ταχύς, Strong's Exhaustive Concordance: New American Standard Bible, updated ed., Lockman Foundation, 1995.
[176] The Dispensational Truth, Clarence Larkin, The imminency of the second coming, pg.15

[177] "tabernacle." <04908> מִשְׁכָּן, Strong's Exhaustive Concordance: New American Standard Bible, updated ed., Lockman Foundation, 1995.
[178] "tabernacle." <4633> σκηνή, Strong's Exhaustive Concordance: New American Standard Bible, updated ed., Lockman Foundation, 1995.
[179] "booth." <05521> סֻכָּה, Strong's Exhaustive Concordance: New American Standard Bible, updated ed., Lockman Foundation, 1995.
[180] Behold He cometh, Herman Hoeksema, The Blessedness of the New Jerusalem pg. 671.
[181] More than conquerors an interpretation of the book of Revelation, William Hendriksen, Chapter 19 We are more than conquerors through Him that loved us, pg. 239-240.
[182] "coming down." <2597> καταβαίνω (katabaino), Strong's Exhaustive Concordance: New American Standard Bible, updated ed., Lockman Foundation, 1995.
[183] "preposition." The Oxford Advanced Learner's Dictionary, Oxford University Press, https://www.oxfordlearnersdictionaries.com/us/definition/english/preposition. Accessed 16 Sep. 2020.
[184] "lowered." <2524> καθίημι Strong's Exhaustive Concordance: New American Standard Bible, updated ed., Lockman Foundation, 1995.
[185] "right." <891> ἄχρι (achri), Strong's Exhaustive Concordance: New American Standard Bible, updated ed., Lockman Foundation, 1995.

Chapter 10 - The Christian Day of Worship
[186] Westminster Confession of Faith Chapter 26 "Of the Communion of Saints" Section 1.
[187] Westminster Confession of Faith Chapter 26 "Of the Communion of Saints" Section 2.
[188] Westminster Confession of Faith Chapter 26 "Of the Communion of Saints" Section 3.

Chapter 11 - Conclusion
[189] "factious." <141> αἱρετικός (hairetikos), Strong's Exhaustive Concordance: New American Standard Bible, updated ed., Lockman Foundation, 1995.

Appendix I - Early Church Fathers on the Sabbath and Lord's Day
[190] The Didache, Chapter XIV.11 —Christian Assembly on the Lord's Day. 14. A.D. 70.
[191] The Letter of Barnabas , The Epistle of Barnabas Chapter II. The Jewish sacrifices are now abolished. A.D. 74.
[192] The Letter of Barnabas , The Epistle of Barnabas Chapter XV. The false and the true Sabbath. A.D. 74.
[193] Ignatius of Antioch, Letter to the Magnesians(shorter) Chapter IX. Let us live with Christ. A.D. 110.
[194] Ignatius of Antioch, The Epistle of Ignatius to the Trallians Longer Versions. Chapter IX. Reference to the history of Christ.
[195] Justin Martyr, Dialogue with Trypho the Jew Chapter XII. The Jews violate the eternal law, and interpret ill that of Moses.
[196] Justin Martyr, Dialogue with Trypho the Jew Chapter XVIII. Christians would observe the law, if they did not know why it was instituted. A.D. 155.
[197] Justin Martyr, First Apology Chapter LXVII. Weekly worship of the Christians. A.D. 155.

[198] Justin Martyr, The Second Apology of Justin for the Christians Addressed to the Roman Senate. Chapter XXIII. The opinion of the Jews regarding the law does an injury to God.
[199] Justin Martyr, The Second Apology of Justin for the Christians Addressed to the Roman Senate. Chapter XLIII. He concludes that the law had an end in Christ, who was born of the Virgin.
[200] Tertullian, An Answer to the Jews Chapter II. The Law Anterior to Moses. A.D. 203.
[201] Tertullian, An Answer to the Jews Chapter IV. Of the Observance of the Sabbath.
[202] Tertullian, An Answer to the Jews Chapter VI. Of the Abolition and the Abolisher of the Old Law. A.D. 203.
[203] Tertullian, Apology Chapter XVI.
[204] Constitutions of the holy apostles, Book V. Sec. III. On Feast Days and Fast Days - Concerning the Watching All the Night of the Great Sabbath, and Concerning the Day of the Resurrection. XIX.
[205] Constitutions of the holy apostles, Book II. Sec. VII. On Assembling in the Church. That Every Christian Ought to Frequent the Church Diligently Both Morning and Evening LIX.
[206] Origen, Against Celsus, Book 8 Chapter XXII.
[207] Peter, Archbishop of Alexandria, The Canonical Epistle Canon XV.
[208] Cyprian, Epistle LVIII.2 To Fidus, on the Baptism of Infants.
[209] Victorinus, The Creation of the World, A.D. 300.
[210] Victorinus, On the Creation of the World, pg. 4.
[211] Eusebius of Caesarea, Ecclesiastical History Book 1 Chapter 4 Section 8, A.D. 312.
[212] Eusebius of Caesarea, Proof of the Gospel 4:16:186, A.D. 319.
[213] Eusebius of Caesarea, Ecclesiastical History, Book 1, Chapter 5, A.D. 315.
[214] Eusebius of Caesarea, Ecclesiastical History, Book 3, Chapter 27, A.D. 315.
[215] Eusebius of Caesarea, Book III. Chapter XXVII, The Heresy of the Ebionites 5 & 6.
[216] Council of Laodicea, Canon XXIX, A.D. 360.
[217] John Chrysostom, Homilies on Galatians 2:17, A.D. 395.
[218] Augustine of Hippo, The Spirit and the Letter 24, A.D. 412.
[219] Augustine of Hippo, Reply to Faustus the Manichæan, Book VI-2.
[220] Augustine of Hippo, Reply to Faustus the Manichæan, Book XVI.-29.
[221] Augustine of Hippo, Reply to Faustus the Manichæan, Book XIX.-9.
[222] Augustine of Hippo, Letters of Augustine Letter XXXVI, Chapter 6. 25.
[223] Augustine of Hippo, Letter LV. Or Book II. of Replies to Questions of Januarius. Chapter 8. 23 A.D. 400.